I0803450

THEY MUST FALL

Muhammad Ali and the Men He Fought

MICHAEL BRENNAN

ACC ART BOOKS

for
Dave Brennan

Contents

Some heroes we forget.

By Simon Van Booy

As Muhammad Ali once said when discussing the term, *killer instinct*, "My intention was to win, but never to kill—even when I knocked a man out—I was happy to see him come back to it."

Boxing is as much a sport, then, as it is a metaphor that embodies a paradox of human nature: the impulse to fight coupled with the equally fierce desire for companionship and comfort. The photographs in this book tell the whole story, for Michael Brennan's pictures are more than a just dazzling record of hooks and jabs—rather, they explore the personal narratives of 25 vastly different men, who all rose to challenge one of the most successful and popular fighters of all time.

Brennan not only pulls viewers into the ring—freezing pivotal moments in boxing history with mesmerizing beauty—but leads them beyond the ropes and across time, into the private lives of men who played vital roles in the history of our ancient sport. Without these individuals, the life of our protagonist, Muhammad Ali, would have been entirely different. In boxing, glamour and success are often braided with catastrophic failure, casting the men in this book (immortalized forever by Brennan) as the unsung heroes of a champion sportsman: fighters whose defeats enabled, or at least played their part in Ali's greatness.

For anyone who has spent time in a gym or been laced into a pair gloves, it's obvious that there is more to boxing than just aggression. In fact, that's only a small part of it. The physical training is intense, perhaps more so than any other sport in the world. It demands a superhuman level of fitness that—in the ring, under the lights—may still not be enough.

Those who excel as pugilists also possess rare artistry. They move about the ring with the grace and precision of a dancer. There is a seamlessness to their actions, a visual harmony made of up of speed, vision, breath, flawless technique, and above all—control. While hobbyists might use boxing as way to release anger, in the professional ring it's discipline that wins bouts. What makes so many of the greatest fighters exciting to watch is that moment they explode, like the uncoiling of a spring. But it's the poise that's thrilling and often so devastating to the opponent.

For the fighters themselves, the journey into the ring is intensively psychological. Visit any boxing gym and you will find that every single person engaged in the sport has a story worthy of a Hollywood blockbuster. For boxing is not only about nurturing the biological instinct that helped ensure the longevity of our ancestors through epochs of bloodshed but also about providing *safe* opportunites for men and women to face an injustice of the past, some unresolved conflict, a relationship left hanging, the torment of abandonment. These are the demons that spectators never see, though rest assured, they are ever-present in every boxing ring throughout the world, from Lagos to Las Vegas.

What makes boxing *safe* is also what imbues it with honor. Strict rules govern engagement. Anger is channeled into aggression, which is then converted into self-discipline, and respect for oneself, one's opponent, the referee, and even for the chattering, jeering crowd, gathered to witness 'a fight' safe in the knowledge that boxing is, at its core, the celebration of life—the chance for victory over one's private gallery of torments.

Photography captures something in boxing that would otherwise be lost forever—actions that occur too quickly to be perceived with any detail by the human brain. For instance, the arc of a fighter's arm a millisecond before the glove makes contact with an unsuspecting opponent's chin. In pictures such as these, we can study a fighter's footwork in relation to a devastating combination of punches. But it's not just the technical aspects of boxing to which Brennan's lens is so attuned—it is also the emotions of the fighters and, of course, the stories of what happened to them in the years after the biggest night of their lives.

Spend some time in these pages and you will soon realize that each photograph is not just a visual landscape to be inhabited momentarily but part of a story we can all relate to—regardless of whether we can throw a punch. For everyone knows that so much of life involves the reconciliation of triumph and defeat.

Simon Van Booy is an award-winning and best-selling author of fourteen books, including The Secret Lives of People in Love (short-listed for the Vilcek Prize), Love Begins in Winter (awarded the Frank O'Connor International Short Story Award) and The Illusion of Separateness. He enjoys hitting the bags at Overthrow Boxing Club in Brooklyn and has trained with Lenny DeJesus at UFC Gym, and with martial artist, David Kaplan.

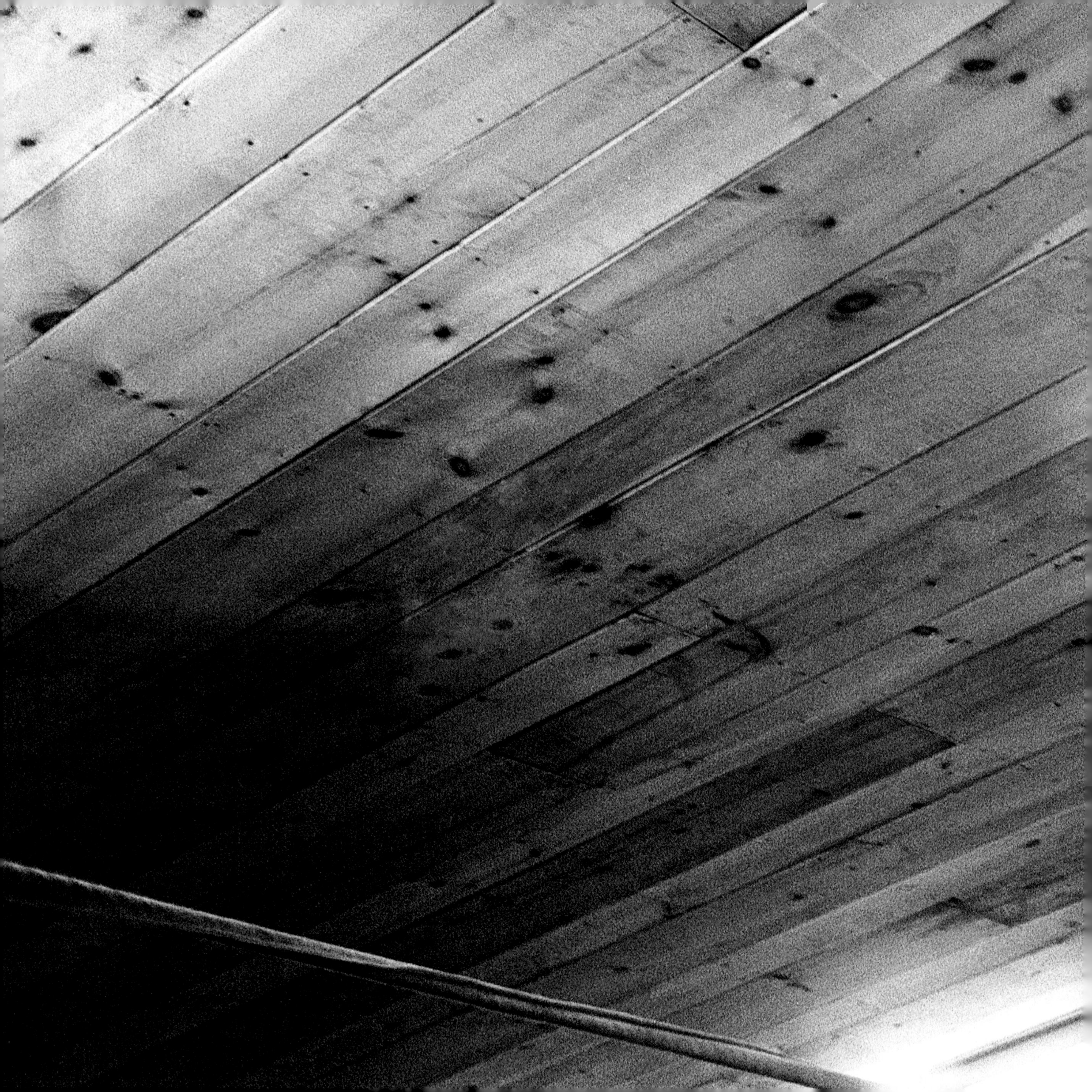

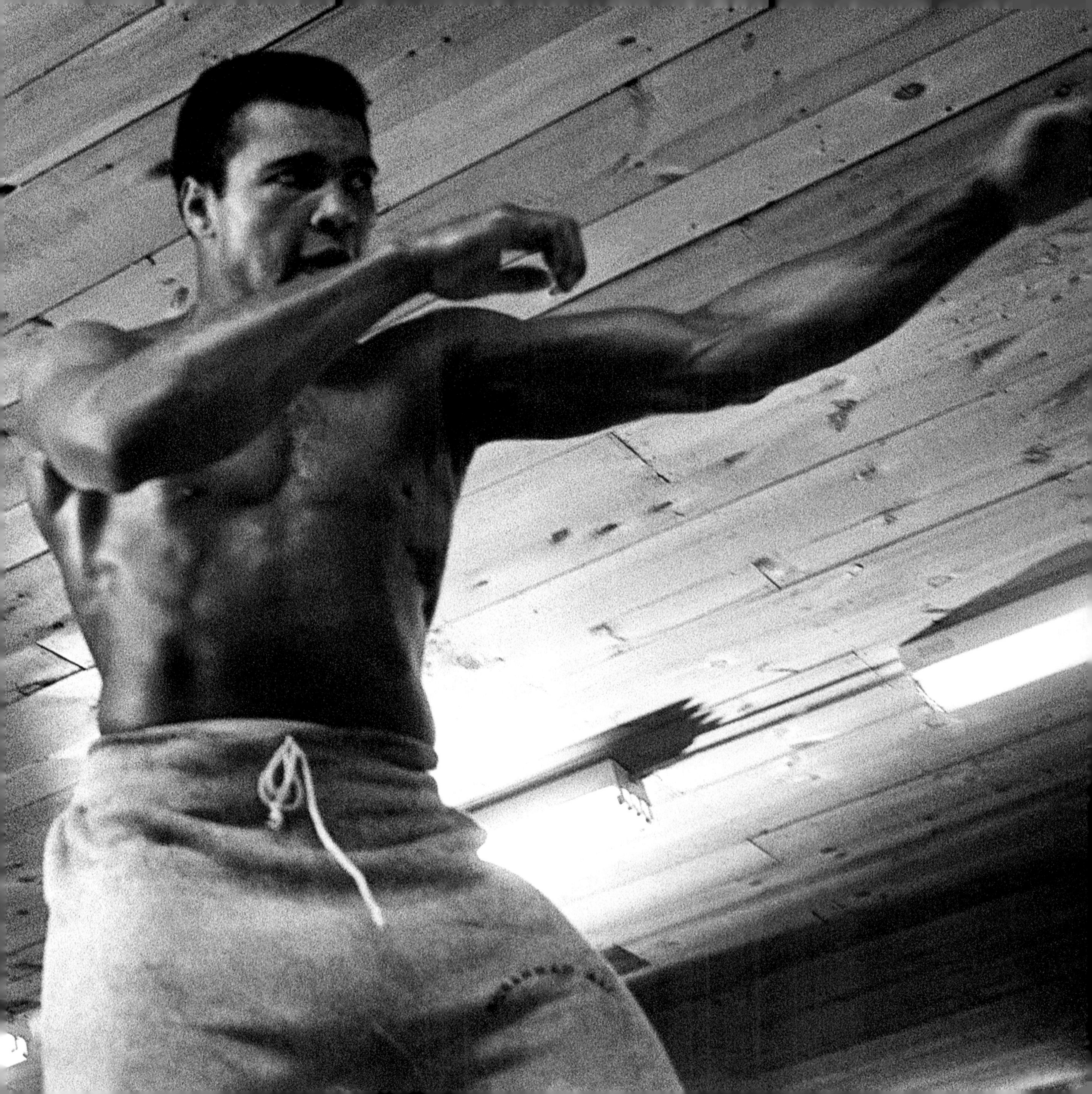

Introduction to Jimmy Breslin.

By Michael Brennan

The noisy and brilliant Jimmy Breslin holds forth about the idiot politicians plus the need to scream about the poor and abused before heading out to confront both. Meanwhile, bartender Fred Percudani couldn't care less since he is more interested in the fifth race at Belmont and whether Breslin will pay his bar tab!

Pulitzer Prize winner Jimmy Breslin was a patron of Costello's Bar & Grill on Manhattan's East 44th Street because of its close proximity to the New York Daily News building where he wrote a daily column. Perhaps its greatest attraction was owner Tim Costello's very liberal attitude to the cashing of personal checks nearly all of which 'bounced' on a regular basis.

For a near thirty years, I resided two blocks further uptown on East 46th and also had use of the check cashing facilities, with the same rubberized consequences. Costello's went out of business in 1996.

I knew Jimmy had written extensively about the then Cassius Clay and his involvement with Malcolm X. After many beers one evening he eventually snapped and said, "Okay Mickey, why don't I write a piece for whatever goddam money-making scheme you are up to." Two years later he delivered this magnificent memory of 'The Greatest.'

Any morning 1986. Around 11.45am, Costello's Bar and Grill, 225 East 44th Street, New York City

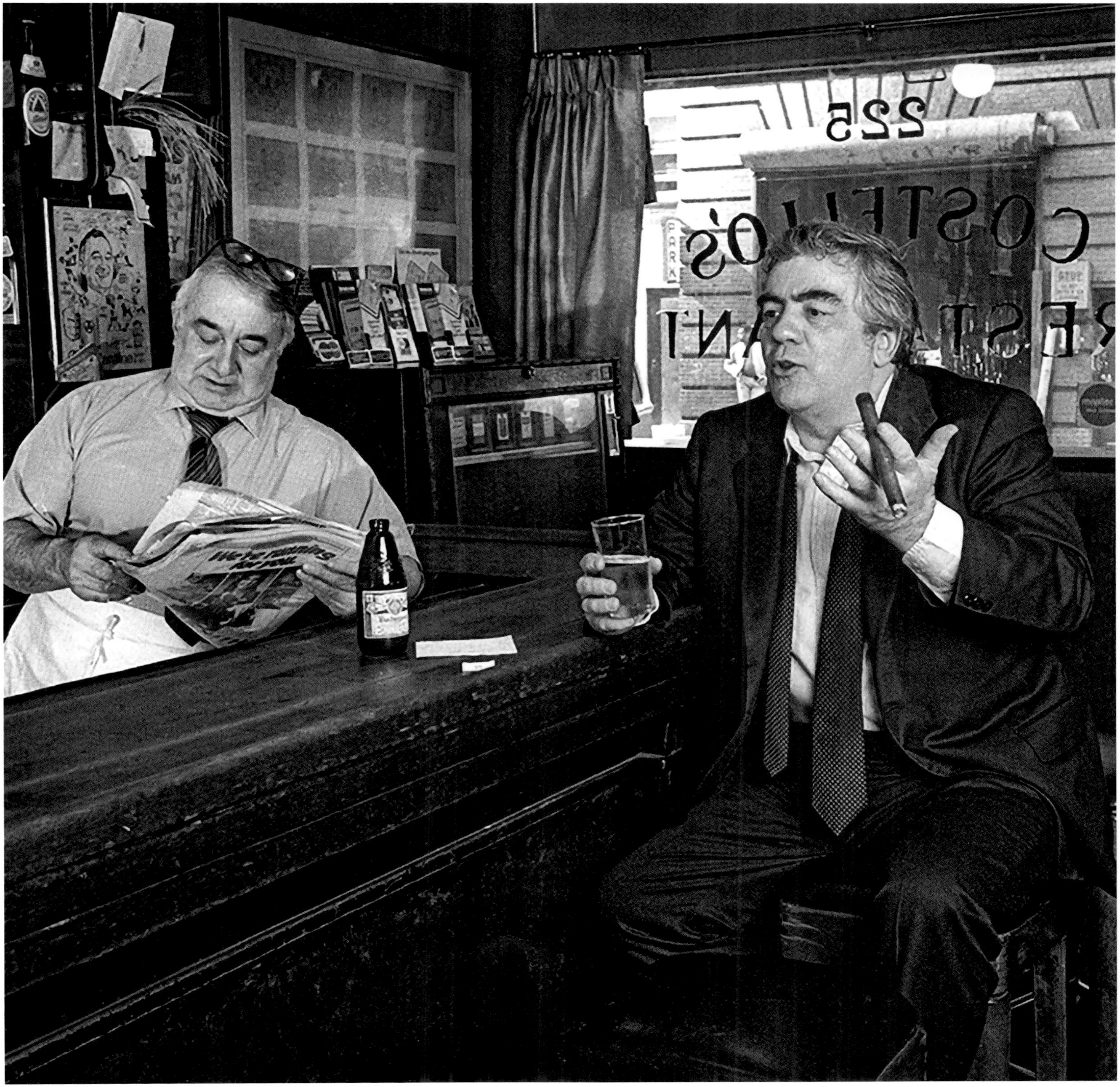

125th Street and Seventh Avenue, 1960.

By Jimmy Breslin, 2006

That night, Officer Johnny McGuire was the first one with a badge to attend Eddie Davis' sermon on the corner of 125th and Seventh Avenue in the heart of Harlem. Davis, bald and bulky, put up his stepladder, with the American flag tied to it, thus making his ladder legal, tucked a Bible under his arm and went up the ladder. He immediately brayed into the Harlem night that whites were robbing the blacks blind.

"Roll on, Brother, Roll On," Johnny McGuire and all the others in the crowed chanted. That was Davis' name on the street corner, Roll On Davis

The second one present with a badge was Cassius Clay, age 18, who had just won the Olympic heavyweight title and had the big gold medallion hanging from a chain around his neck. He was tall and with a young handsome face that upon each glimpse in the mirror caused him to cry, "I'm beautiful!"

He was from Louisville, where white businessmen treated him so well because he was champion and a deferential one at that. But now Cassius Clay was shocked to see a crowd of blacks clap and shout when Roll On Davis said:

"The white man is a rapist!"

Clay was in disbelief. A black man was saying this about whites and there were no police with clubs storming into them. The person who had brought Clay to Harlem was Dick Schaap, a sports writer who told Clay, "Of course you can say this. You're in America."

On this night, the "Yassuh" fell out of Cassius Clay and the bright mind of a black came out.

And here in Miami Beach on February 25, 1964, was the last of Cassius Clay taking these long swift steps around the ring while Liston, the heavyweight champion, his face without expression, trailed him. Liston's feet made a thump. That was the sound of his life. He trained with a beaverboard that made great sound when Sonny jump-roped to 'Night Train.' And now, feet pounding, he came after this fresh young Clay. This time, Sonny's head snapped back as Clay's jab, a big strong left arm that whipped so fast it could hardly be seen. Liston loaded up with a right hand. Clay packed it off and jabbed. Once, twice. Then his legs moved him away. He had trouble in the fourth and fifth round when an ointment from somewhere, his corner, Liston's, got in his eyes and had him shrieking. But that jab whisked out and he hooked off it so quickly Liston didn't know what it was all about. He was tiring. He could figure one thing: he was on the verge of getting a major beating. He went back to his corner and quit.

The new champion went to a motel where Malcolm X of New York announced that Clay was becoming a Muslim and his new name was Muhammad Ali. Eddie (Roll On) Davis had started it on a street corner and now Muhammad Ali made it international.

As Ali, he went to Houston and was drafted for the service but did not take a step forward and never went in. Anybody else would have been arrested. Ali was too much to handle.

The rematch was in Lewiston, Maine. The training was at Poland Springs where, on a morning, Ali came to a press conference. He came in military style. The black draft resister marched and then went, "Right flank!" and his body wheeled, then marched over the grass to "Column Left!" and the body swung. He infuriated the fat patriots here to see a fight or made everybody laugh.

The fight was on May 25th of 1965. My friend Jack O'Neill from New York came with a group of thieves and took over my room for a card game with local car dealers. One of them, in an electric wheelchair, tried dealing seconds. This was taken for as a green light by the thieves with O'Neill. They took all but the batteries from the wheelchair. Robert Goulet, who had been tremendous fun with us all week, forgot the words to the 'Star Spangled Banner.' He was right and the song was wrong. Moments before the first round, Ali stood in his corner and gave the hand motions of his new faith and from the stands came a wail:

"Muuuuhammaddd!"

He caught Liston with a short right hand in the second round, so short most people never saw it. Liston went on his back. Ali stood over him and screamed for him to get up, Liston wasn't rising.

Ali screamed that he was the greatest, that he was beautiful. He said that the punch was one he had learned from watching Jack Johnson in fight films. It didn't matter where it was from he took that punch and a name that showed utter contempt for white rulers and the chanted, "I am the Greatest!" and "I'm Beautiful!" and the world loved it and made Muhammad Ali the one everybody in the world knew and loved. There was nobody else. He was alone.

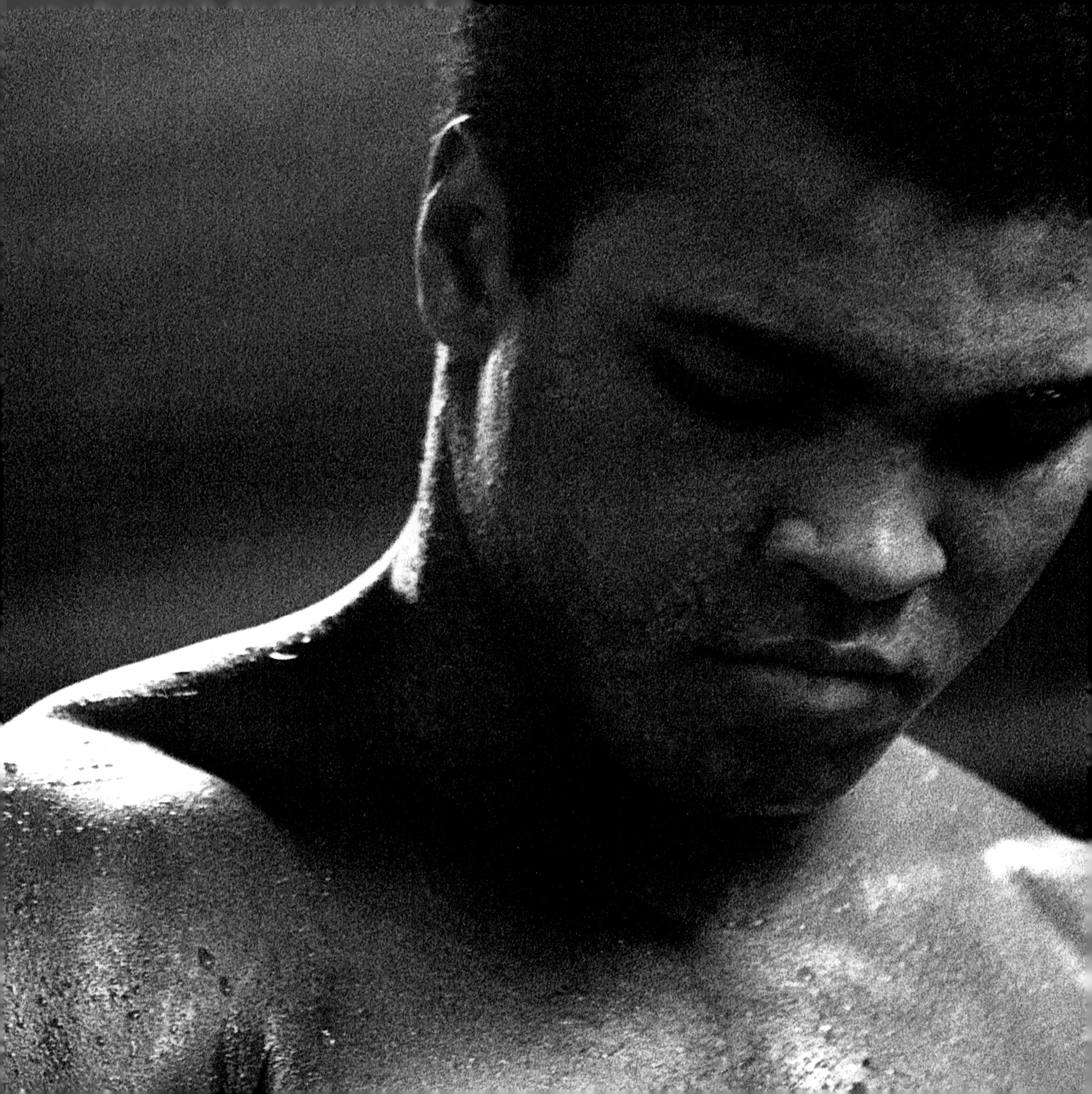

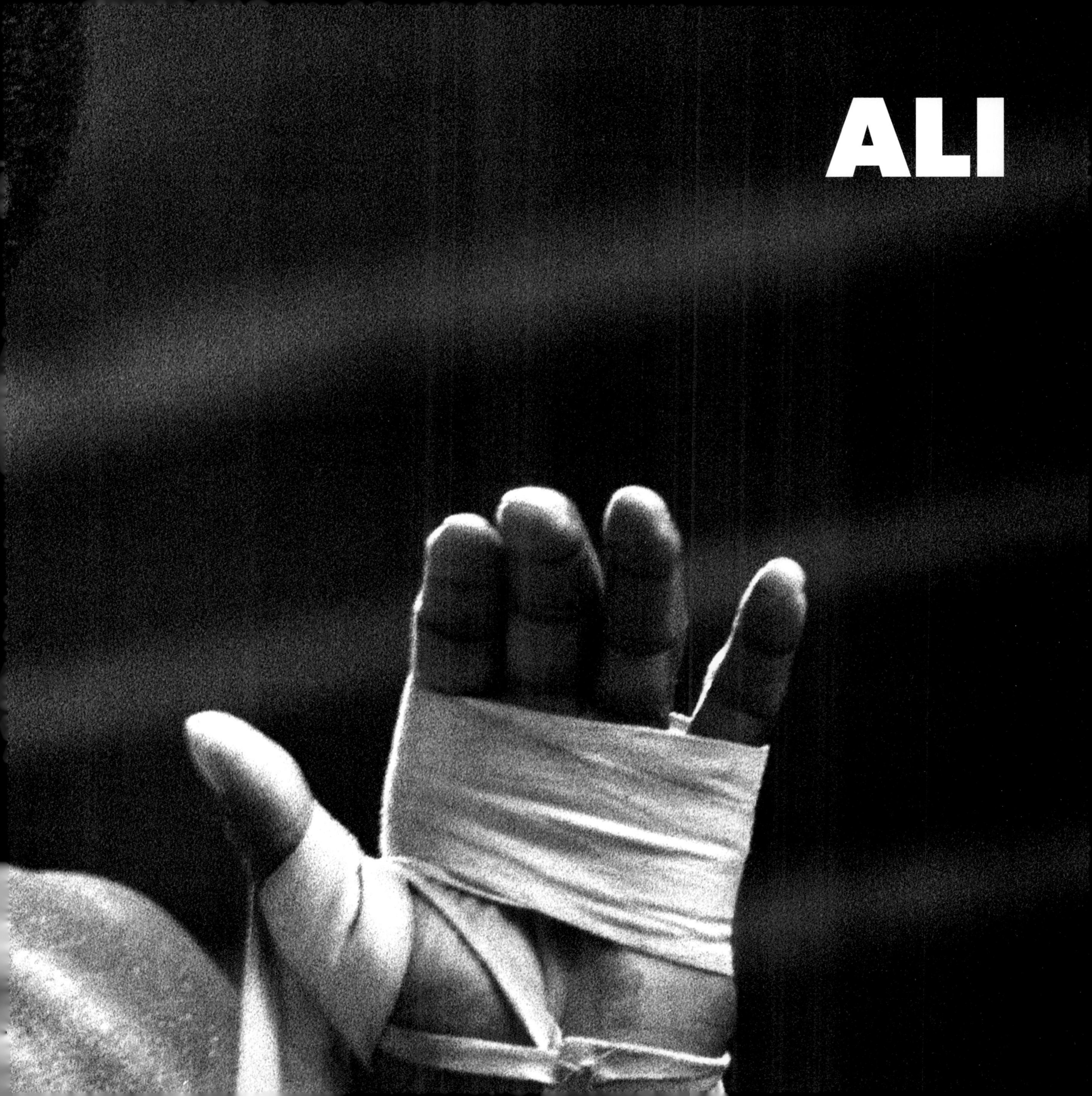
ALI

Muhammad Ali v Joe Frazier 2
Final press conference
Wig & Pen restaurant, New York City
Thursday January 17, 1974

Muhammad Ali; a promoter's dream. My first experience of Ali's promotional skills: Tucking into a free steak dinner, Ali suddenly jumps up and says to Joe Frazier, "Okay sucker, let's get it on now"… end of the much-anticipated freebie.

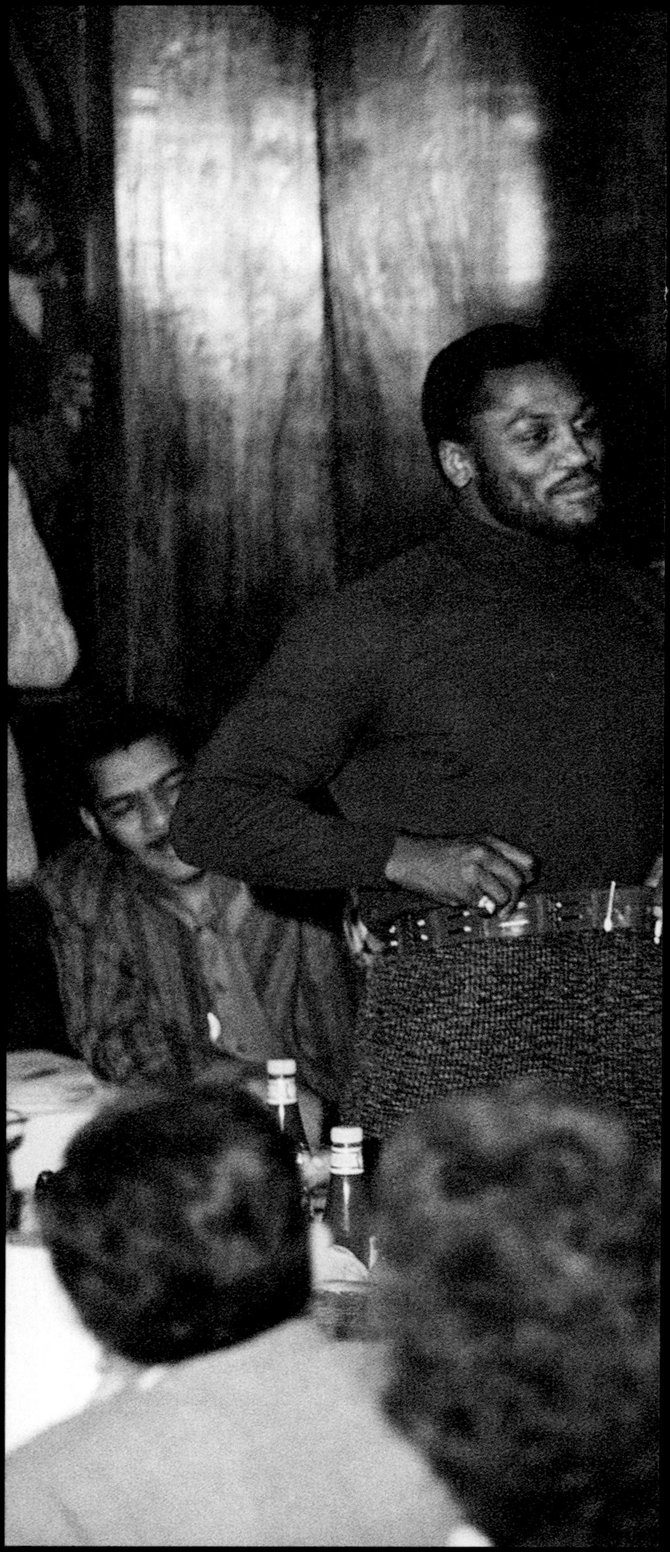

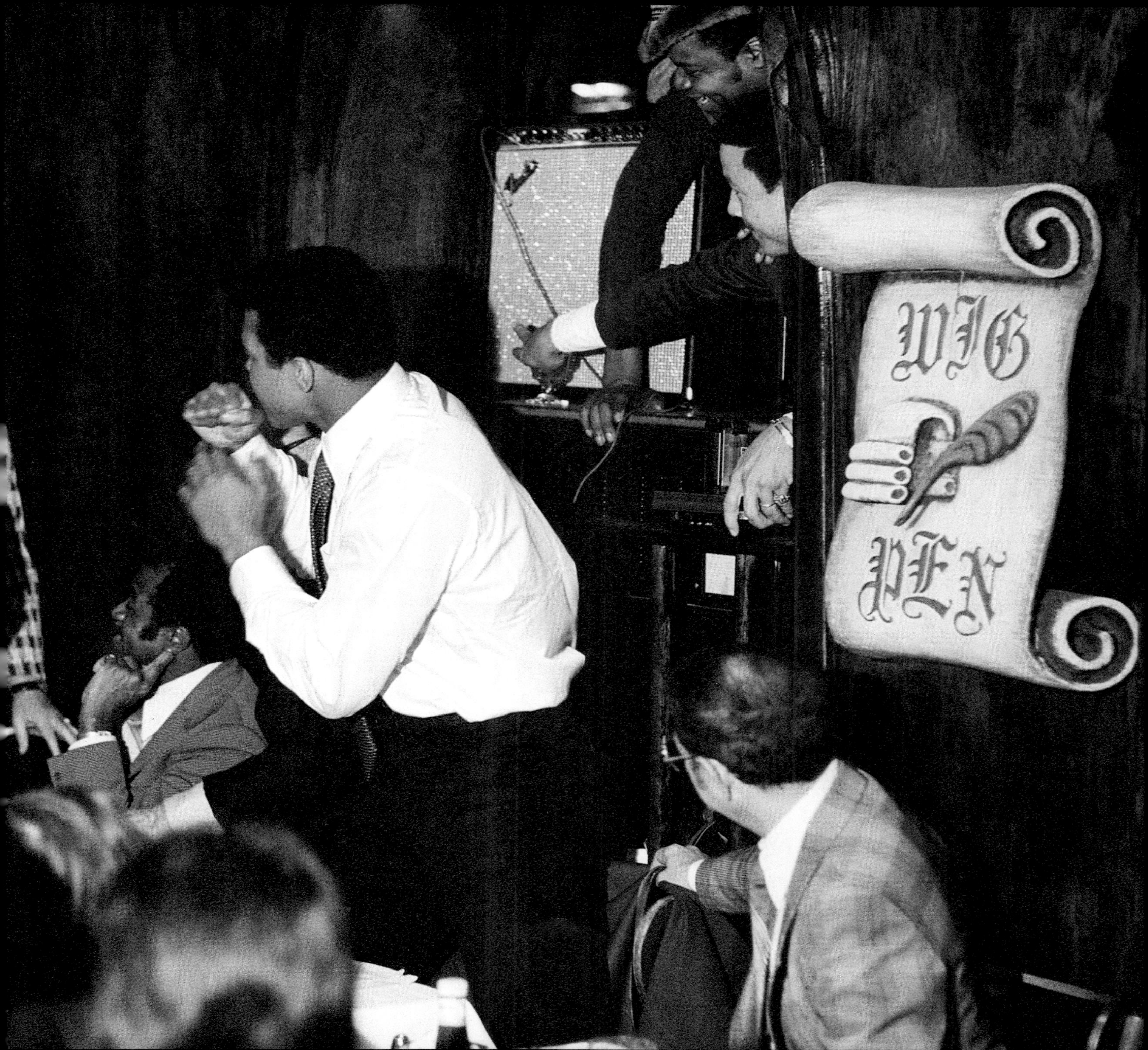
WIG
PEN

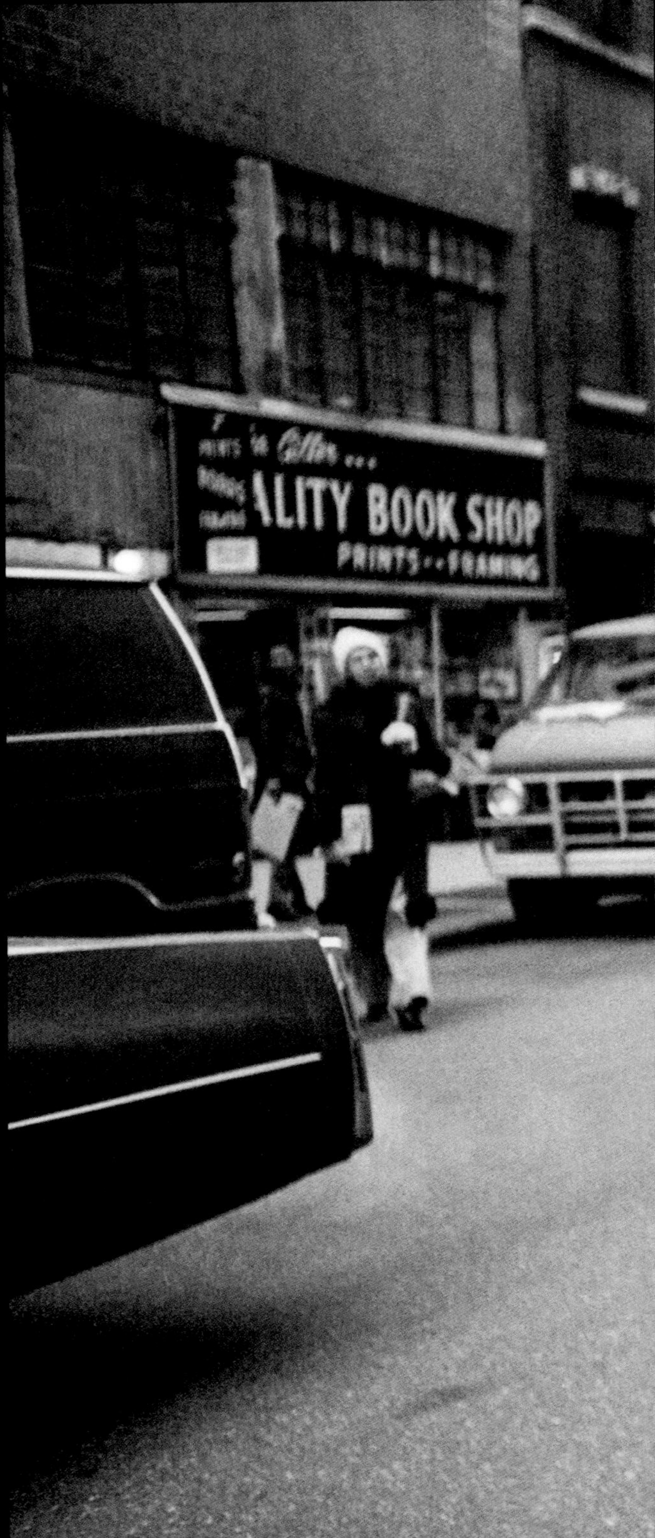

Muhammad Ali points to the side-view mirror and tells Joe Frazier to take a look and see how ugly he is after a press conference to announce their second fight in Manila
West 47th Street, near Madison Square Garden, New York City
January 1974

It would seem that a camera, any camera anywhere would have Muhammad Ali turn into a promotional automaton. Unfortunately, many recipients of those well-meaning tirades found it tiresome. Joe Frazier most times tolerated Ali's creative insults. However, on this occasion it became obvious that had his trainer Eddie Futch and press representative Dave Wolf not intervened, Frazier would have responded. You might have seen Ali v Frazier 2 on the streets of Manhattan.

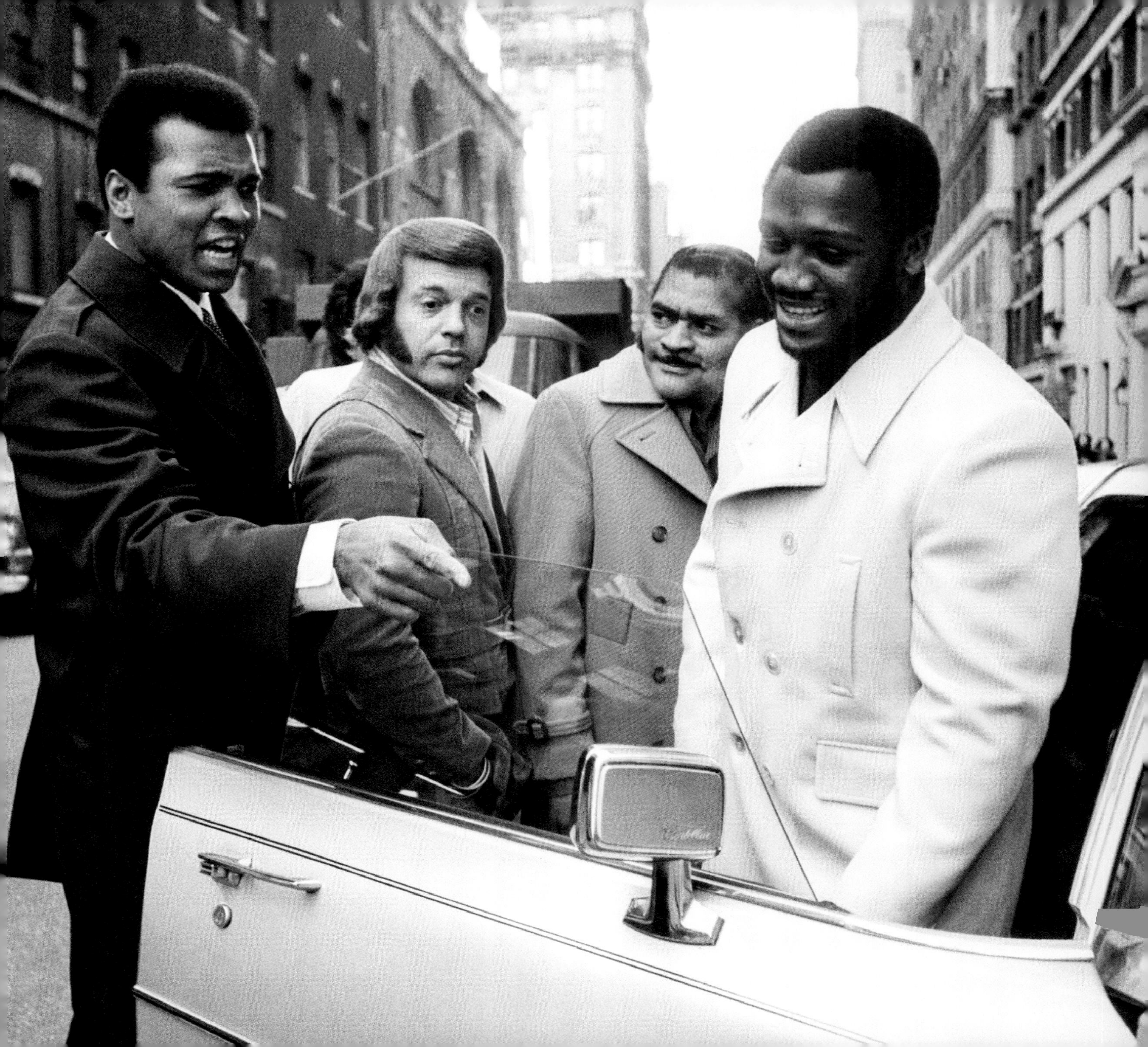

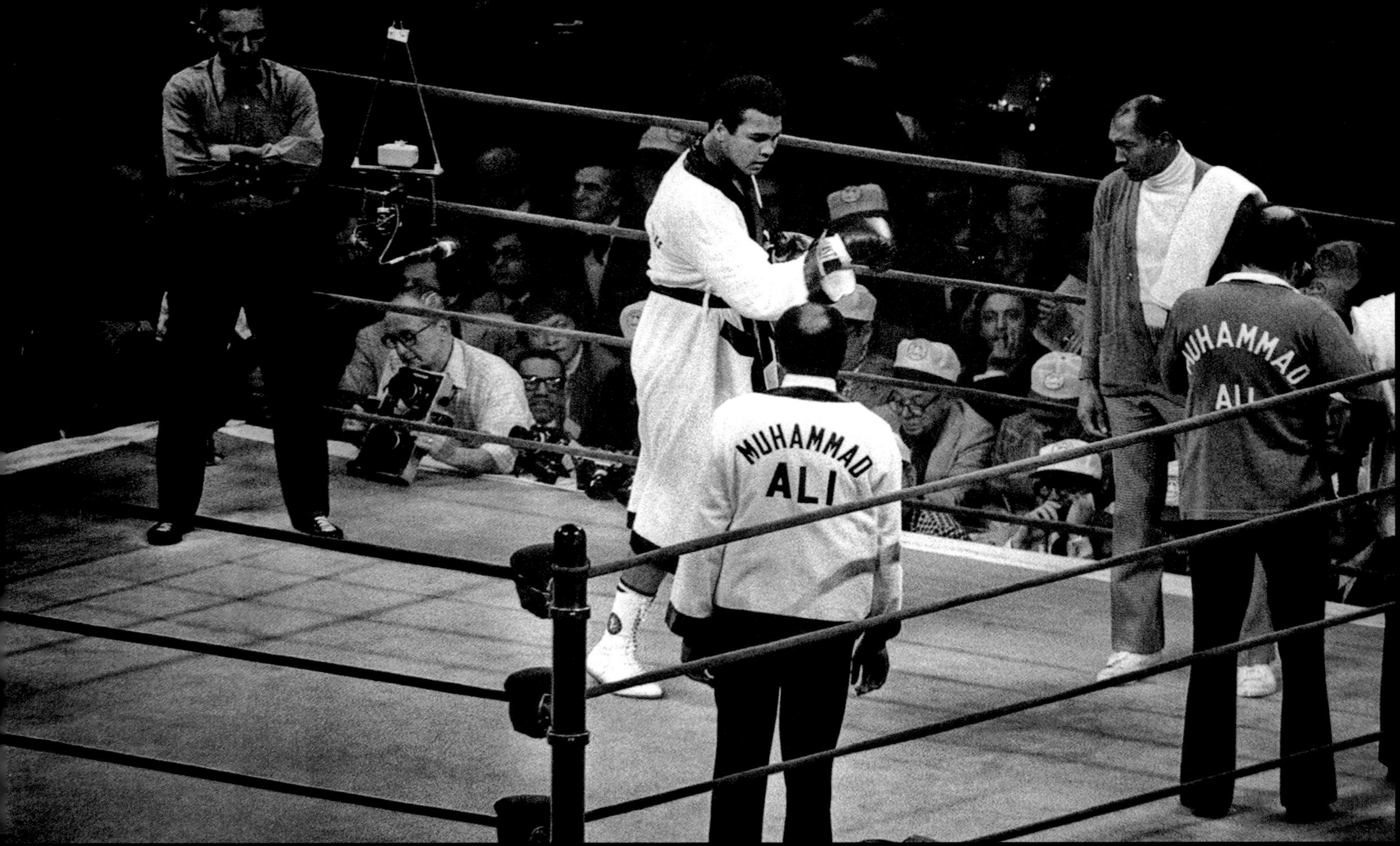

Muhammad Ali v Joe Frazier 2
Frazier lost to Ali by UD
Madison Square Garden, New York City
Monday January 28, 1974

Although the atmosphere in The Garden was electric, those patrons who attended the first collision were less enthusiastic about the outcome. Myself, being at 'The Garden' at a fight between Ali and Joe! Should it have all ended there…I would have been seriously fed-up!

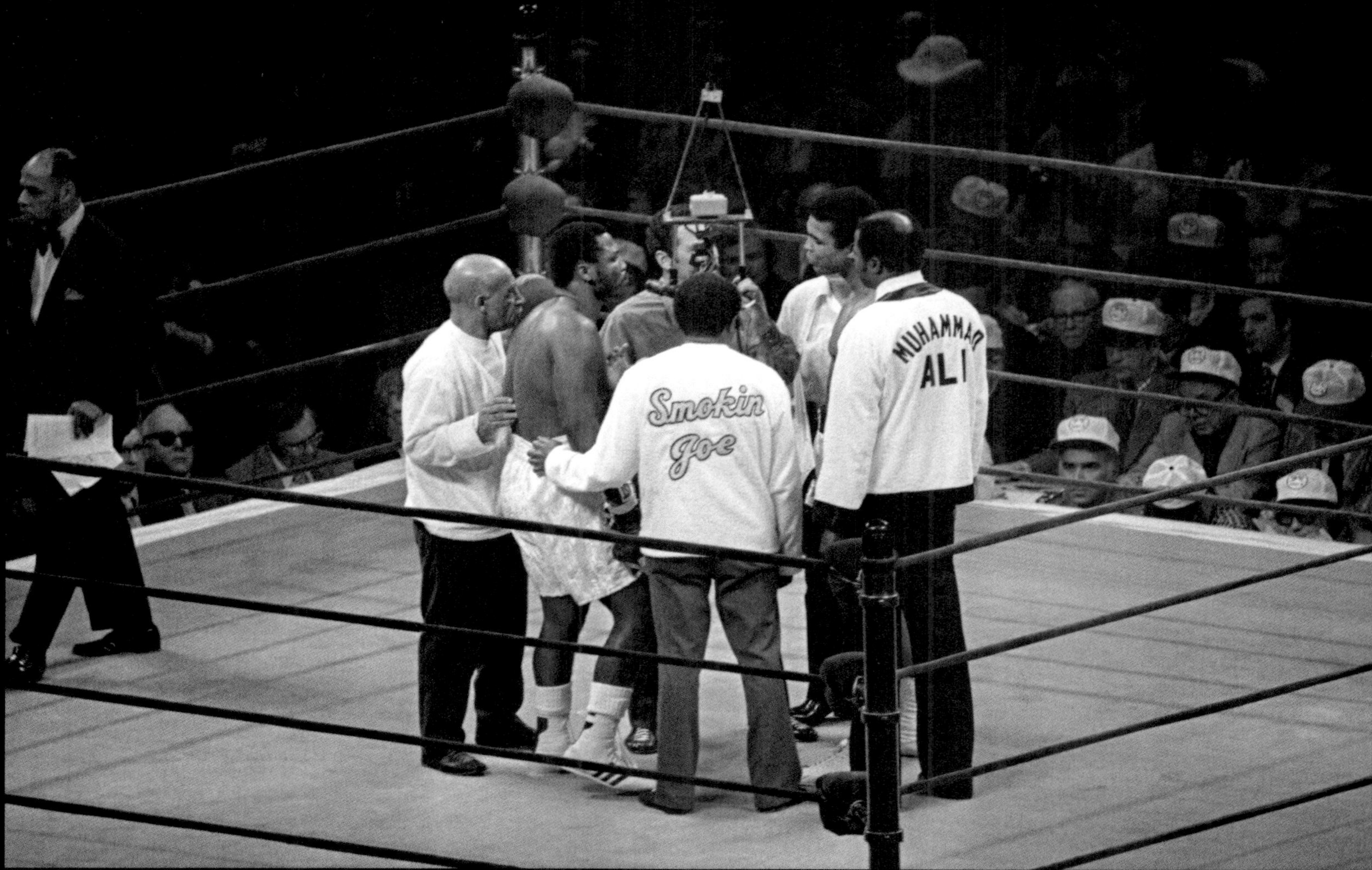
Smokin
Joe
MUHAMMAD
ALI

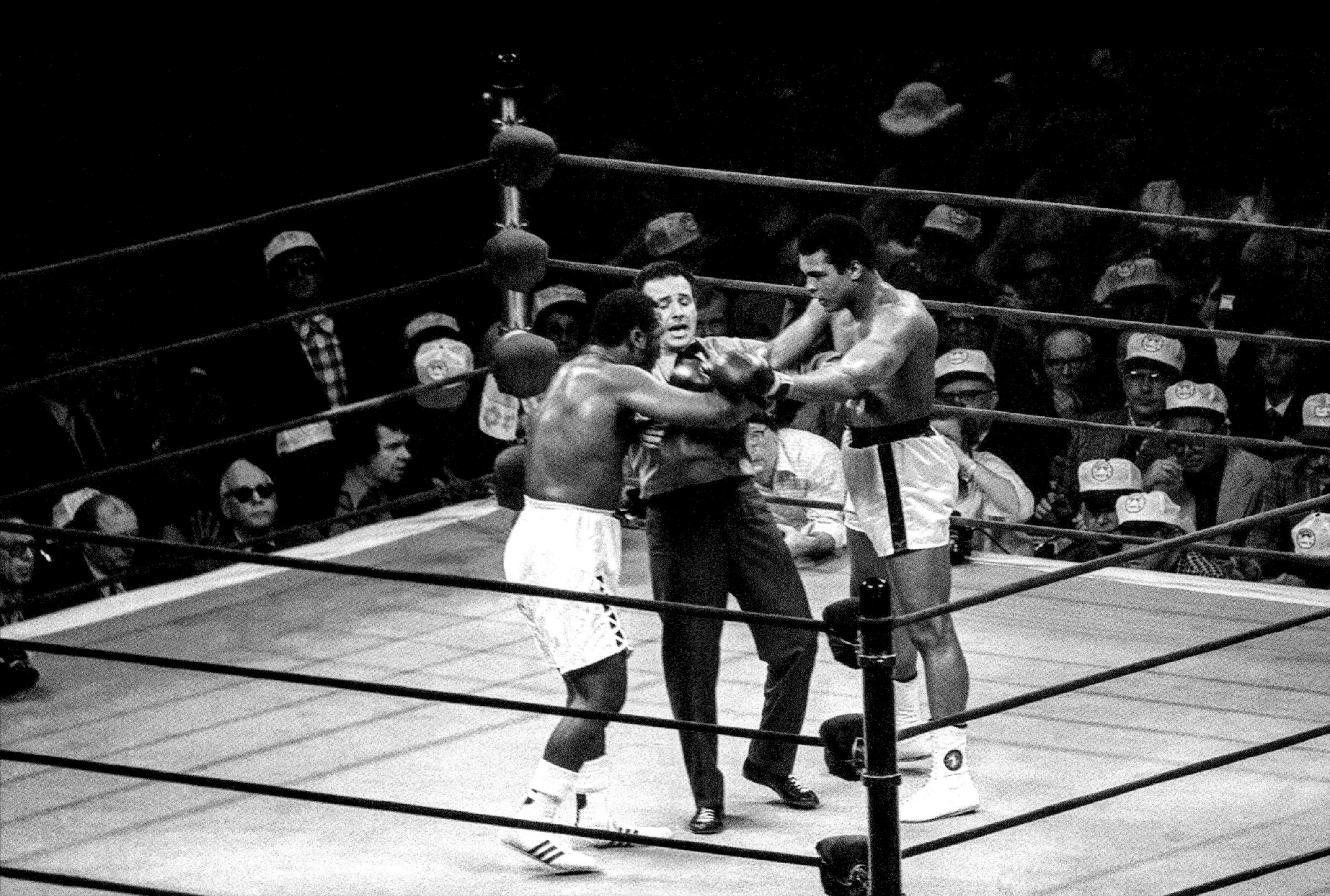

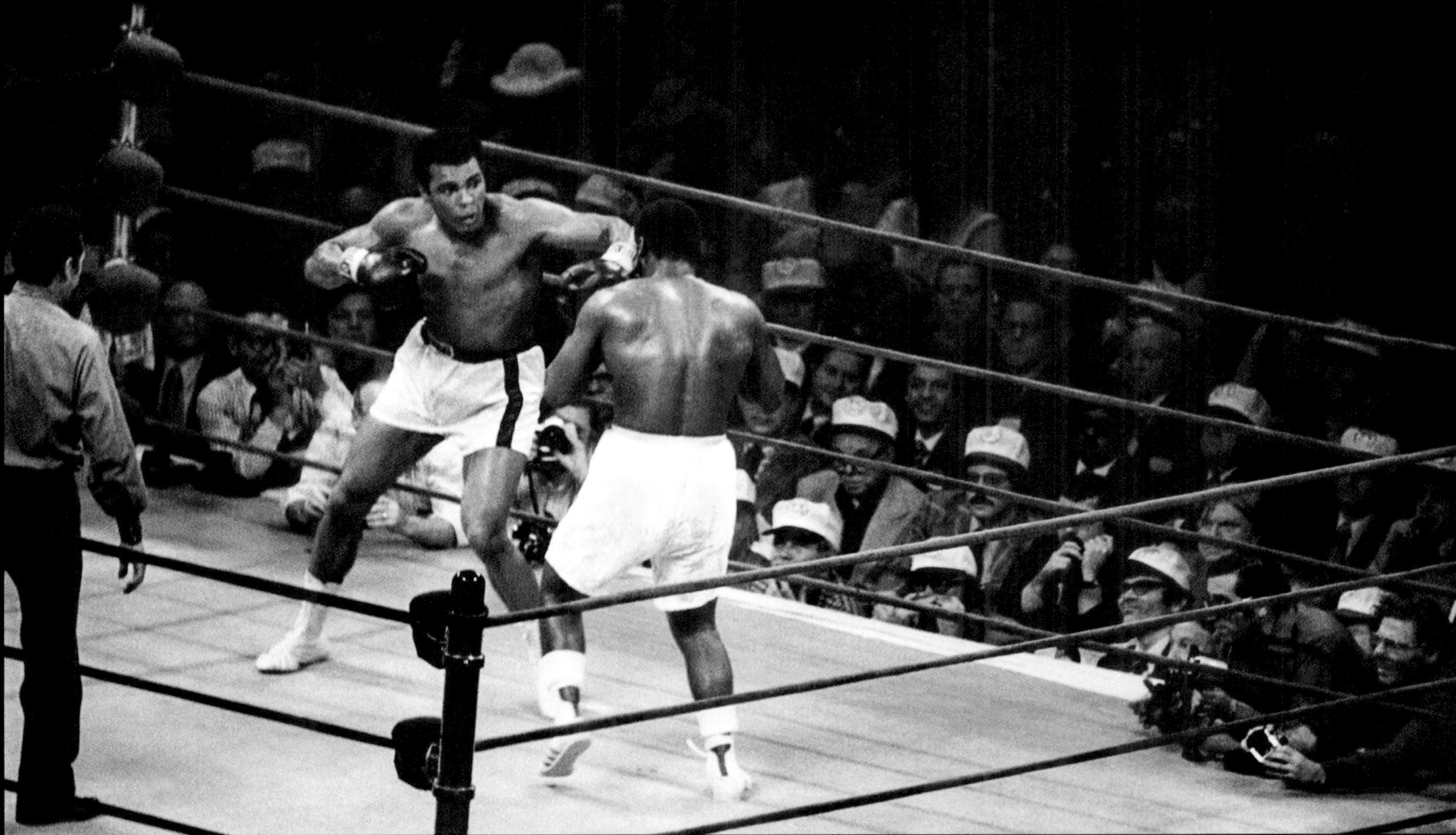

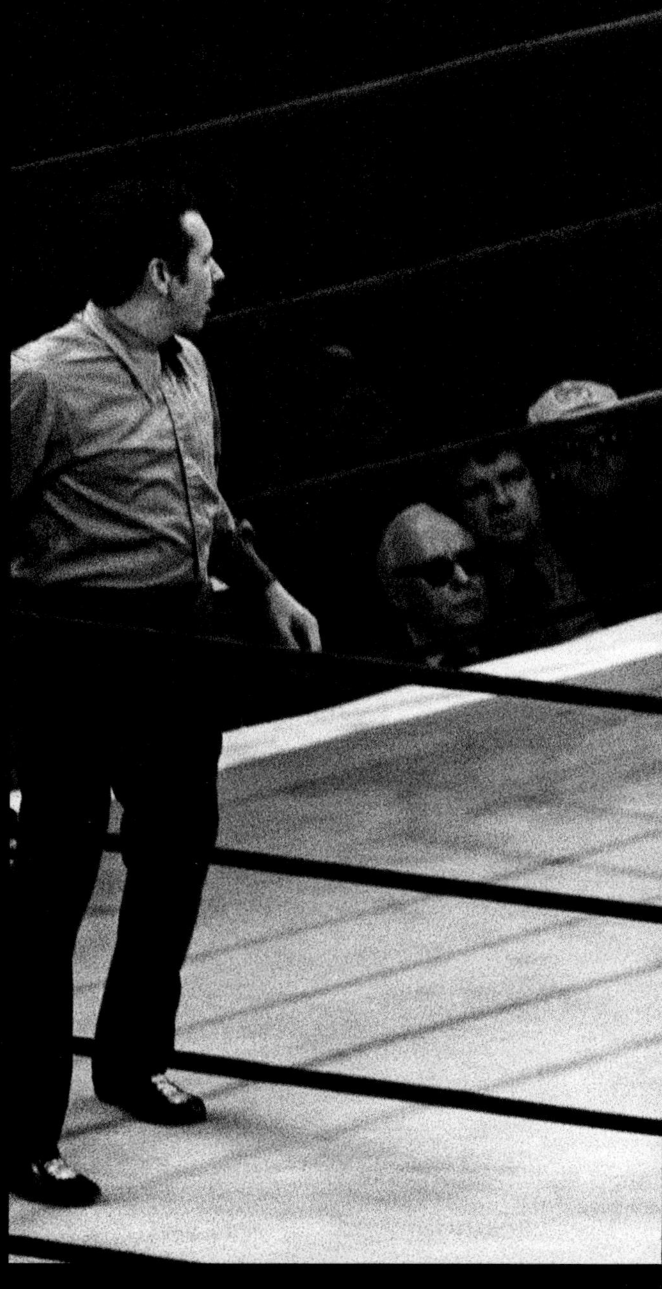

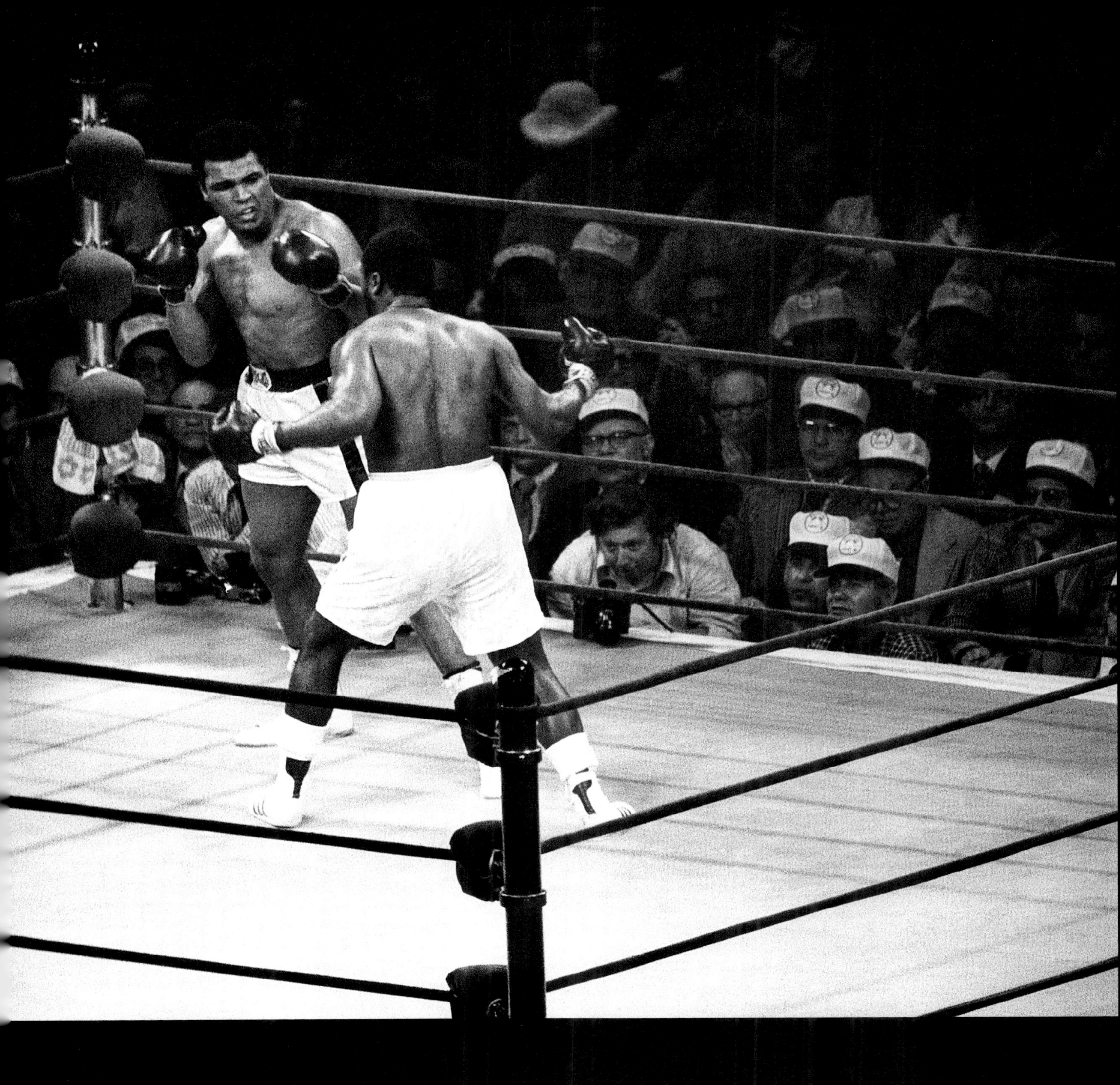

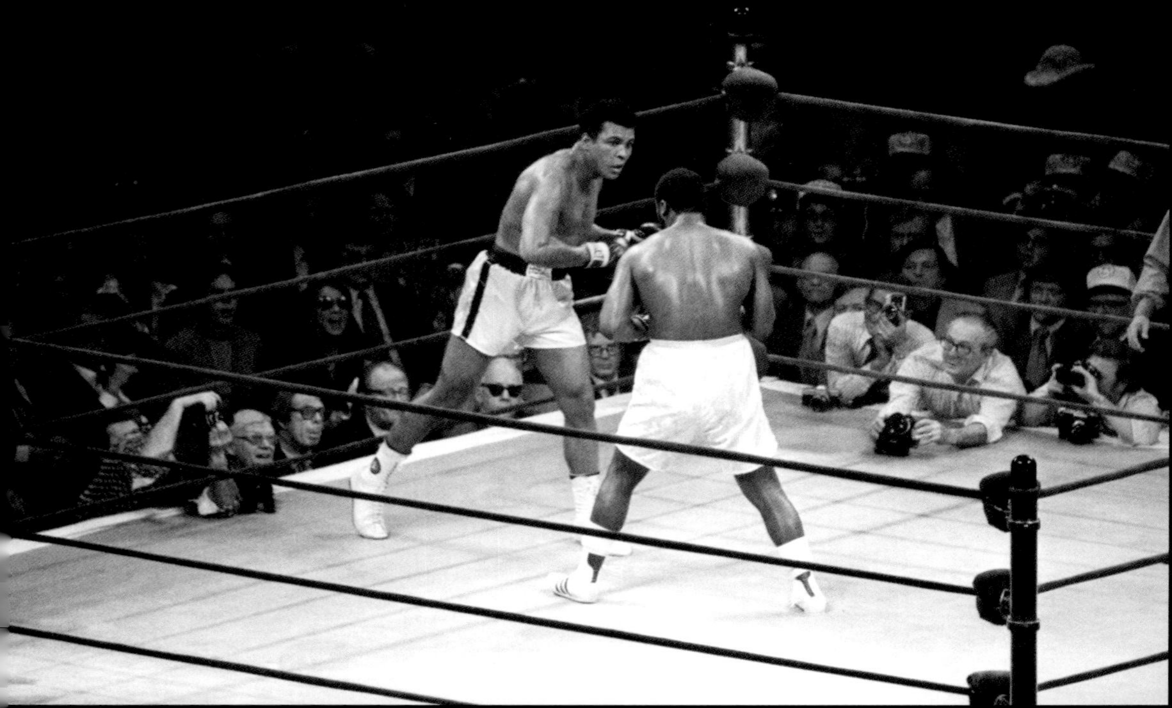

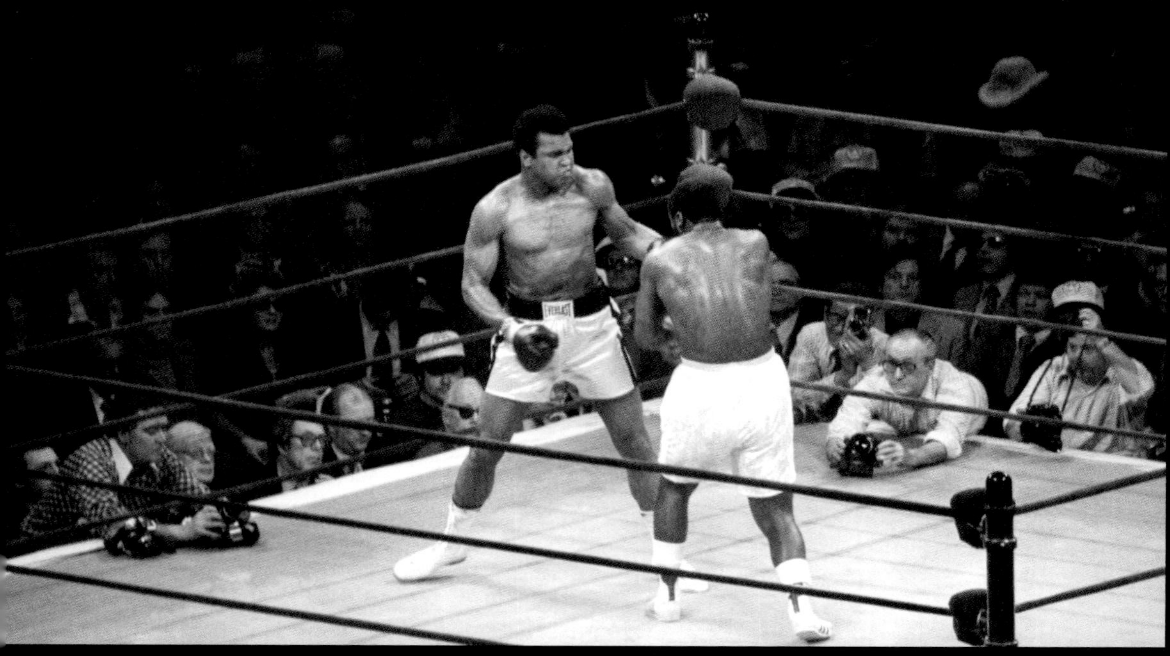

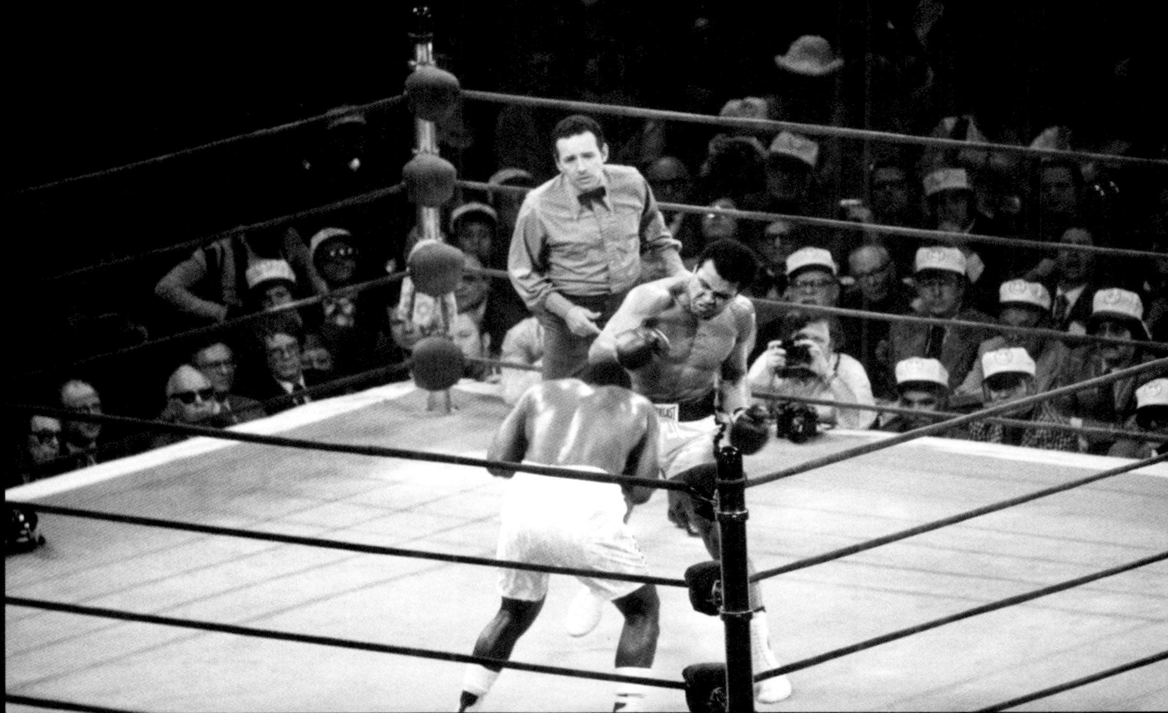

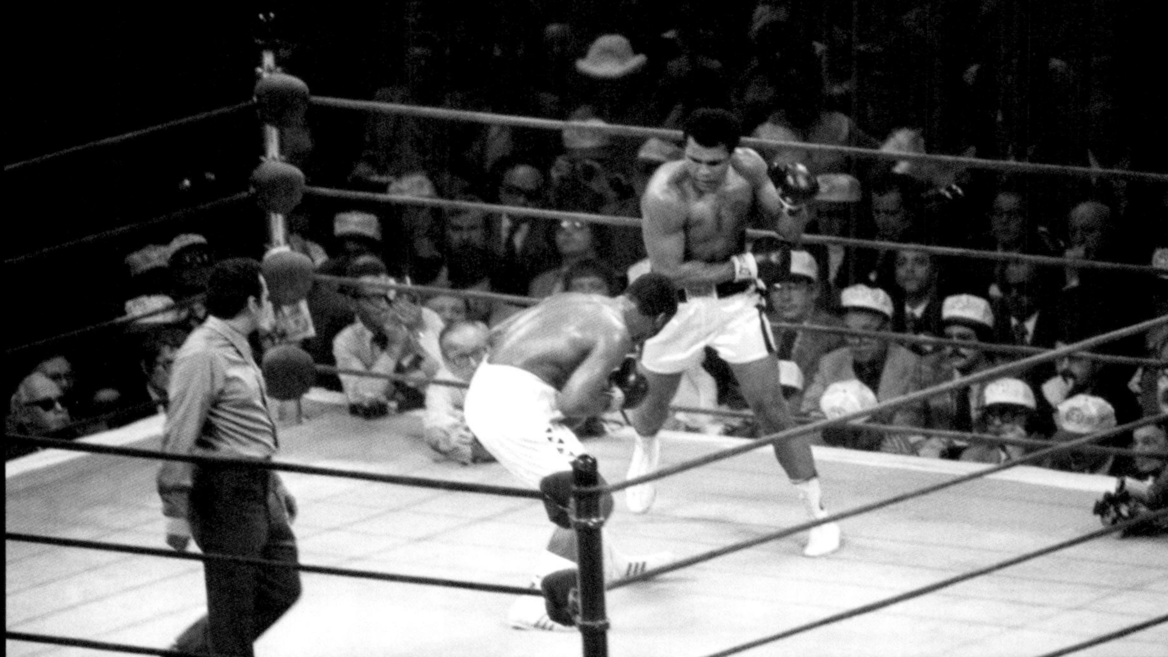

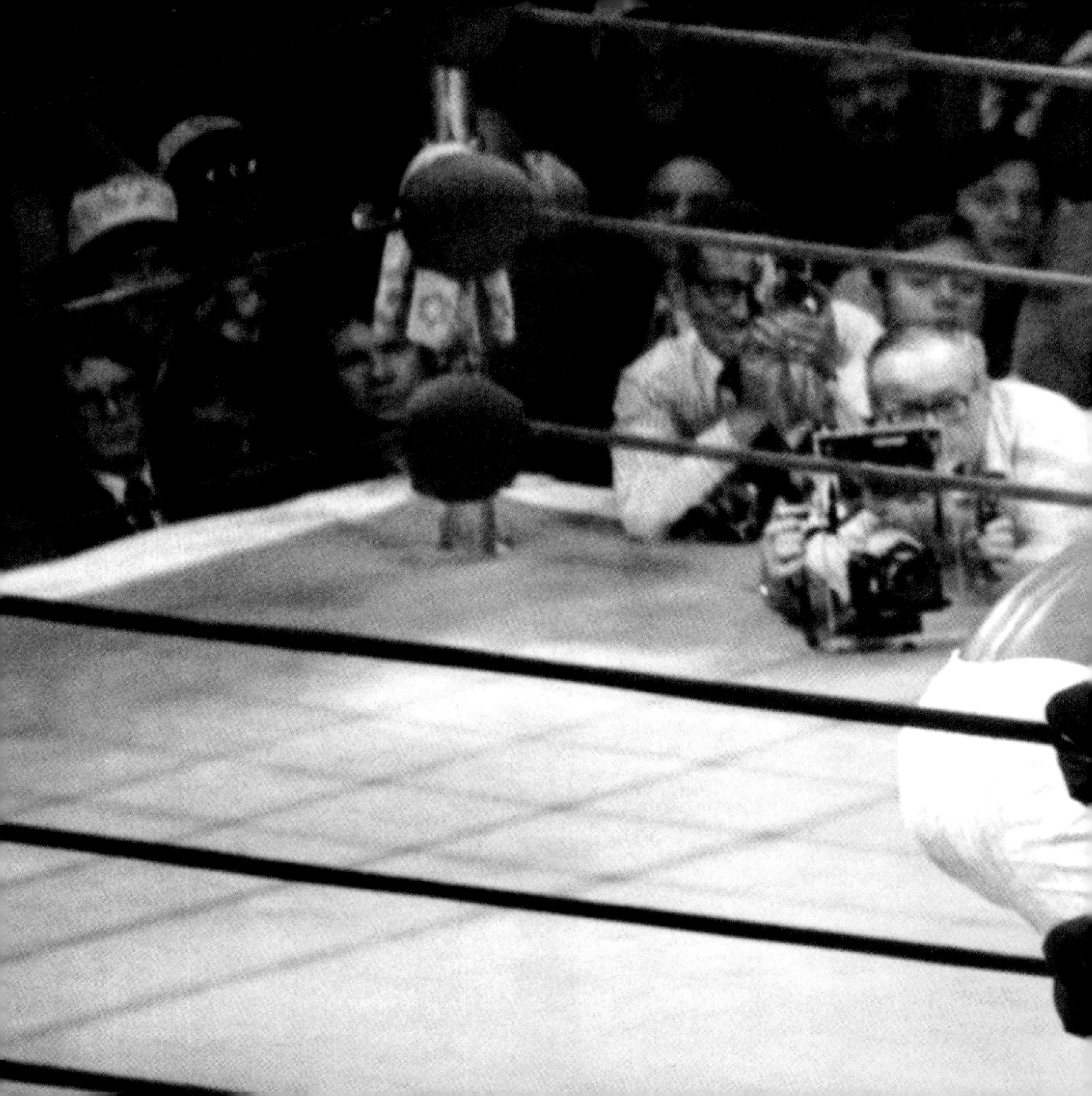

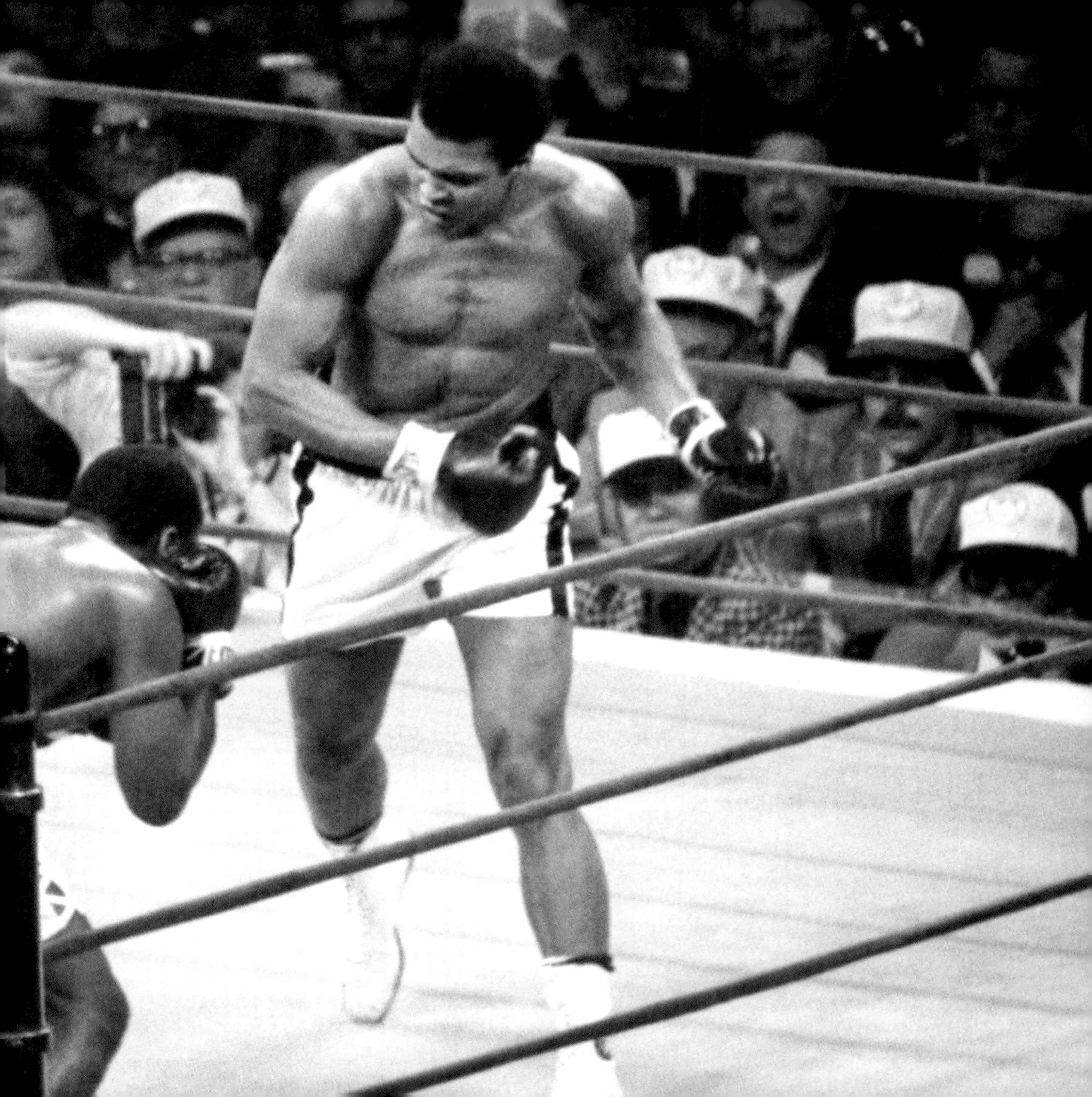

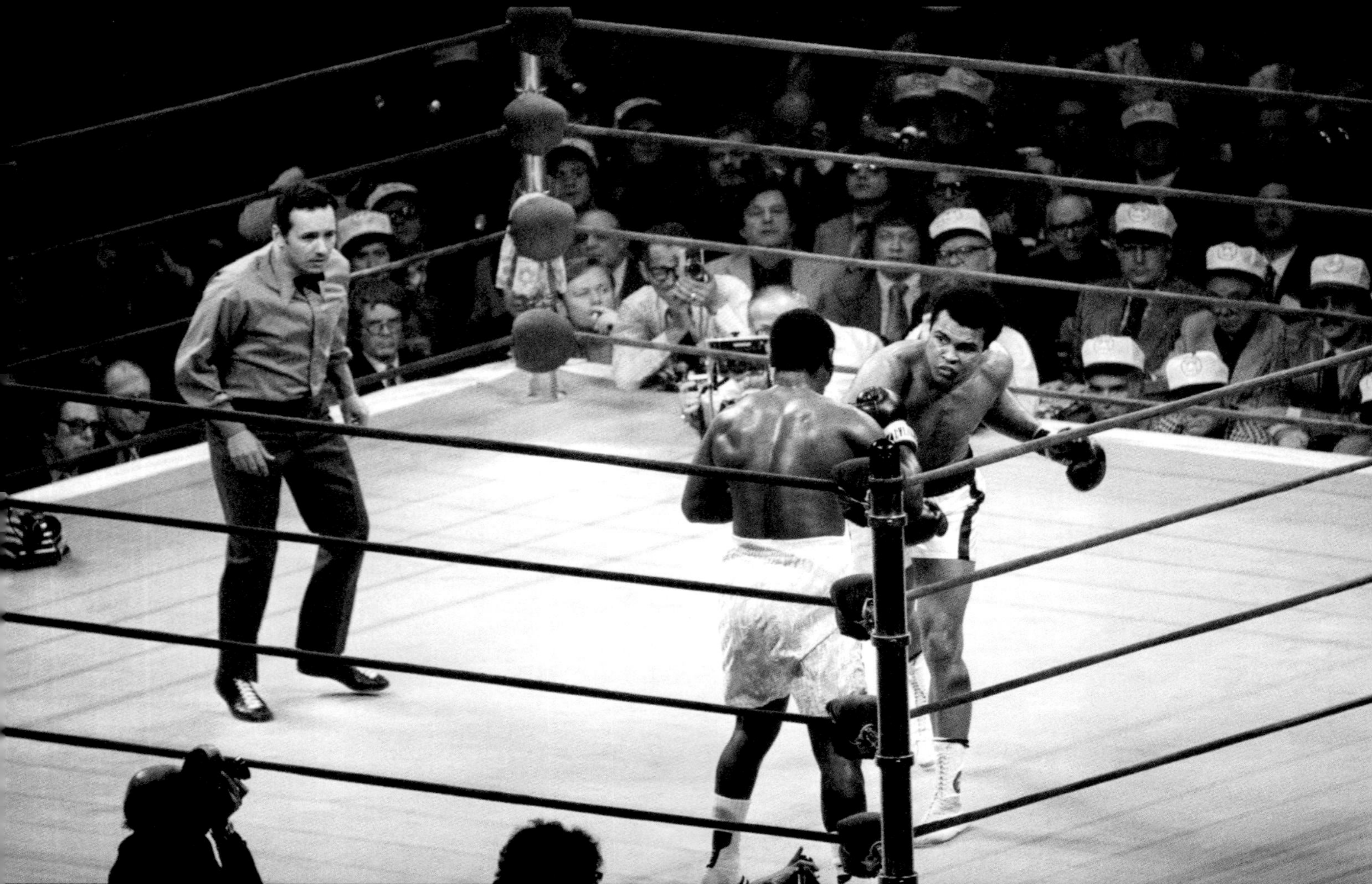

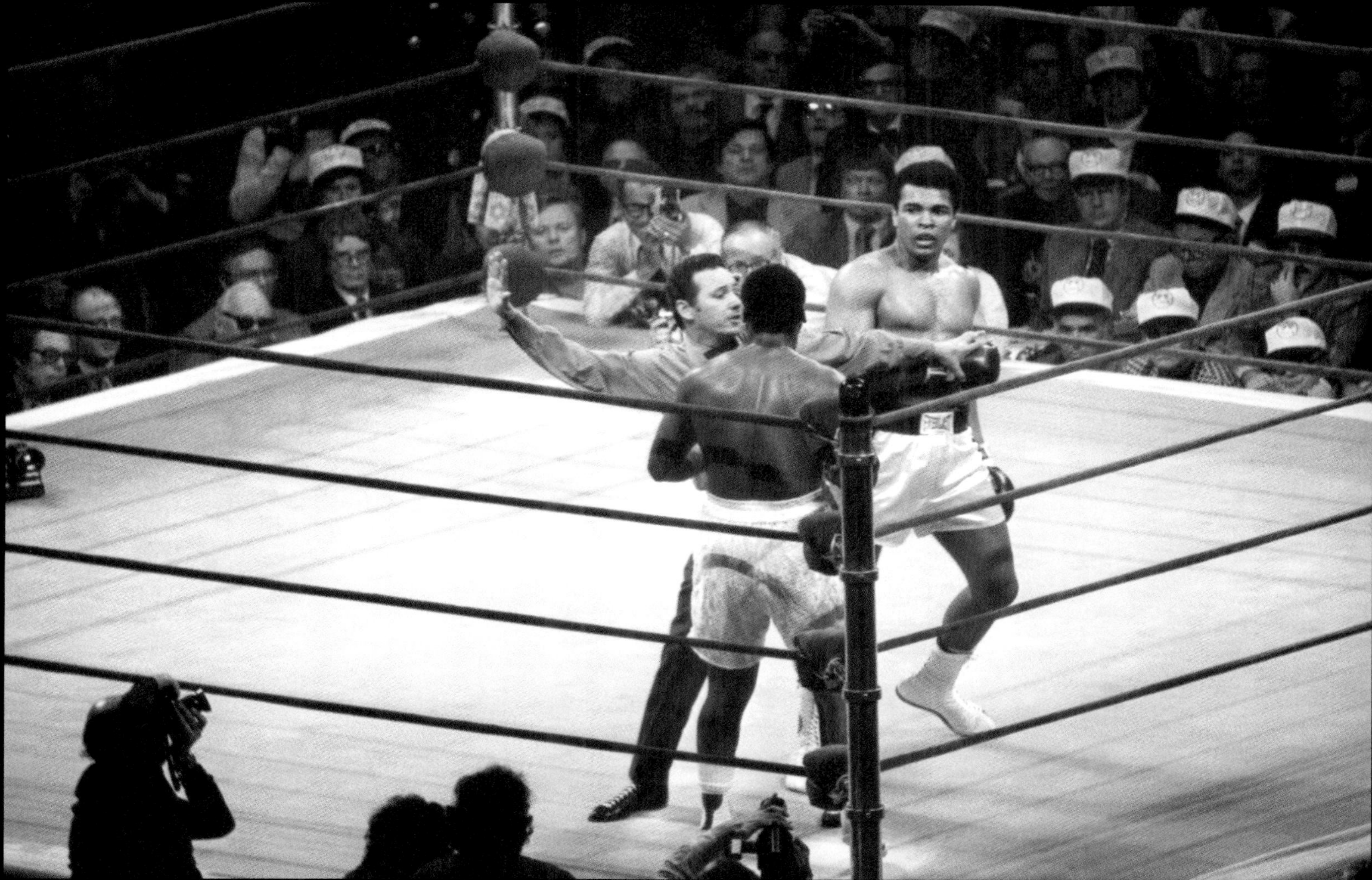

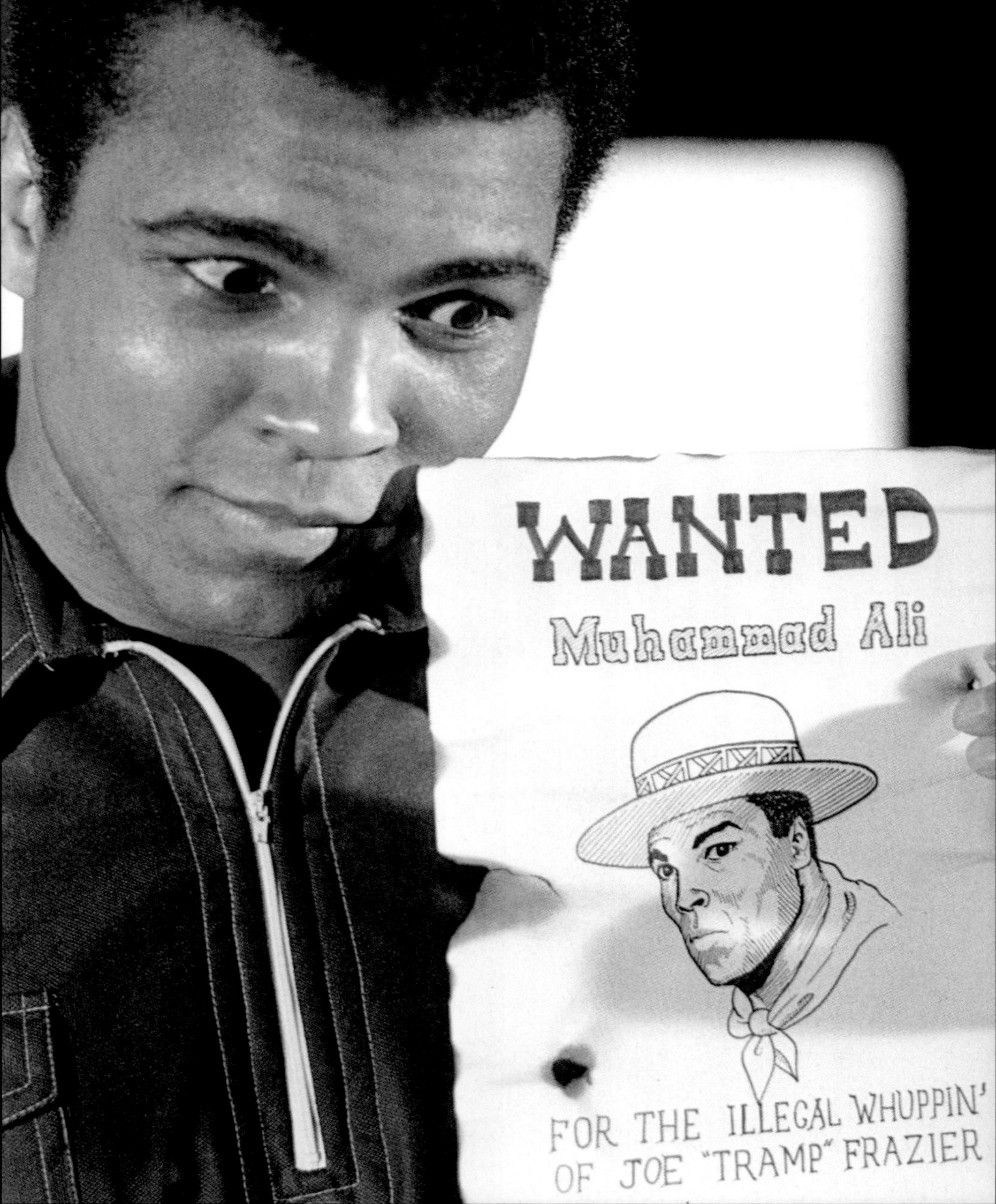
WANTED
Muhammad Ali
FOR THE ILLEGAL WHUPPIN'
OF JOE "TRAMP" FRAZIER

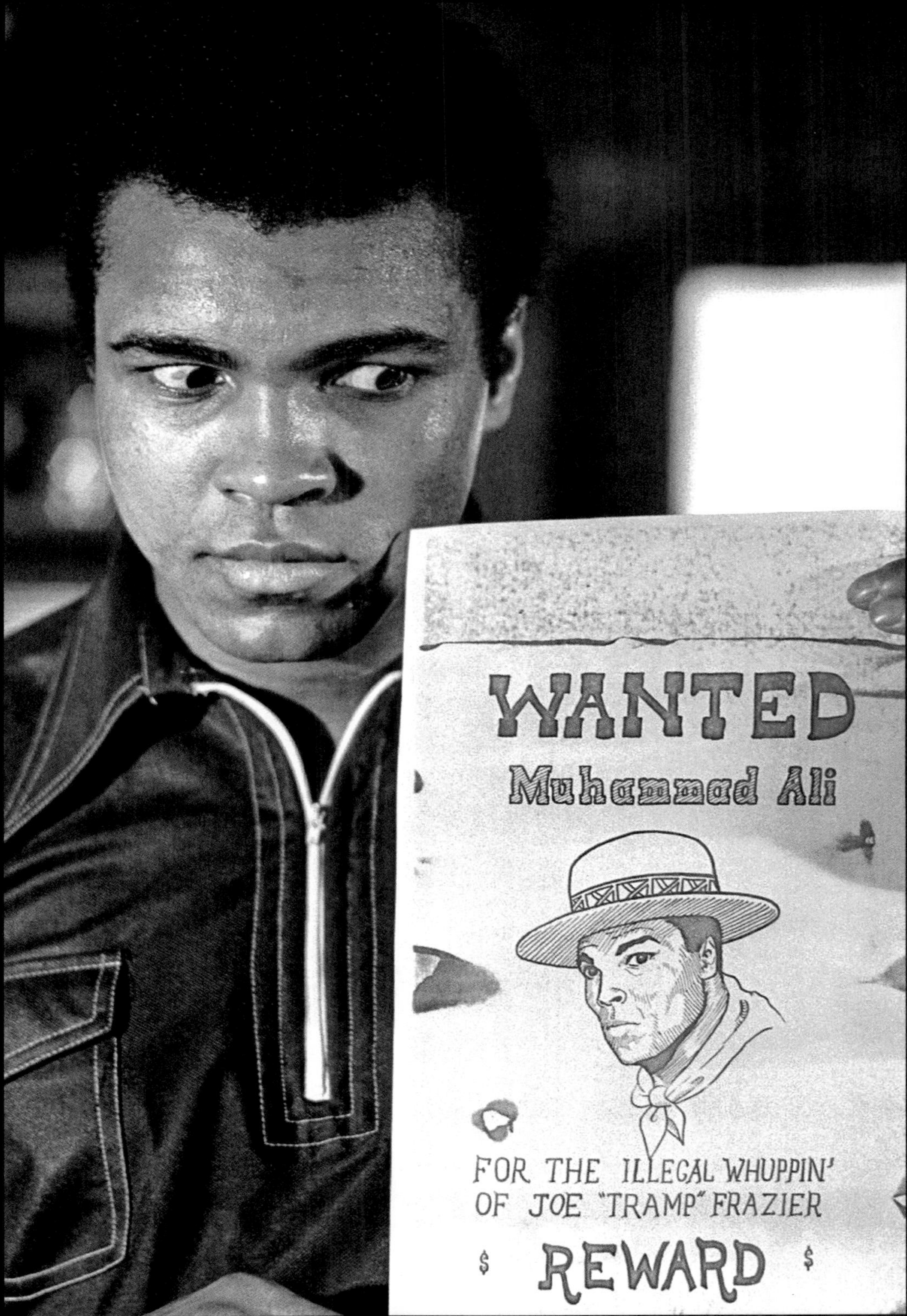
WANTED
Muhammad Ali
FOR THE ILLEGAL WHUPPIN'
OF JOE "TRAMP" FRAZIER
$ REWARD $

34

Muhammad Ali trains for his fight with George Foreman
Muhammad Ali training camp, Deer Lake, Pa.
Wednesday August 7, 1974

Ali had the world's media in the crowded gym at Deer Lake, Pennsylvania, that day. He proclaimed, "I got The New York Times, I got Dick Young, I got Red Smith, I got NBC, CBS, ABC. I even got some folk come from England. The Queen of England told 'em you better go report on Muhammad Ali."

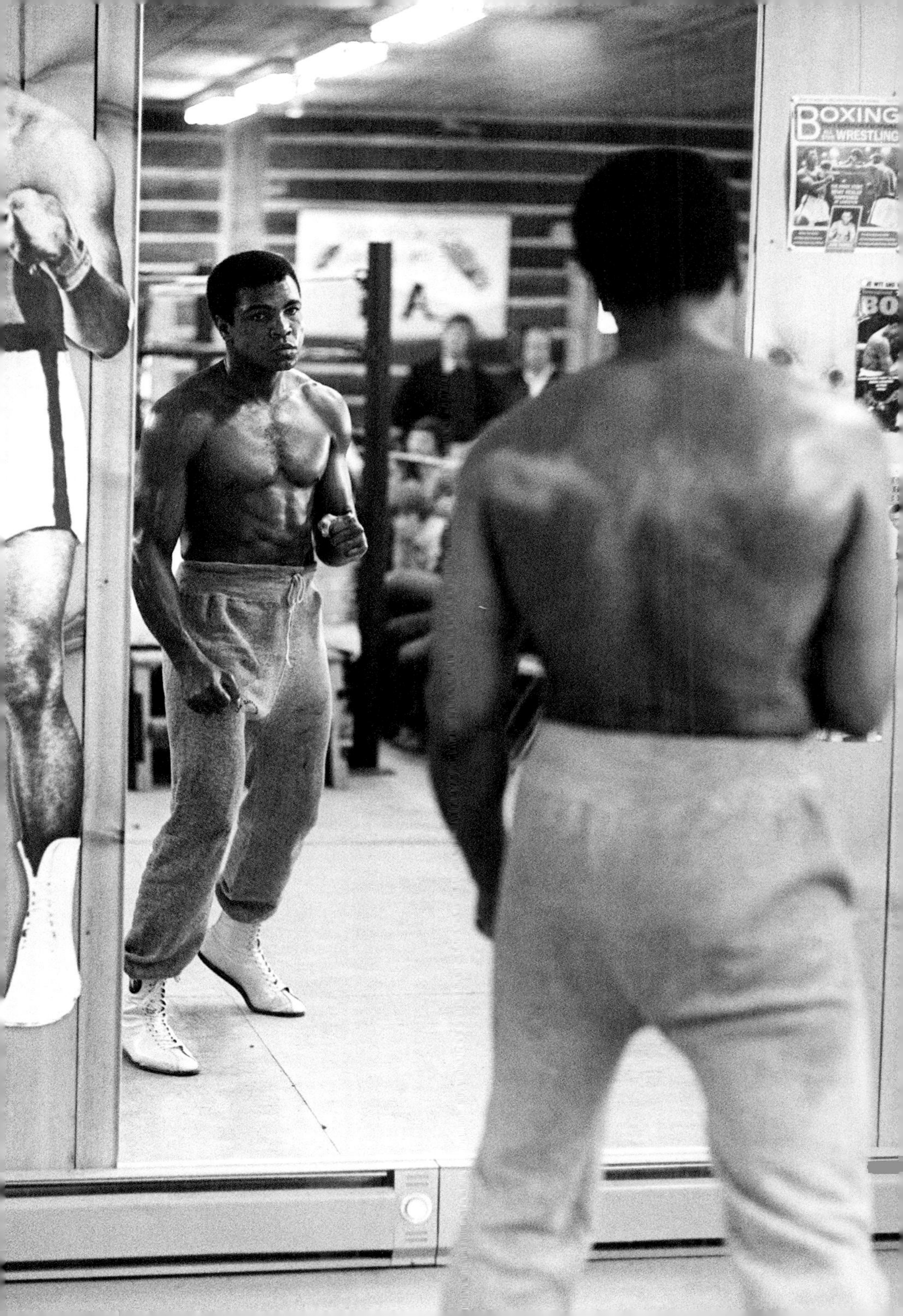
BOXING
WRESTLING

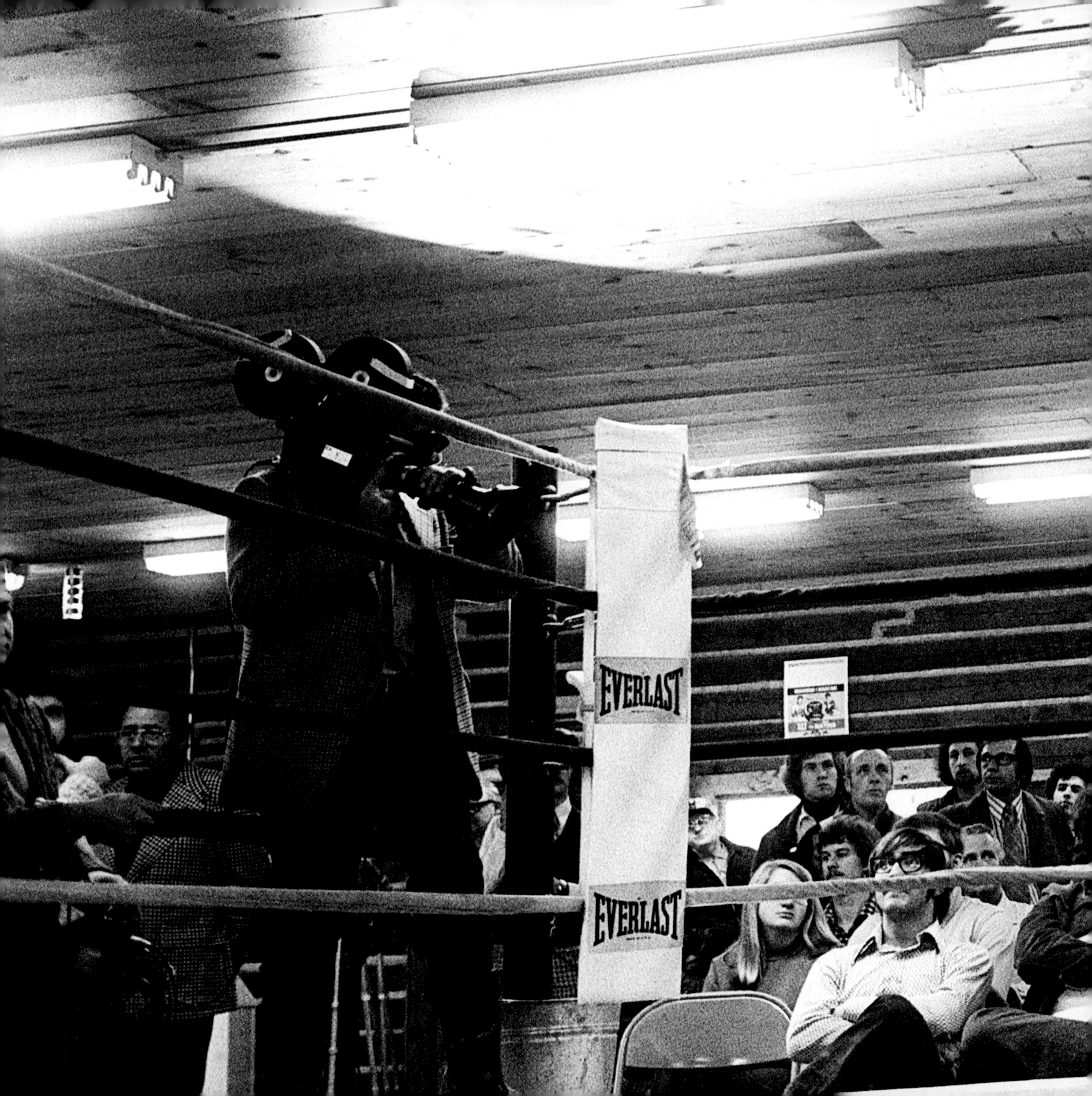
EVERLAST
EVERLAST

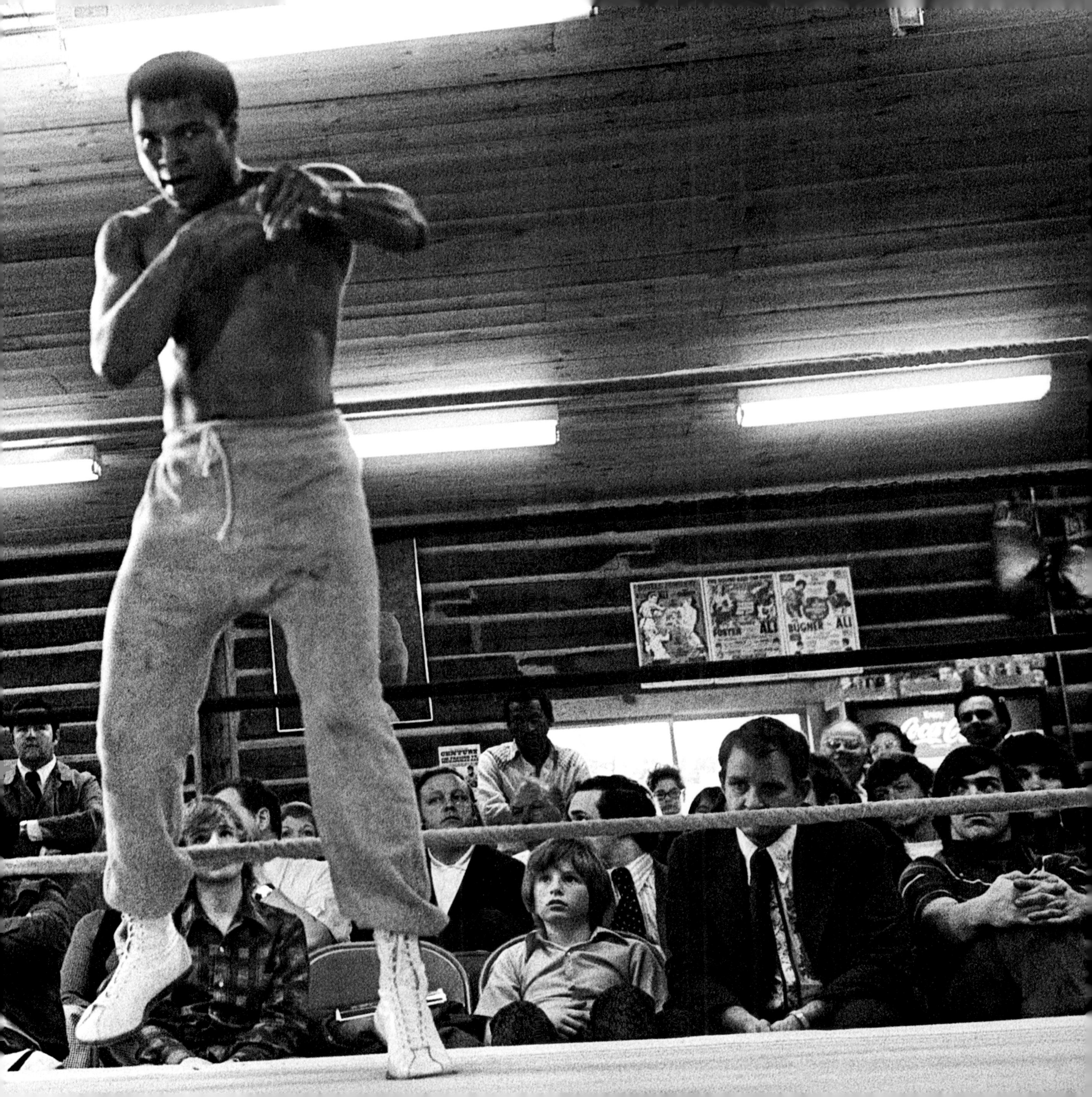
FOSTER
ALI
BUGNER
ALI

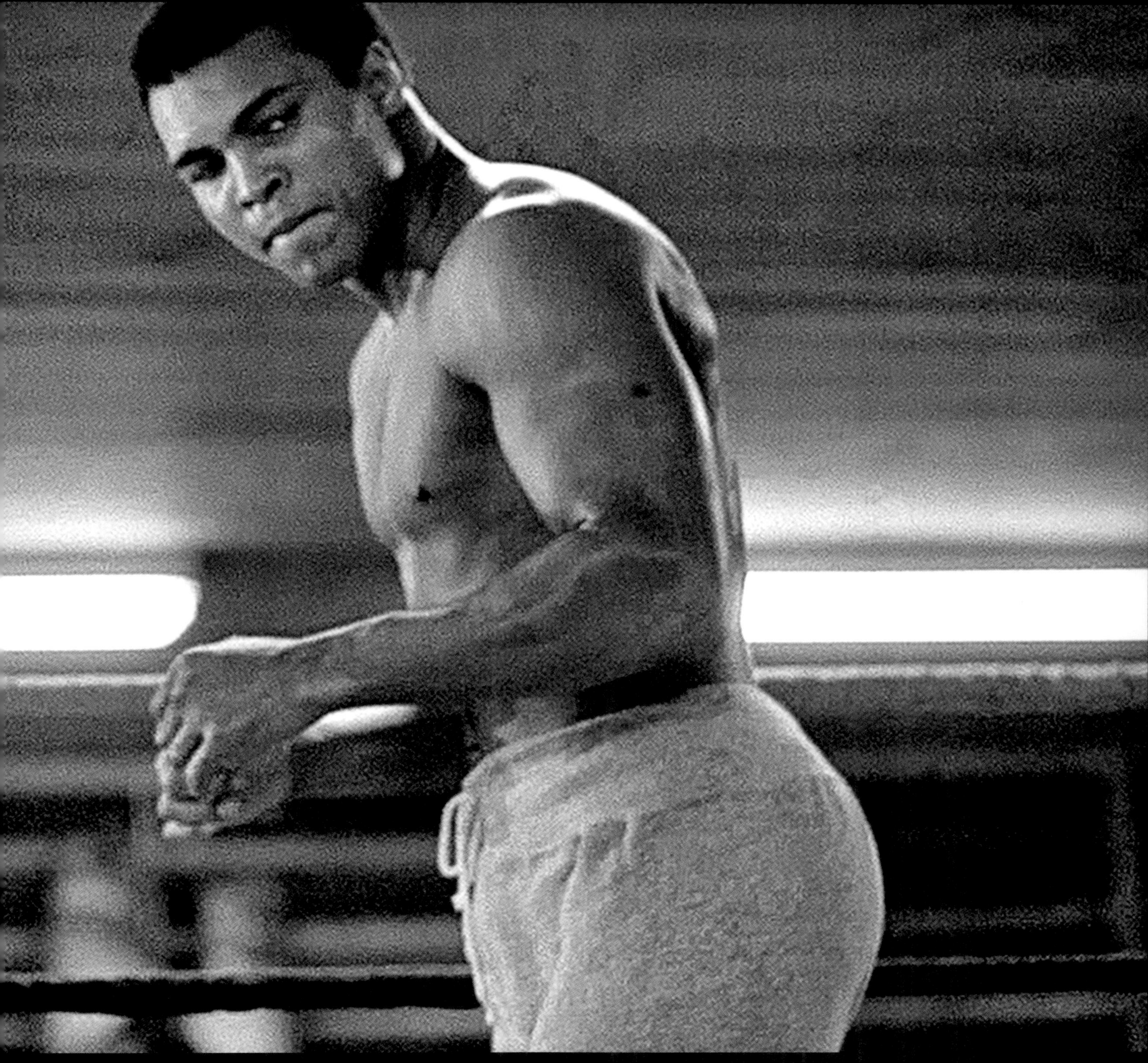

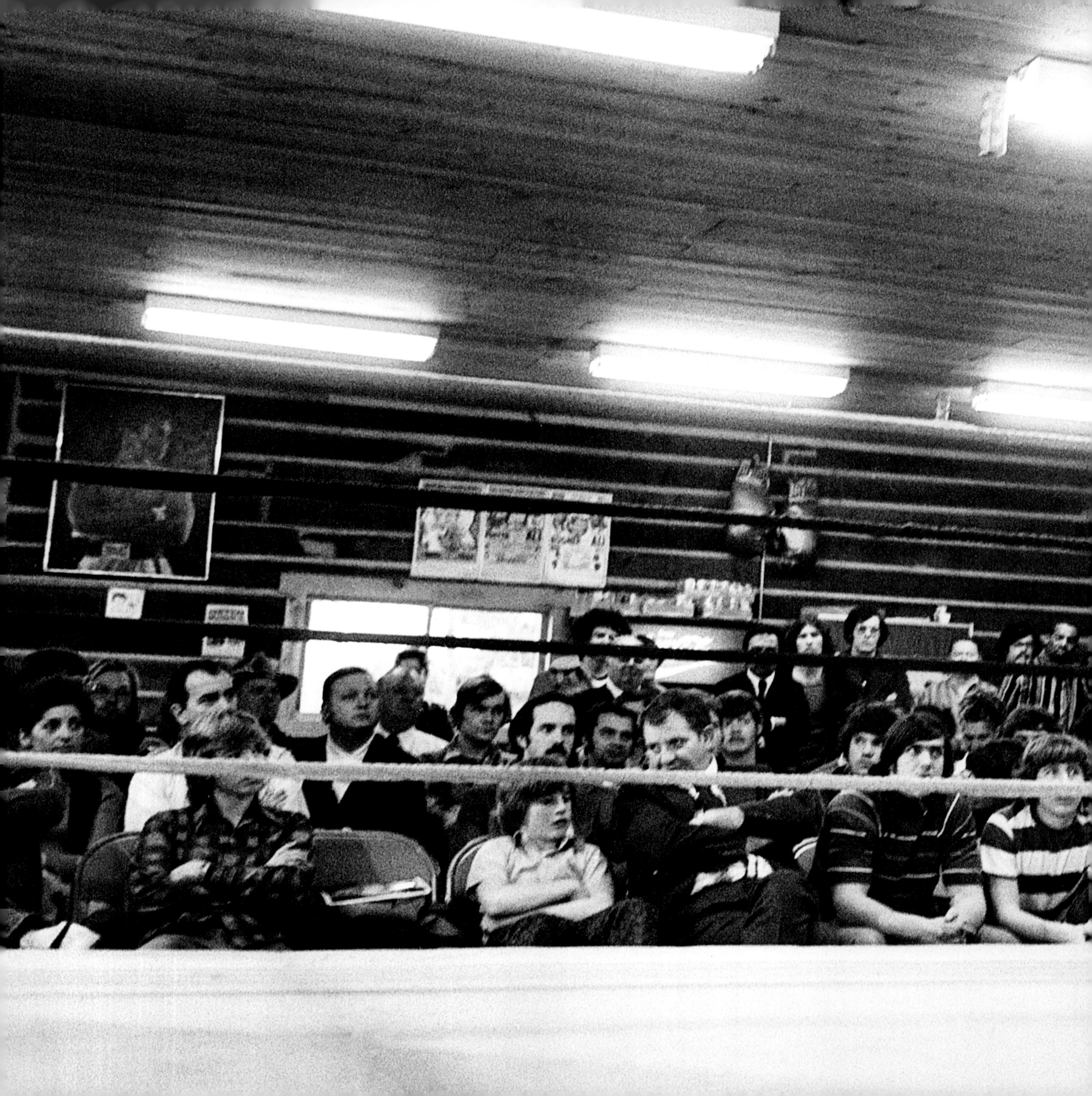

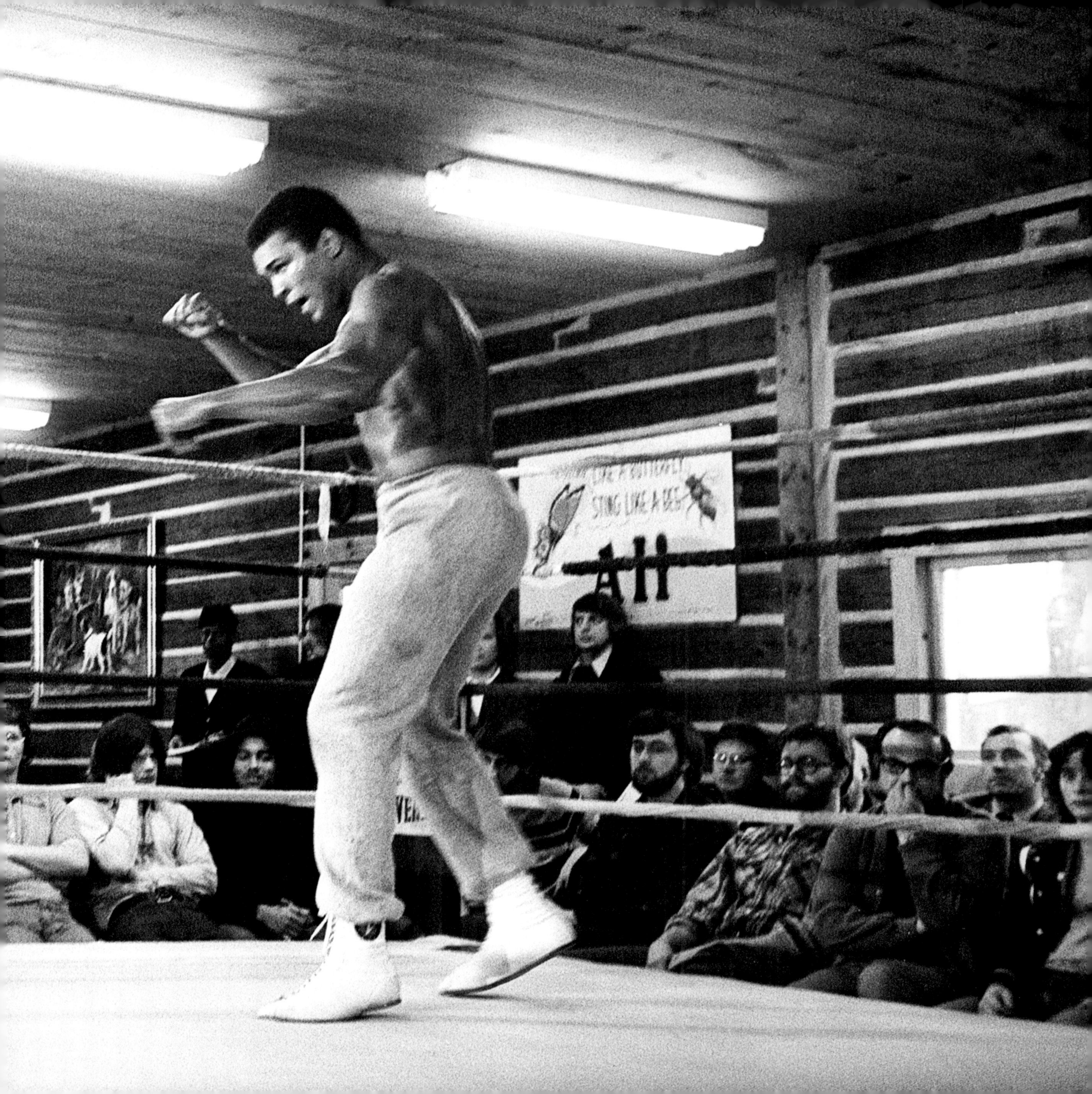
STING LIKE A BEE
ALI

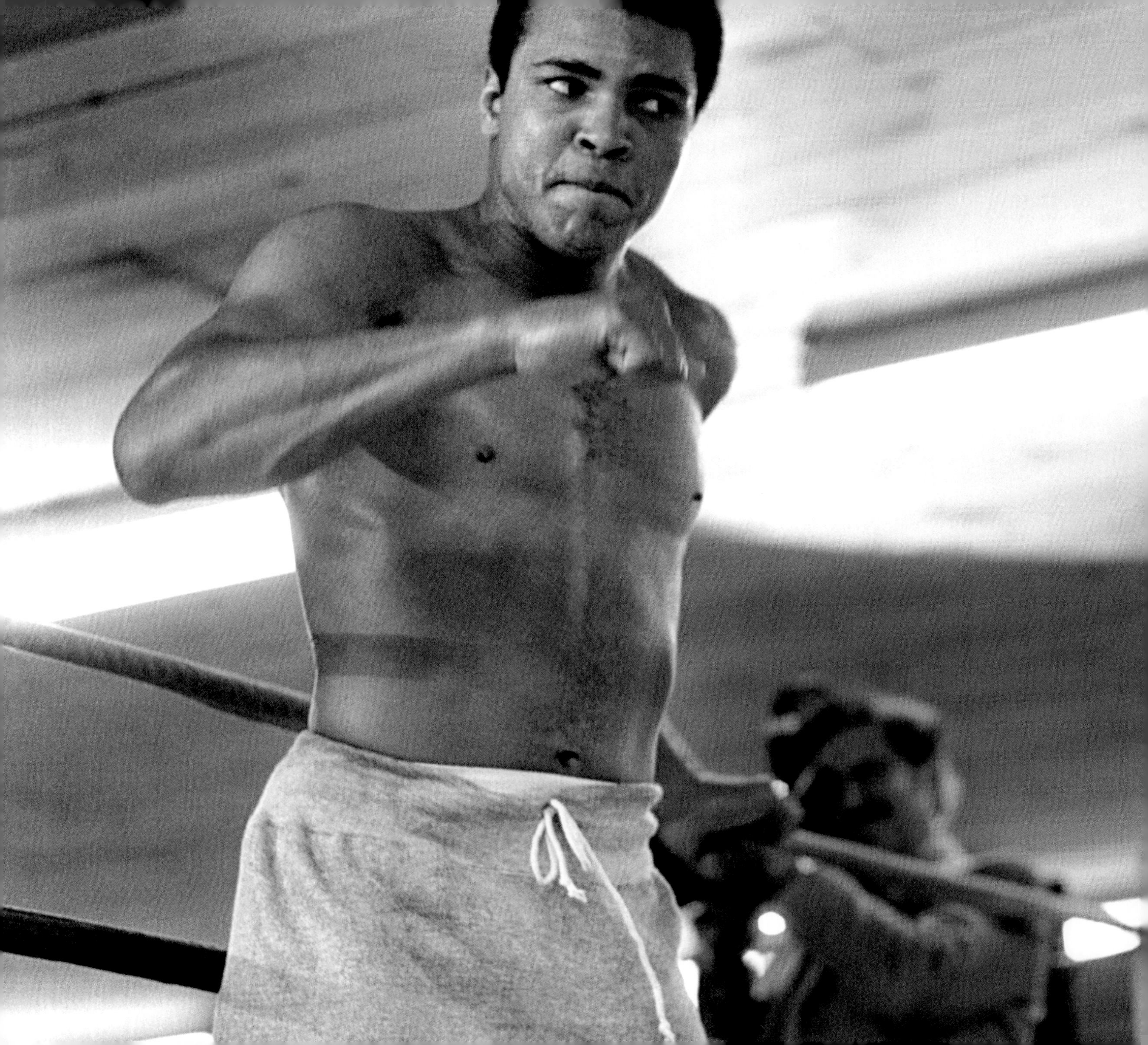

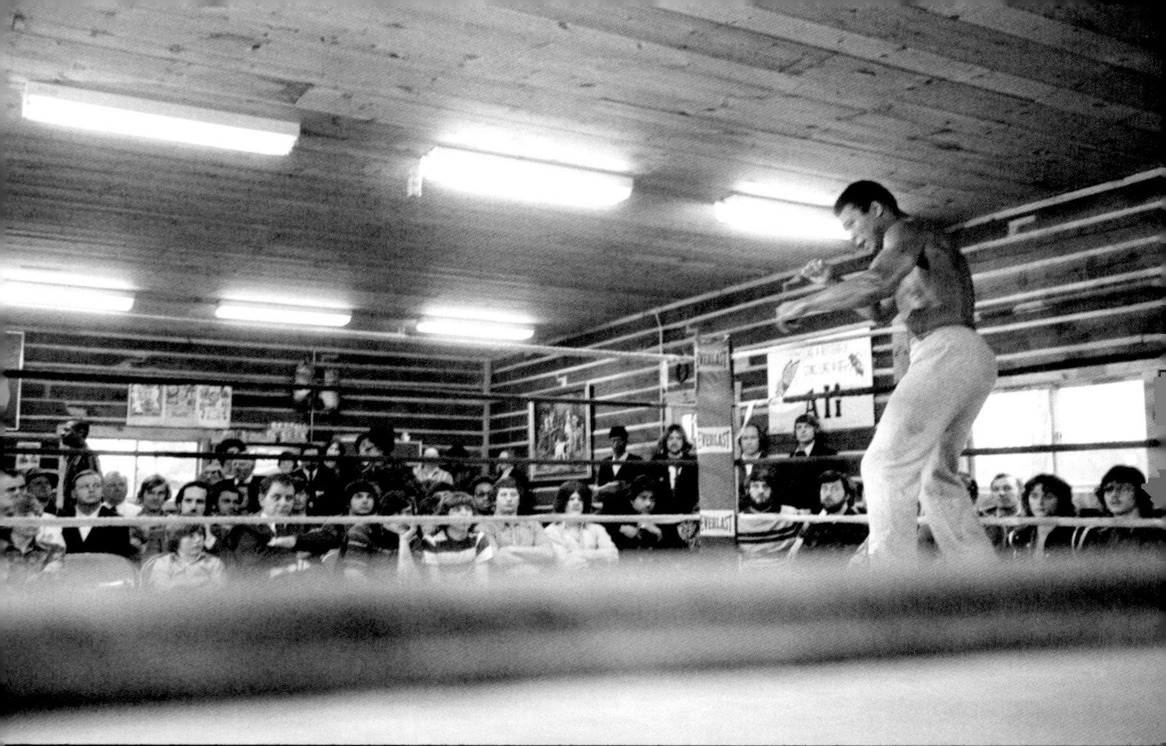
EVERLAST
Ali
EVERLAST
EVERLAST

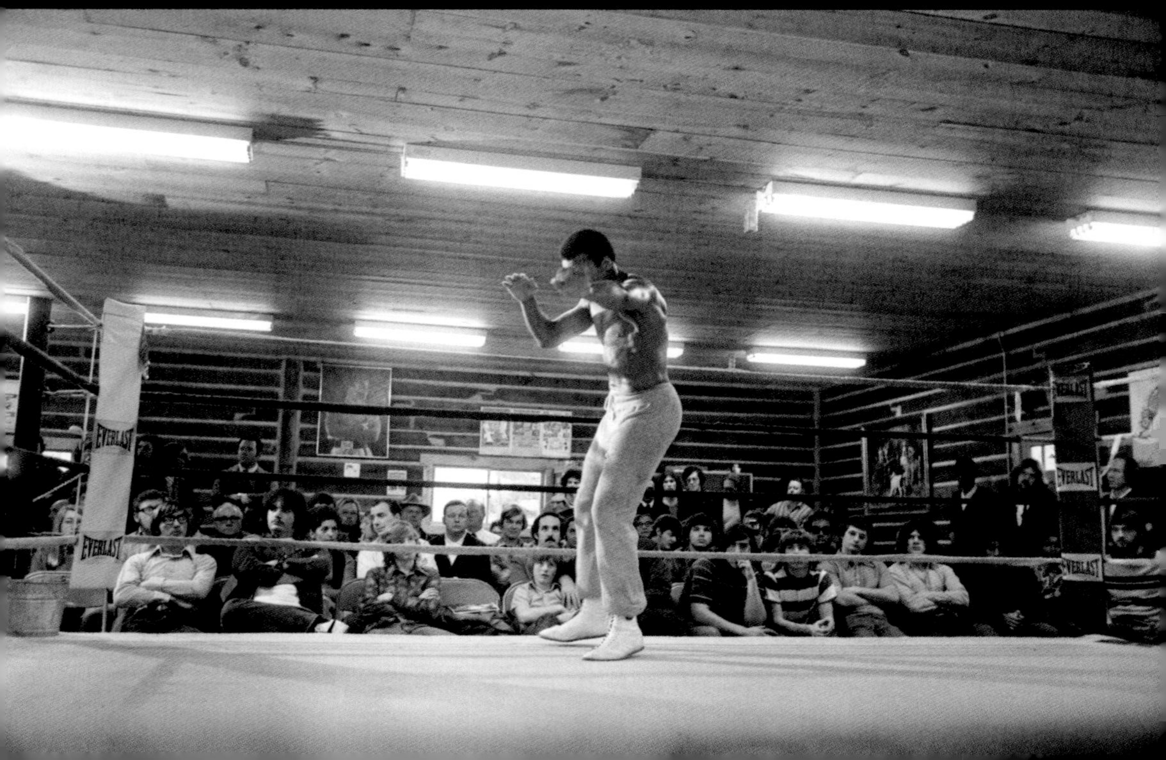
EVERLAST
EVERLAST
EVERLAST
EVERLAST
EVERLAST

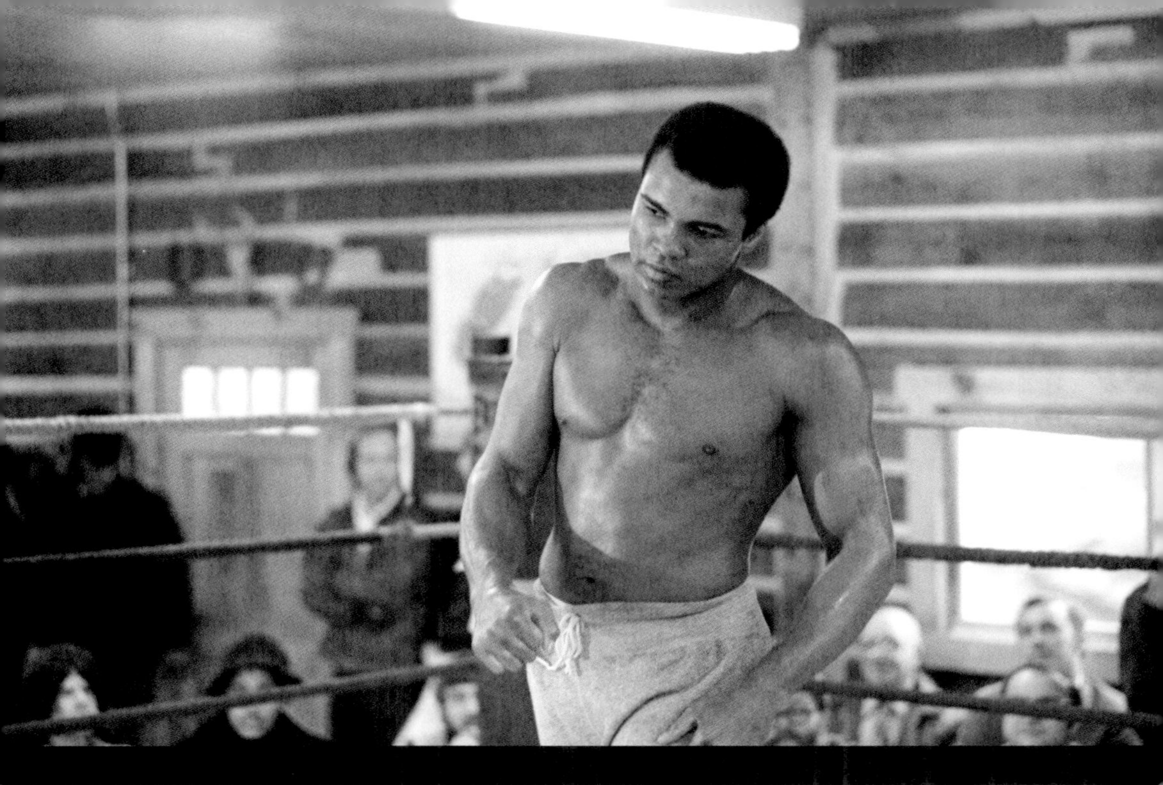

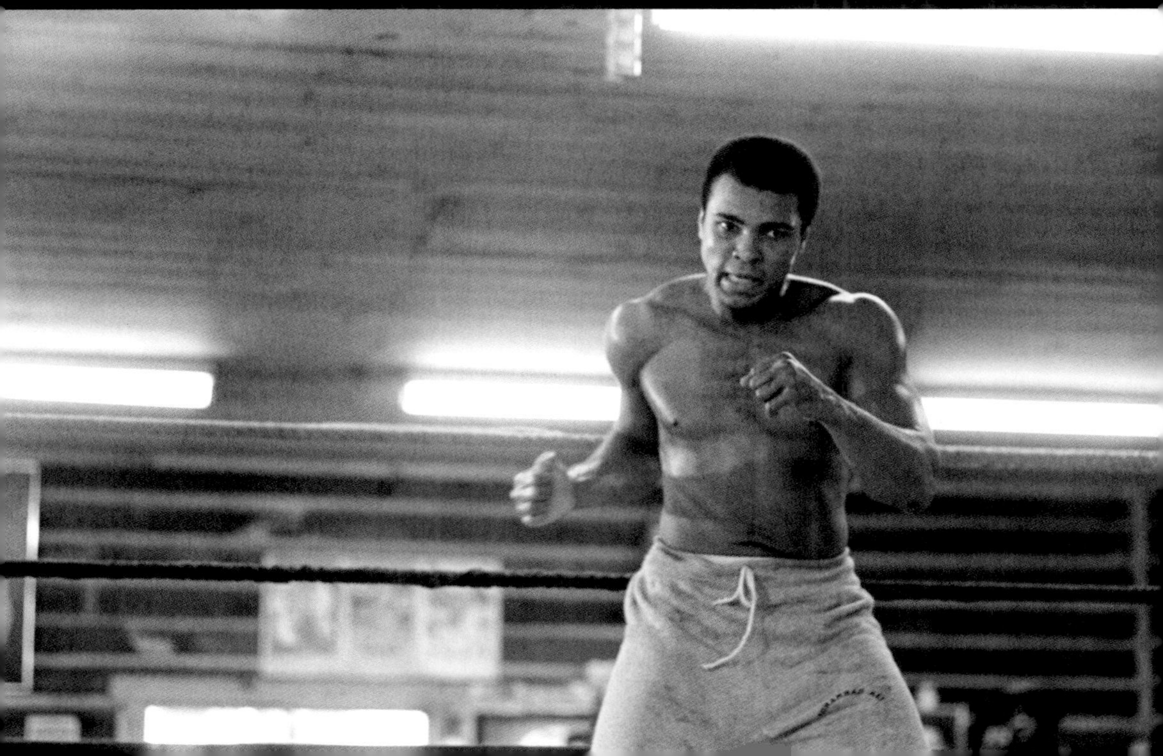

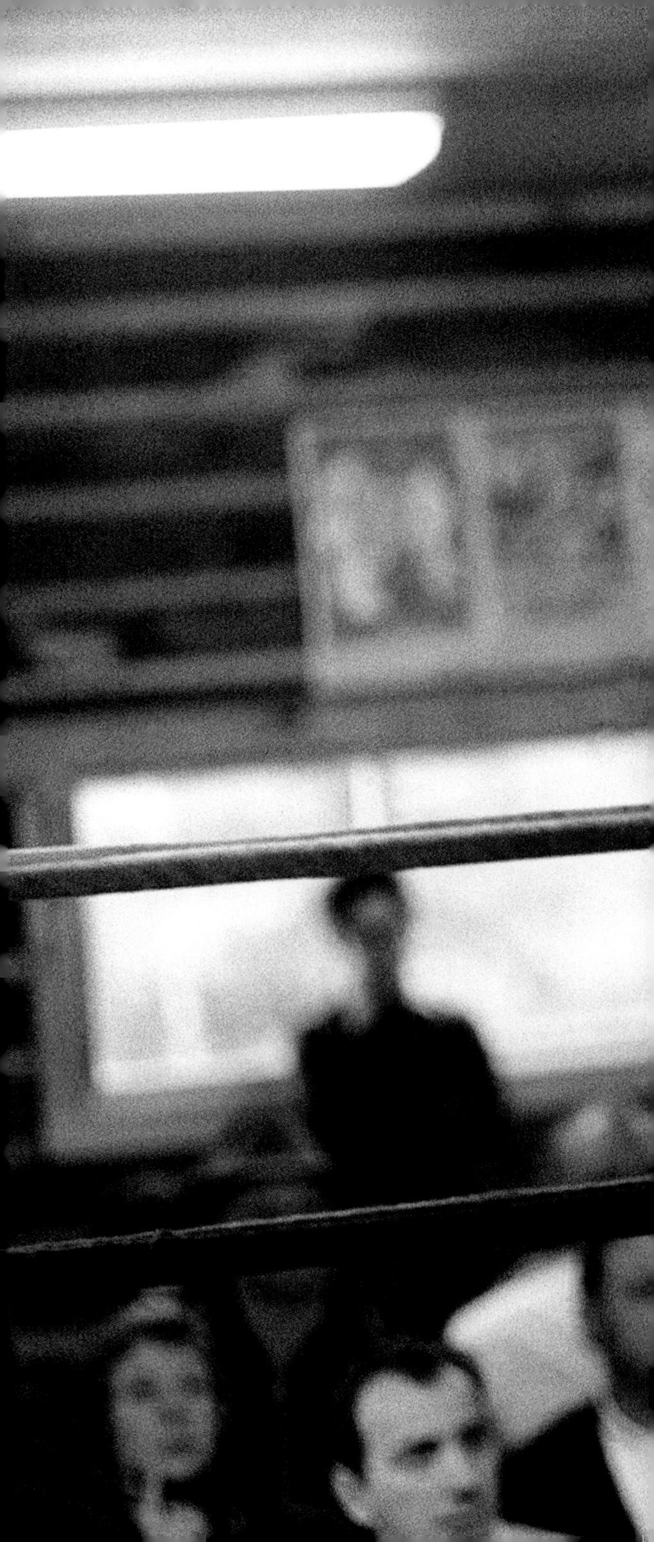

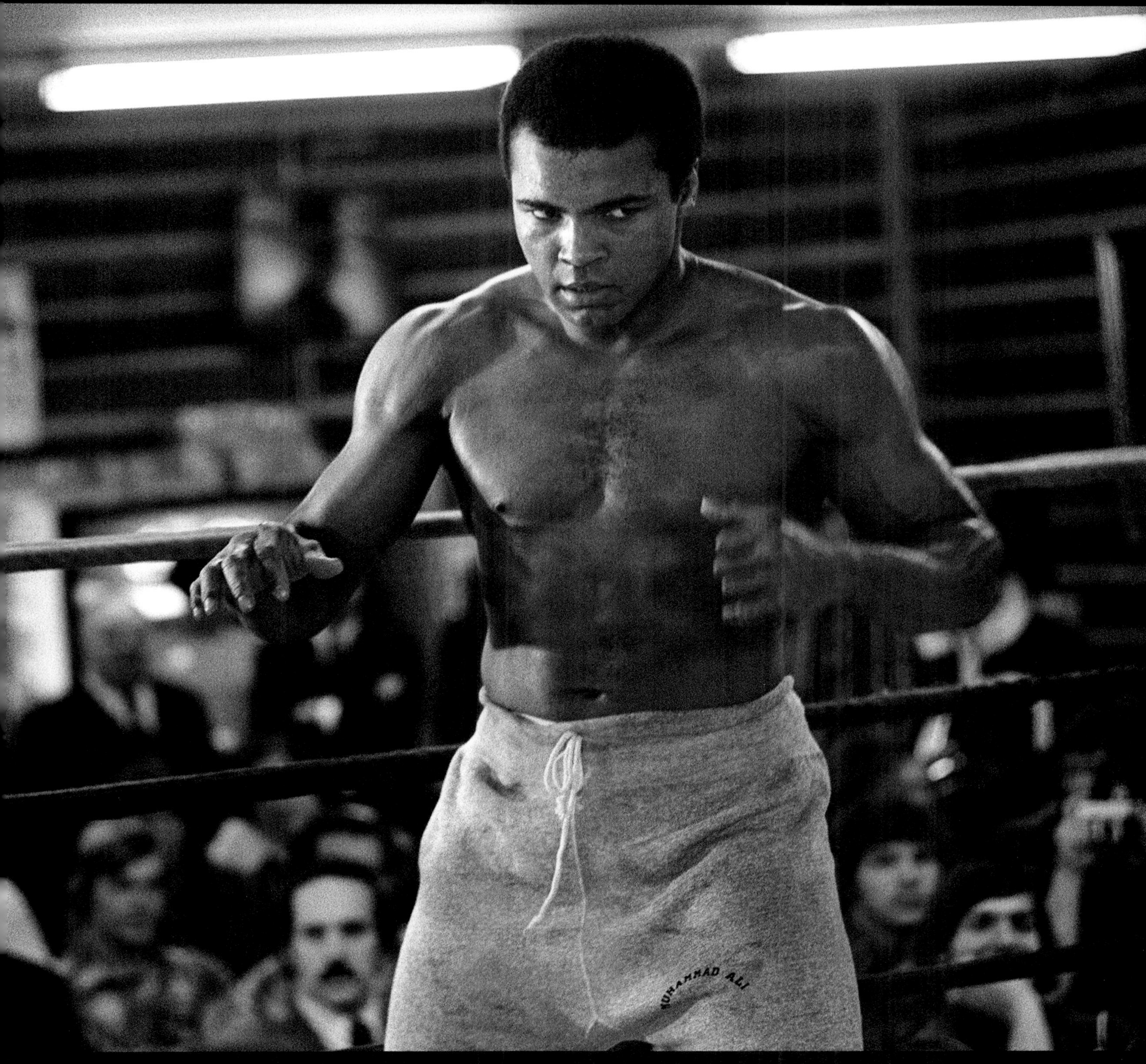
MUHAMMAD ALI

8

Muhammad Ali trains for his fight with George Foreman
Muhammad Ali training camp, Deer Lake, Pa.
August 1974

While most observers were worried that Ali could be seriously hurt during the fight against George Foreman, Ali devised a plan to confuse Foreman and have him punch himself out. Ali absorbed Foreman's mighty punches by just covering up so the bigger man would tire. It worked so well that Ali had enough firepower left to demolish the exhausted Foreman. Leading up to the fight, Ali had said that he had a secret plan. When I looked back at my negatives, I realized we had all been witnesses to this secret plan … the "rope-a-dope" was later described by one sportswriter as one of sport's greatest sleights of hand.

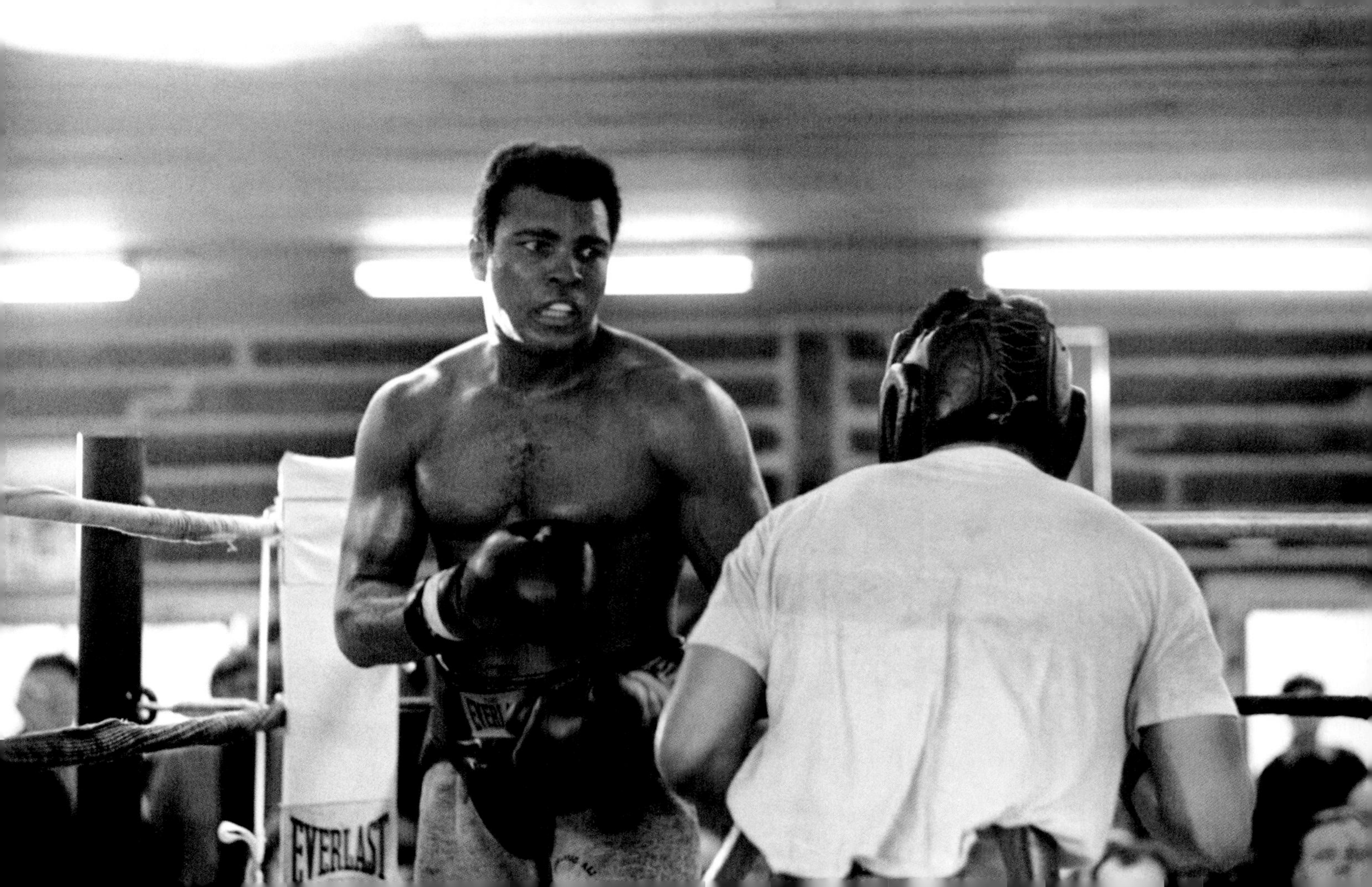
EVERLAST

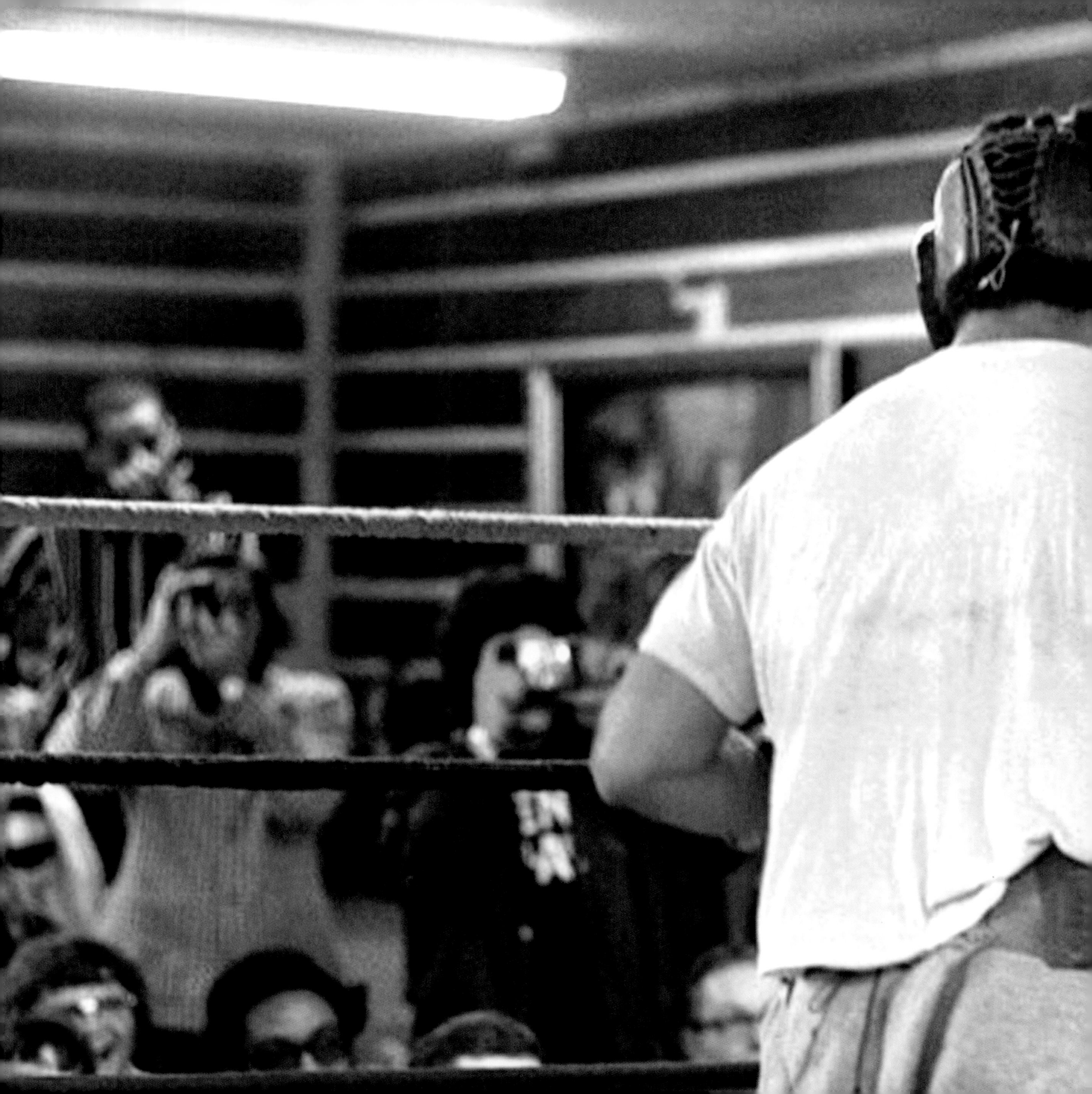

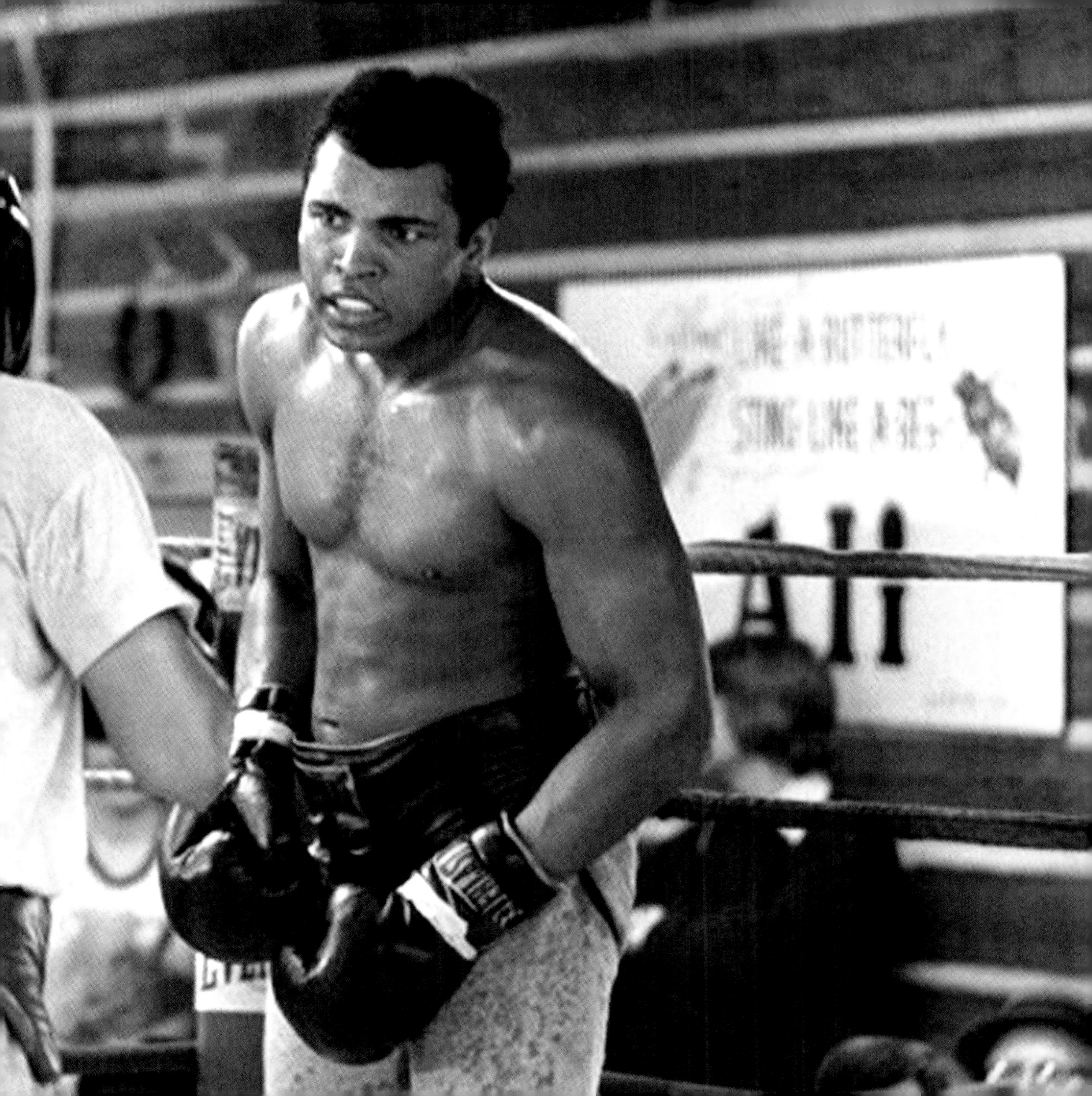

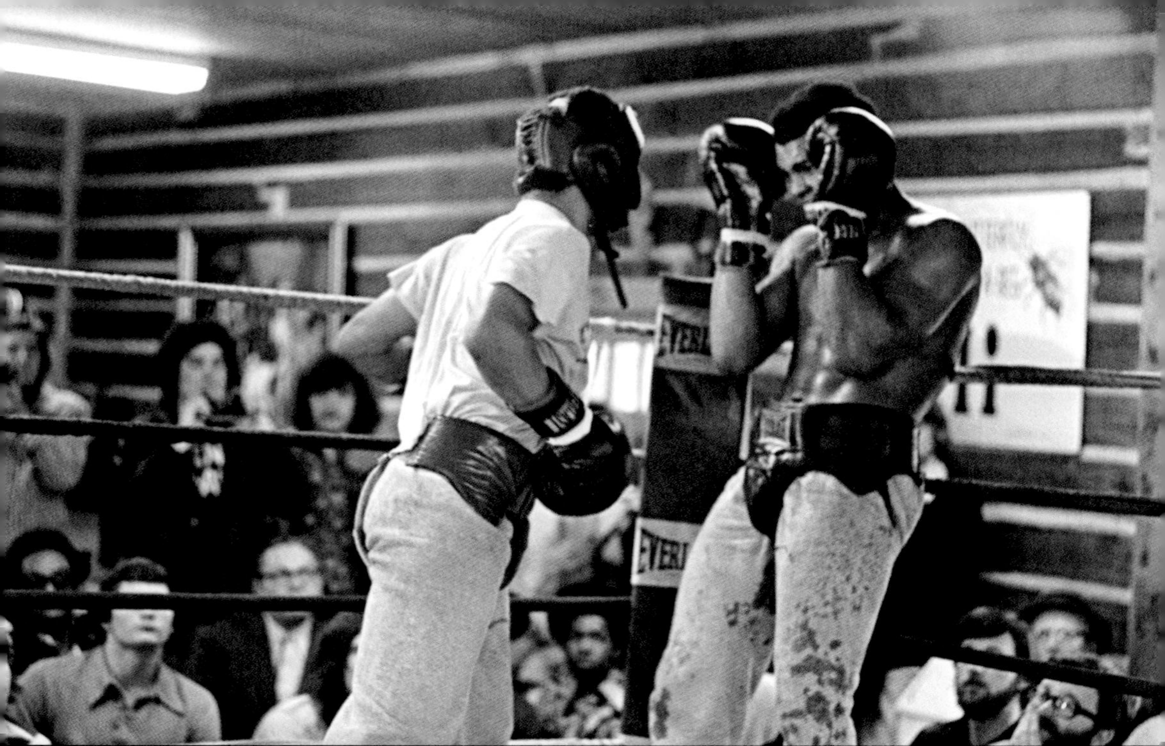

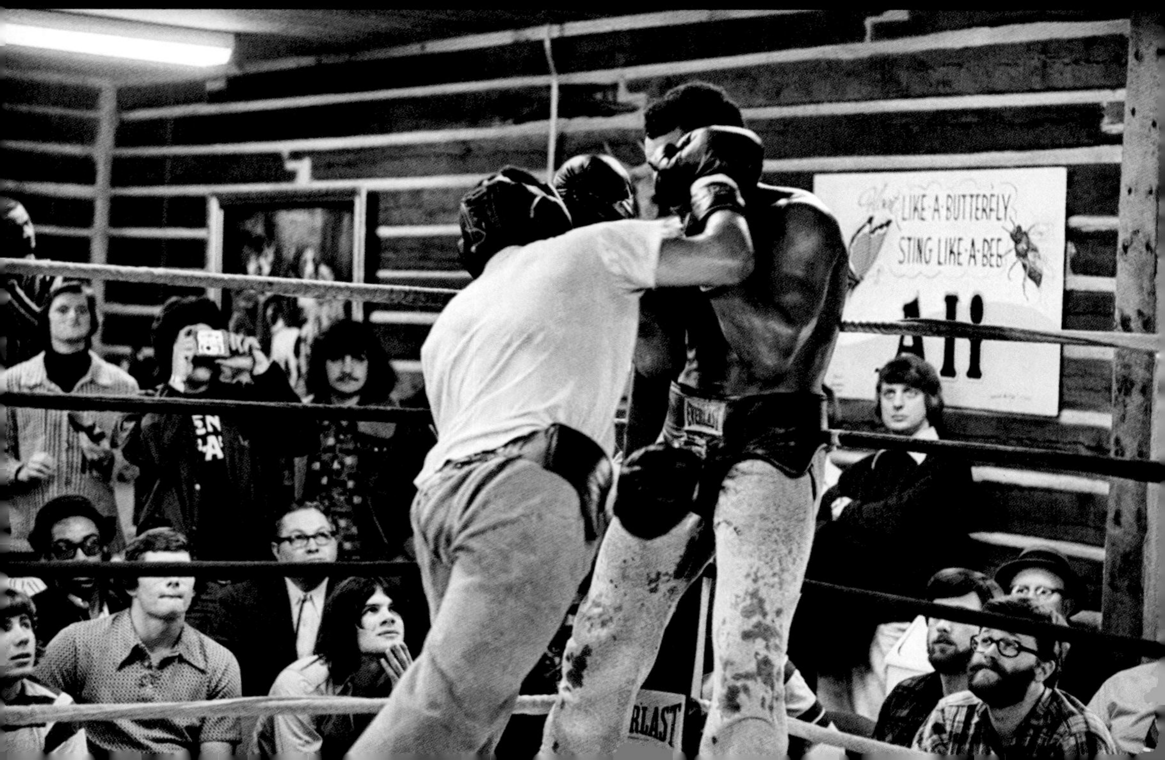
LIKE-A-BUTTERFLY
STING LIKE-A-BEE
Ali
EVERLAST

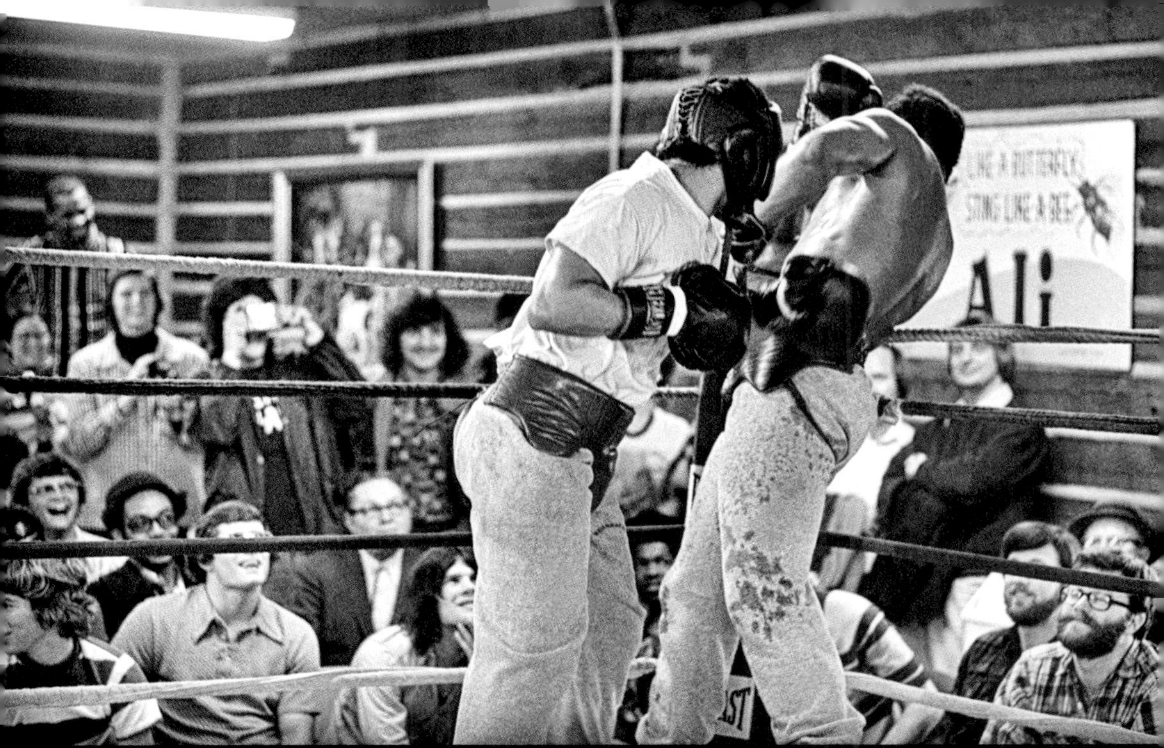
STING LIKE A BEE
Ali

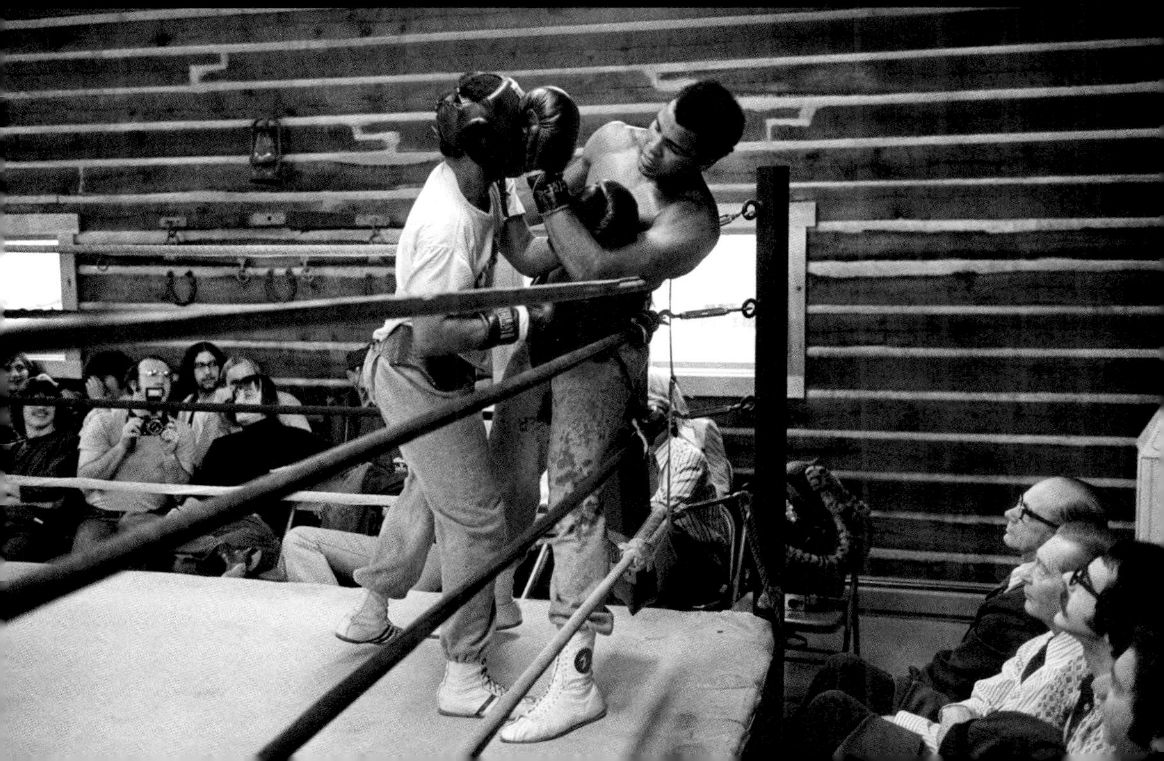

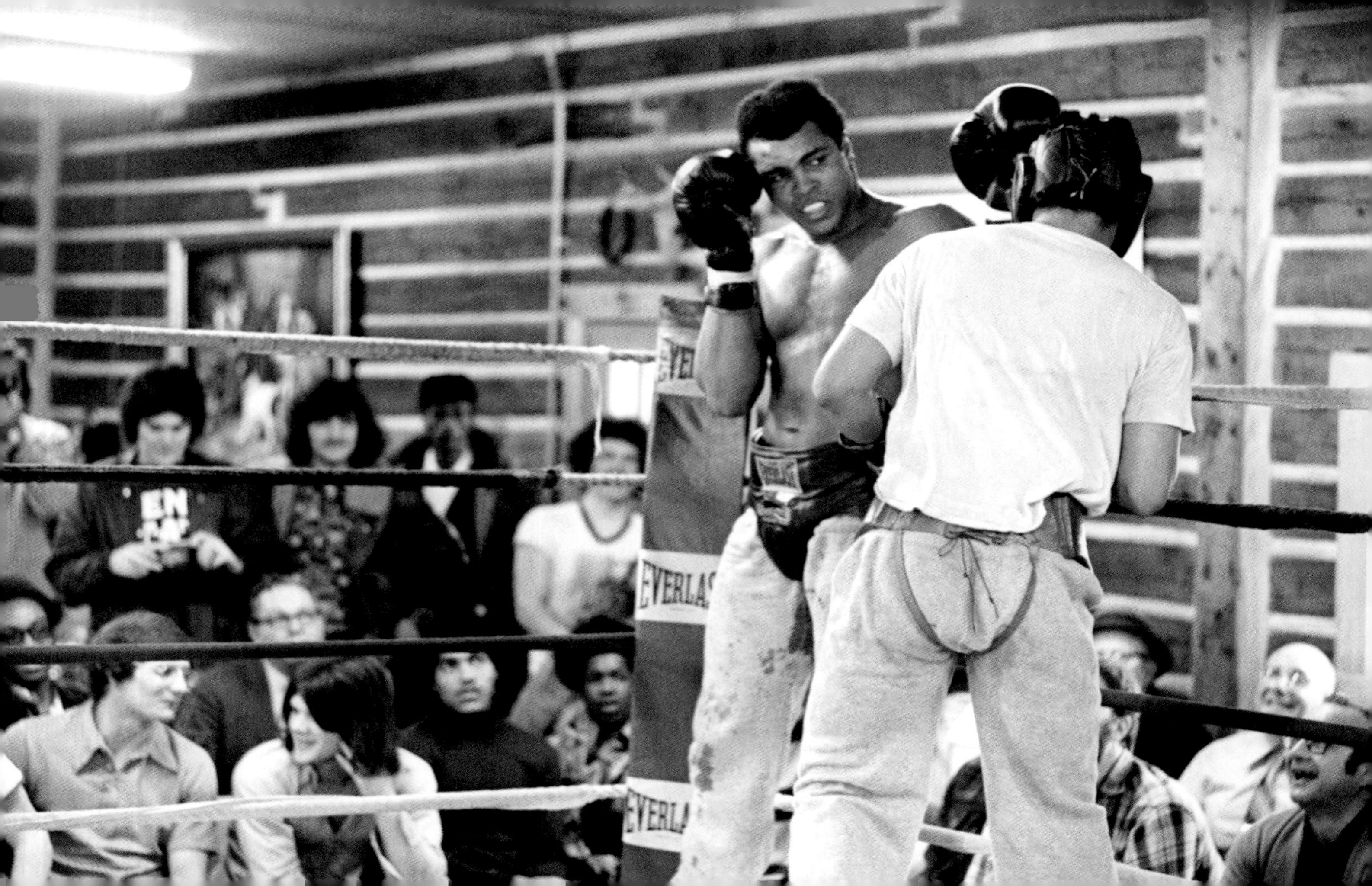

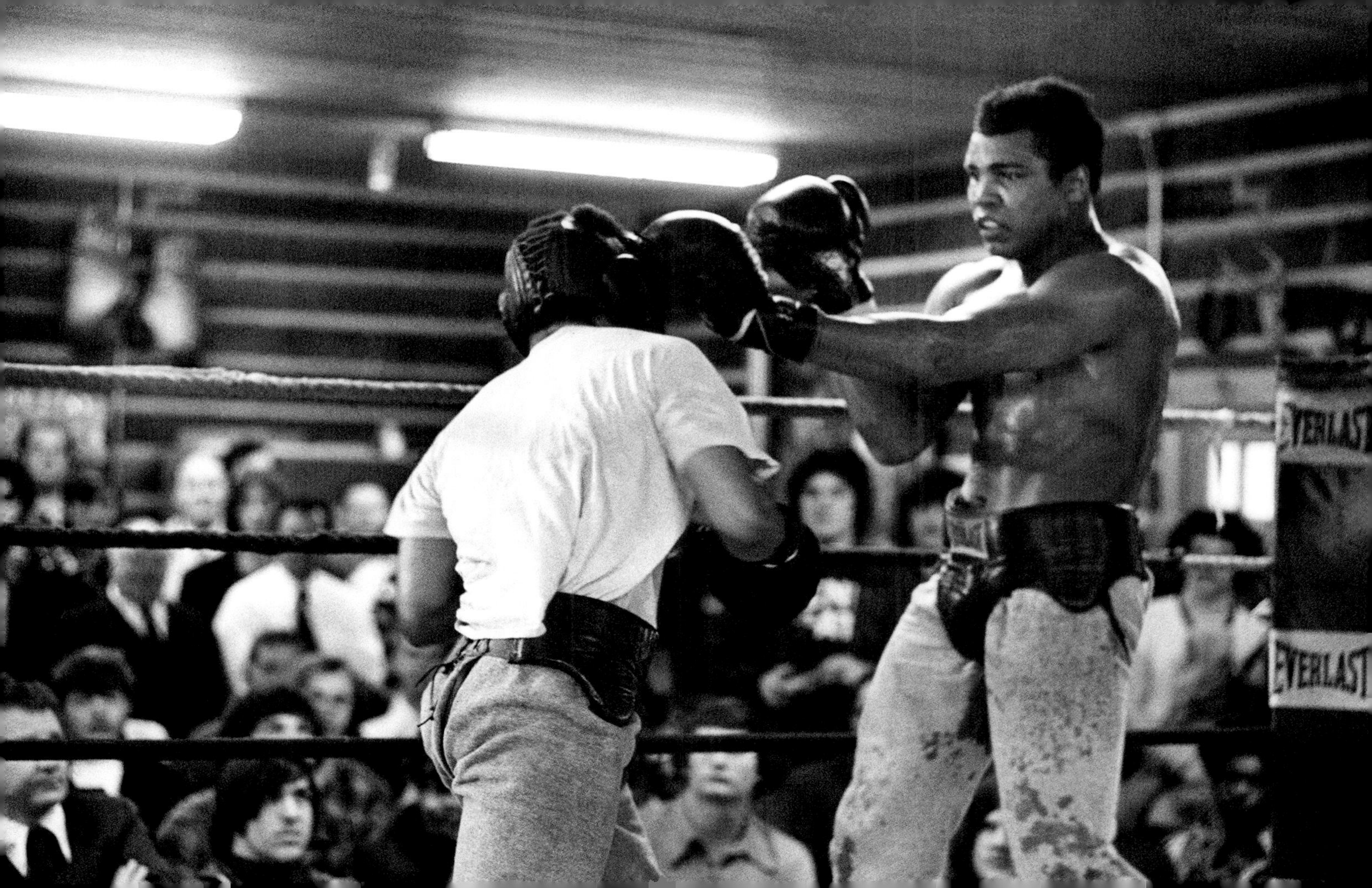
EVERLAST
EVERLAST

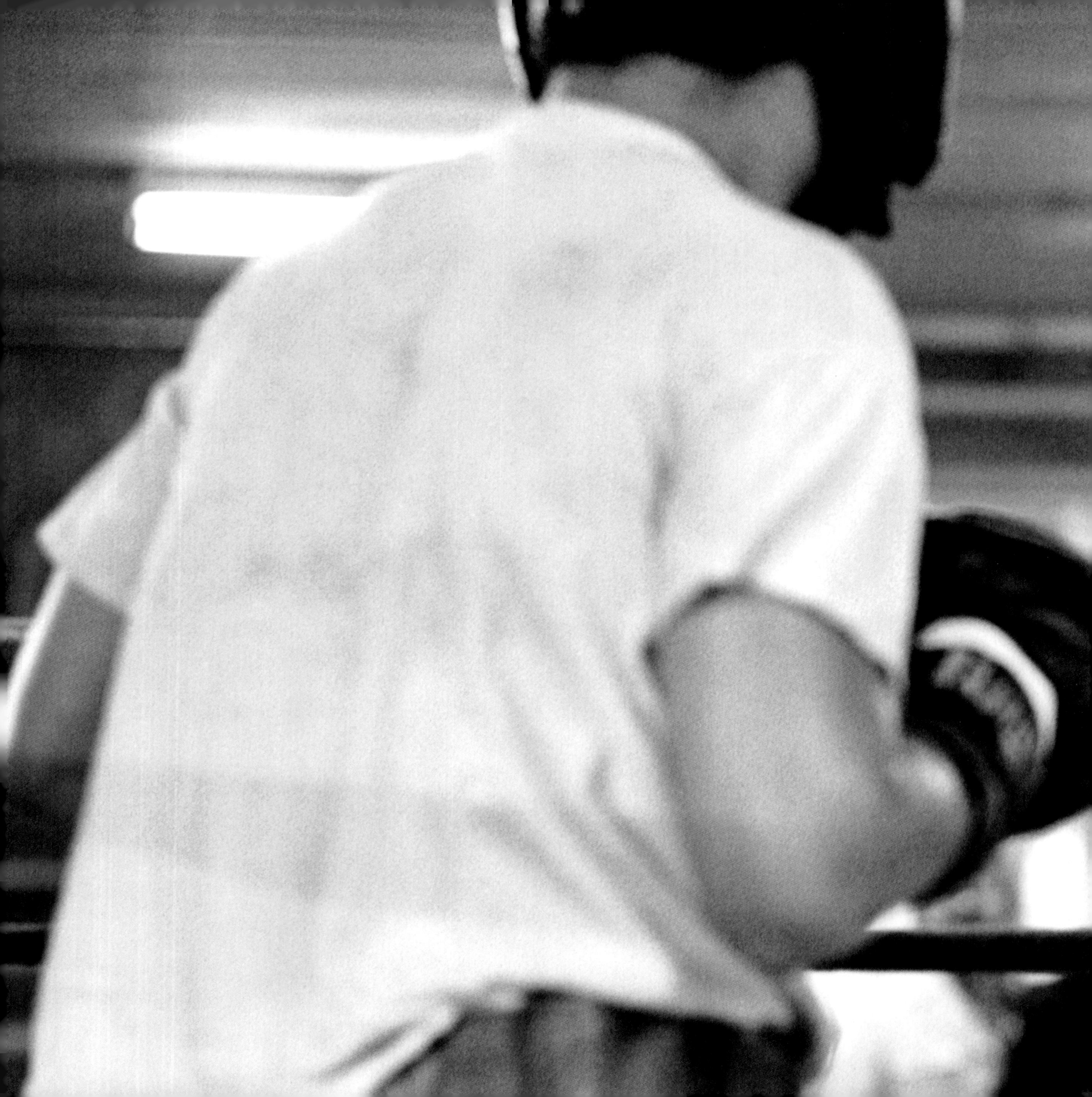

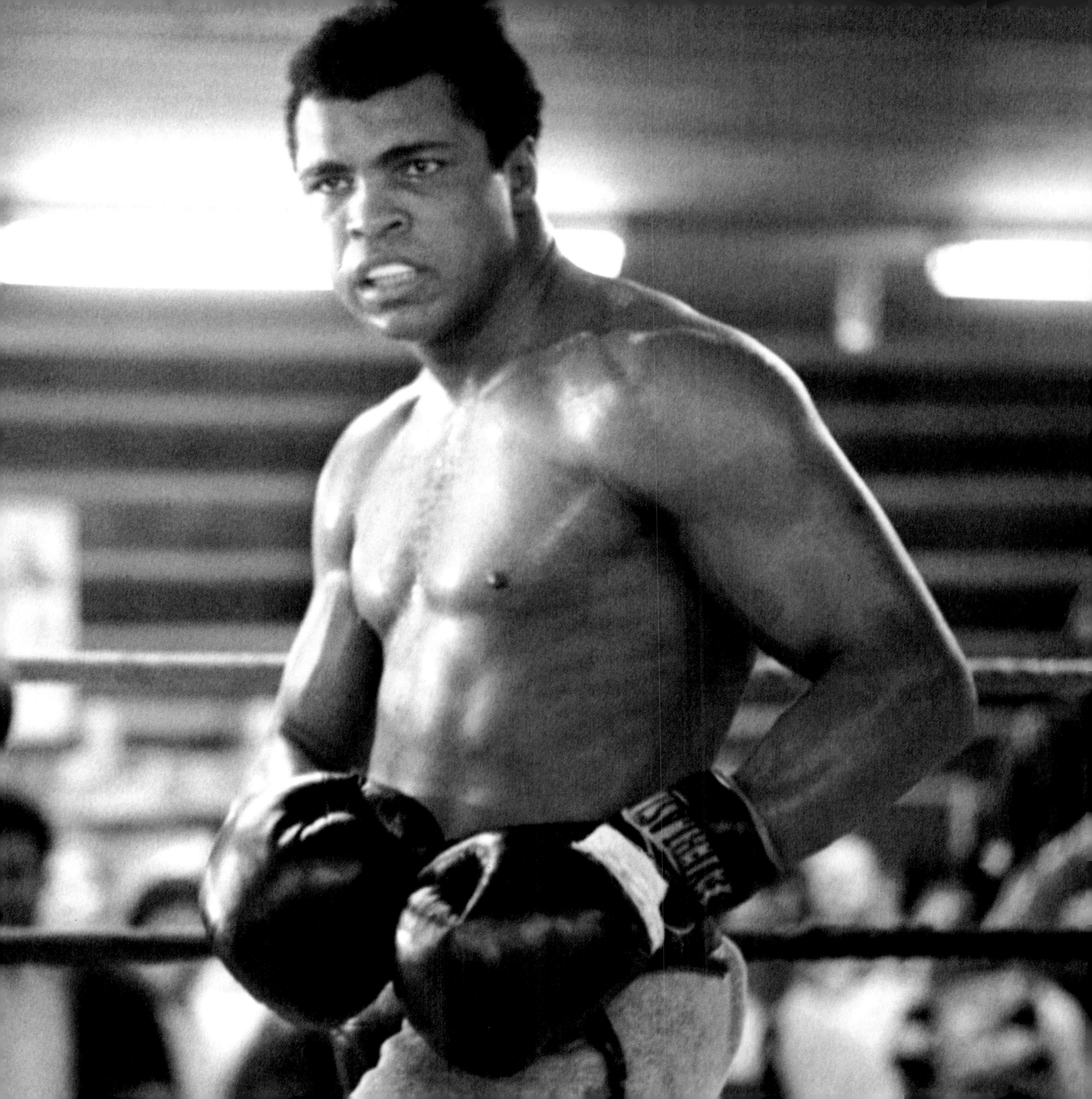

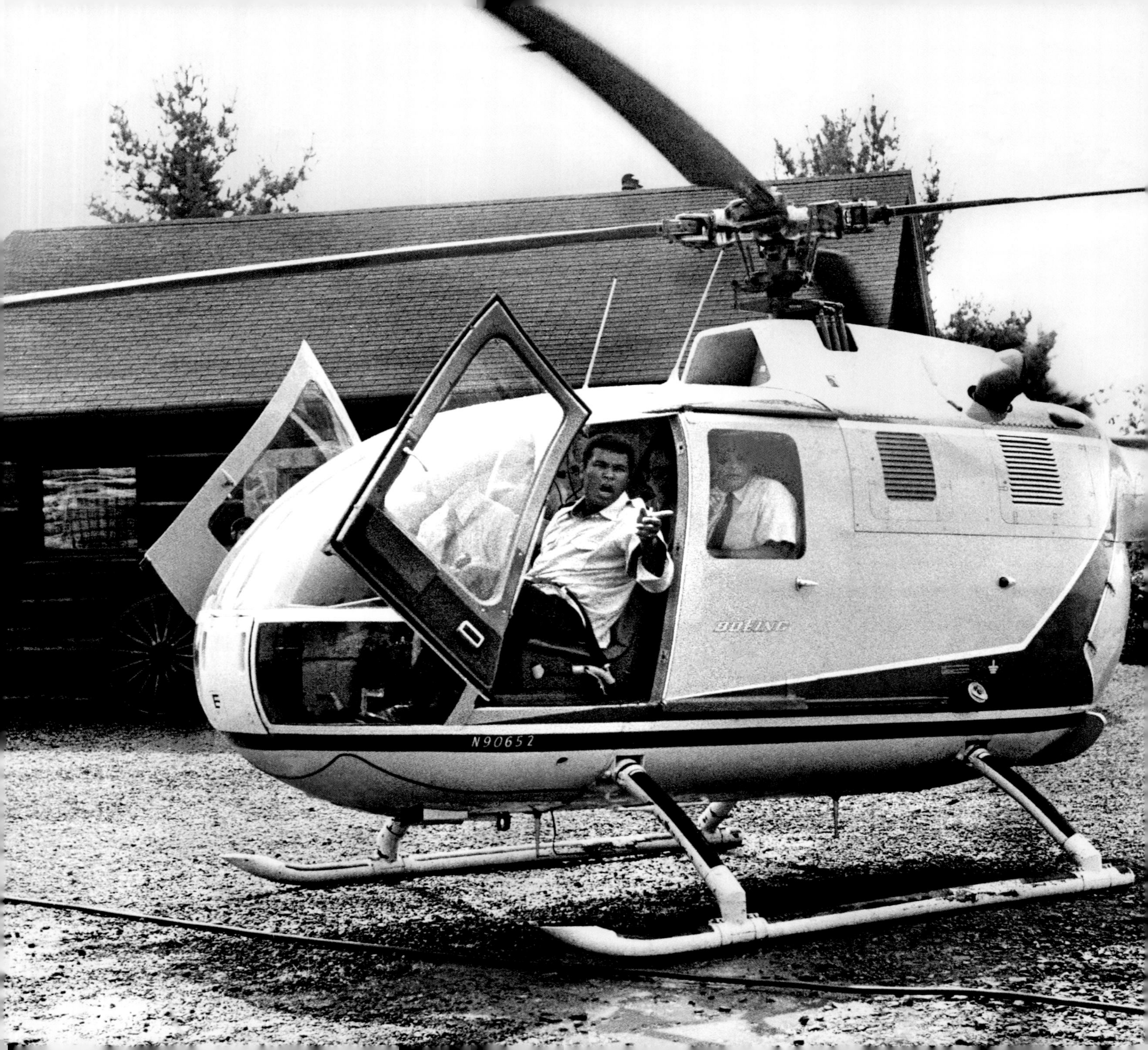
BOEING
N90652

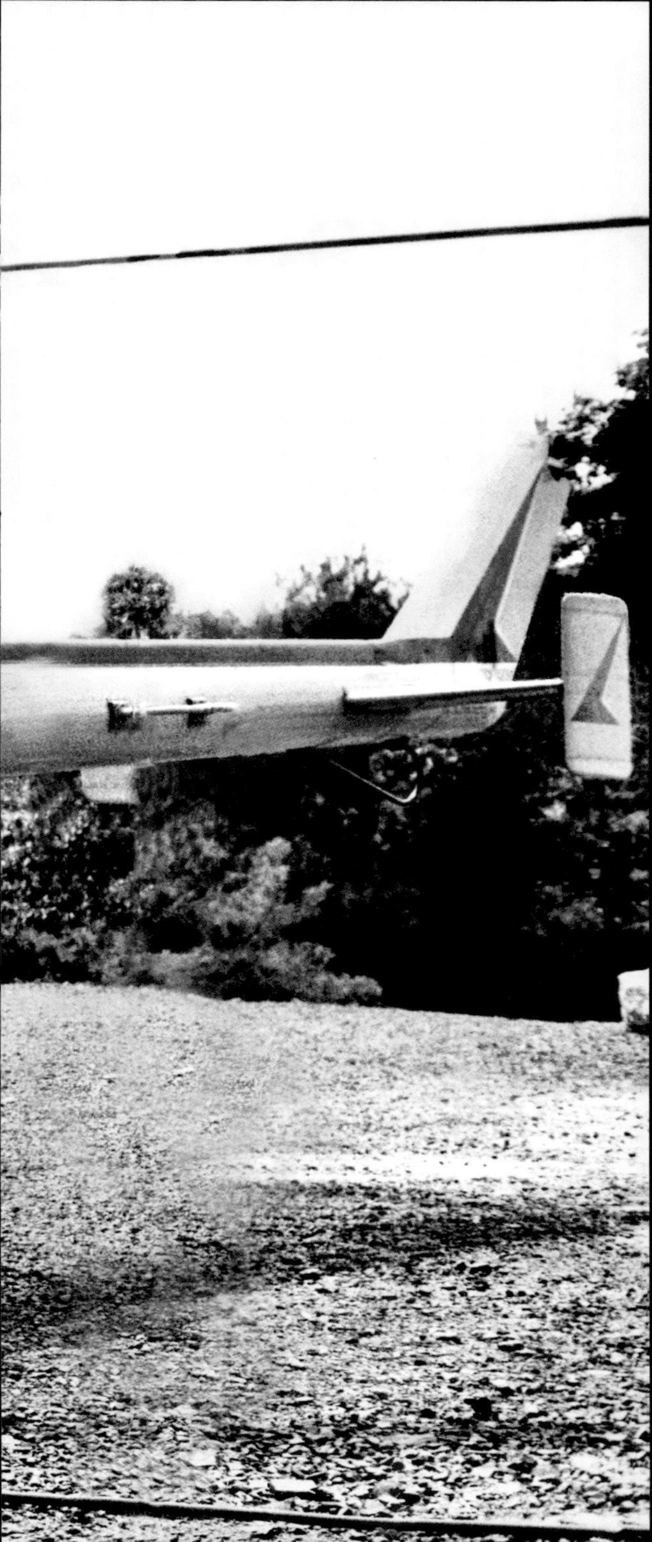

Muhammad Ali trains for his fight with George Foreman
Muhammad Ali training camp, Deer Lake, Pa.
Tuesday August 20, 1974

Ali lands back at Deer Lake in a helicopter after an overnight flight from Los Angeles to Philadelphia and the helicopter to Deer Lake. The quick trip to LA was to announce his upcoming fight with George Foreman in Zaire.

This purported and much reported Ali quote: Just before take-off on an airplane flight, the stewardess reminded Ali to fasten his seat belt. "Superman don't need no seat belt." replied Ali. "Superman don't need no airplane either," retorted the stewardess.

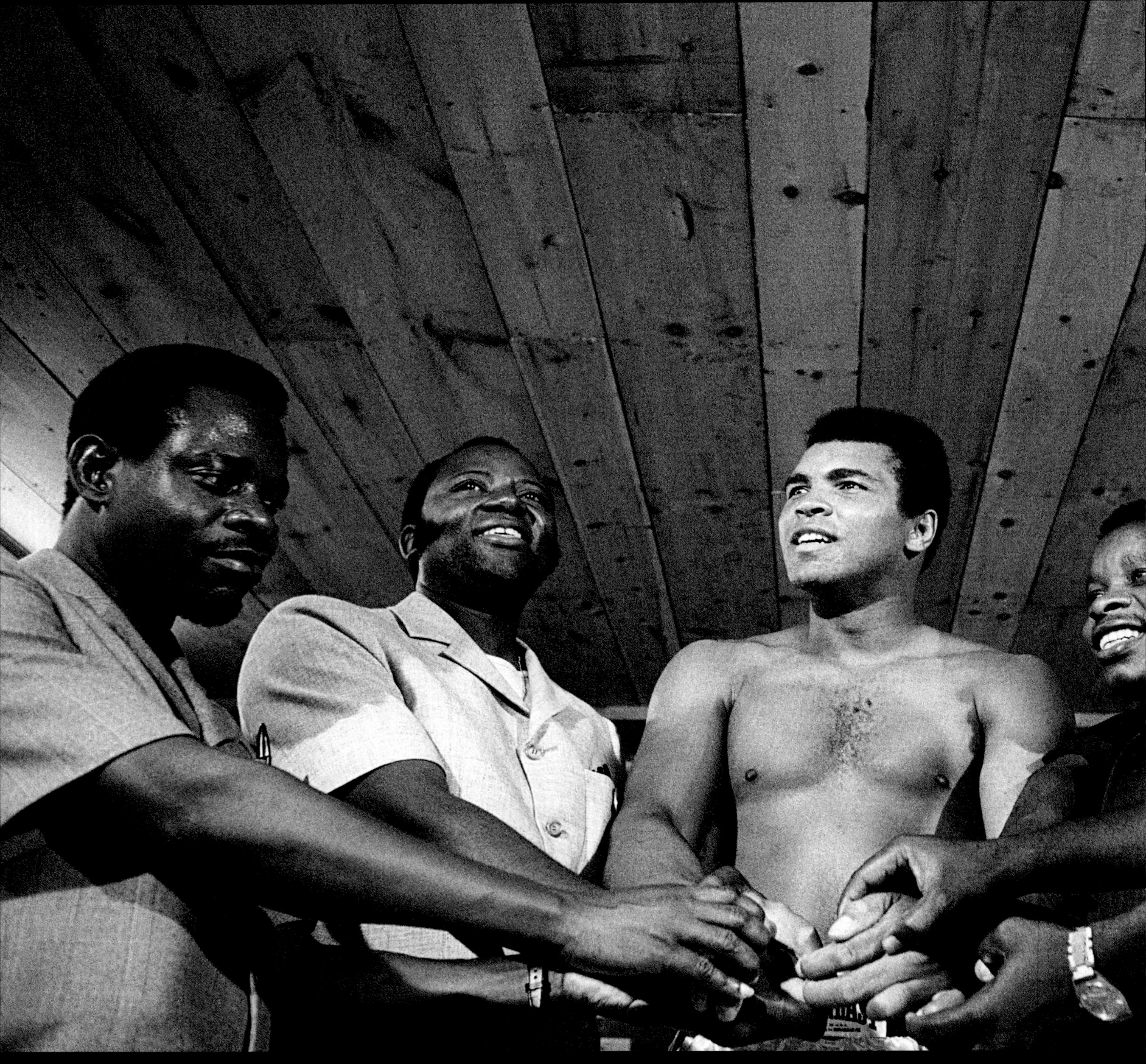

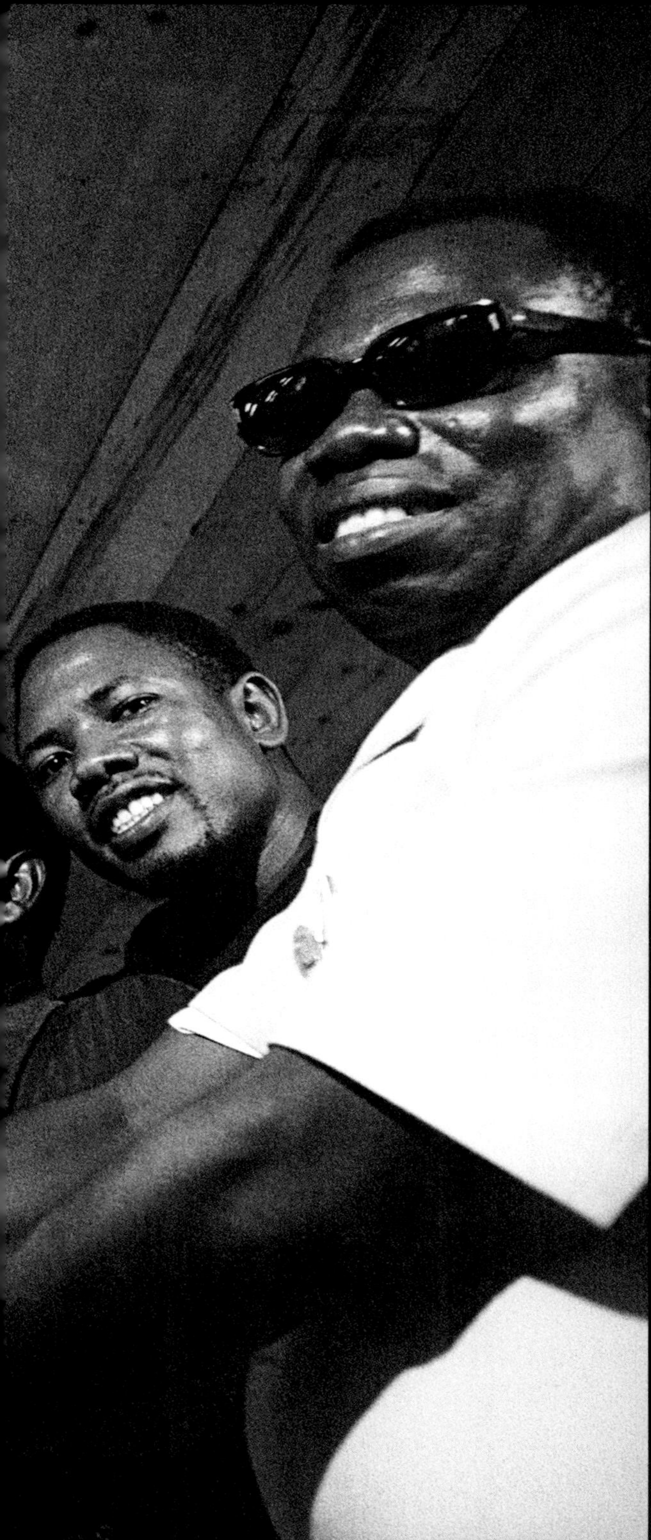

Ali with a delegation from Zaire

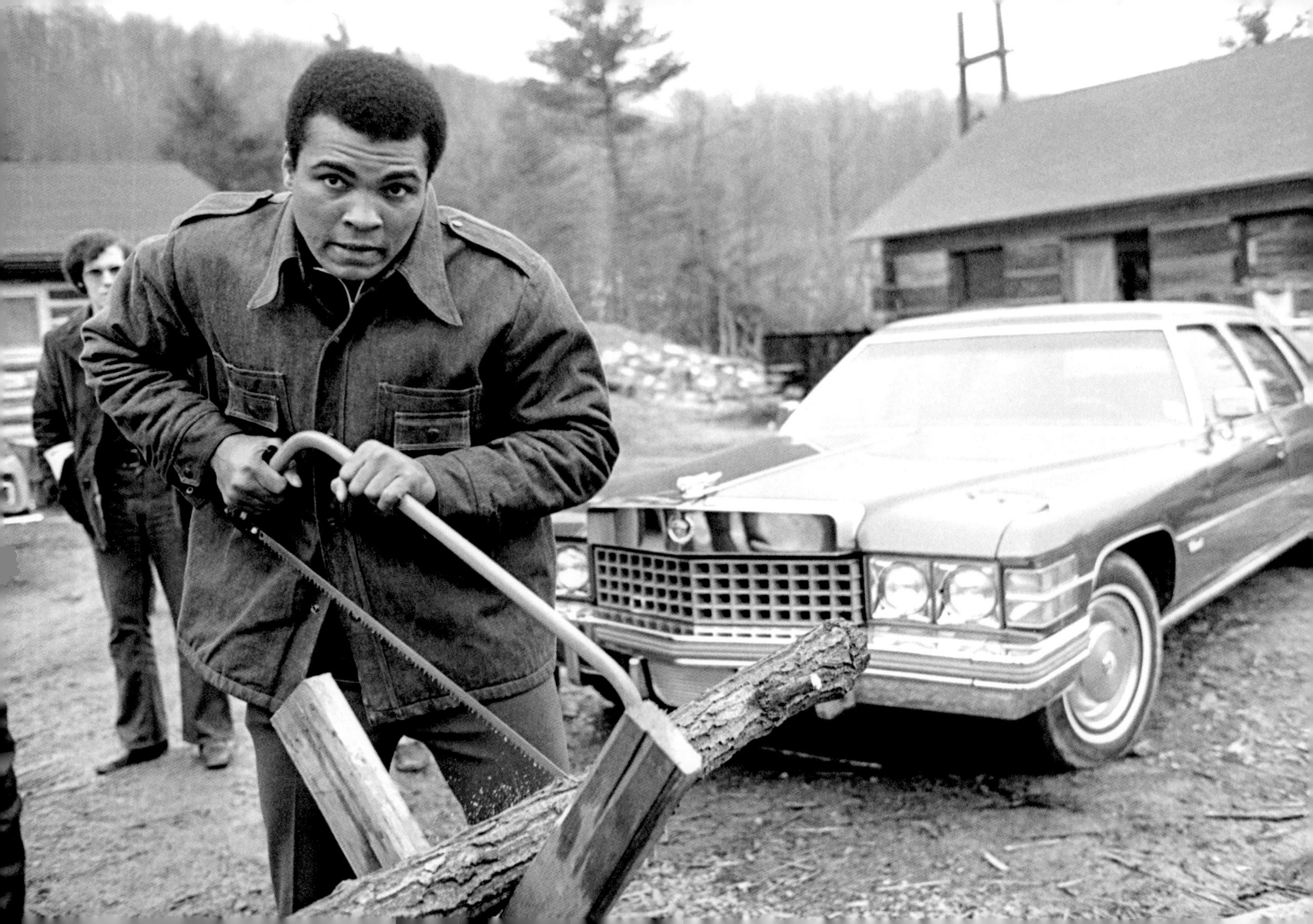

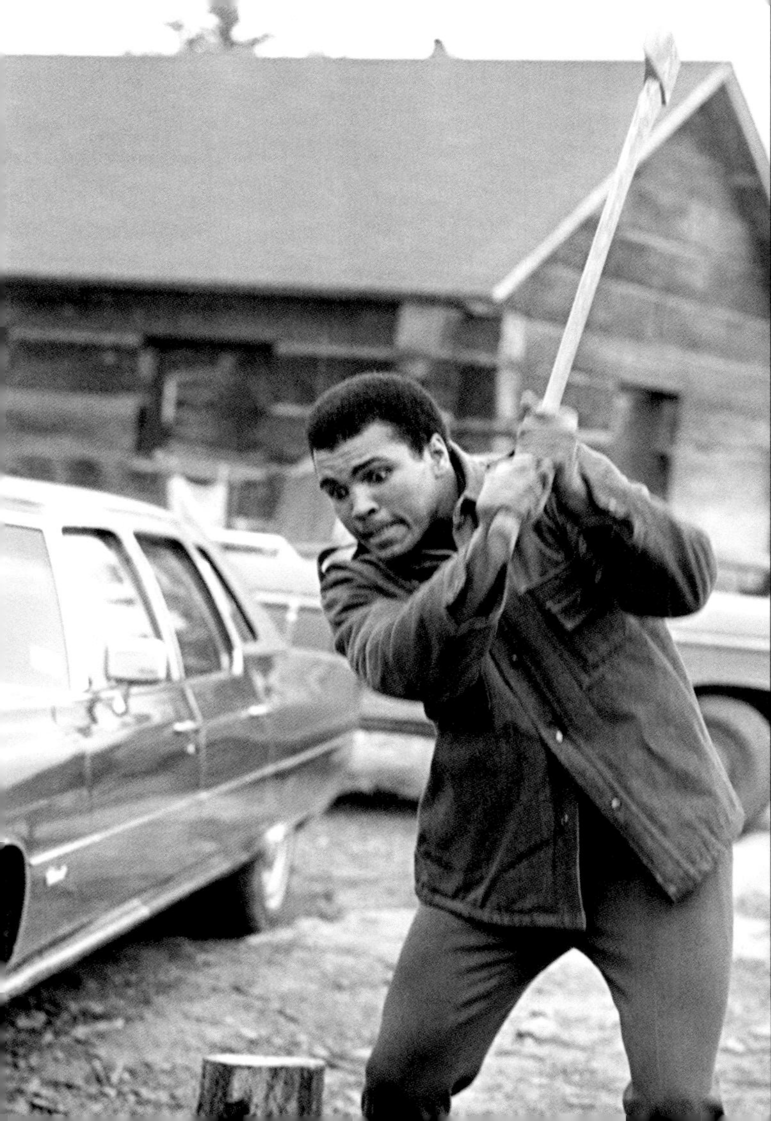

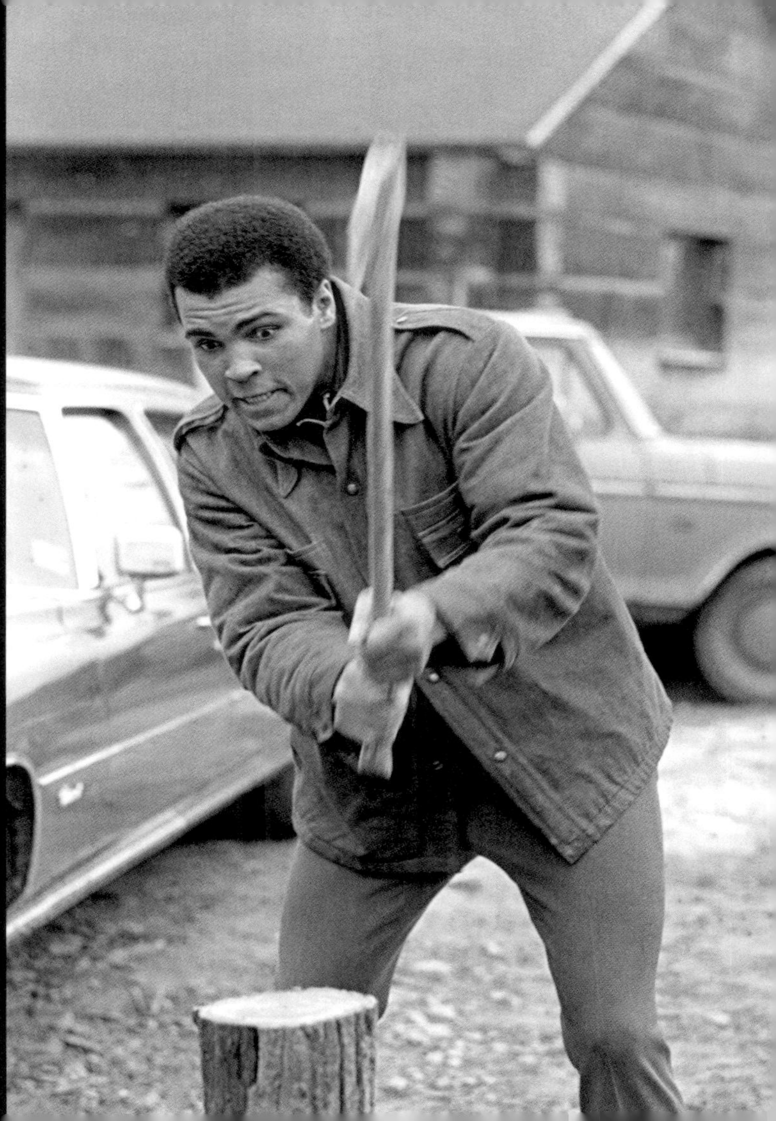

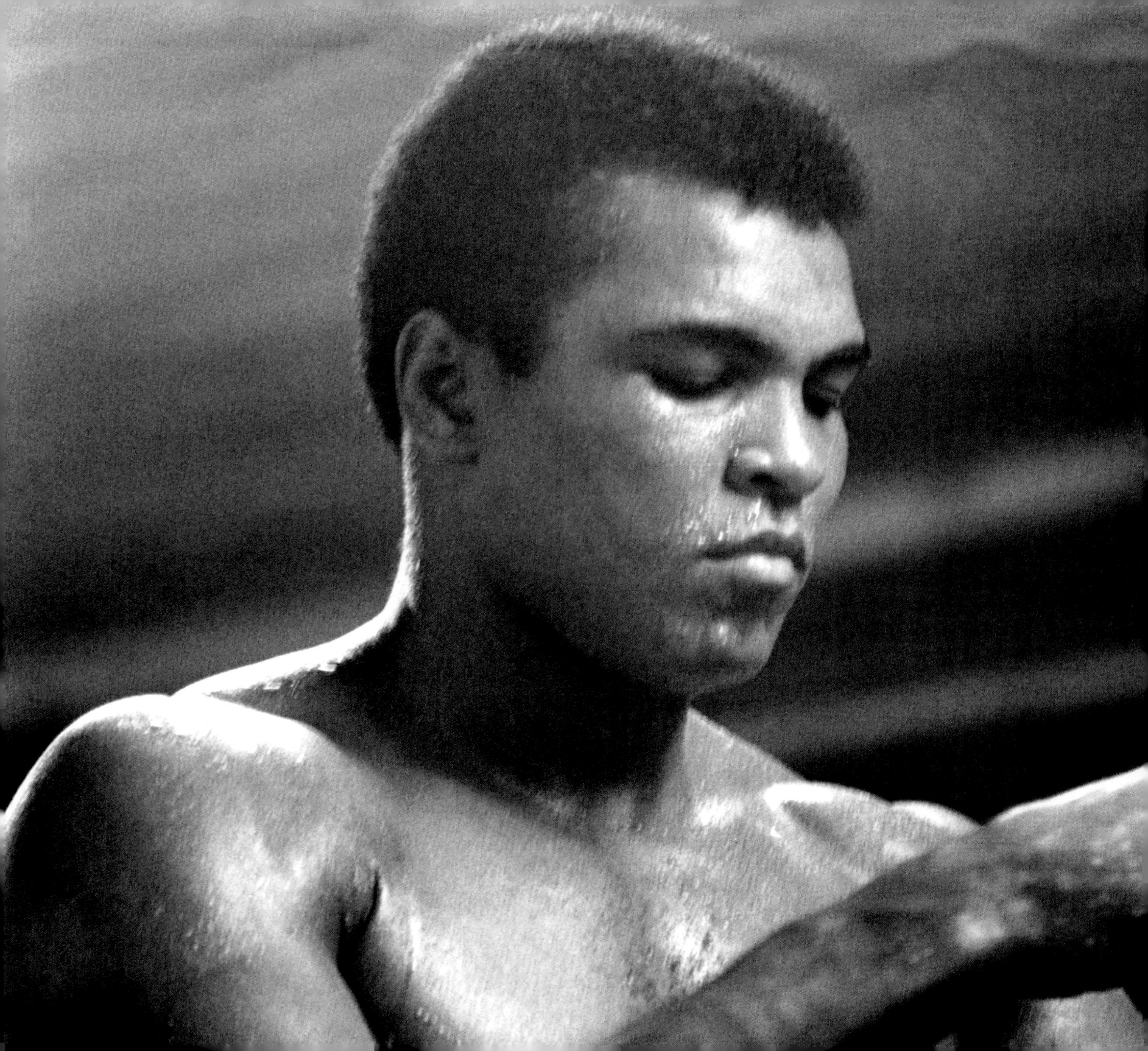

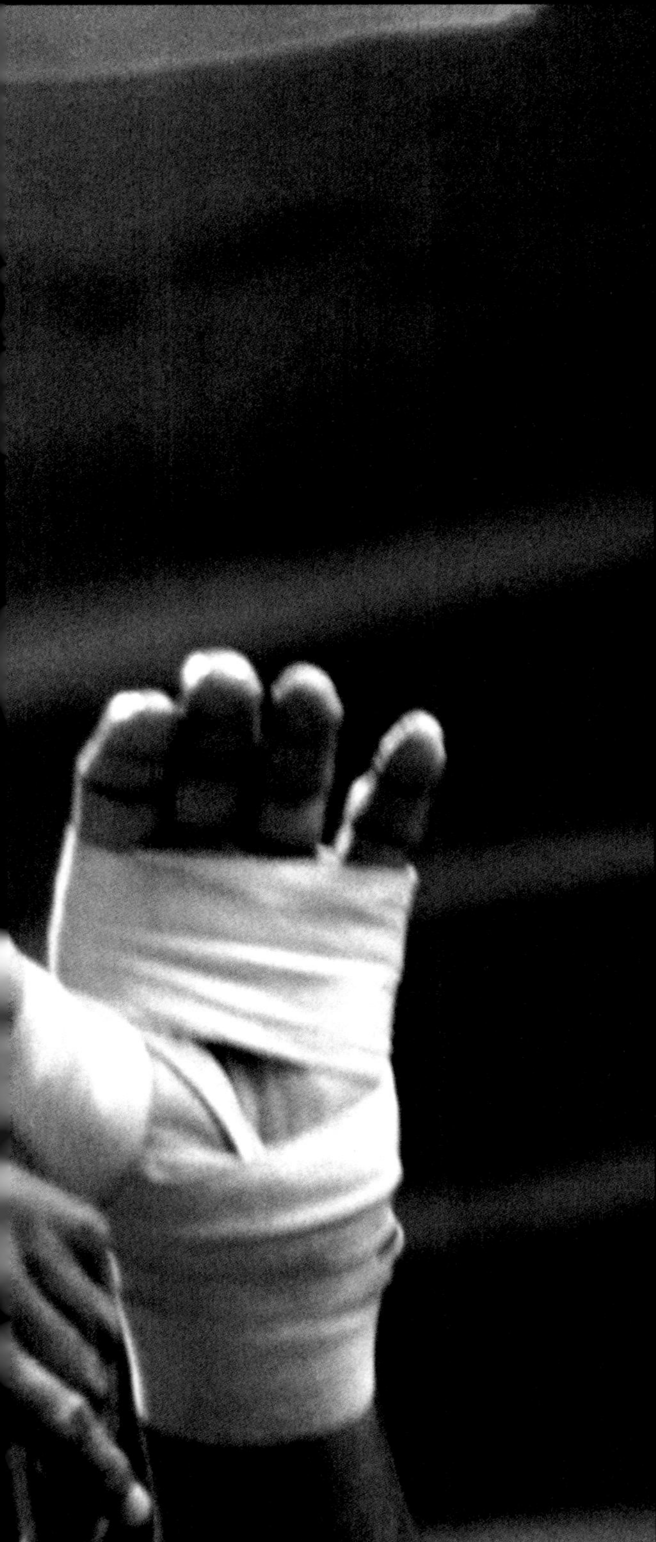

Muhammad Ali trains for his third fight with Joe Frazier
Muhammad Ali training camp, Deer Lake, Pa.
Wednesday September 3, 1975

There is a time, and I have noticed it with many fighters when they are alone, when their thoughts belong only to themselves. Muhammad Ali would stand, bandaging his hands, just him with his innermost thoughts. Anyone with half a brain wouldn't approach a man ignoring surrounding chaos and surely that person being Muhammad Ali!

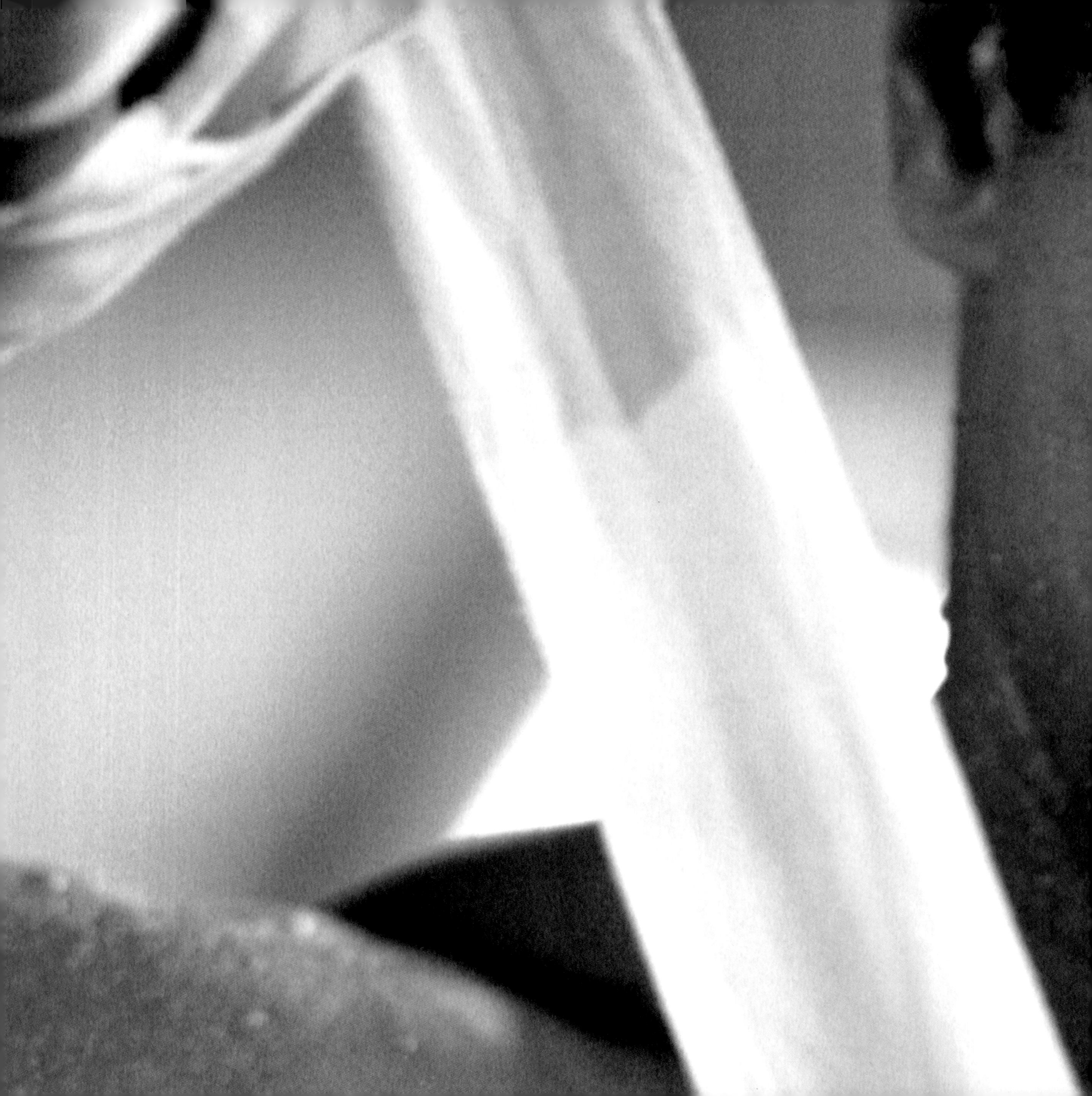

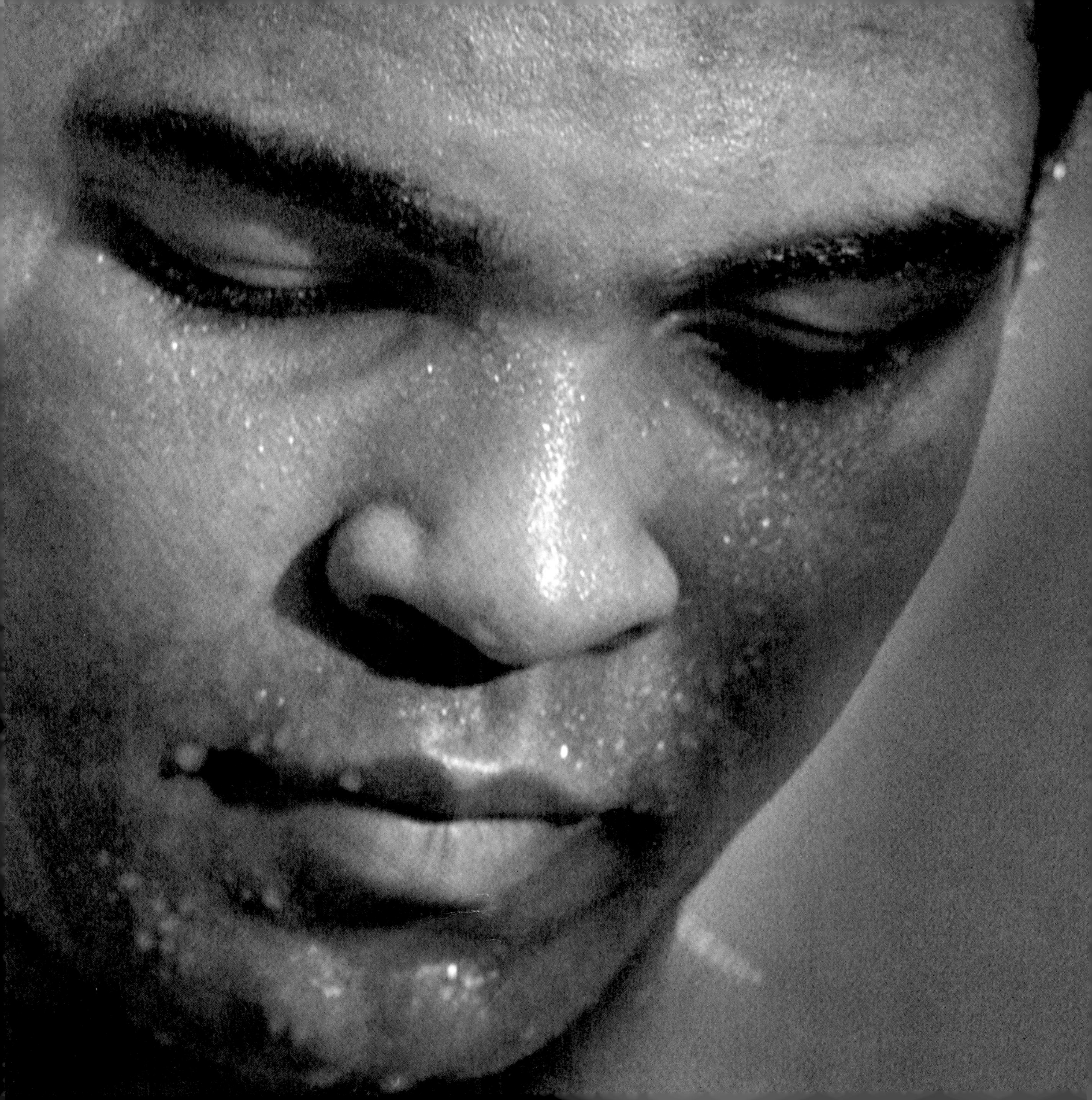

68

Muhammad Ali
Deer Lake, Pa., 1975

After an altercation the previous evening in New York City, I arrived back at Deer Lake with two black eyes. Arriving early, I wandered into the gym to find Ali already preparing for his training session. I tried to focus my cameras wearing sunglasses but being the height of the summer, the perspiration was rolling over the lenses. I raised the glasses to reveal the two 'shiners.' Ali looked up and casually said, "Limey, you taken up fighting?" Without missing a beat, I said, "yes." Cracking up he said, "Well, looks like you ain't doin' too good so far."

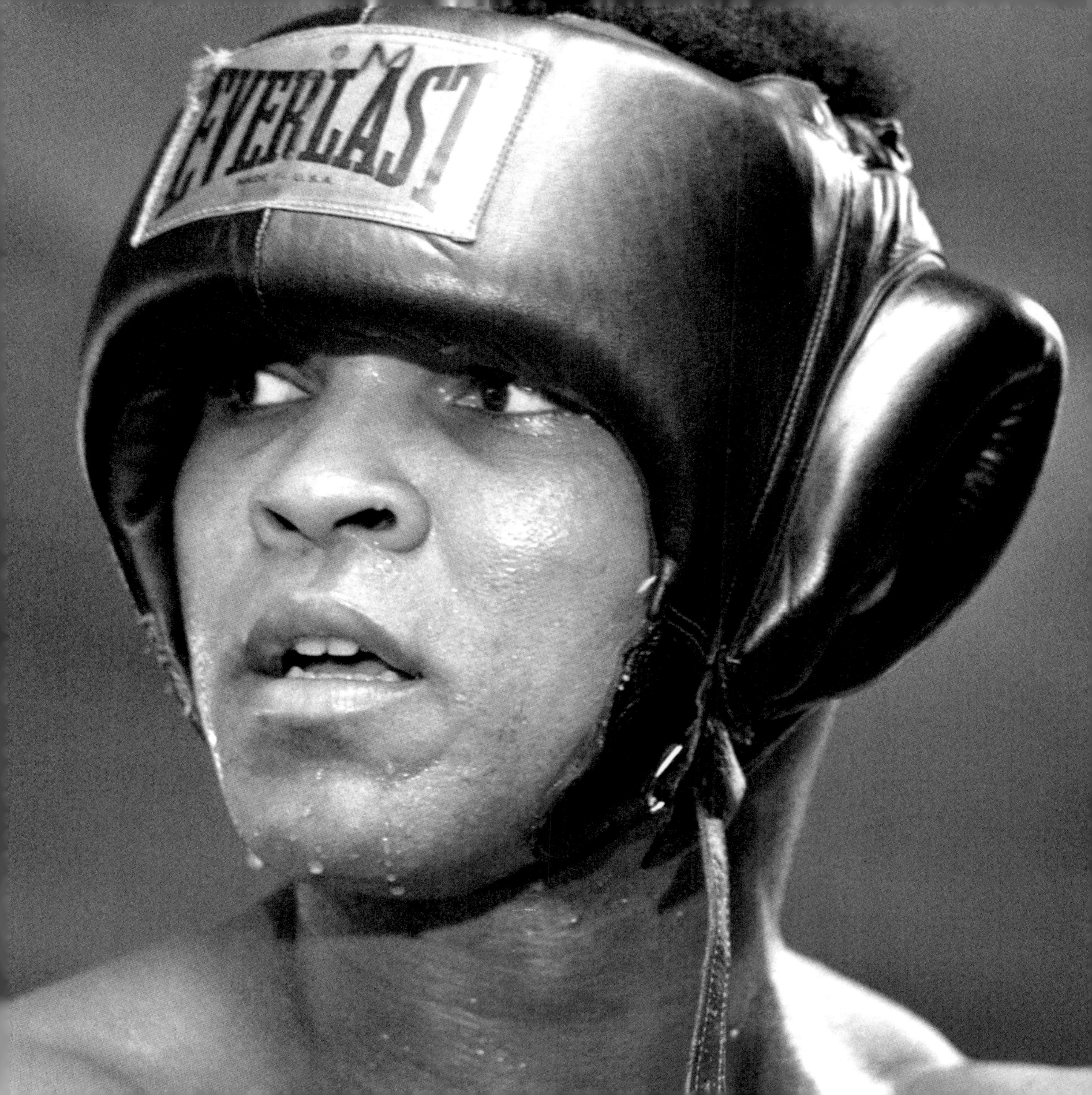
EVERLAST

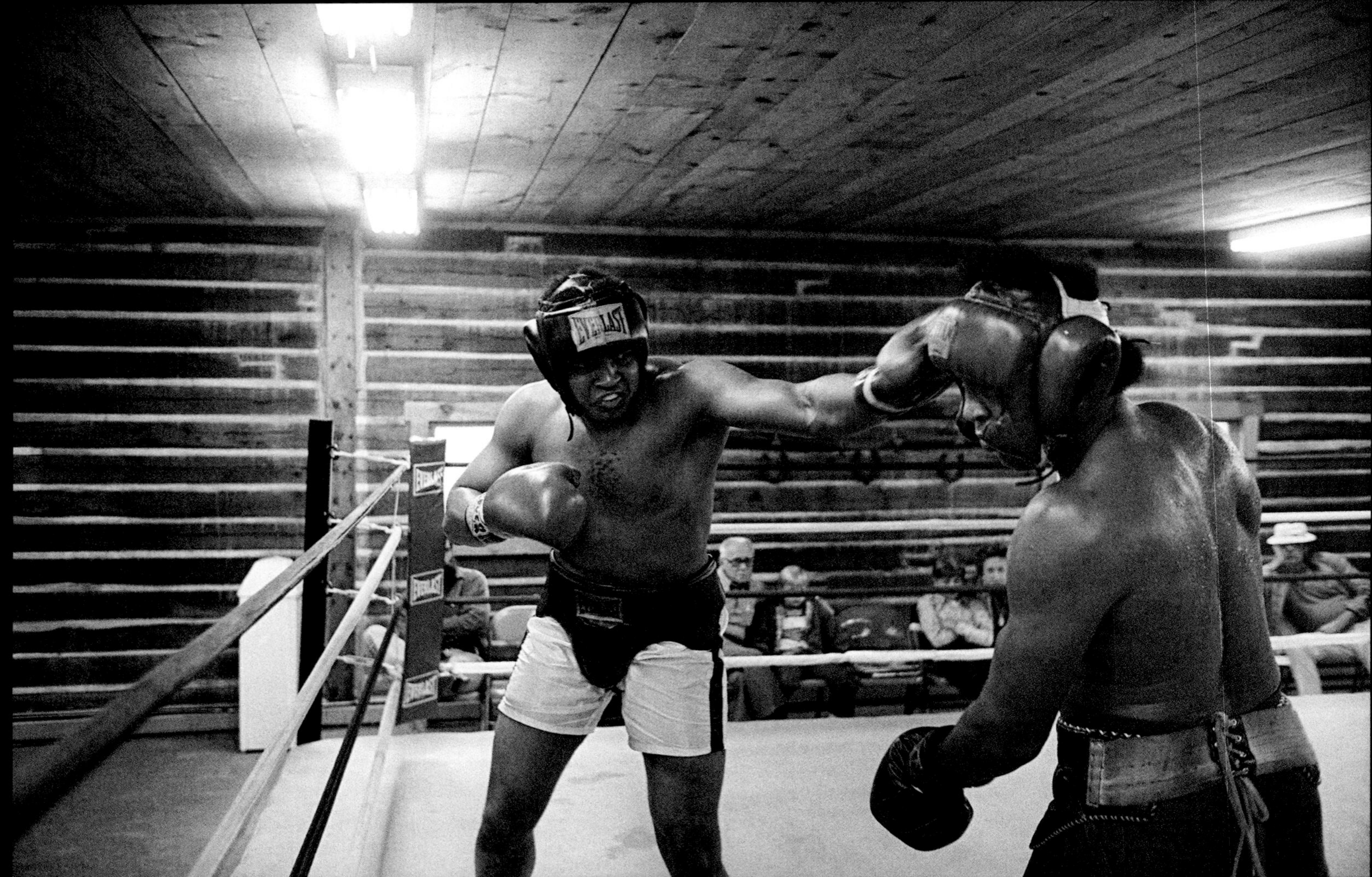
EVERLAST
EVERLAST
EVERLAST
EVERLAST

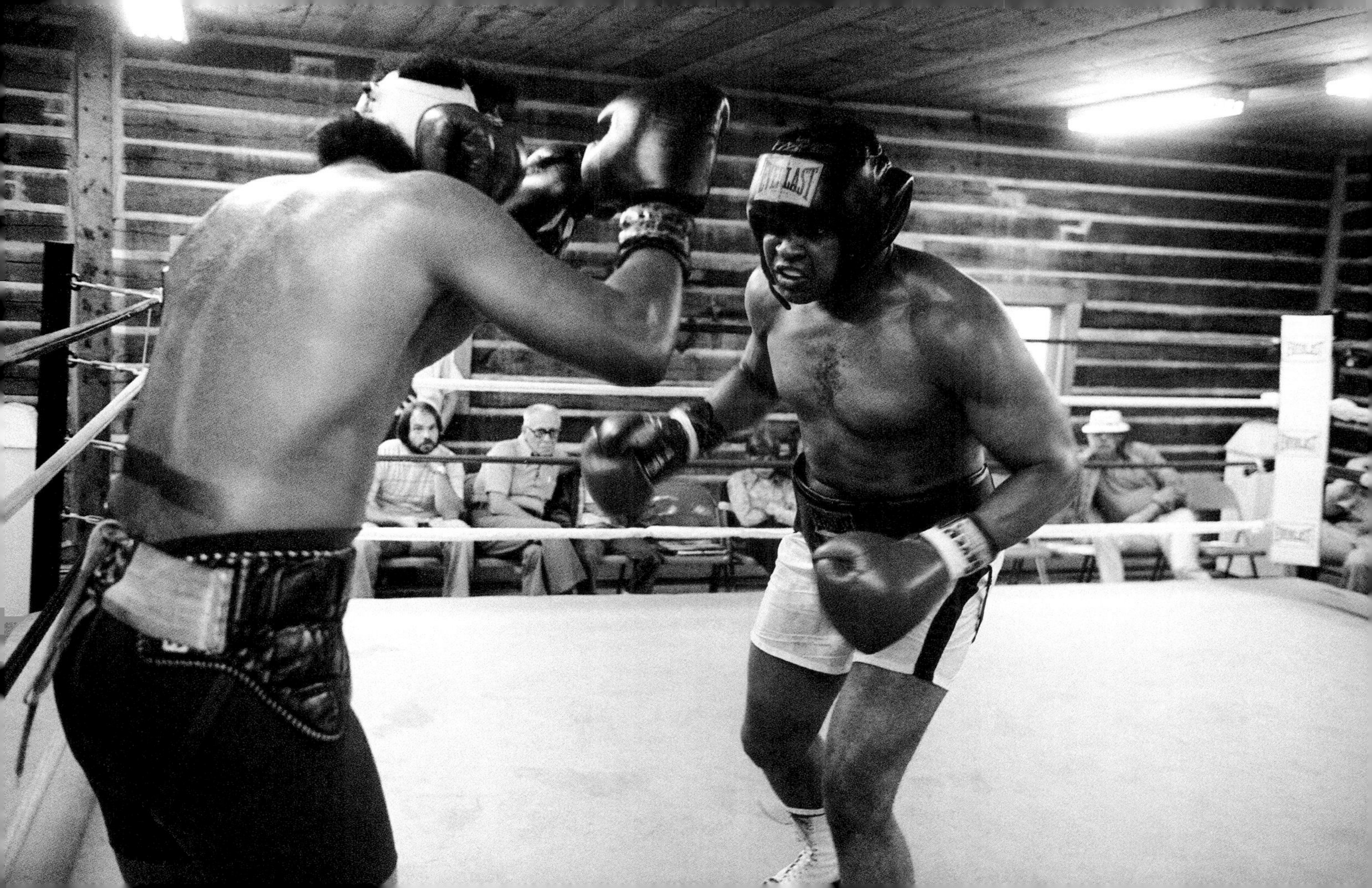
EVERLAST

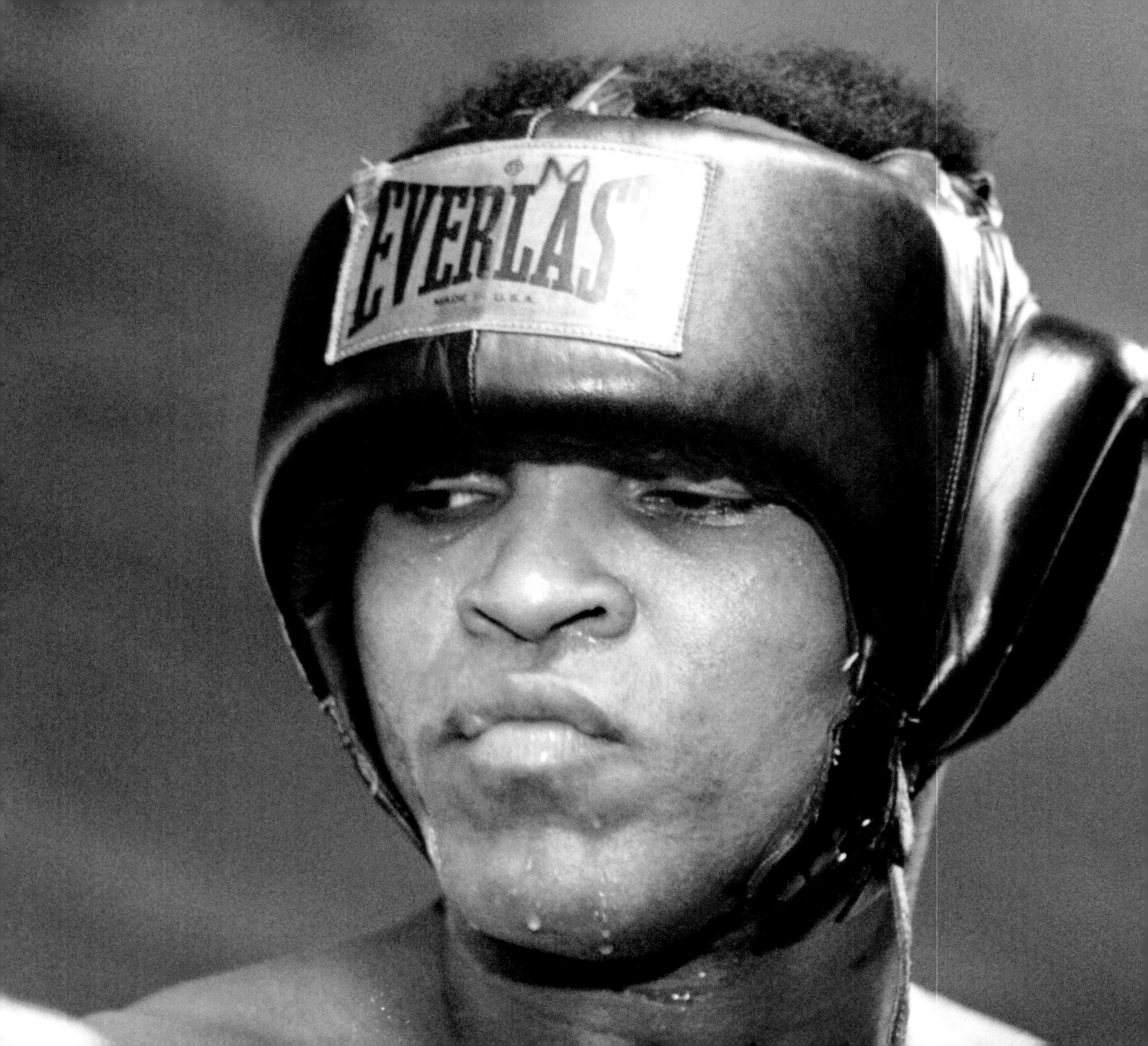
EVERLAS

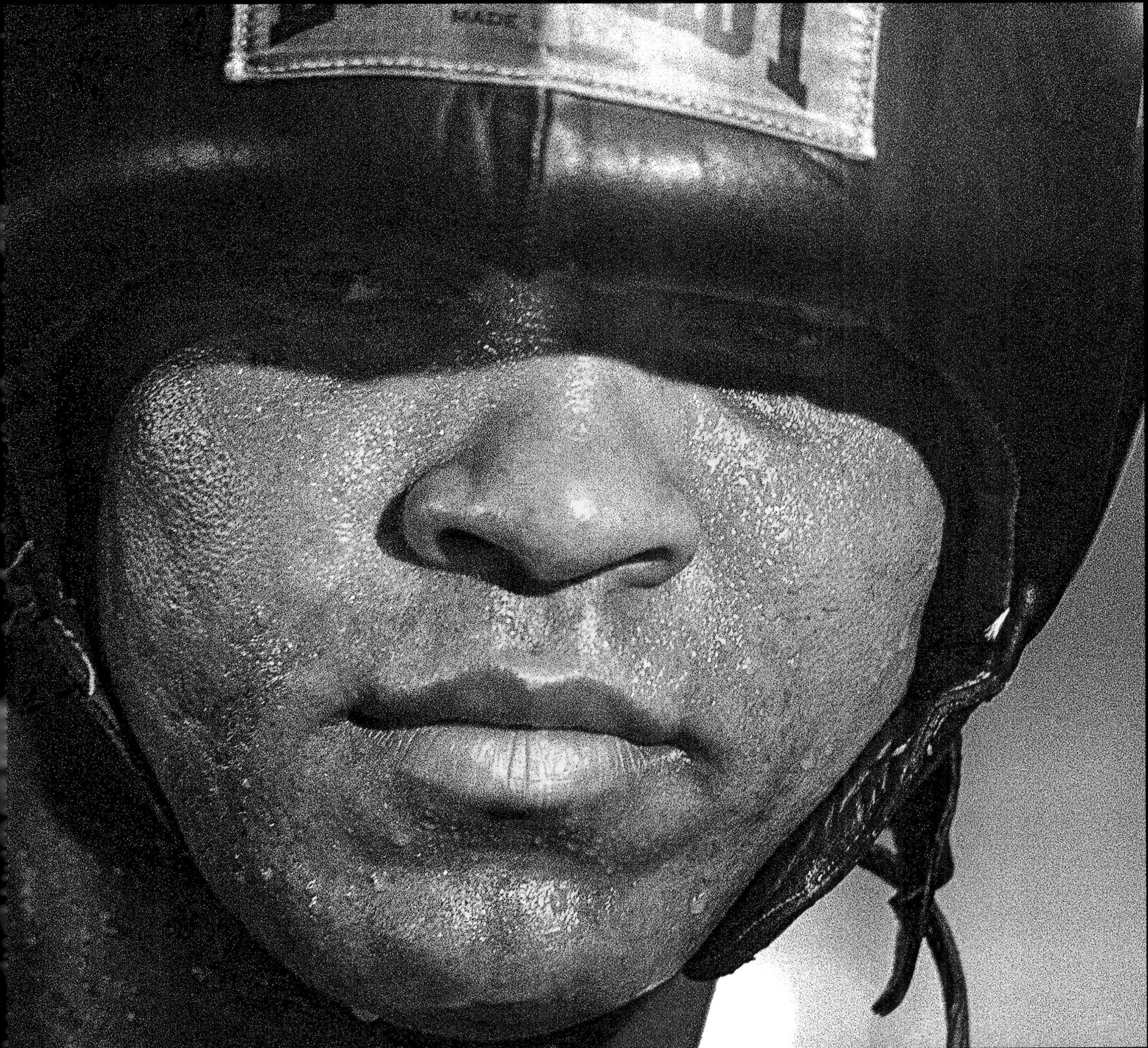

76 **Muhammad Ali trains for his fight with Jimmy Young**
Muhammad Ali training camp, Deer Lake, Pa.
Monday March 22, 1976

Of all the marvellous experiences when visiting Muhammad Ali at Deer Lake, the best was his absolute joy at having kids around. Ali's long-serving friend and advisor Gene Kilroy tells a moving story about a young fan with cancer who had been to the camp. Ali signed a picture of the two of them together with "I'm gonna beat George Foreman and you gonna beat cancer." Soon after the meeting the little boy was dying in the University of Pennsylvania hospital. Ali and Kilroy secretly went to see him. When Ali whispered to the stricken child, "I told you that you gonna beat cancer." He replied, "No I'm going to meet God and I'm going to tell him I'm a good friend of yours."

Three days later the boy died. At the viewing, the lad lay in the casket along with the picture of he and Ali and the inscription "I'm gonna beat George Foreman and you gonna beat cancer." Gene Kilroy says that both he and Ali were so choked-up they couldn't talk all the way back from the hospital to Deer Lake.

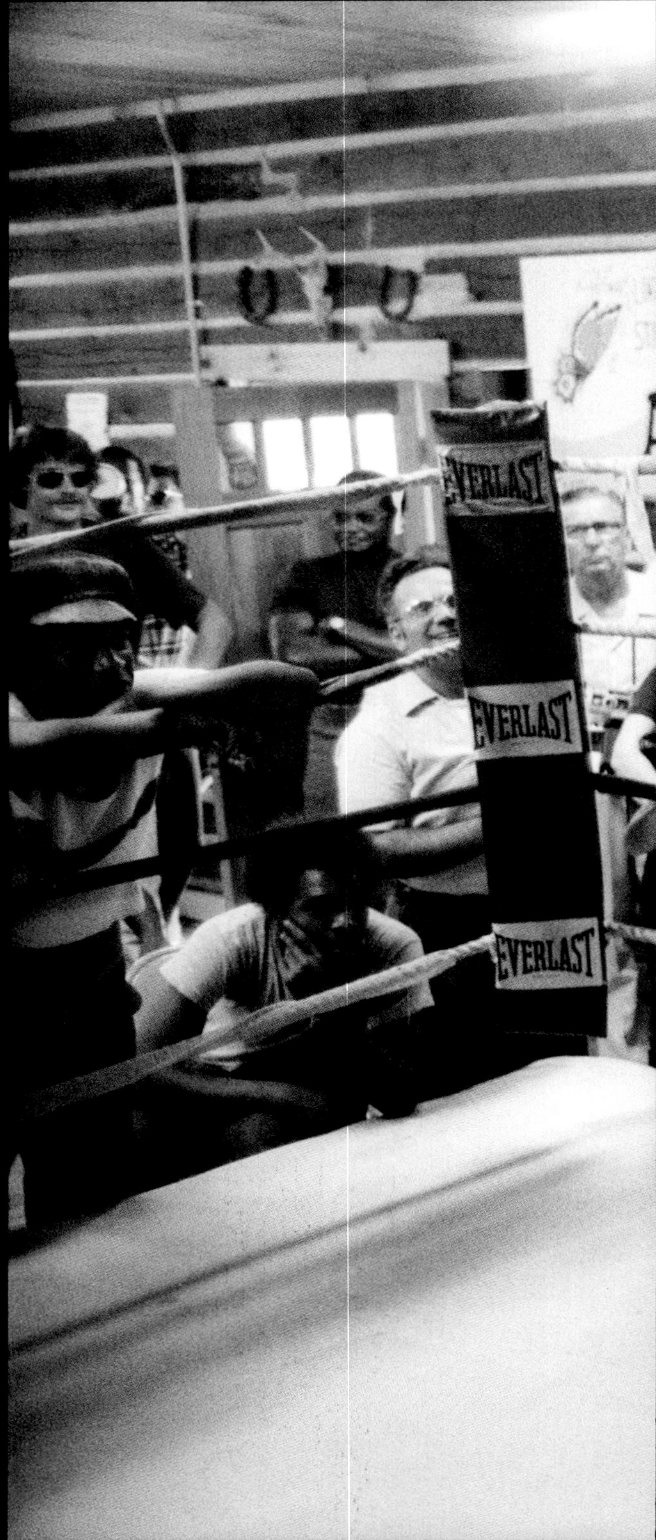

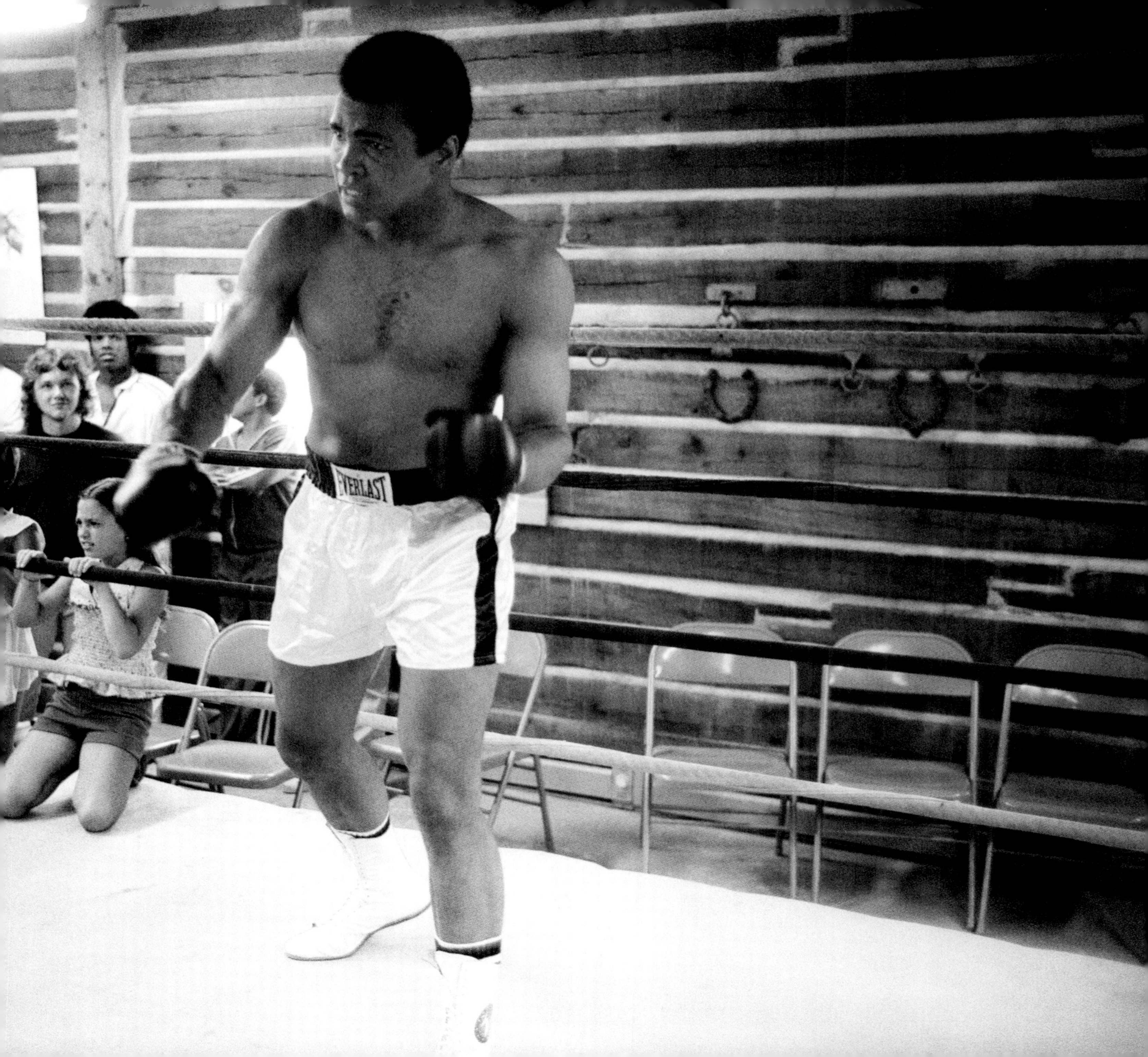
EVERLAST

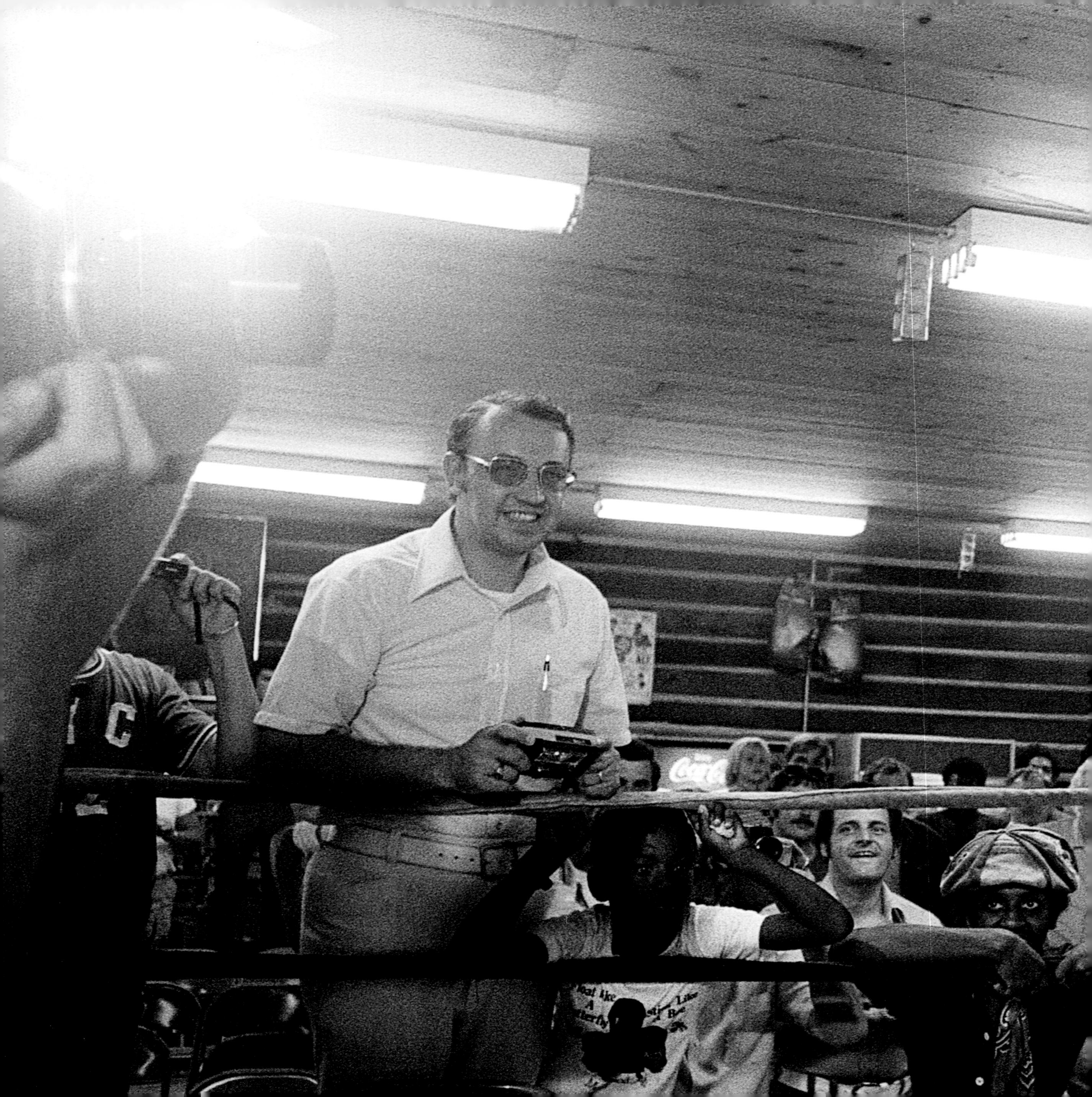

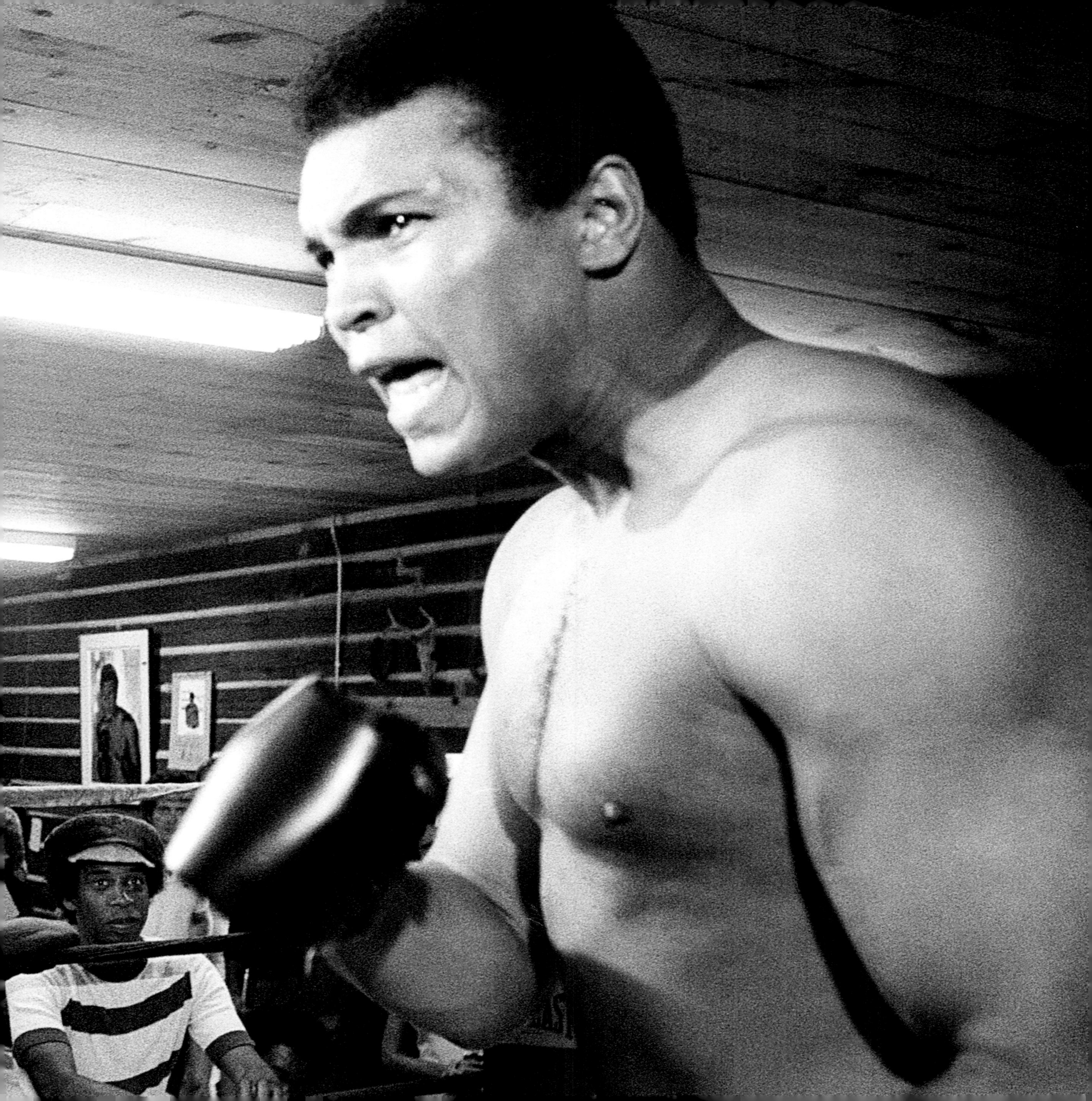

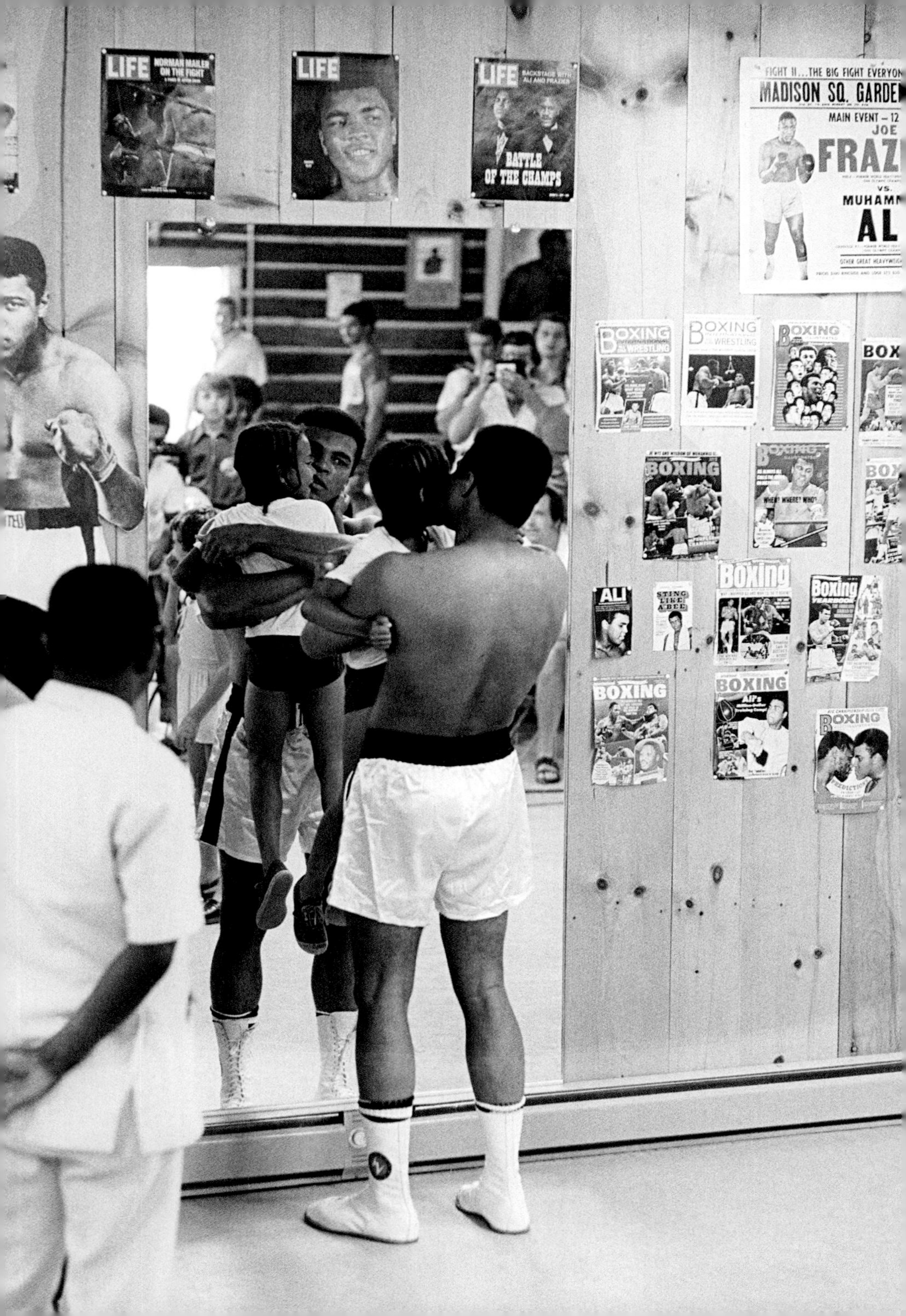
LIFE
NORMAN MAILER ON THE FIGHT
LIFE
LIFE
BACKSTAGE WITH ALI AND FRAZIER
BATTLE OF THE CHAMPS
MAIN EVENT
JOE
VS.
BOXING
WRESTLING
BOXING
WRESTLING
BOXING
BOXING
WHERE? WHERE? WHO?
ALI
STING LIKE A BEE
Boxing
Boxing
YEARBOOK
BOXING
BOXING
PREDICTION

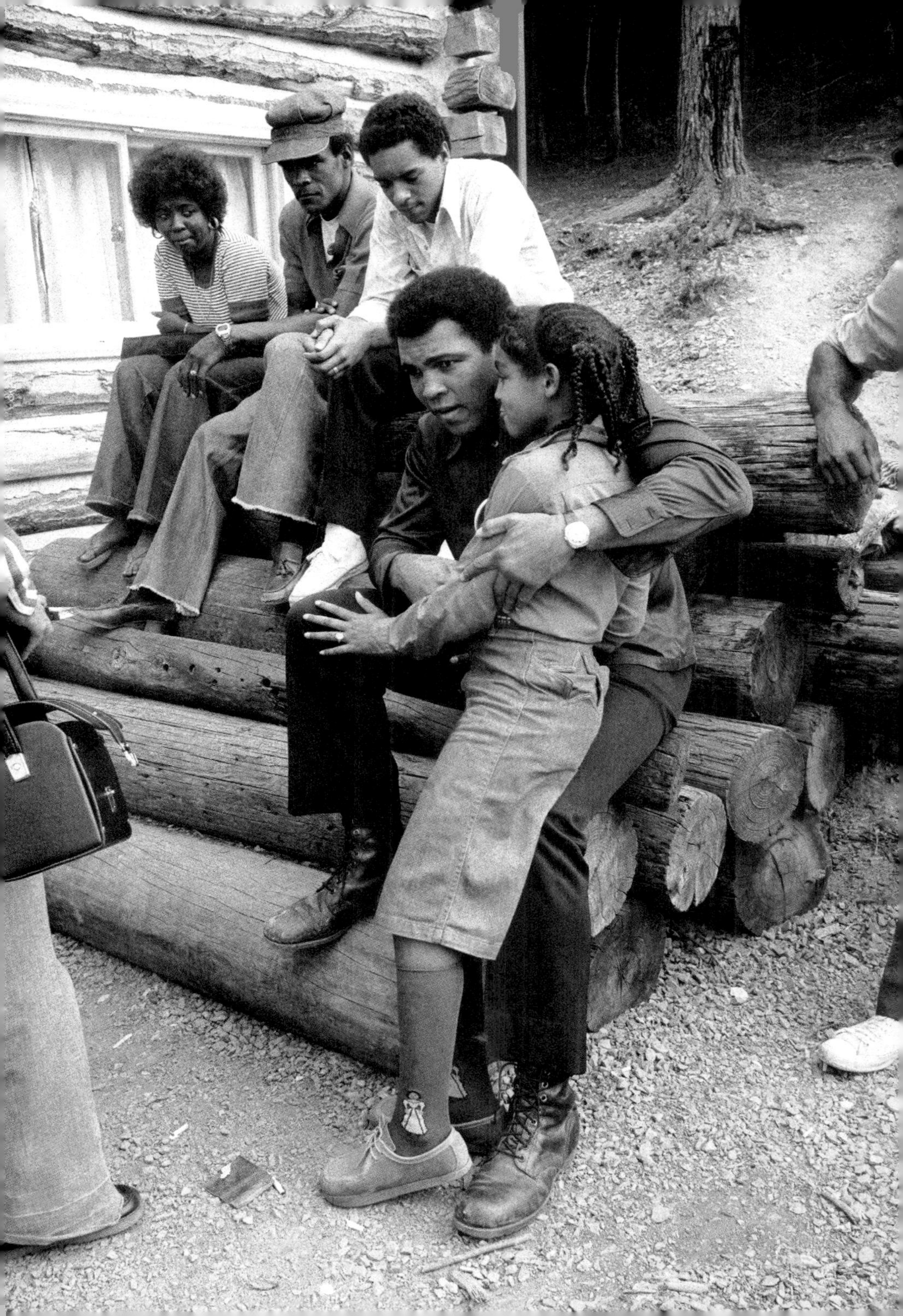

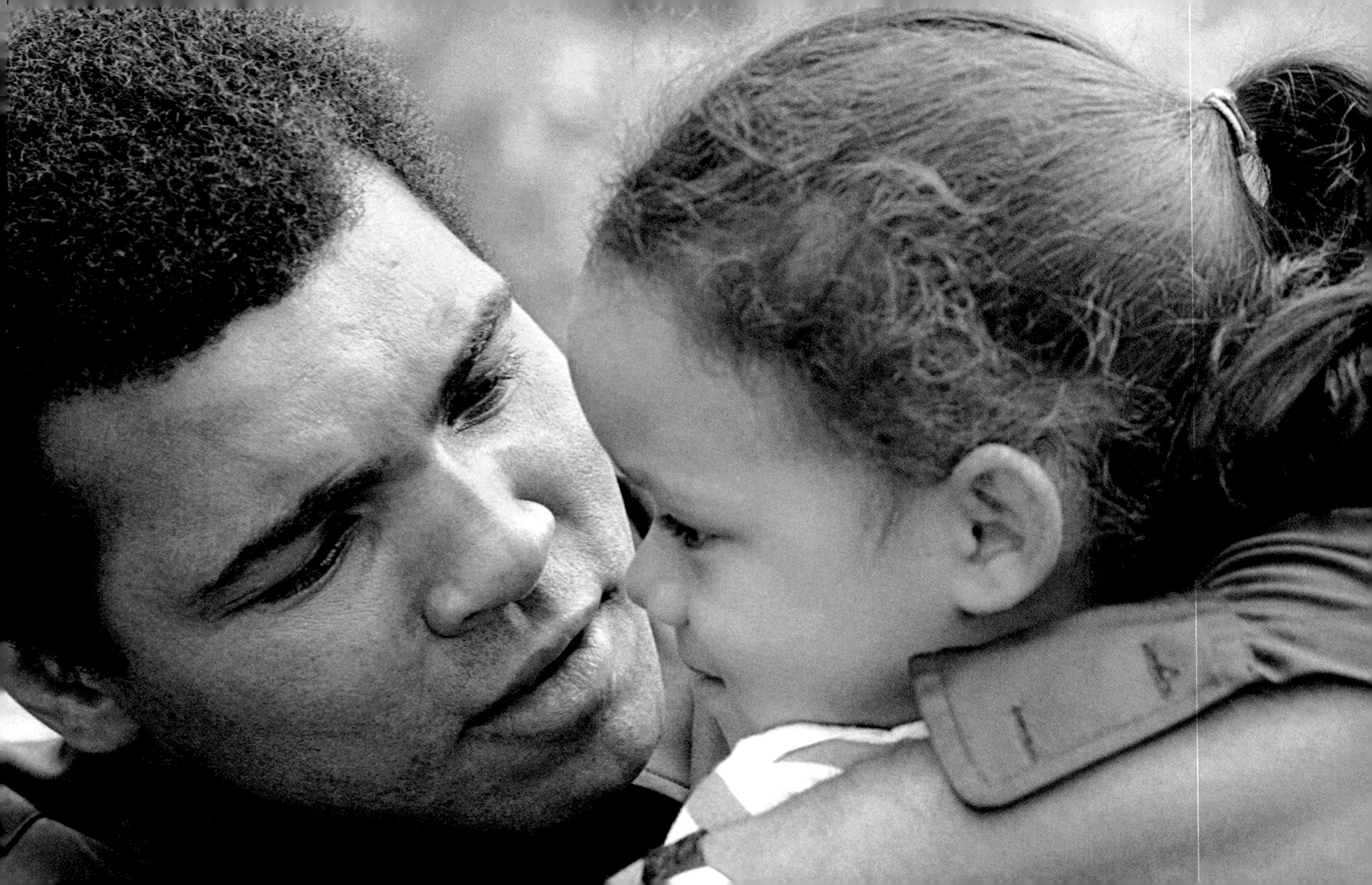

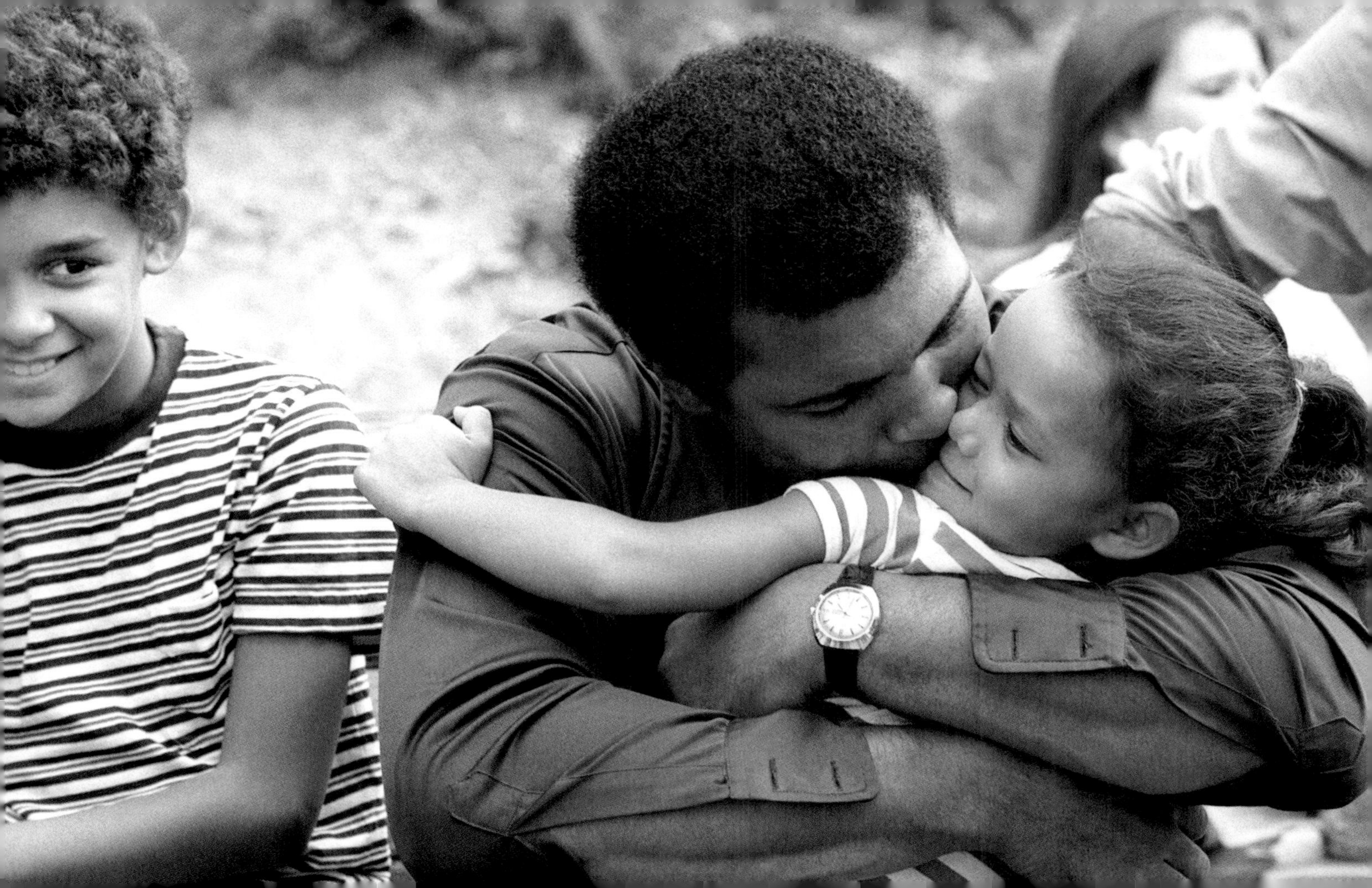

Ali and the handlers
1974 -1977

Ali was surrounded by a group of dedicated handlers, including sparring partners ready to take blows from the great fighter, his younger brother, Rahman Ali, cornerman Drew Bundini Brown and Luis Sarria, Ali's long-time masseur and cutman, known as "The Silent Cuban."

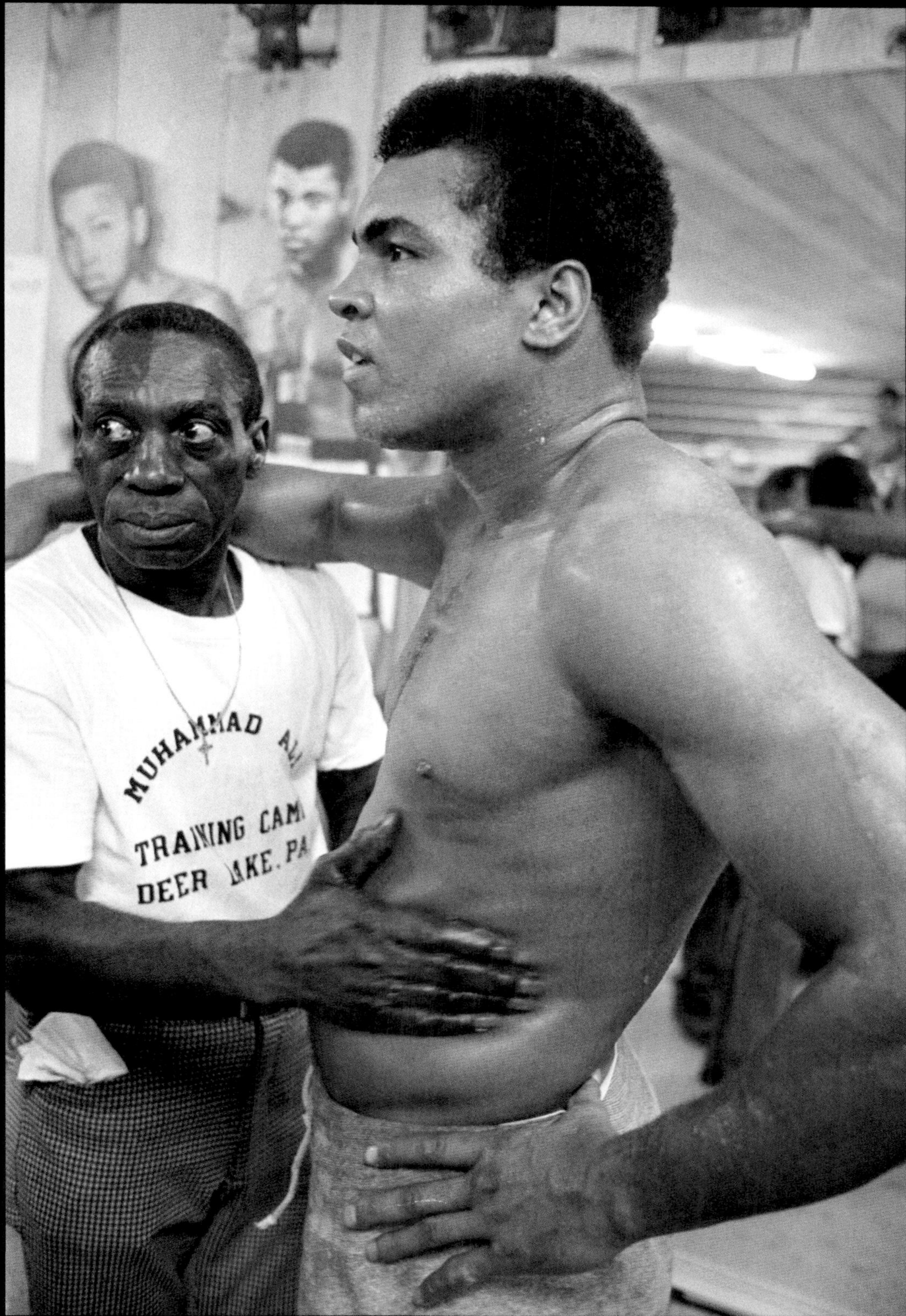
MUHAMMAD AL
TRAINING CAM
DEER LAKE, PA

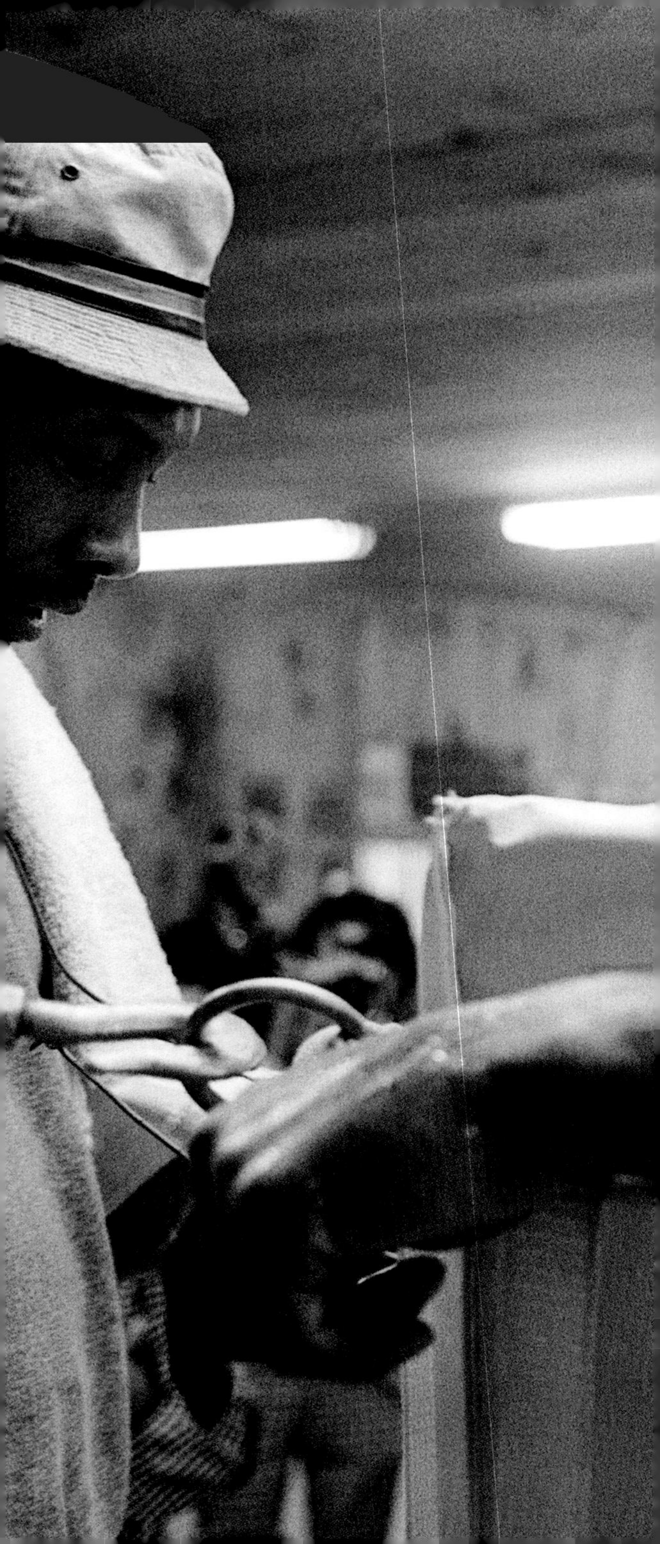

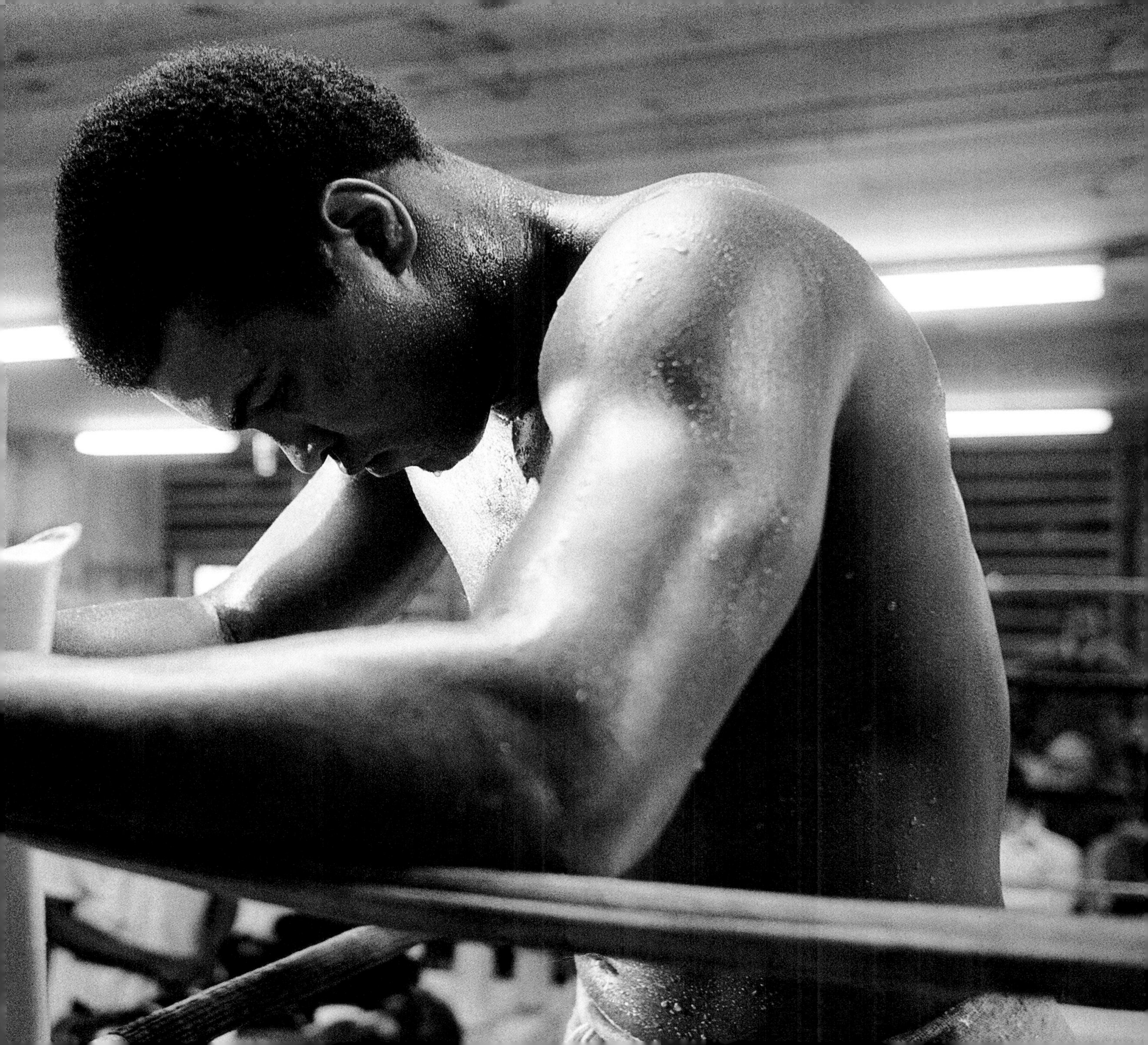

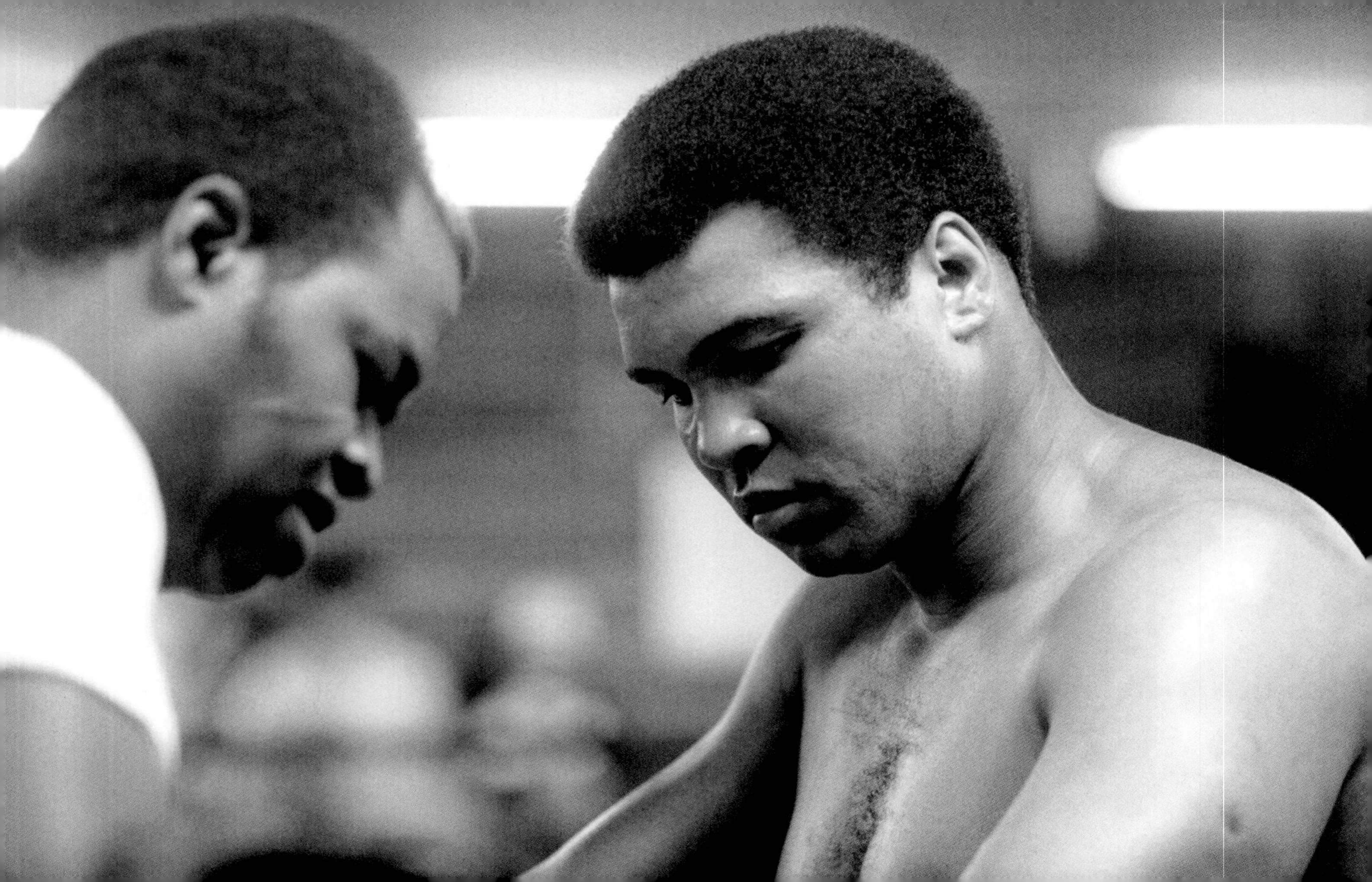

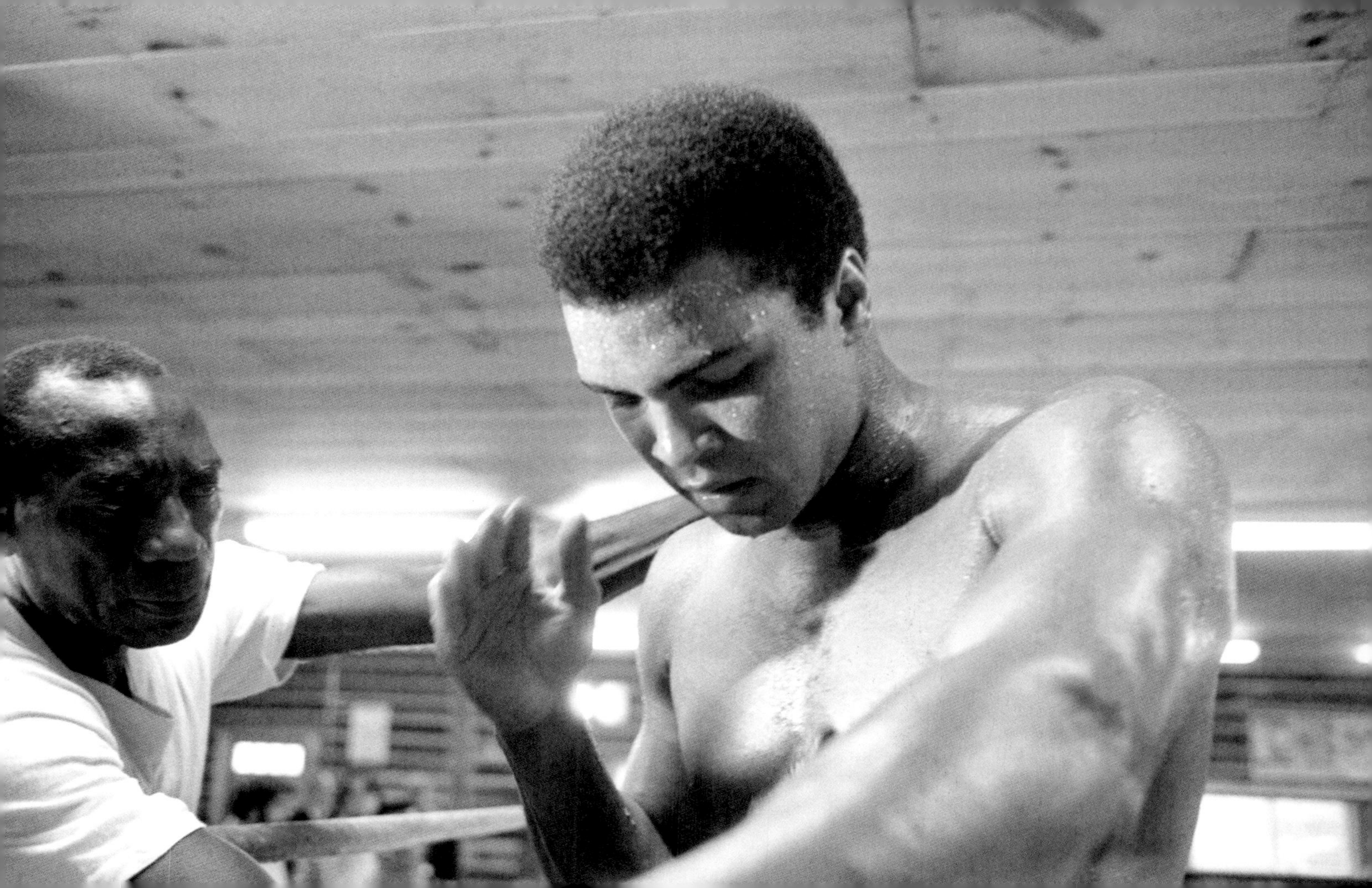

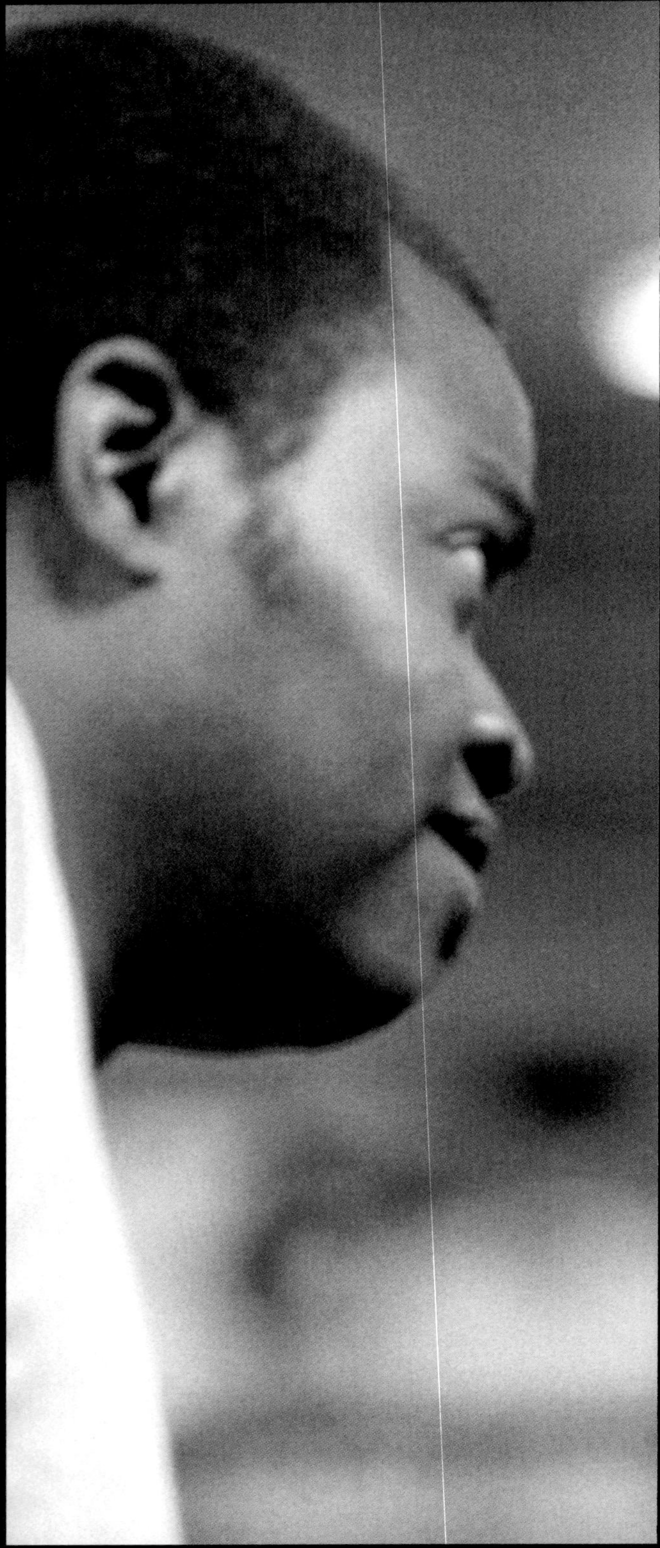

Ali with Drew Bundini Brown

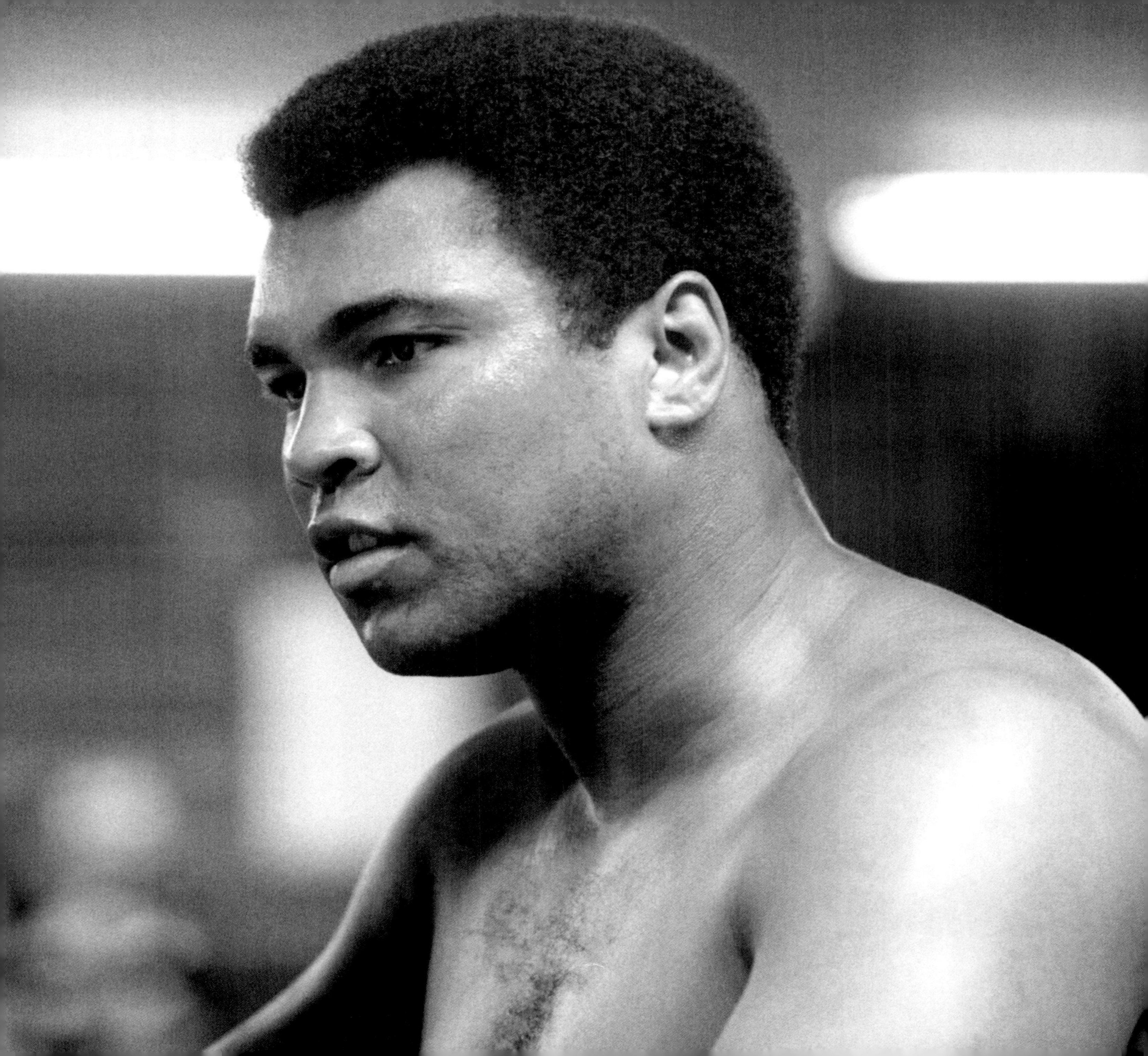

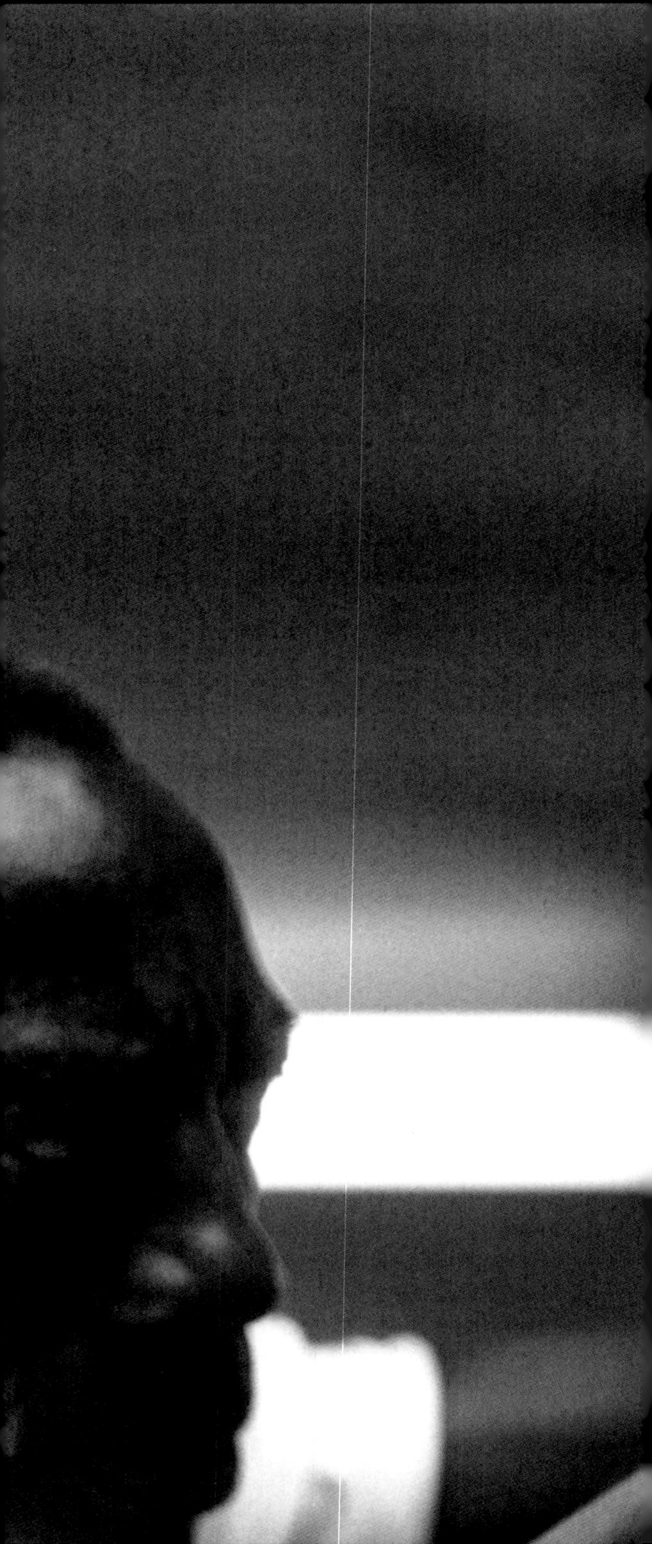

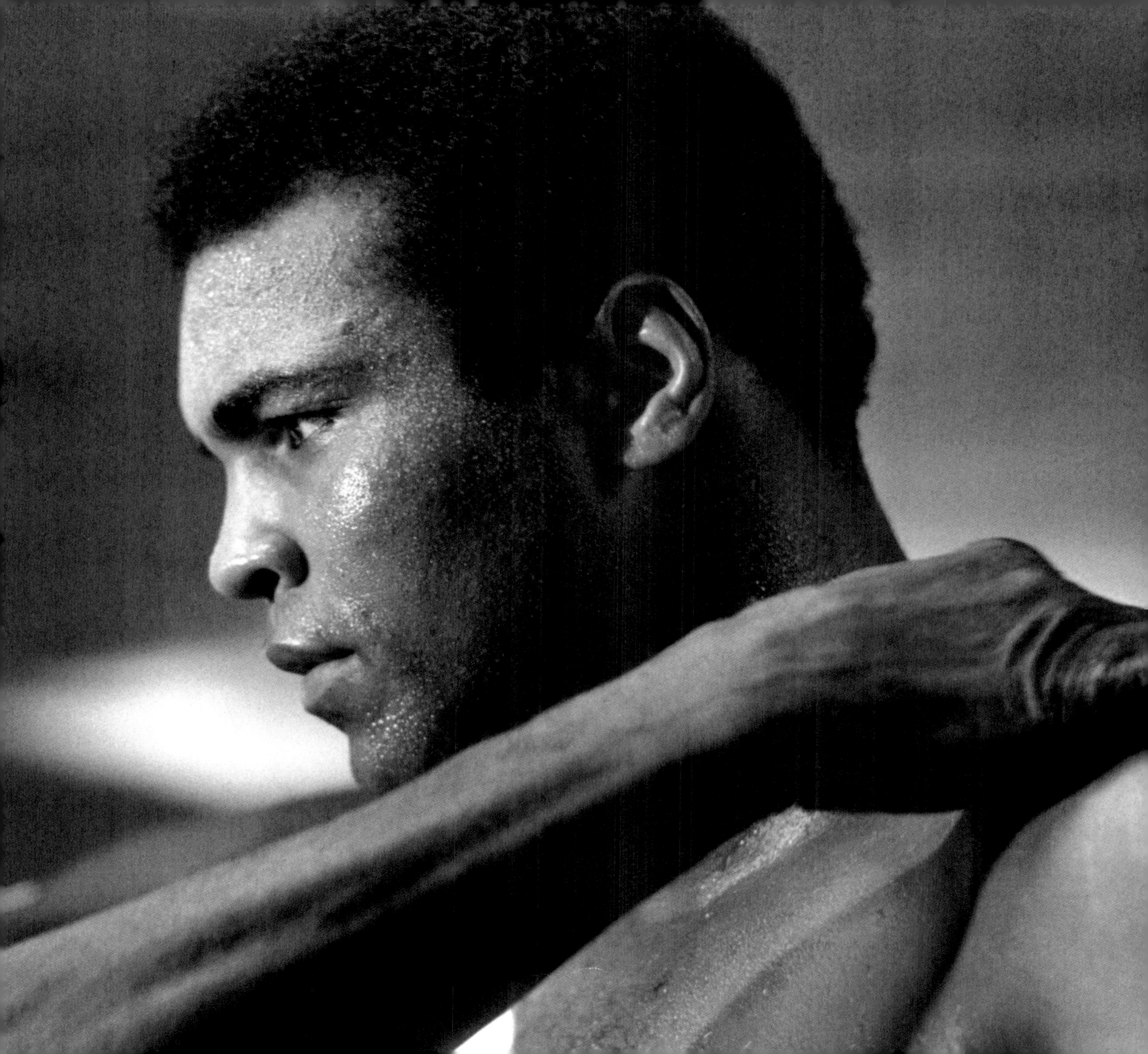

94

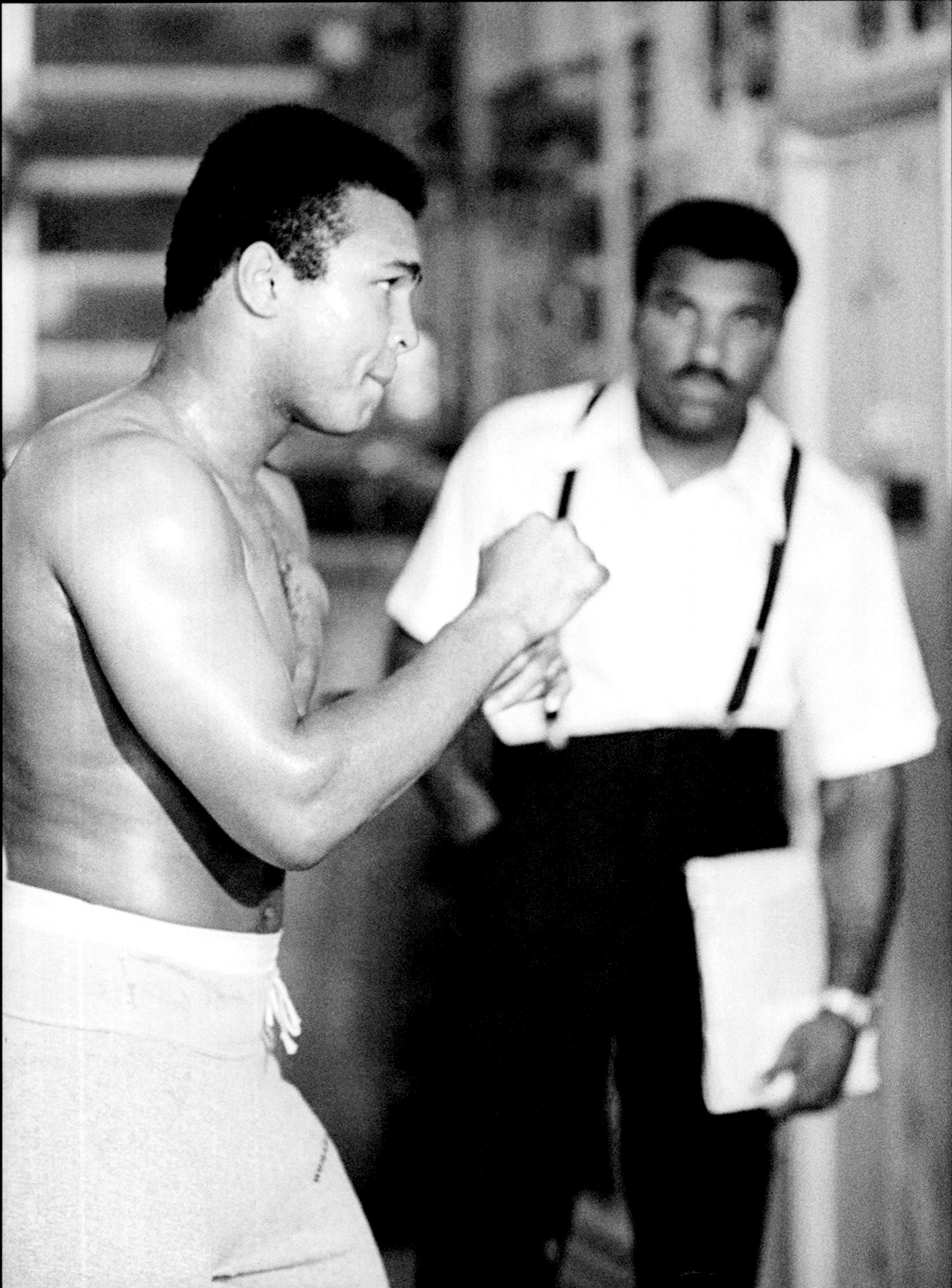

Ali with his younger brother, Rahman Ali

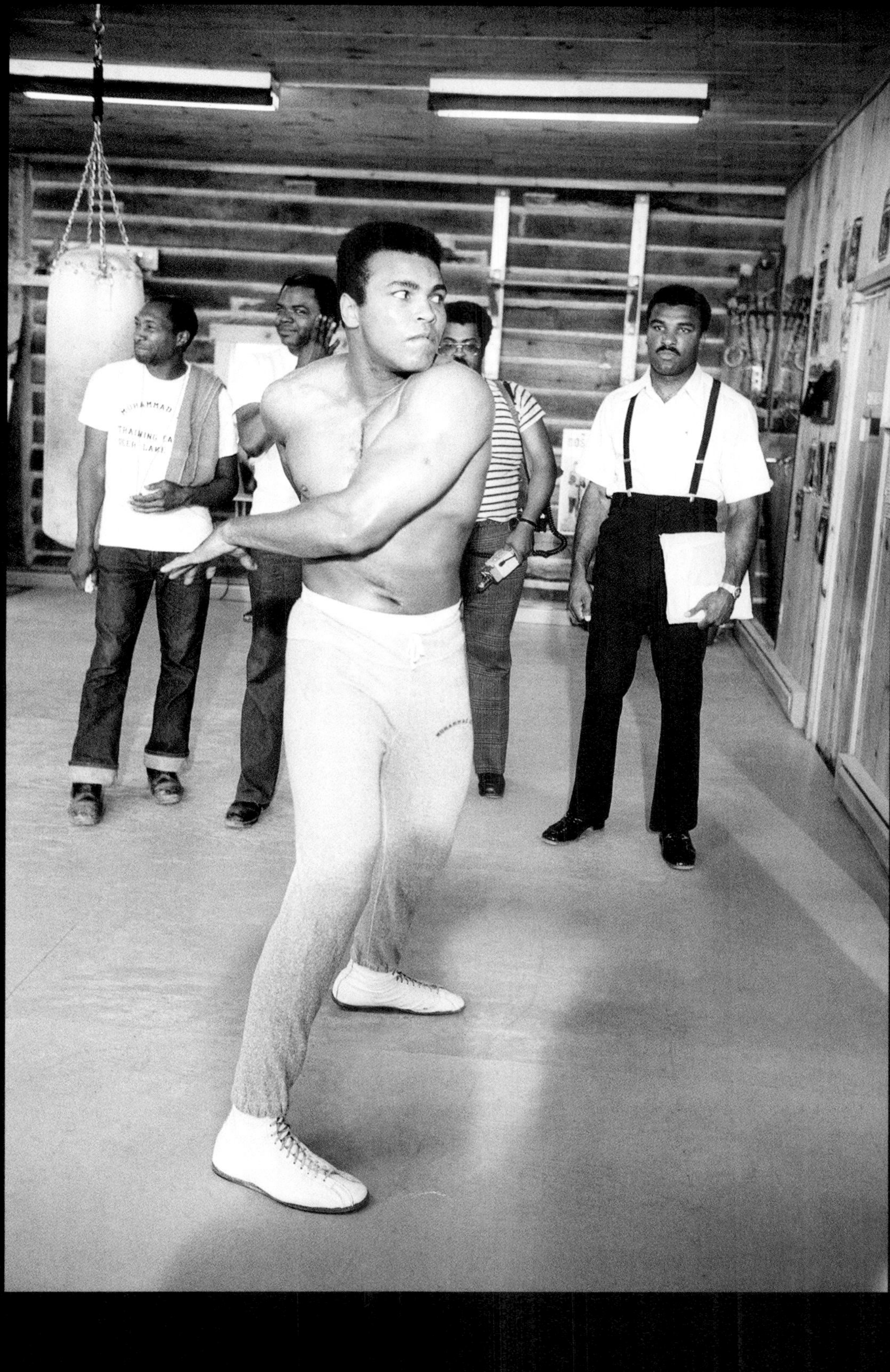

Muhammad Ali training camp, Deer Lake, Pa.
Saturday September 17, 1977

For a Muhammad Ali training session, the gym was surprisingly quiet. Ali had carried out his usual routine involving light shadow boxing, alone, lacing his gloves in a contemplative silence. However, this was no ordinary training session, in twelve days Ali was up against a fearsome, hard-hitting heavyweight named Earnie Shavers in New York's Madison Square Garden. Three sparring partners were selected for their similarities of style, toughness and roughness akin to the rugged Shavers. The late summer heatwave had left the gym uncomfortably hot, likely a bonus for Ali since he would need to shed a little poundage to come in at the right weight. Just an opened door near one of the corners of the ring allowed some early afternoon light and much needed ventilation into the stuffy surroundings. Ali's strenuous workout with the three chosen sparring partners left him exhausted. He ripped off his famous Everlast headguard and leaned into the corner post with his head cradled in his arms facing the open door. At that moment a cameraman from ABC TV flooded the scene with a direct, searing, bright piercing light. Ali, never one to ignore a camera—whether still or movie—slowly raised his head and looked straight into the ABC lens, which by then was shooting over my left shoulder. A split second I will never forget. The exhausted, sweaty head shot has always been pretty much a stereotype but this was Muhammad Ali, arguably the most recognised face in the world. Using a Nikon F2 with a 200mm f/4 lens with the focus racked as close as possible and with the cameraman's piercing strobe-like light combined with the soft daylight from the open door shooting at 1/250th s at f/4, the result was this '1977' image. Some years later I showed Ali the picture I had taken. He was training in The Bahamas for a shabby farewell fight against an opponent called Trevor Berbick. He traced his right index finger over the sweat beads in the photograph and mumbled, "All them years, all them years of hard work."

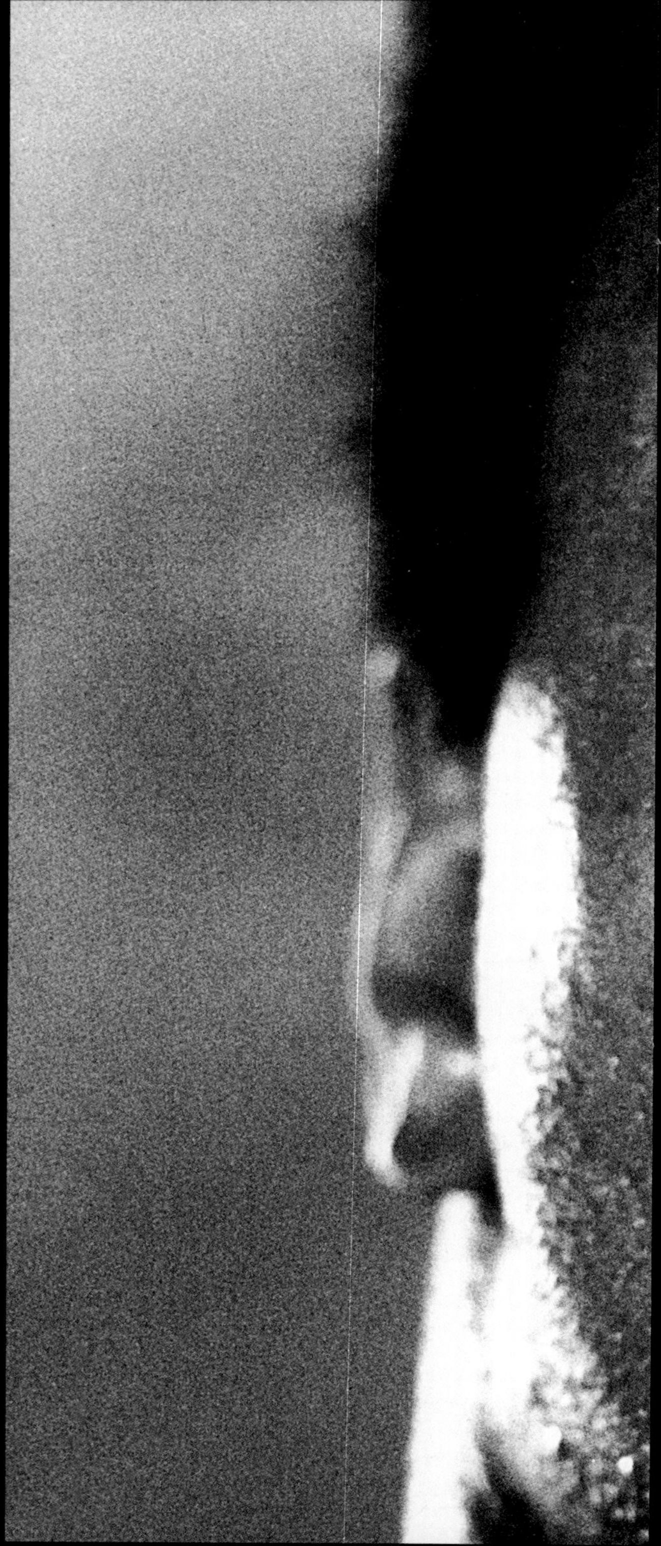

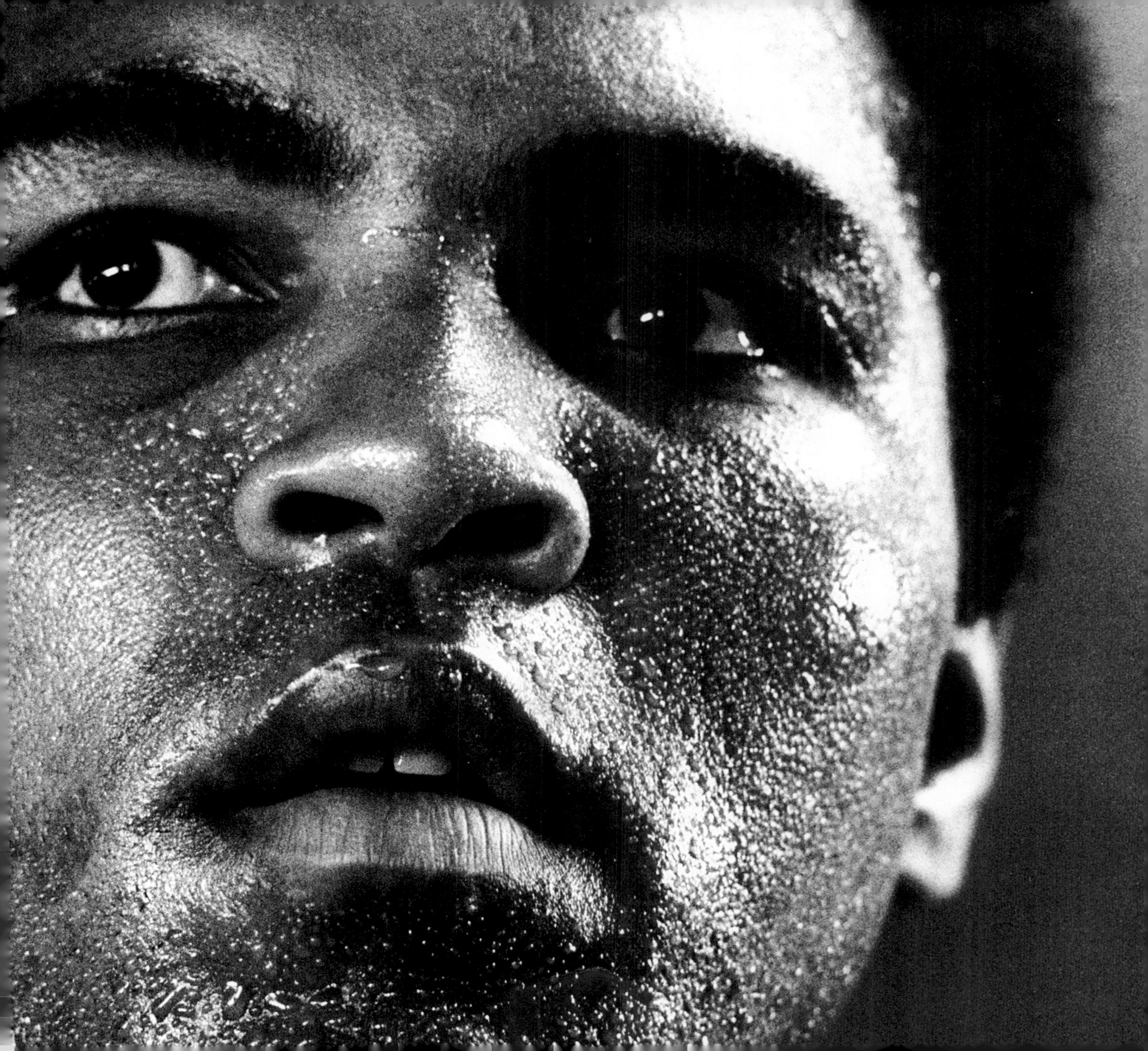

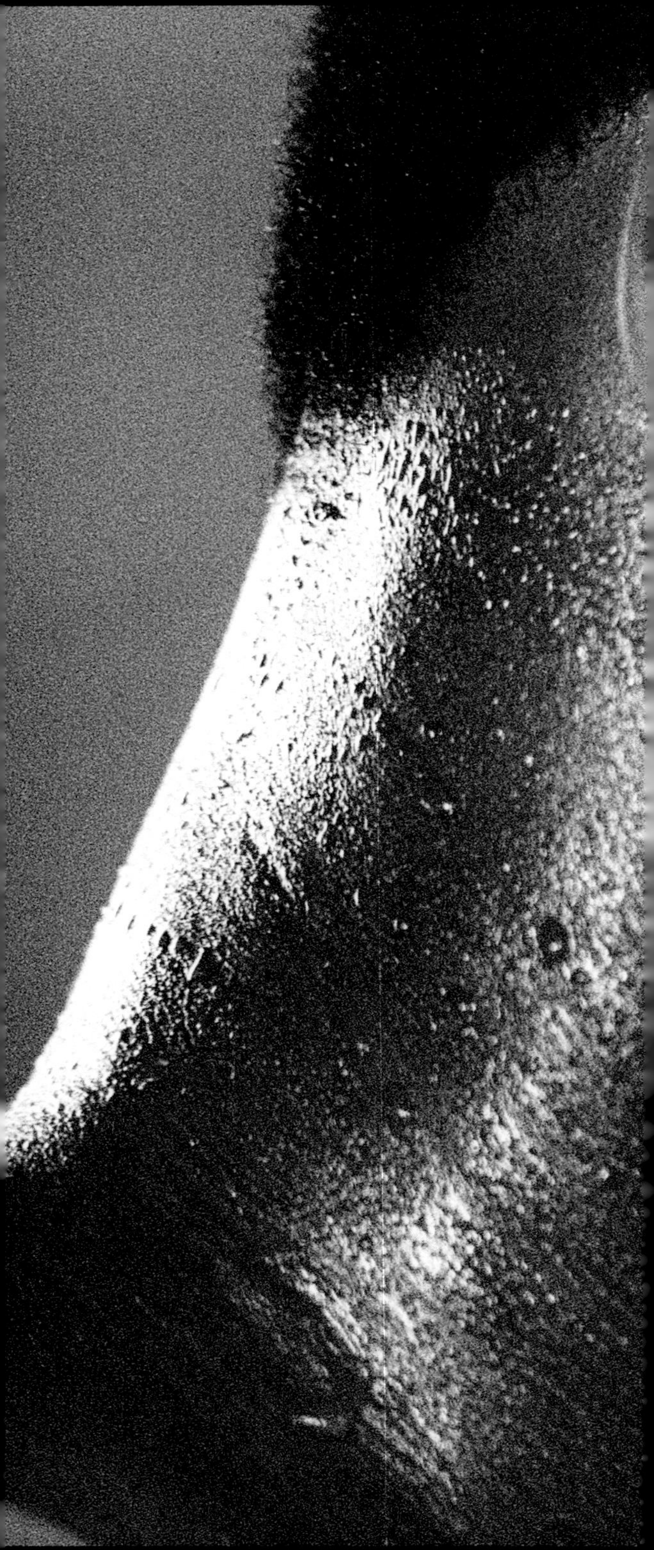

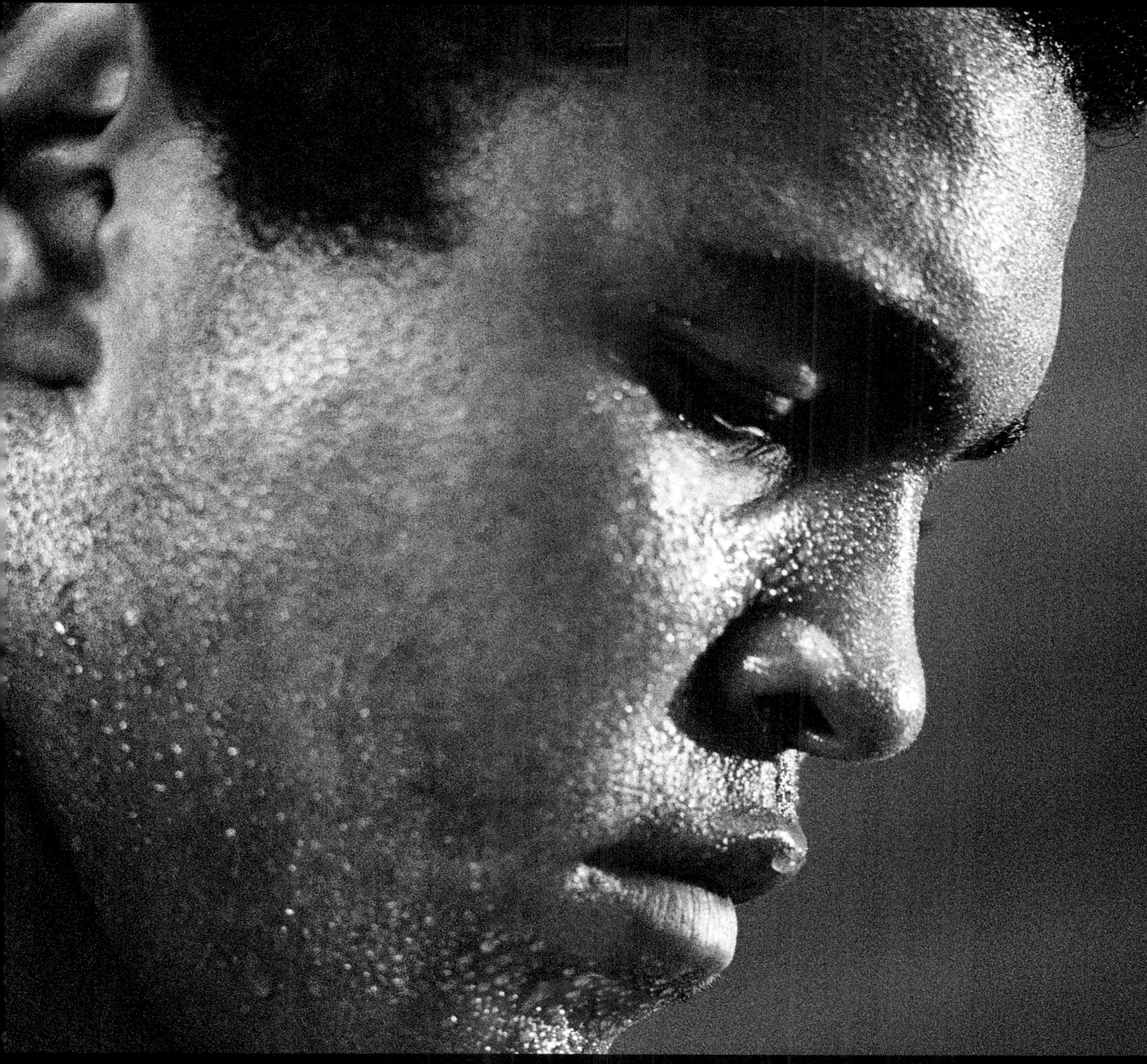

Muhammad Ali trains for his fight with Larry Holmes
Muhammad Ali training camp, Deer Lake, Pa.
Tuesday July 29, 1980

For nearly 20 years Muhammad Ali has been imposing an extravagant fantasy upon his life but somewhere, surely, reality is crouching in ambush, waiting to take revenge. It would seem that Larry Holmes is about to give reality some vigorous assistance. Ali has come back, less than four months short of his 39th birthday, and after two years of debilitating retirement, insisting that next Thursday the most remarkable fist-fight ever to break out in a car park will make him the heavyweight champion of the world for the fourth time.

from *The Hardest Game: Hugh McIlvanney on Boxing*

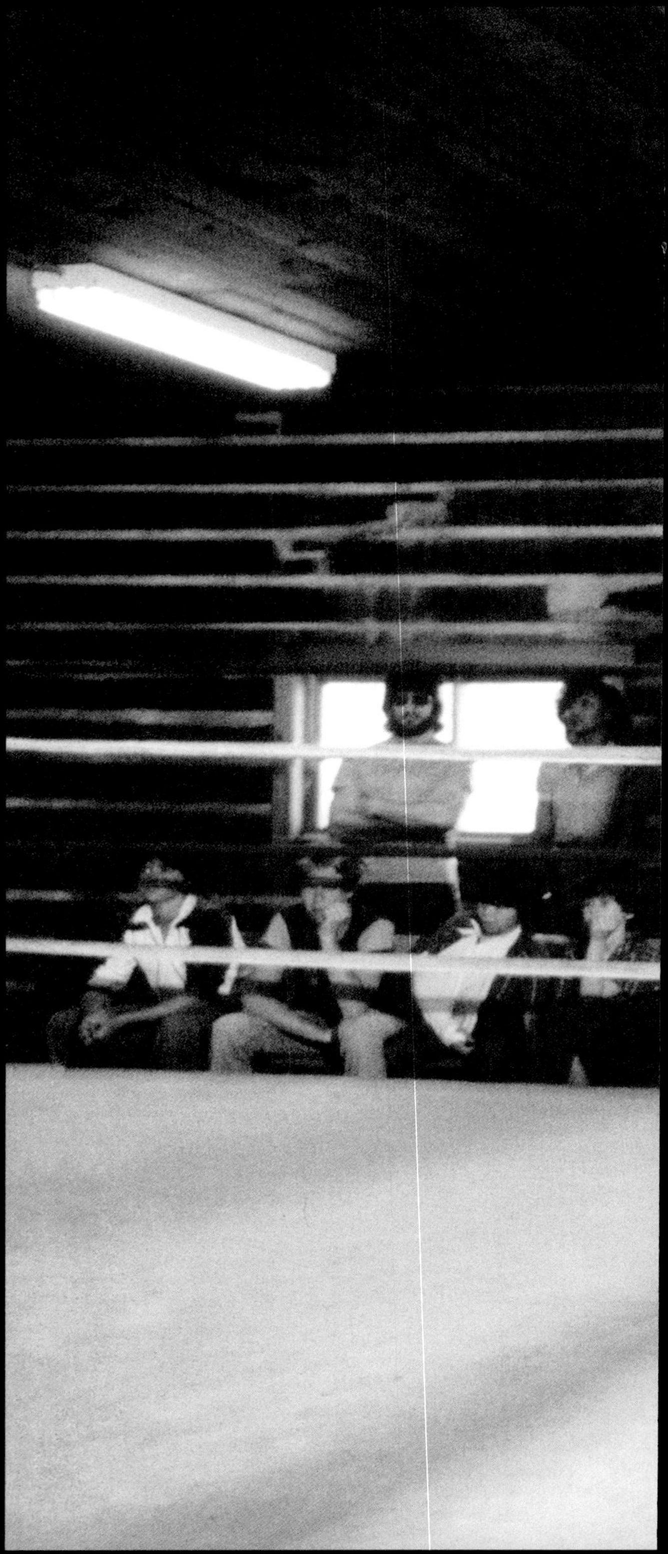

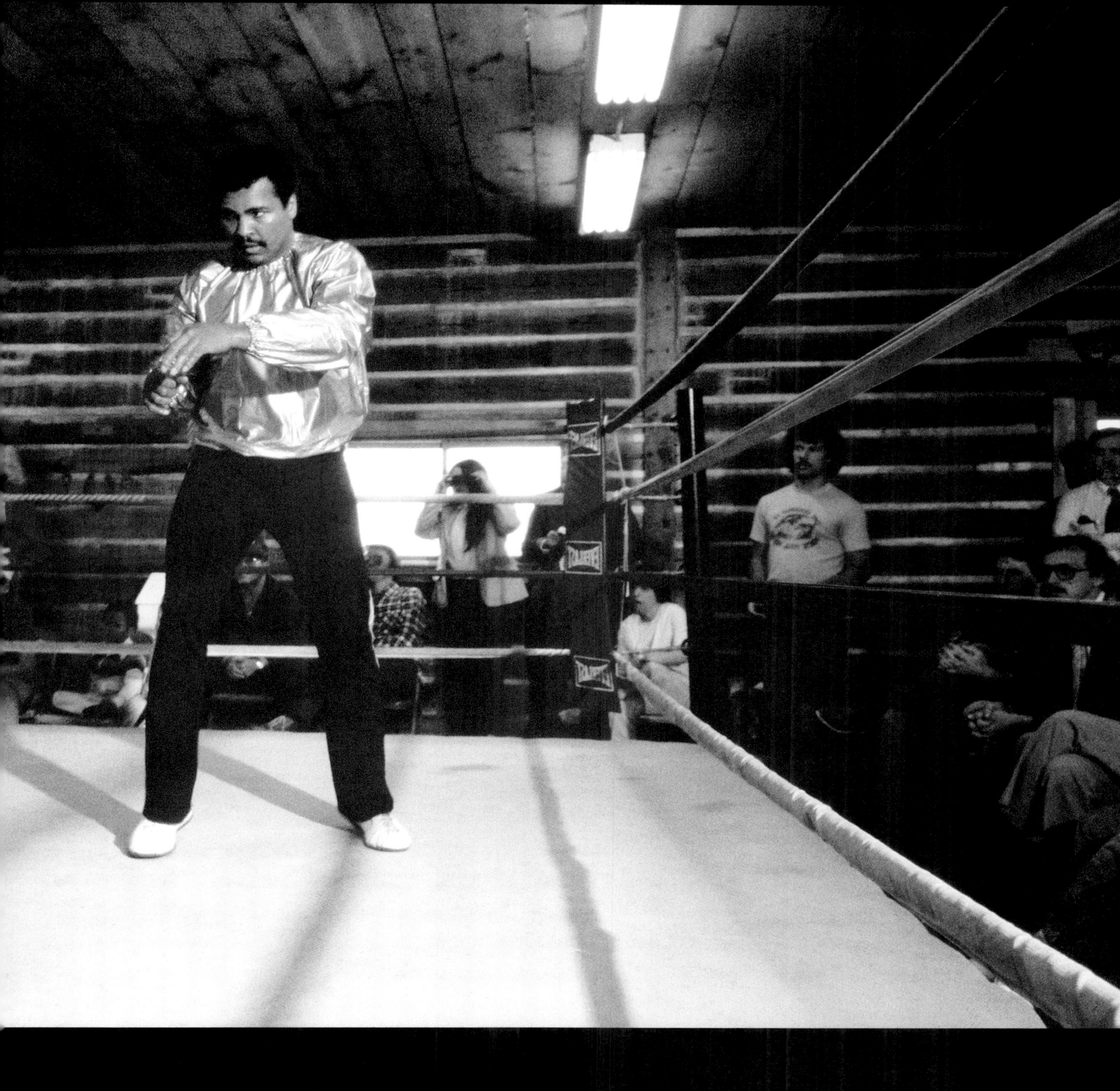

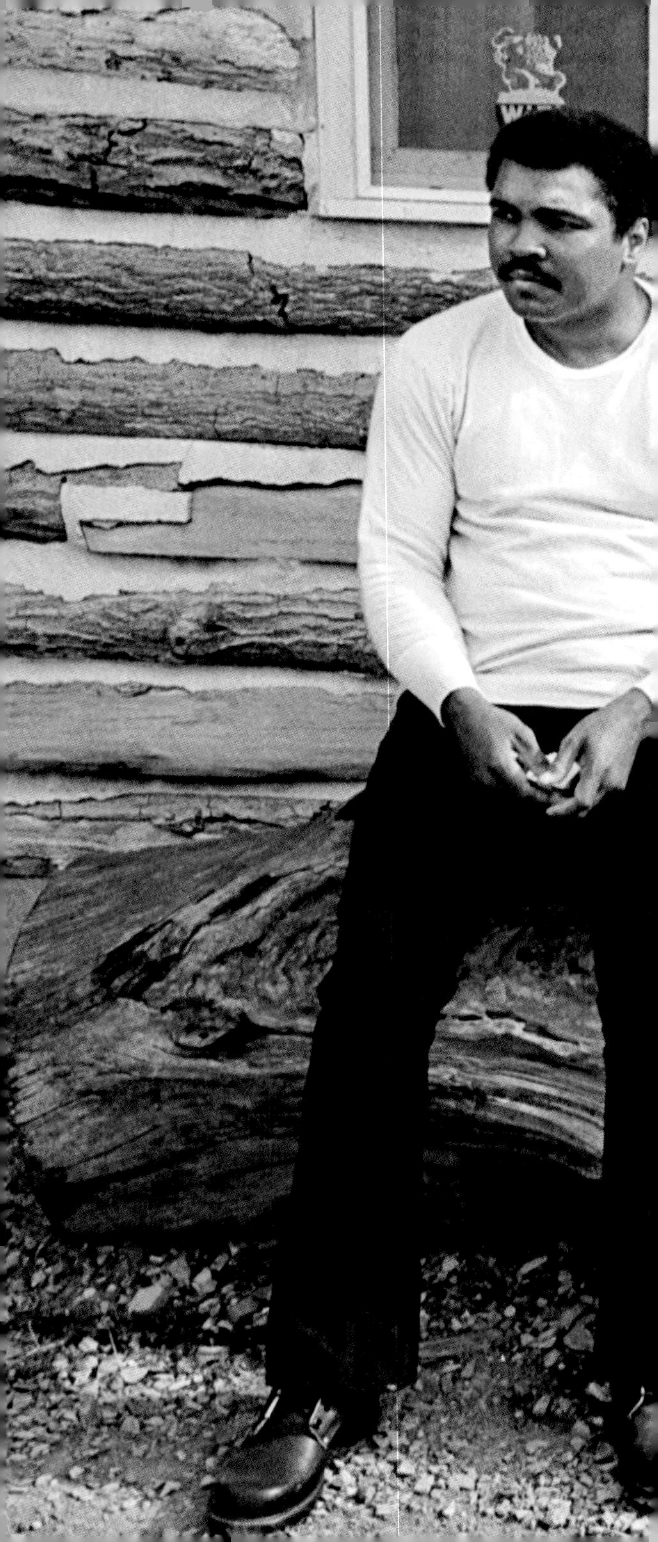

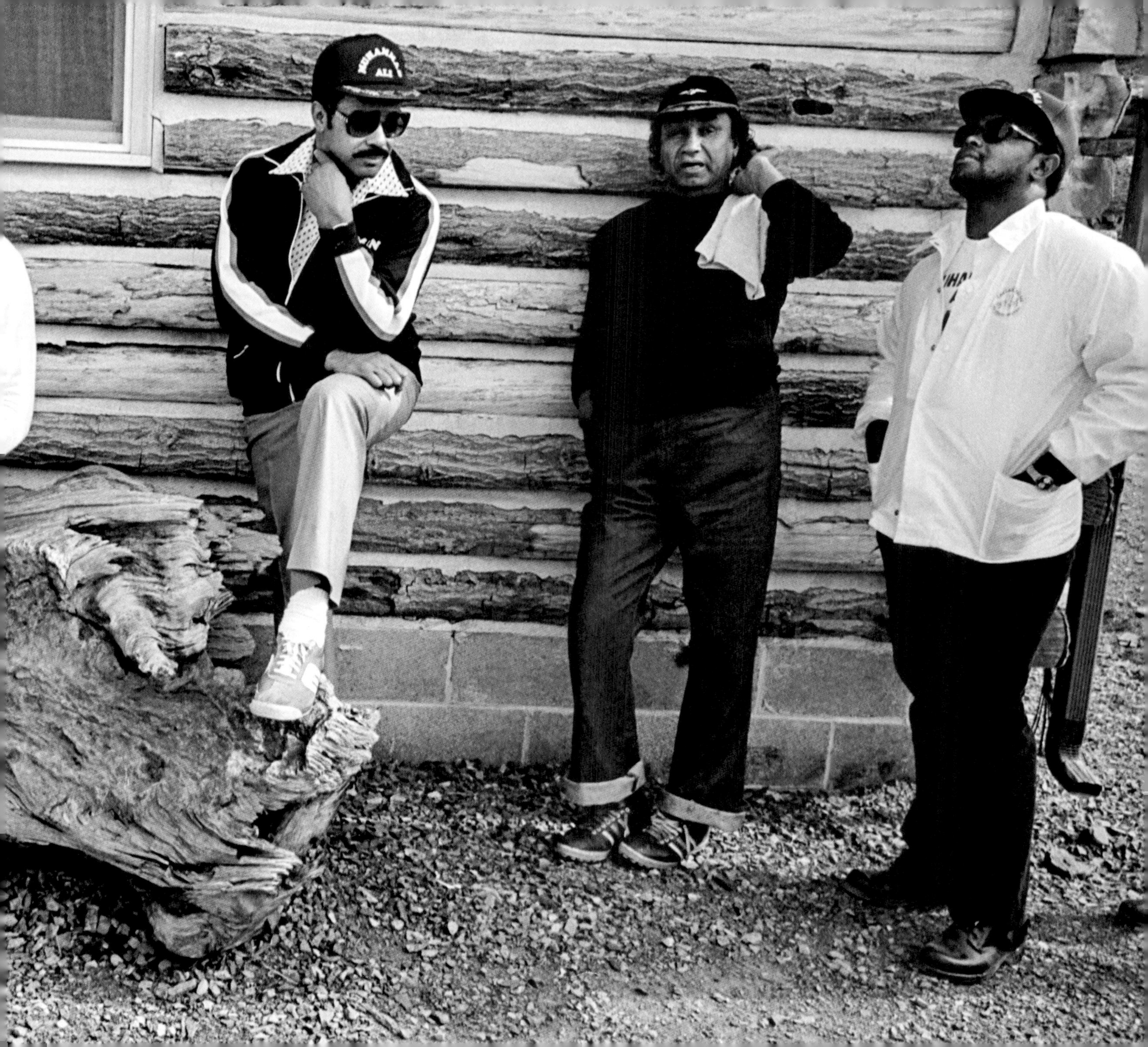

Muhammad Ali as "Dark Gable"
Thursday September 11, 1980

Prior to his disastrous October 1980 fight with Larry Holmes, Muhammad Ali slimmed down from 254 pounds to 217 ½. In preparation for the forthcoming event, *Sports Illustrated* were running a large, several pages long piece of mine about what happened to all of Ali's old opponents. They needed an up-to-date picture of the great man. After a night out at Elaine's in NYC, my assistant Brian (who was the bartender and later my accountant) and I drove (Brian drove) to the Pottsville training camp in Pennsylvania. To my dismay, Ali had grown an elegant moustache and decided to call himself "Dark Gable." Six days before the piece and my photographs were due to run in *SI*, Ali shaved the offending appendage off. Ali's photographer pal Howard Bingham quickly had to provide the latest 'clean-shaven' portrait. Interesting though, when we arrived at the camp Ali was shooting a Public Service Announcement to stop folks from using public fire-alarm boxes for hoax calls. That was about the only endorsement I ever remember seeing him involved with. Different times.

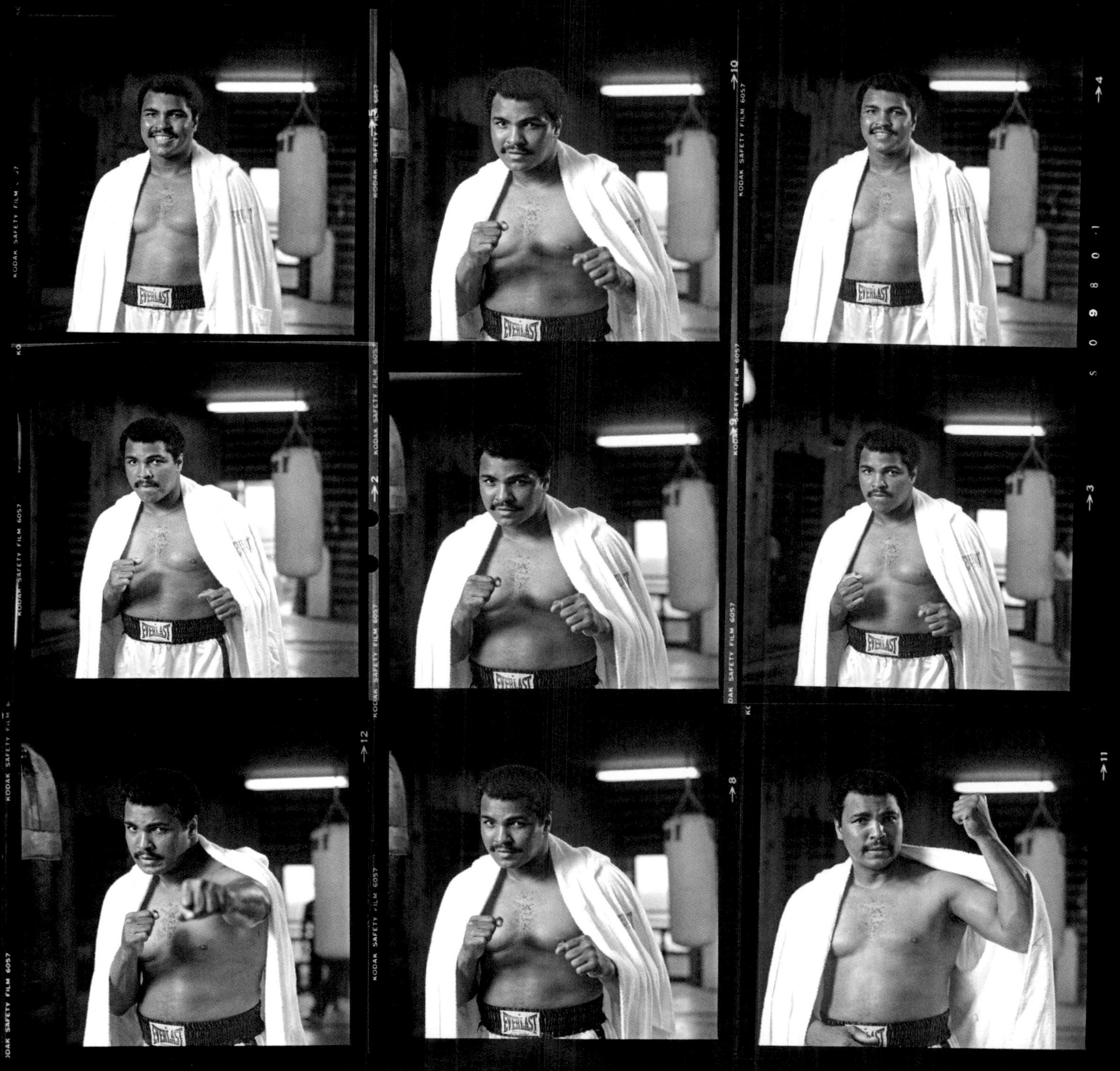
KODAK SAFETY FILM 6057
EVERLAST

Muhammad Ali v Larry Holmes
Caesars Palace Hotel & Casino, Las Vegas, Nevada
Thursday October 2, 1980

Should you wish to view a disaster in slow motion it is, in my opinion best viewed from 'up in the gods' (for those not familiar with showbiz parlance, the highest and cheapest seats in a theater). Caesars Palace Hotel & Casino converted its car park to accommodate the Larry Holmes v Muhammad Ali heavyweight
06 boxing match on October 2, 1980. My position was very high up and very far away from the 'action' in the ring but a 600mm lens brought the participants a little closer!

The Greatest had nothing to offer. He hardly threw a punch. His much publicised 30lb weight loss had taken its chemical toll on his stamina and any ring skills he had left. Cheerleader and Ali cornerman Drew Bundini Brown and savvy trainer Angelo Dundee, who had been in Ali's corner since the 1960s, stopped the fight in the time between the 10th and 11th rounds. Later, some of the writers were of the opinion that it was fortunate the opponent was Holmes. He knew of Muhammad Ali's past greatness having been a sparring partner and so limited his destructive intentions; a younger boxer might have keen to make a name for himself.

After the fight Holmes said, "I went to his room and he was lying on the bed being massaged. I said, 'I love you man.' He says. 'If you love me, why you beat me like that?'"

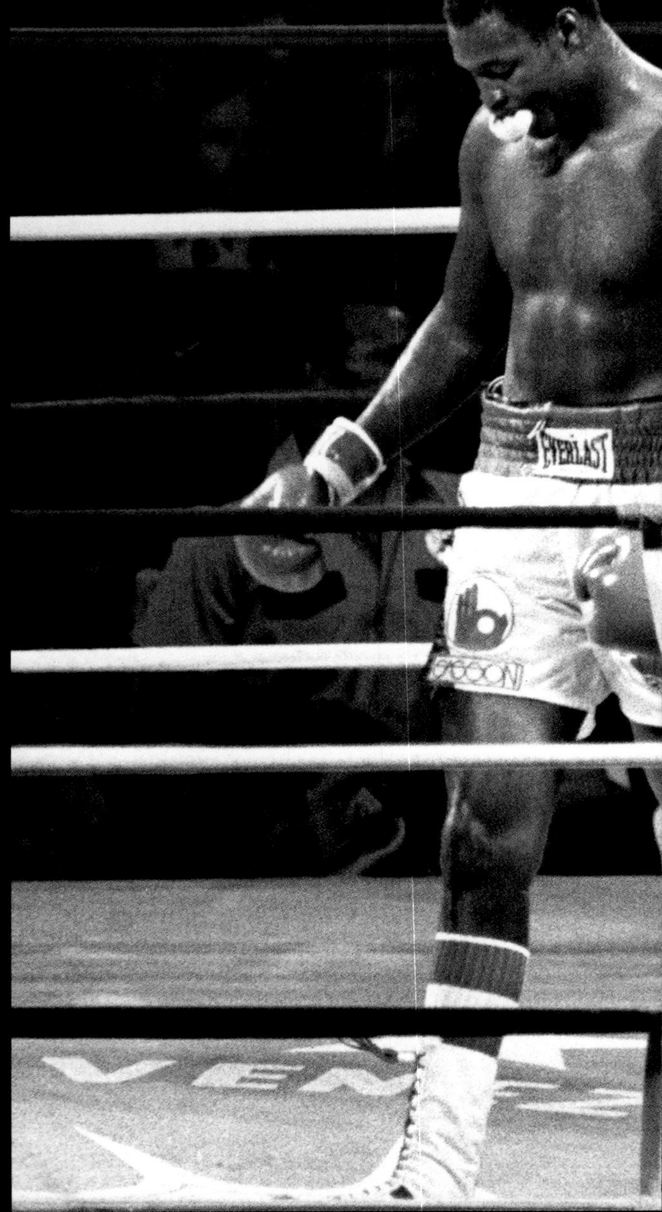

Larry Holmes turns and walks away from Muhammad Ali at the end of the 10th round

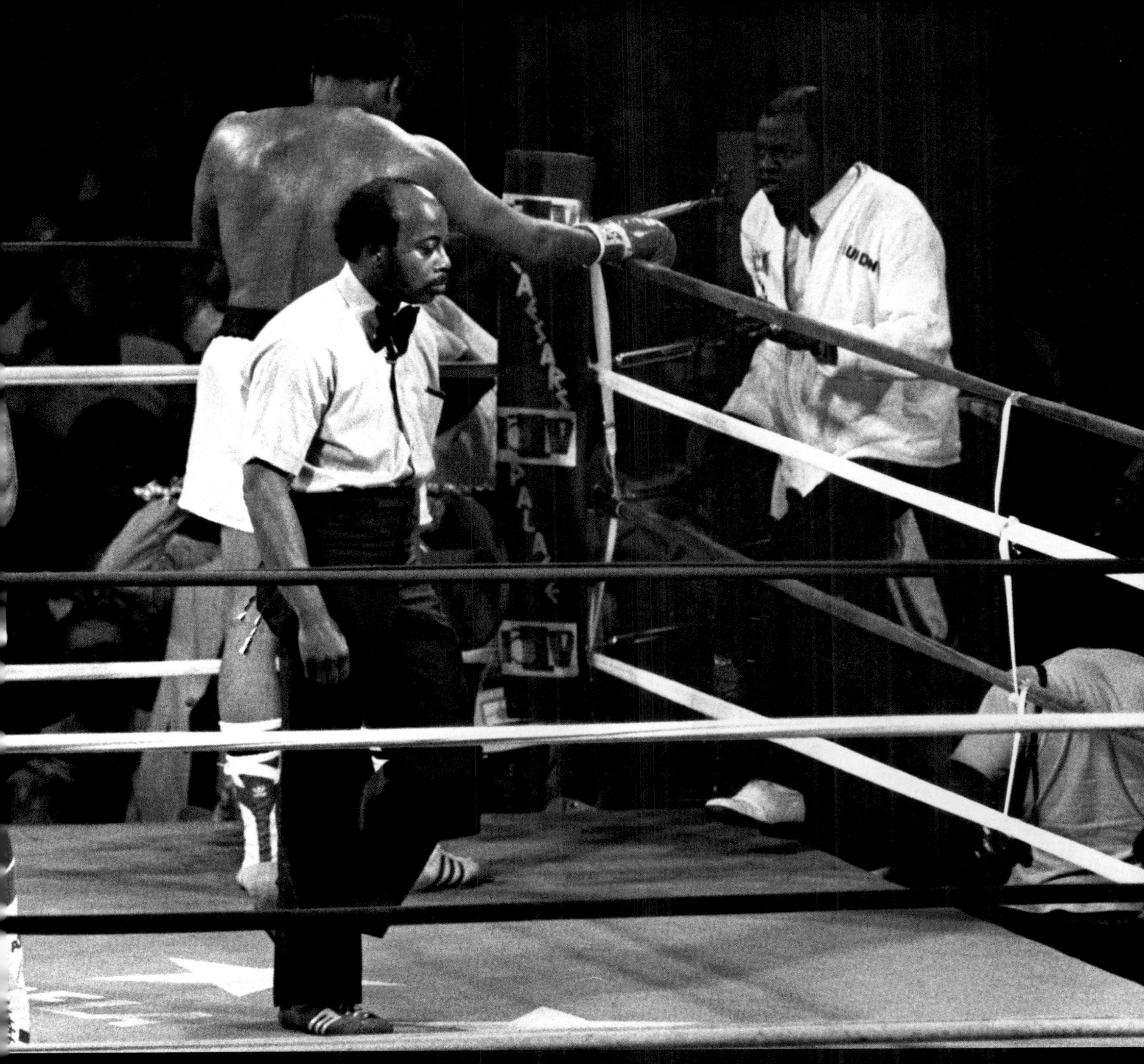

Muhammad Ali v Trevor Berbick

Queen Elizabeth Sports Center, Nassau, The Bahamas
Friday December 11, 1981

The early 1980s were arguably Muhammad Ali's quietest years. His last ring appearance had been a shambles held in Nassau in The Bahamas, billed as 'Drama in Bahama.' Just a few weeks shy of his 40th birthday, he had been coerced by dubious promoters to fight a 27-year-old brawler named Trevor Berbick.

Such was the chaos of the promotion that at the last moment it was discovered nobody had bothered to provide sporting equipment.

The jangle of a cow-bell rang the end. A tawdry affair where even the bell, it was rumored, had been lifted from an unsuspecting bovine grazing somewhere in The Bahamas.

A gaggle of sports writers gathered yet again in a makeshift dressing room, most had been around for years. The AP's Ed Schuyler spoke directly to Ali, "Muhammad it's been a hell of a ride, thank you."

Ali lifted his head and with his wide-eyed look of mock astonishment, he proclaimed, "I will return..........to Los Angeles!"

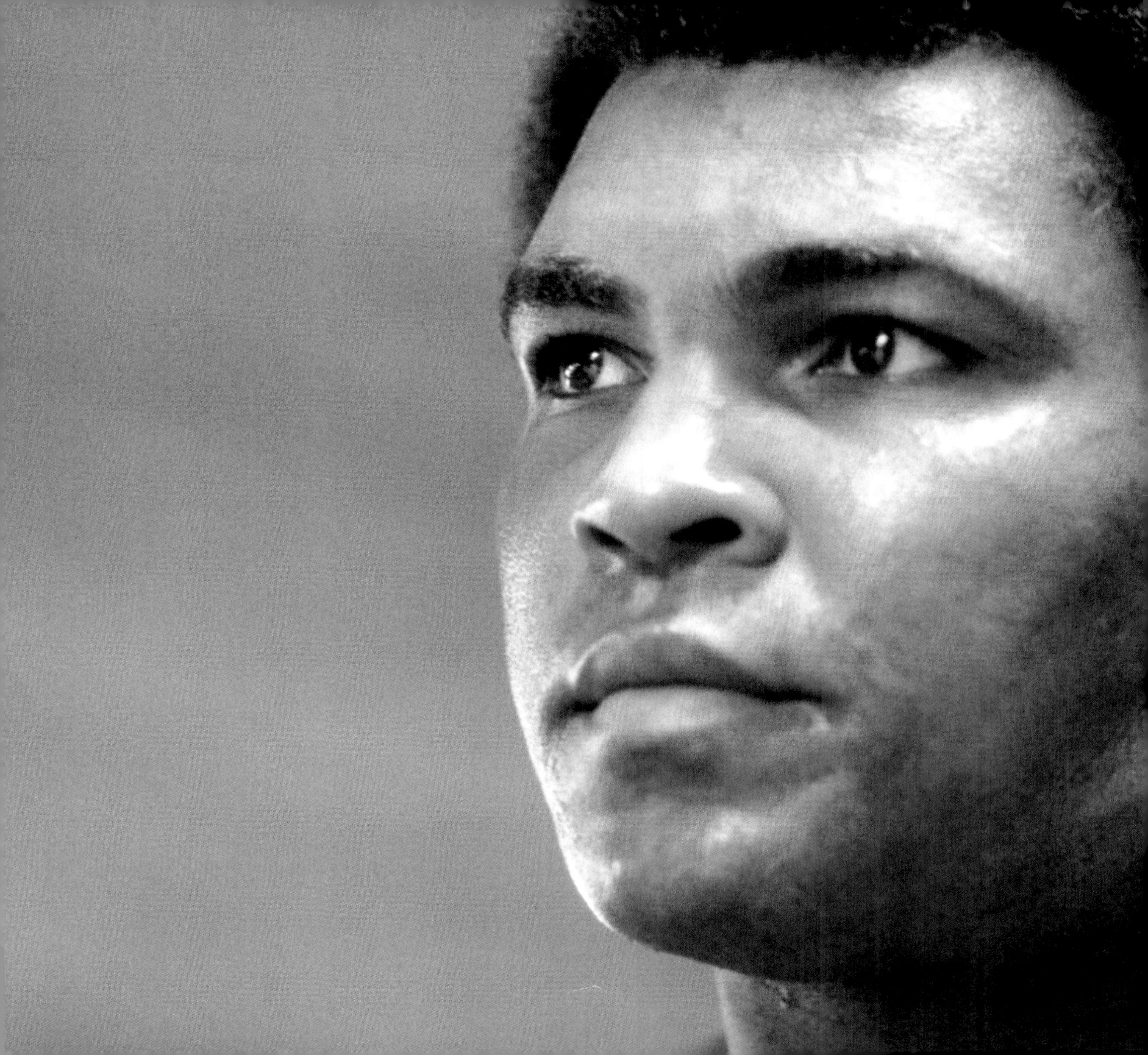

THE OPPONENTS

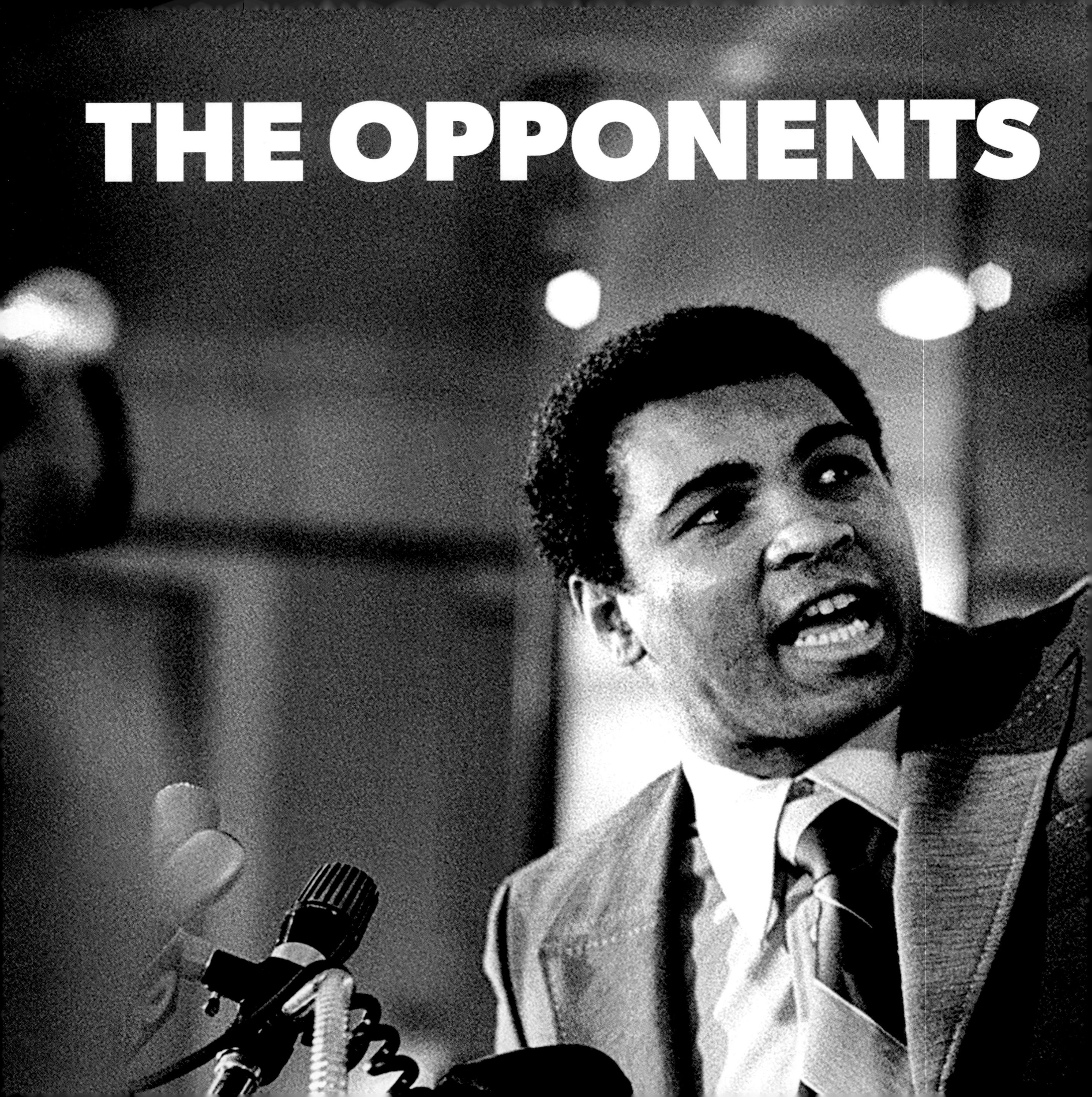

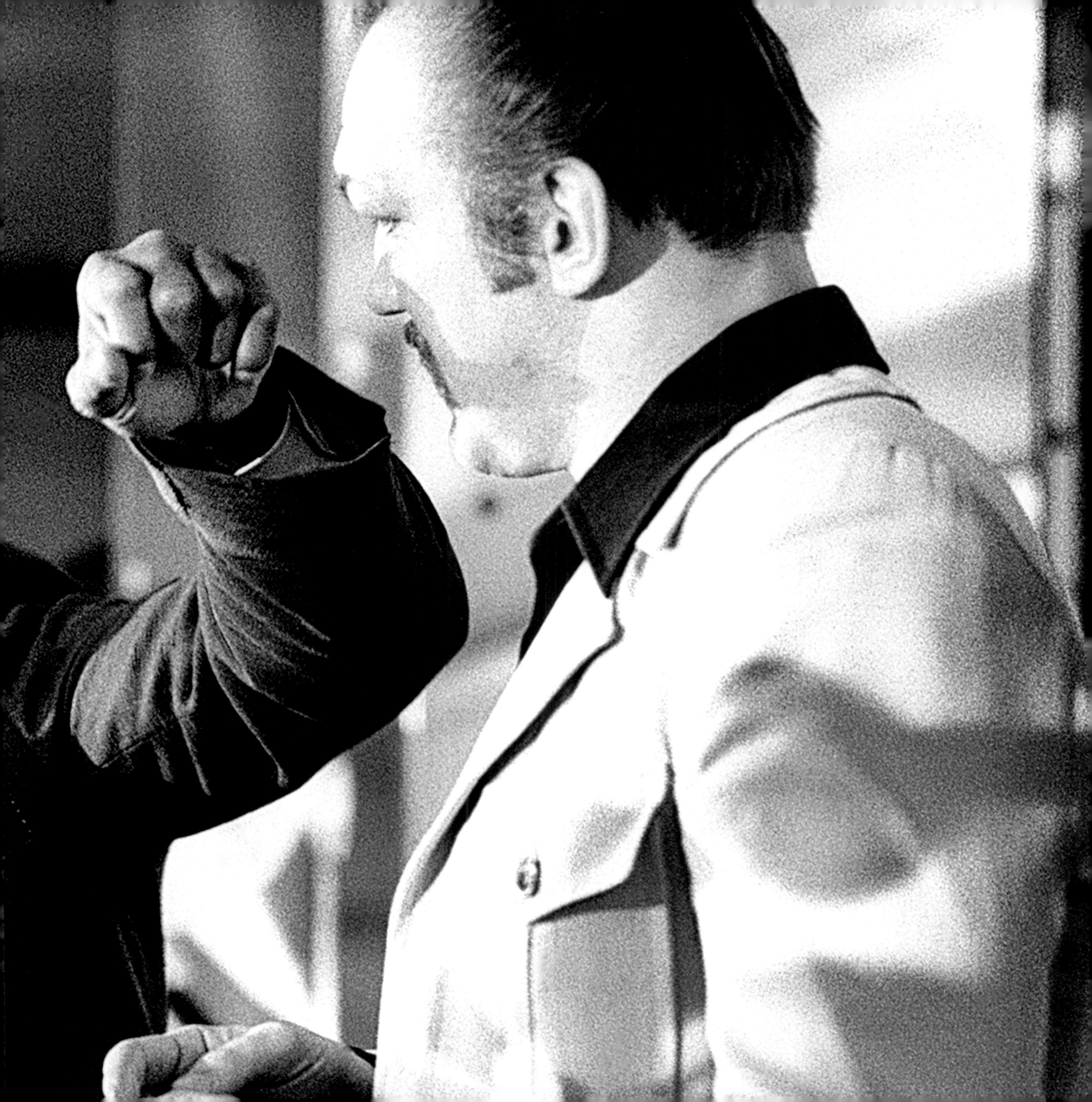

Tracking them down.

"It was George Foreman that got me thinking. It was 1977, right after his punishing loss to Jimmy Young in Puerto Rico. Foreman had a near-death experience, found God and he took up preaching. I thought – if this is what George Foreman is doing – I wonder what happened to the others."

That question led Michael Brennan on a journey to track down as many of Ali's "old opponents" as he could find. Using phone directories, calls and conversations, one tip led to another and Brennan was on his way. The results might be surprising to some readers, as the stories of the former opponents range from successful businessmen to cops, prison sentences and to Leon Spinks working at a McDonald's thirty years after winning the Gold Medal at the 1976 Olympics. The initial results of Brennan's quest were published in an extensive 14-page feature in *Sports Illustrated* on September 22, 1980, but his pursuit didn't end there. Brennan would continue to photograph Ali's former opponents, including a return visit to George Foreman in 1991 in the West Indies, Floyd Patterson in 1995 and Larry Holmes in Easton, Pa., in 2006, to name only a few.

"The money back then wasn't what it is today," Brennan comments. "Today, to step in a ring at that level would result in a substantial payday. But that wasn't the case back then when some of the fighters only got a few hundred bucks, if that, to face Ali in the ring." Many of the men Brennan tracked down were working in jobs completely unrelated to their former glory days of trading punches with The Greatest, making tracing their whereabouts an even tougher job. LaMar Clark was working as boss in a mine in Salt Lake City. Alex Miteff drove limousines in New York City. "Finding Buster Mathis took about 40 calls and confusing leads. But I finally found him – only seven years after he retired from boxing, working as a truck loader in Grand Rapids in 1979. He told me that life after boxing wasn't easy, but he was still proud of where he ended up. He died in 1995 of a heart attack, tipping the scales at 500lbs. A few months later, his son, Buster Jr., got into the ring himself in a match against Mike Tyson."

"I am the greatest. Not only do I knock 'em out, I pick the round."

Muhammad Ali

As challenging as finding Buster was, the most difficult opponent to track down was Jim Robinson. It was Brennan's photo shoot with Herb Siler—who had lost to Ali in 1960—in a Dade County, Fla. correctional facility, serving time for shooting his girlfriend, that gave Brennan the first leads on "Sweet Jimmy" Robinson's whereabouts. "Siler told me Robinson was living somewhere in northwest Miami, at that time, not an area you'd go unprotected. I made a few anxious trips to no avail. I waited until Siler was out of prison and asked him if he'd start asking around for me."

Robinson fought Ali—still Cassius Clay at the time—in 1961 as a last minute replacement on the card. Likely due to Siler's prompting, Robinson turned up at Brennan's hotel late on a Friday night in November 1979. "We had a good conversation and he told me how he and Ali were good friends back in the 1960s. I could tell things weren't going well for him, so after I took some photos and our conversation ended, I slipped him twenty bucks. I was told years later that I might have been the last man to see Jimmy alive. There's been rumors and whispers about Robinson's whereabouts, but nothing confirmed."

Previous spread: *Muhammad Ali with Chuck Wepner at a press conference prior to their fight*

114

George Foreman
Fought Ali in Zaire on October 30, 1974 at a fight that would be known as 'The Rumble in the Jungle'
KO'd in the 8th round

Foreman retired in 1977 and went on to become an ordained Christian minister. He returned to the ring in 1984 to reclaim the title of Heavyweight Champion of the World, becoming the oldest champion in history (aged 45). After retiring for a second time, he became the spokesperson for the George Foreman Grill.

Foreman became the inspiration for the 'old opponents' venture. After having nearly been baptised by George sitting on the plane back to NYC in 1977, I thought "if that's what George is doing, what are the other opponents up to?"

Foreman at home in Houston following his defeat, November 21, 1974

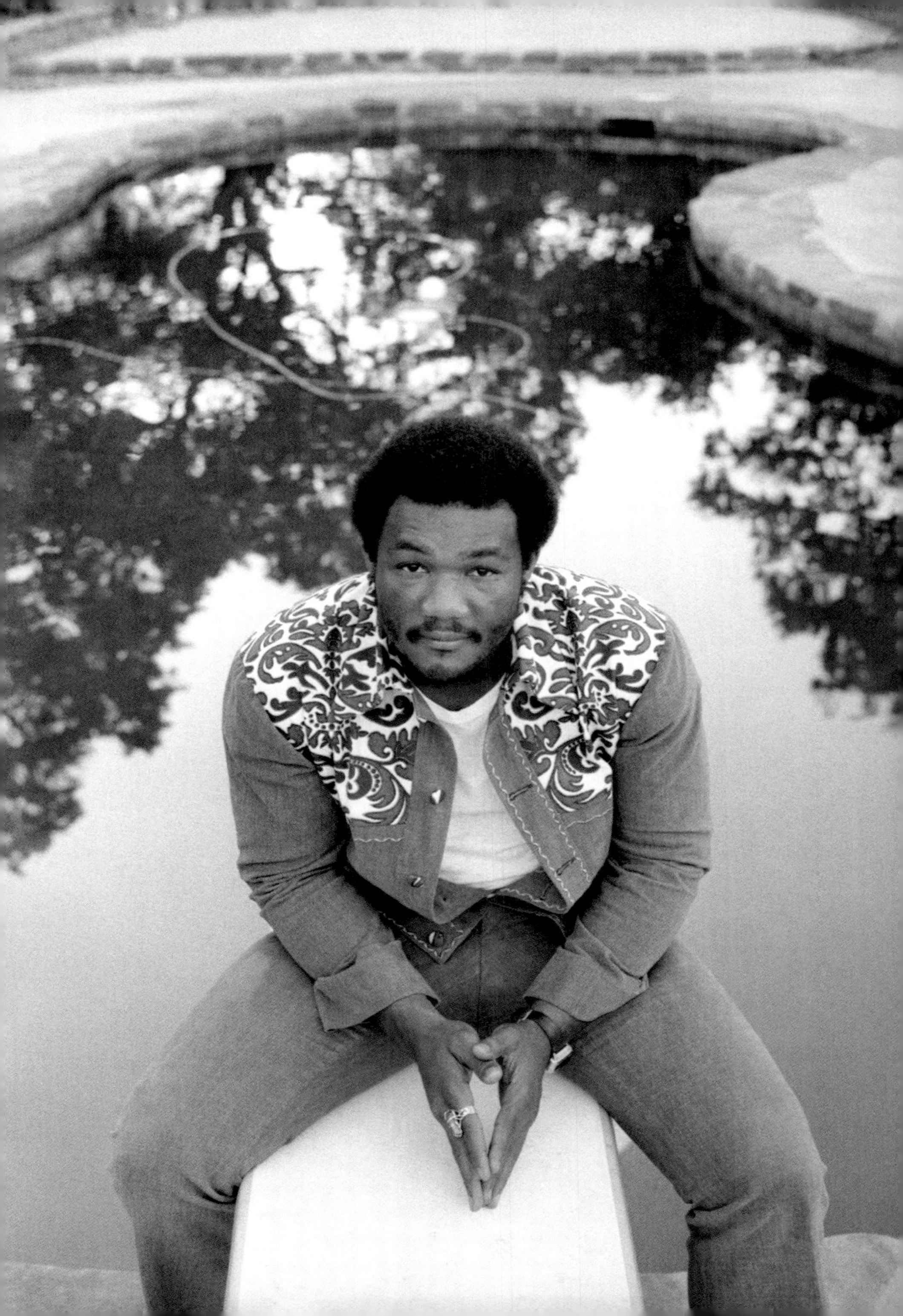

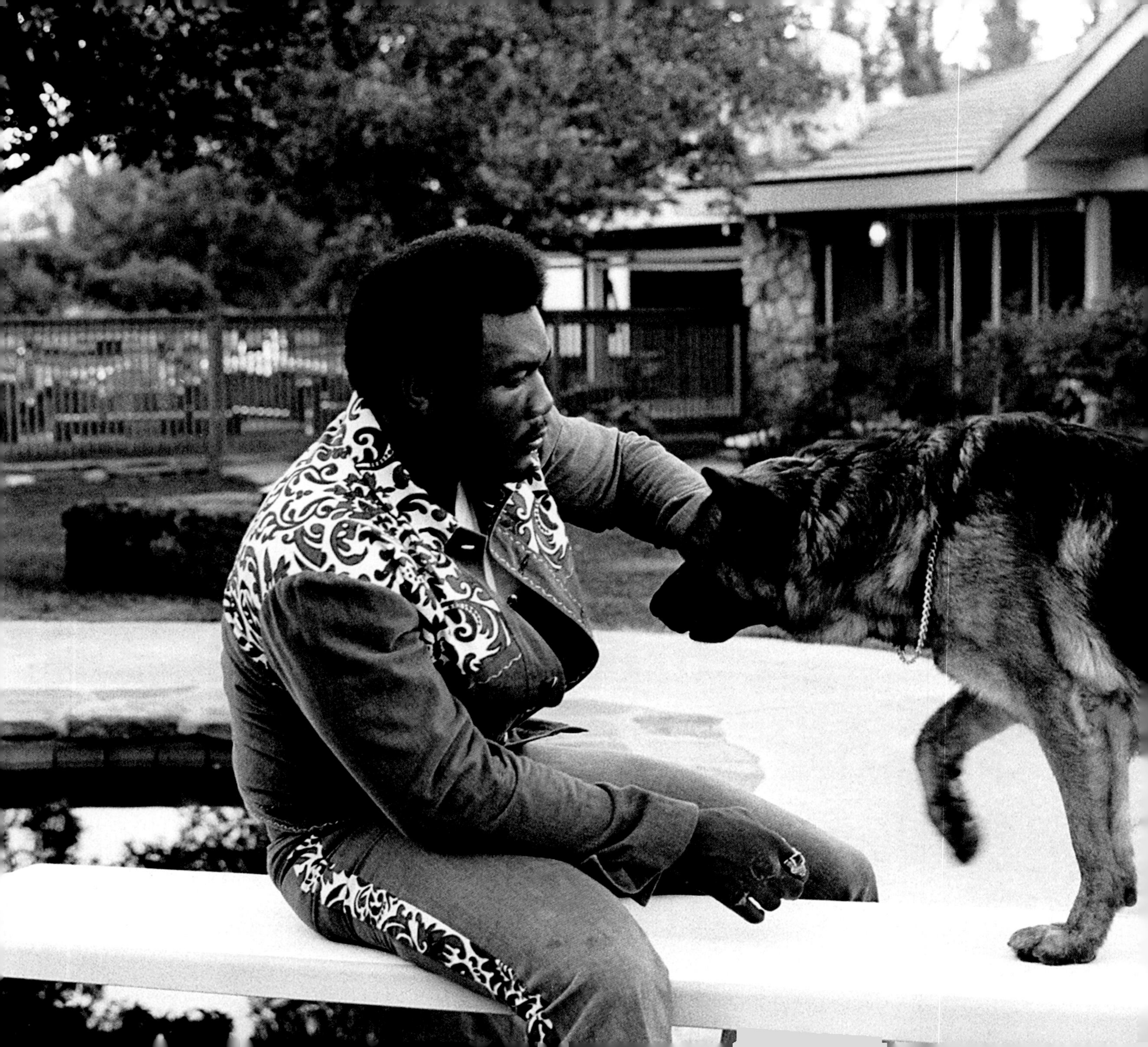

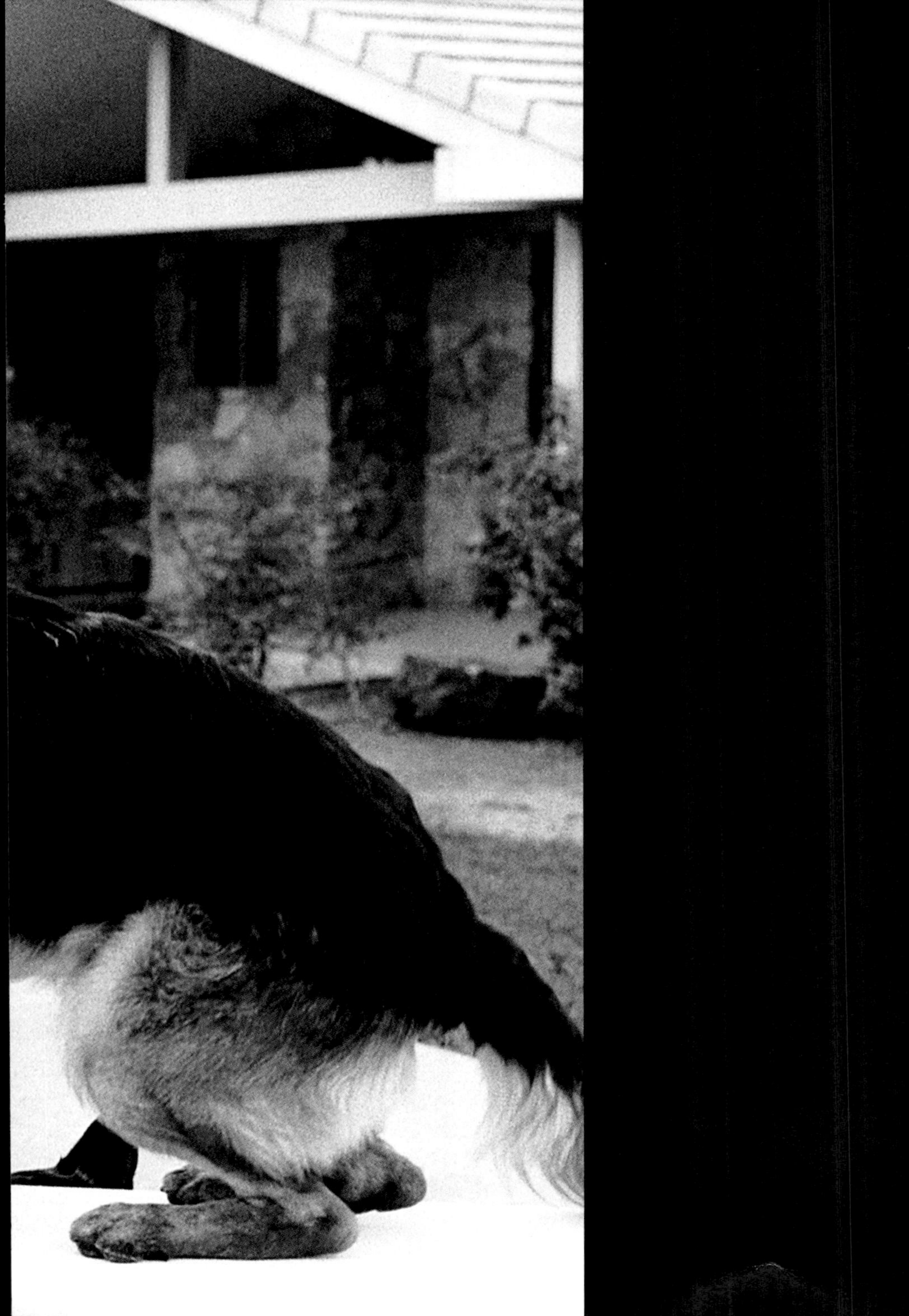

Foreman at home

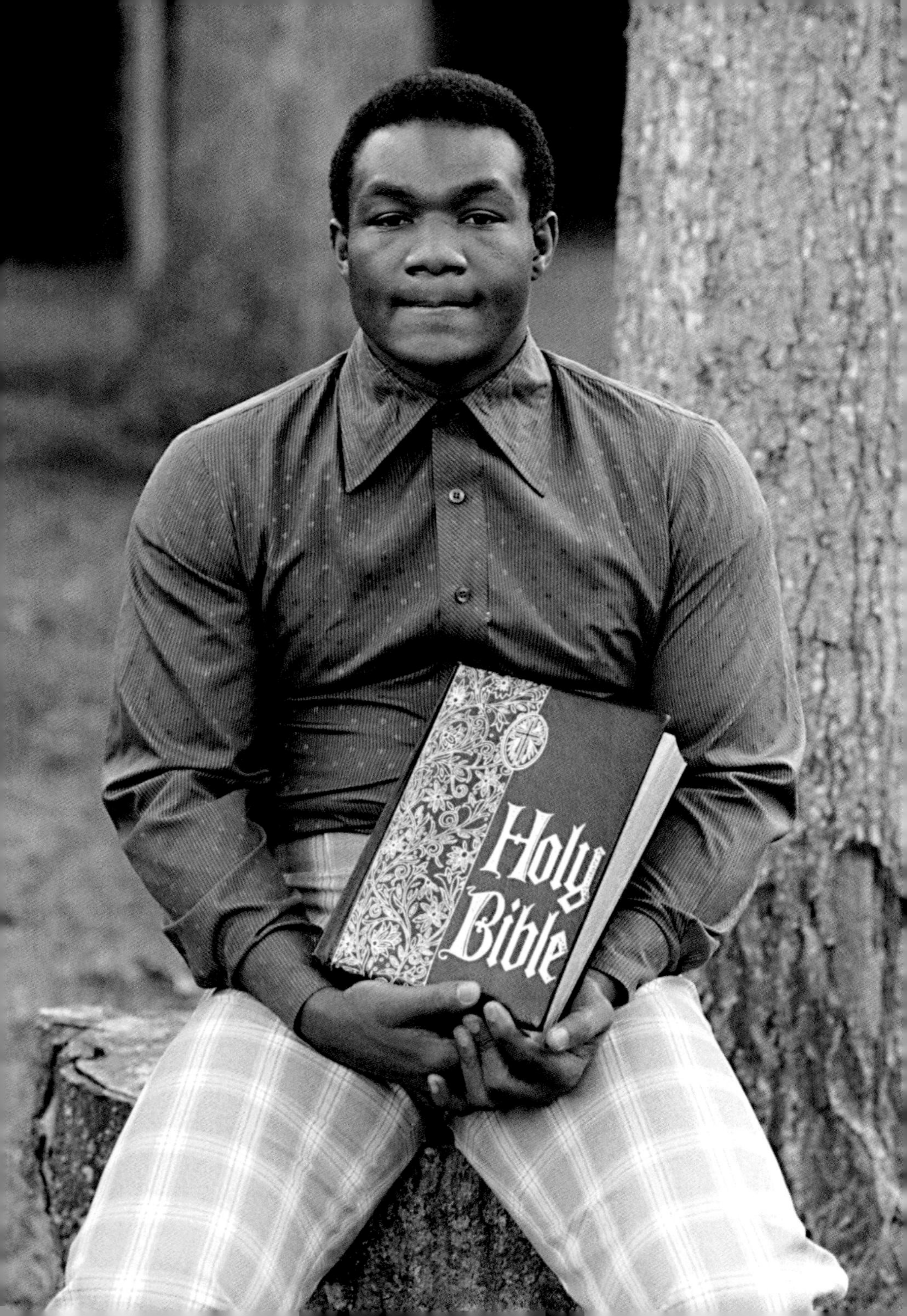
Holy
Bible

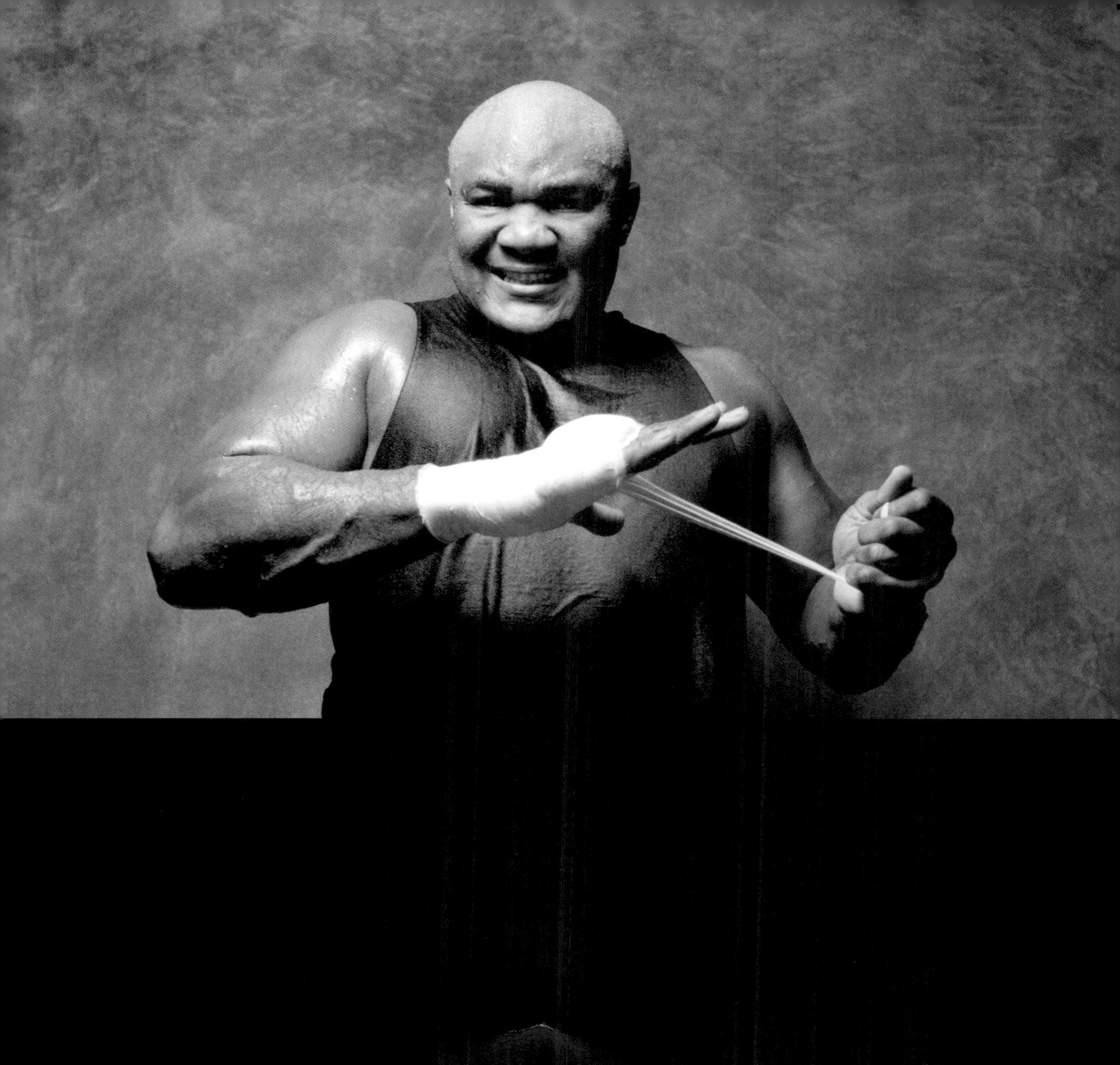

eft: *December 10, 1977*

Above: *St Lucia, West Indies in March 1991*

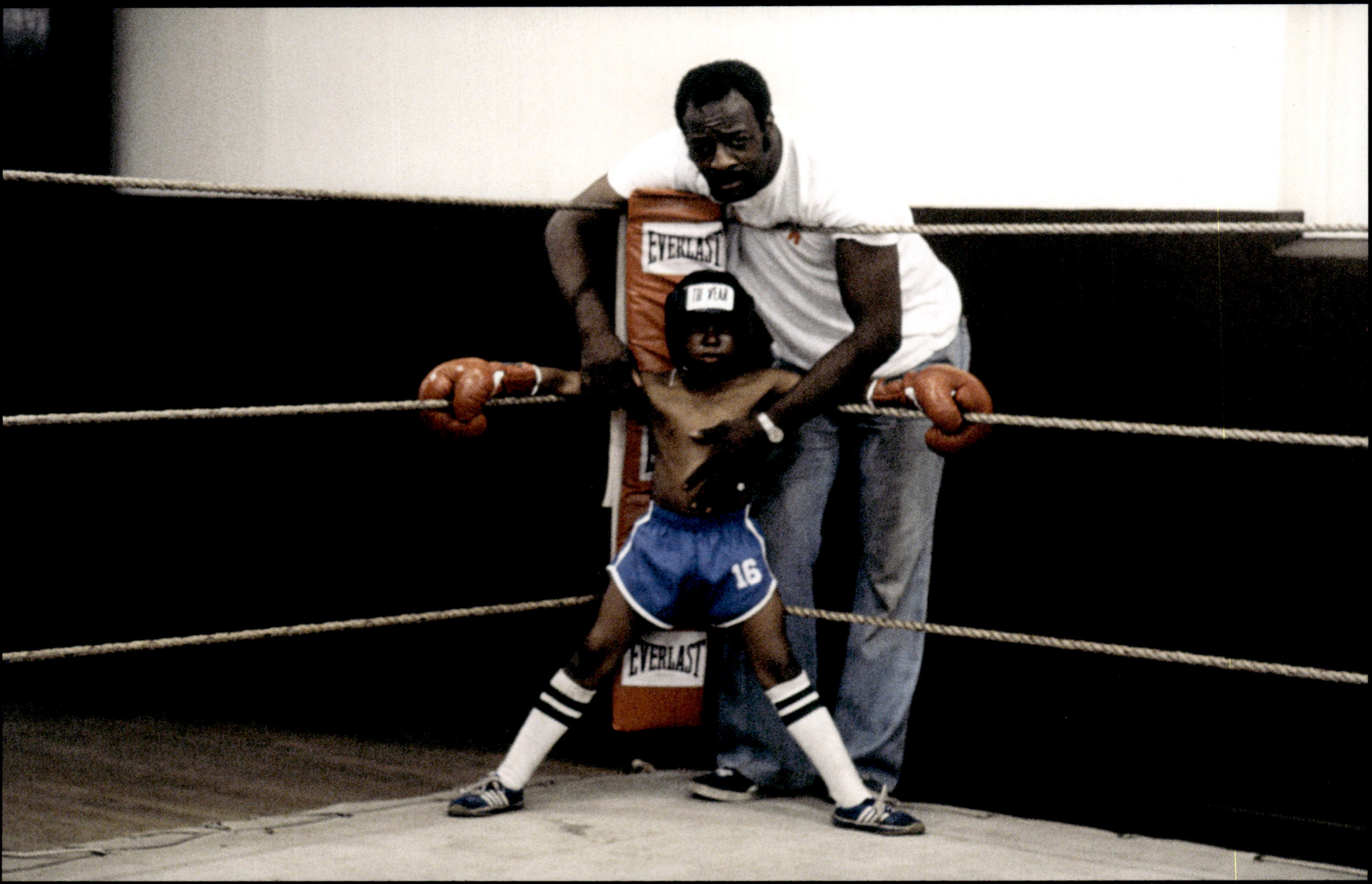

Alvin "Blue" Lewis
Fought Ali in a non-title fight in Dublin in 1972
Lost in the 11th round in a TKO

"Look at them kids, just take a look. Maybe there's a Muhammad Ali or a Blue Lewis among them." Alvin "Blue" Lewis

Photographed at the Wheeler Center, Detroit, Michigan, July 6, 1979

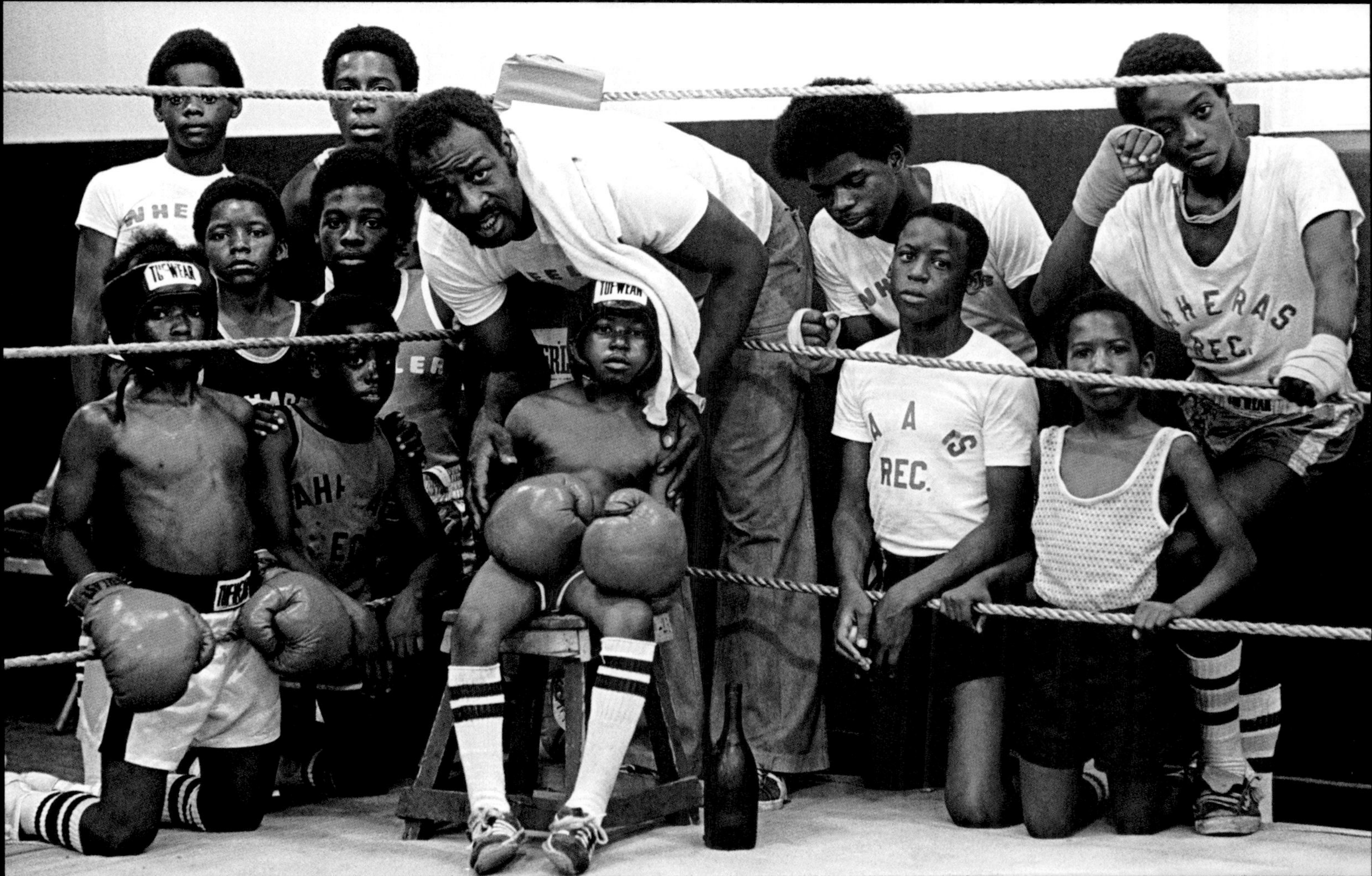
TUF WEAR
TUF WEAR
HERAS
REC.
REC.

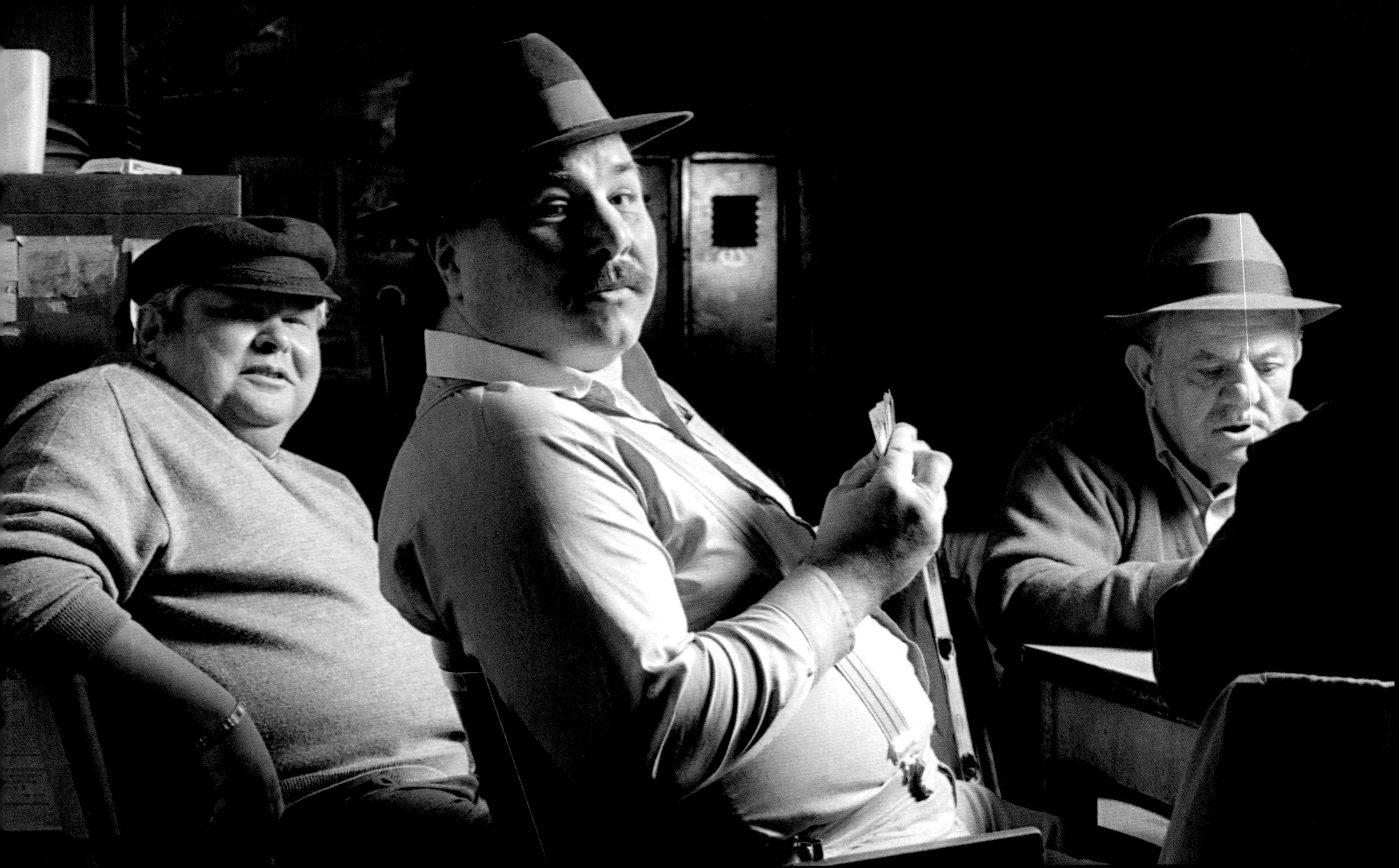

George Chuvalo
Fought Ali twice: once in 1966 for the Heavyweight title, then again in 1972
Went the distance both times and lost both times

Chuvalo lives in Toronto, Canada and travels lecturing to kids on the dangers of drugs.

"The judges voted for Ali, but he had to be taken to hospital afterwards – while I went dancing with my wife."
George Chuvalo after losing to Muhammad Ali, March 29, 1966

Photographed at the Lansdowne Gym, Toronto, Canada, January 16, 1991

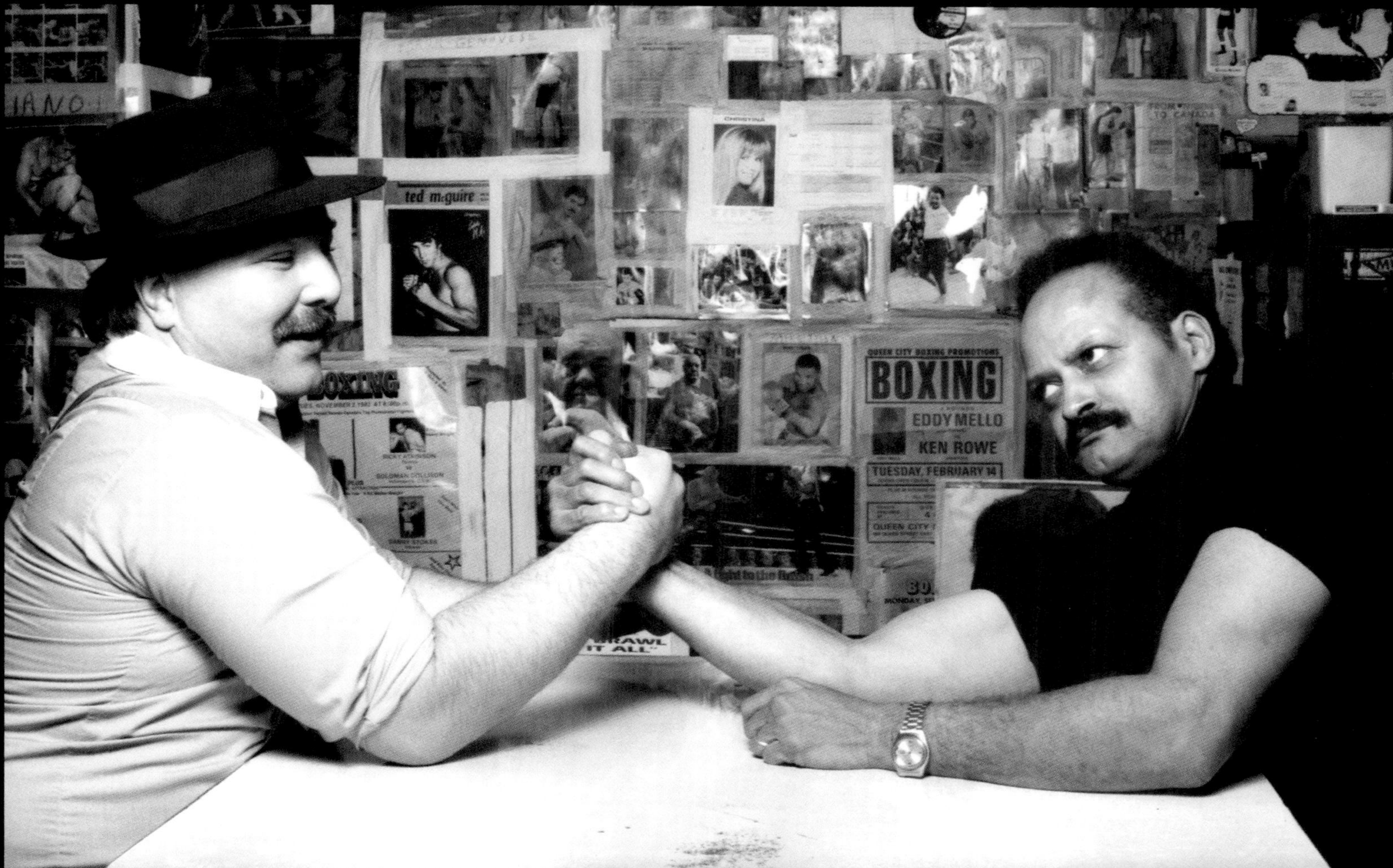
ted mcguire
BOXING
QUEEN CITY BOXING PROMOTIONS
BOXING
EDDY MELLO
KEN ROWE
TUESDAY, FEBRUARY 14

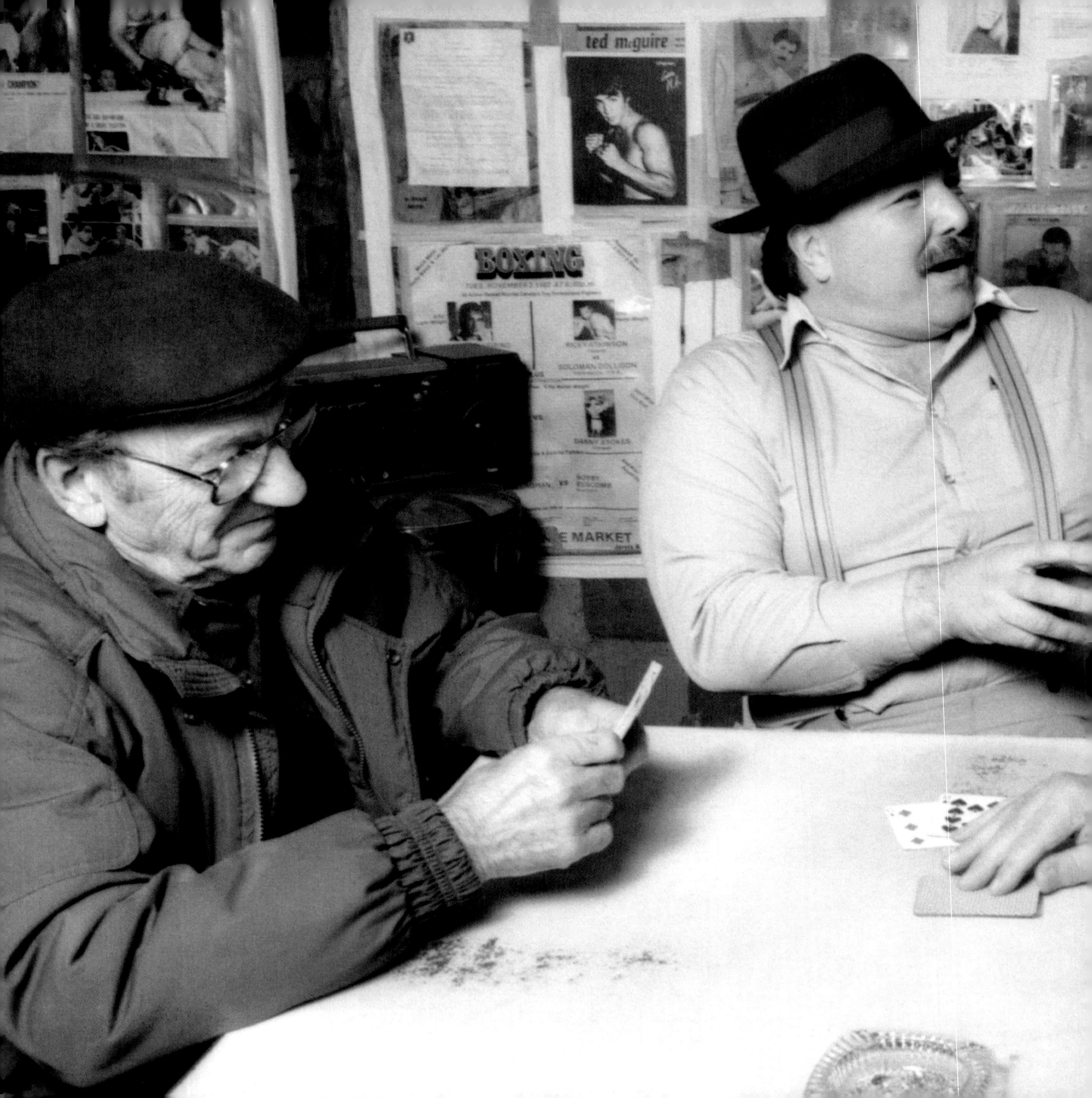
ted mcguire
BOXING
MARKET

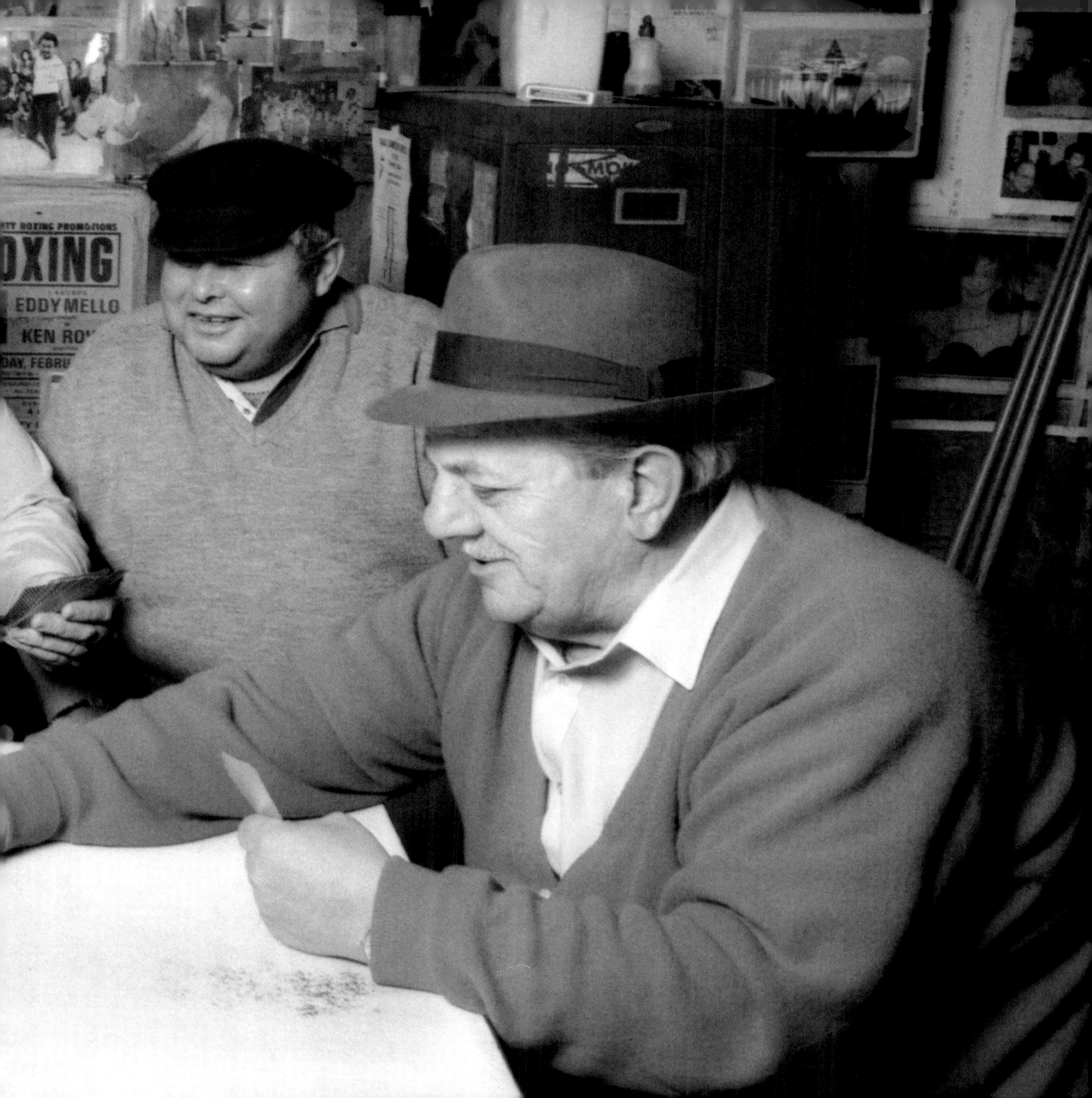
BOXING PROMOTIONS
OXING
EDDY MELLO
KEN RO

Chuck Wepner
Fought Ali in Cleveland on March 24, 1975 for the World Heavyweight title
KO'd in the 15th round

Known as "The Bayonne Bleeder", he later became a liquor salesman and was rumored to be the inspiration for the *Rocky* franchise.

"Chuck Wepner is to climb into the ring against the great Muhammad Ali, Chuck hands his wife $100 'What's this for, honey?' Mrs. Bayonne Bleeder inquires.

'Baby, you run down to Frederick's of Hollywood, or one of them other fancy places and get the sexiest lingerie you can find. Why? Because after this fight, honey, you will be sleeping with the heavyweight champion of the world.'

Mrs. W went and bought her sexy outfit and put it away.

The fight is over and Chuck is sitting in his room covered by ice packs. His face is blue, purple, black and two or three other colors. His whole body aches.

'Honey,' his wife asks, 'I have a question.'
'What?' the bruised and battered Bleeder answers.
'Do I go up to Ali's room or will he come down here?'
The Bayonne Bleeder had to laugh"

Mike Marley, *fightnightnews.com*

Bayonne, New Jersey, June 14, 1979

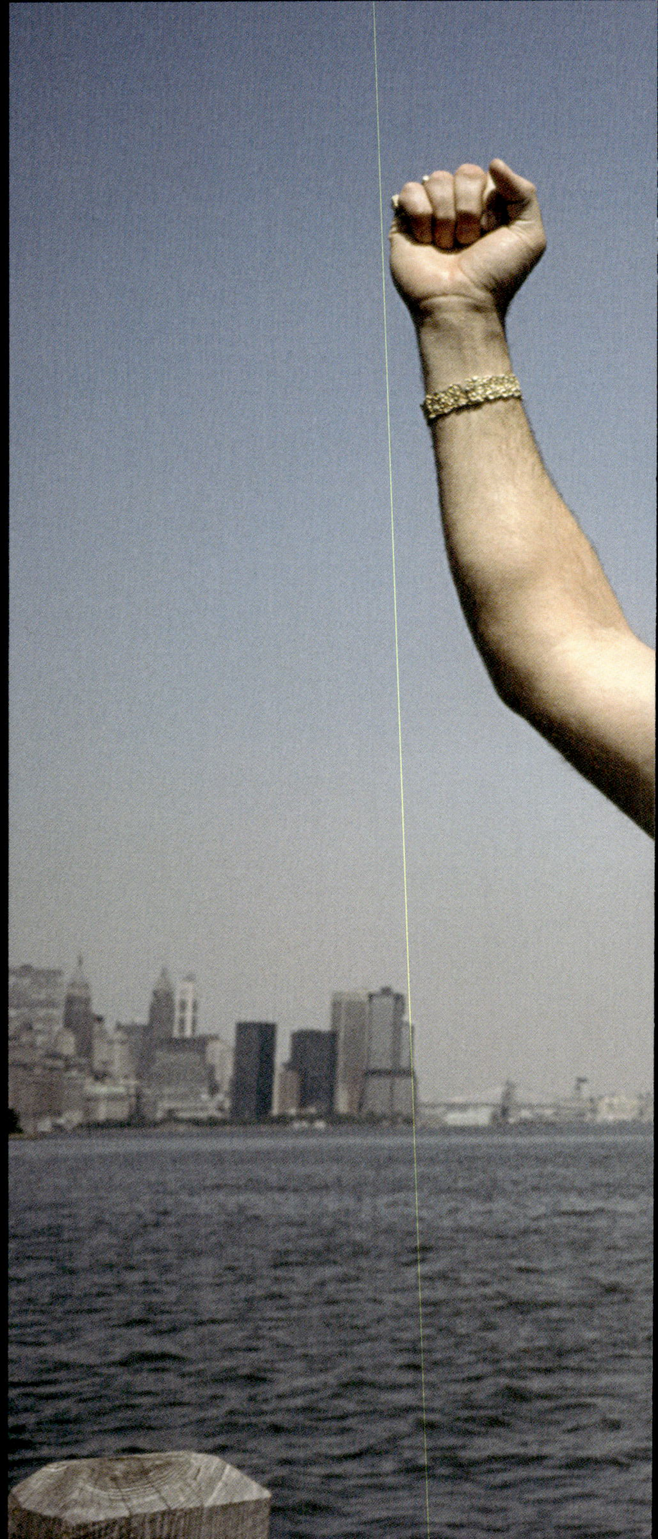

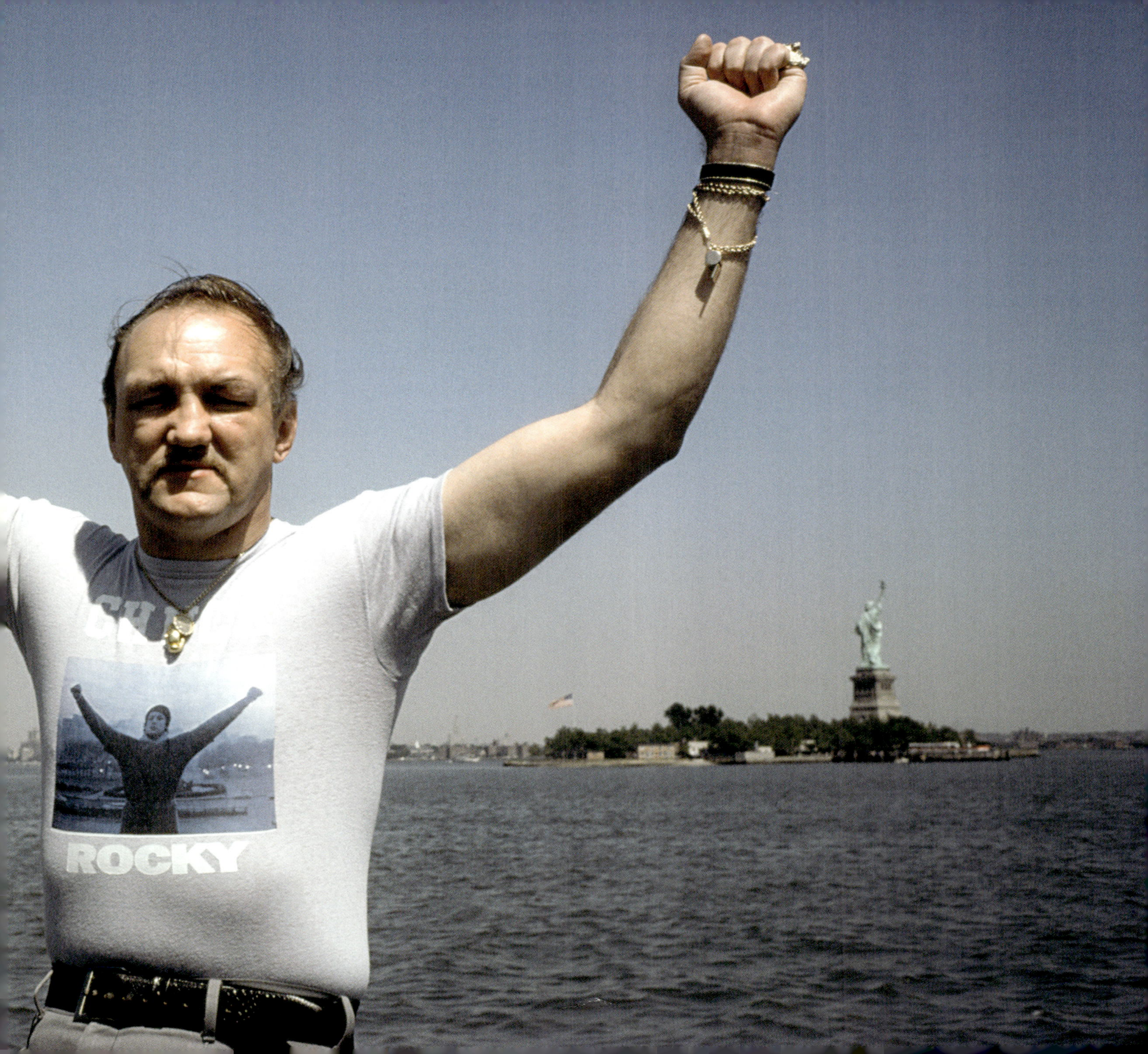
ROCKY

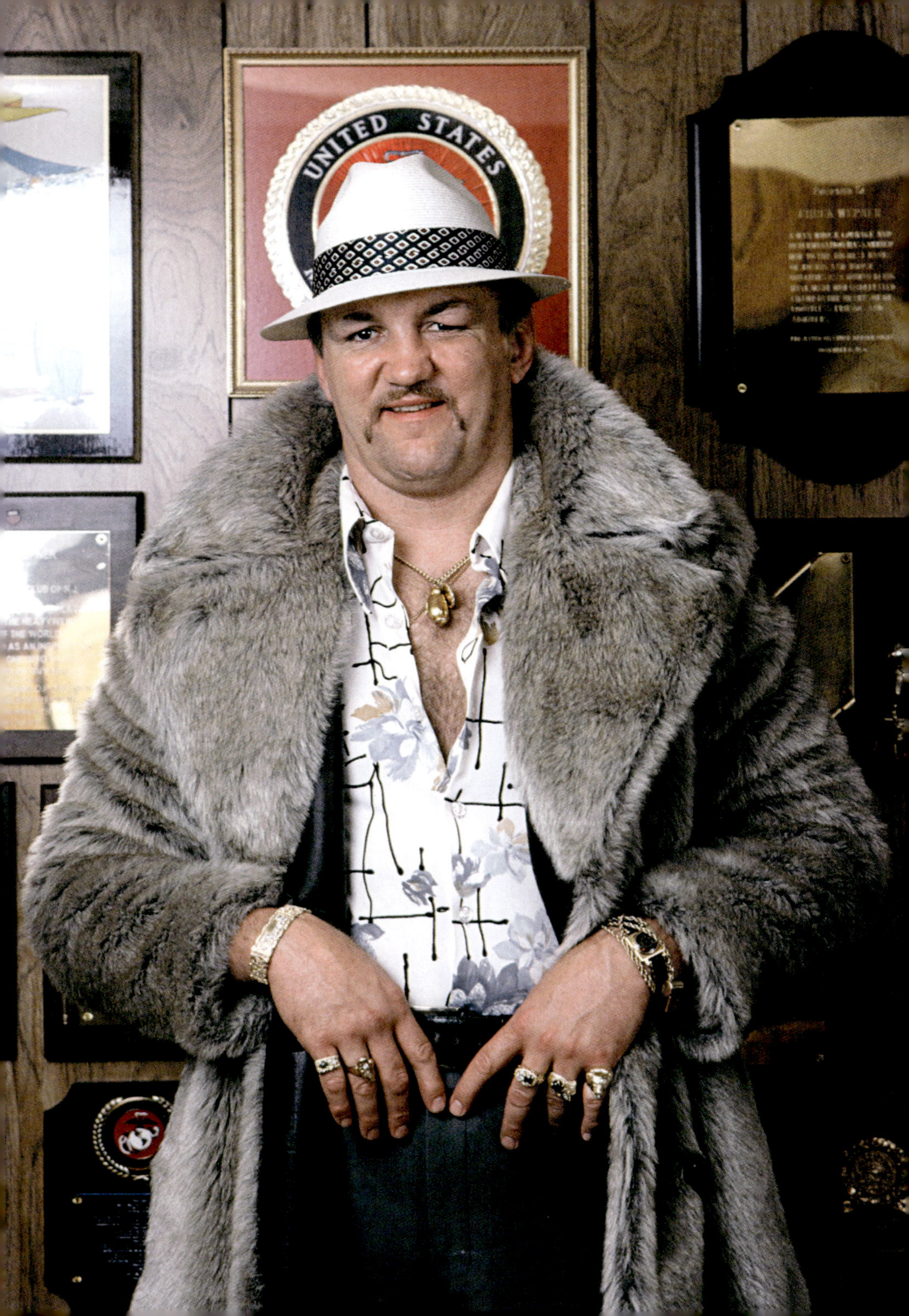
UNITED STATES

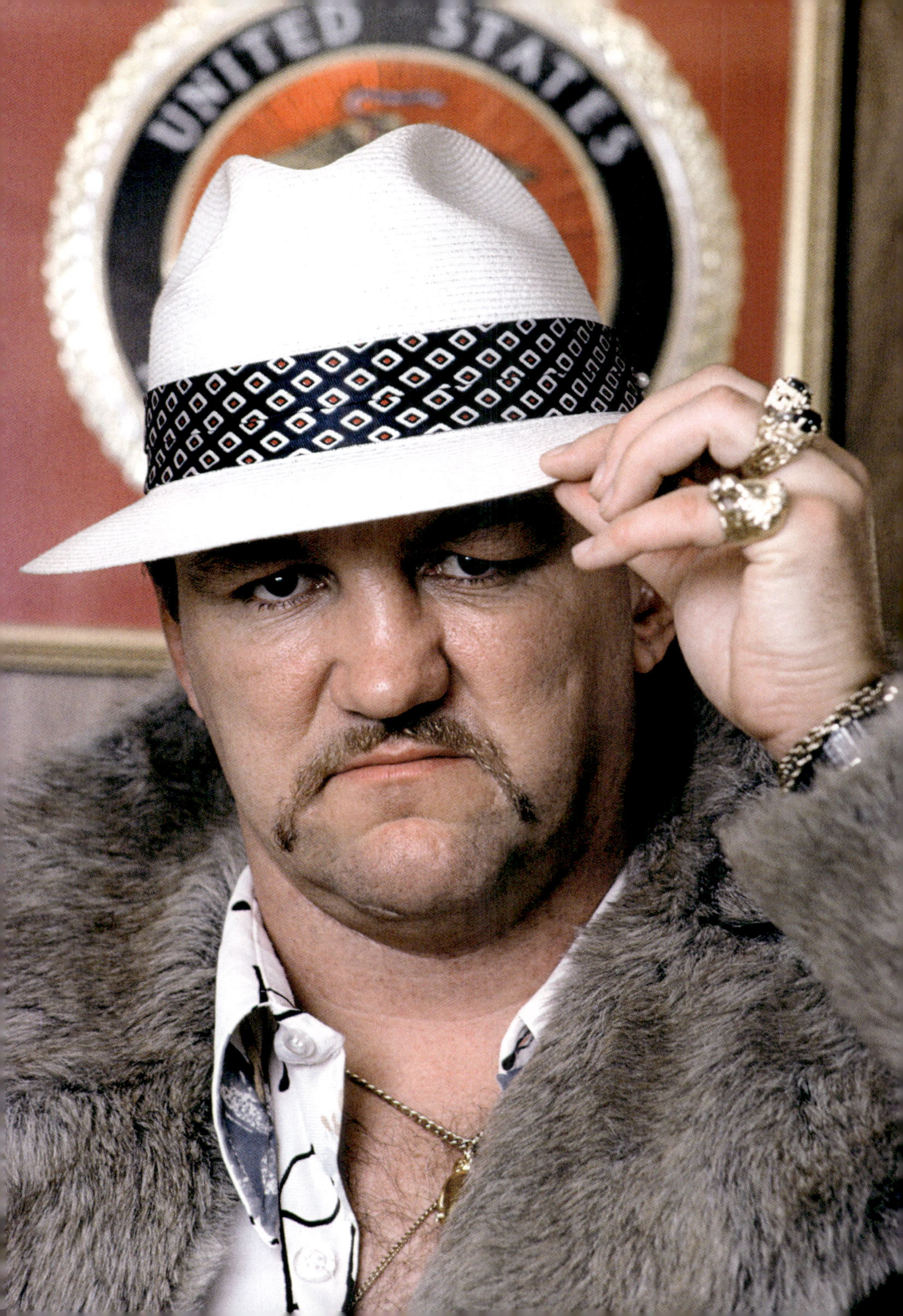
UNITED STATES

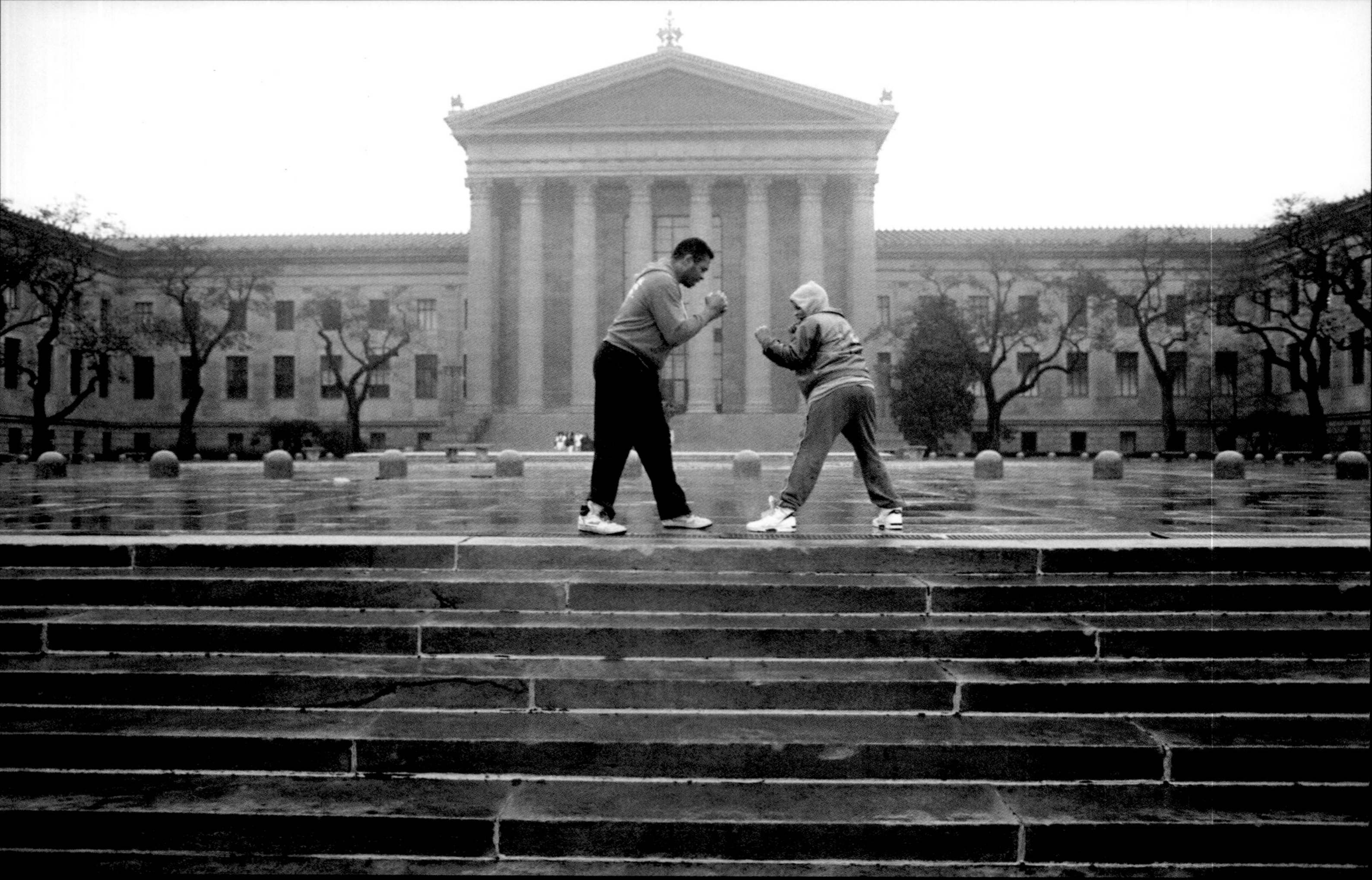

Jimmy Young
Fought Ali in Maryland, April 1976

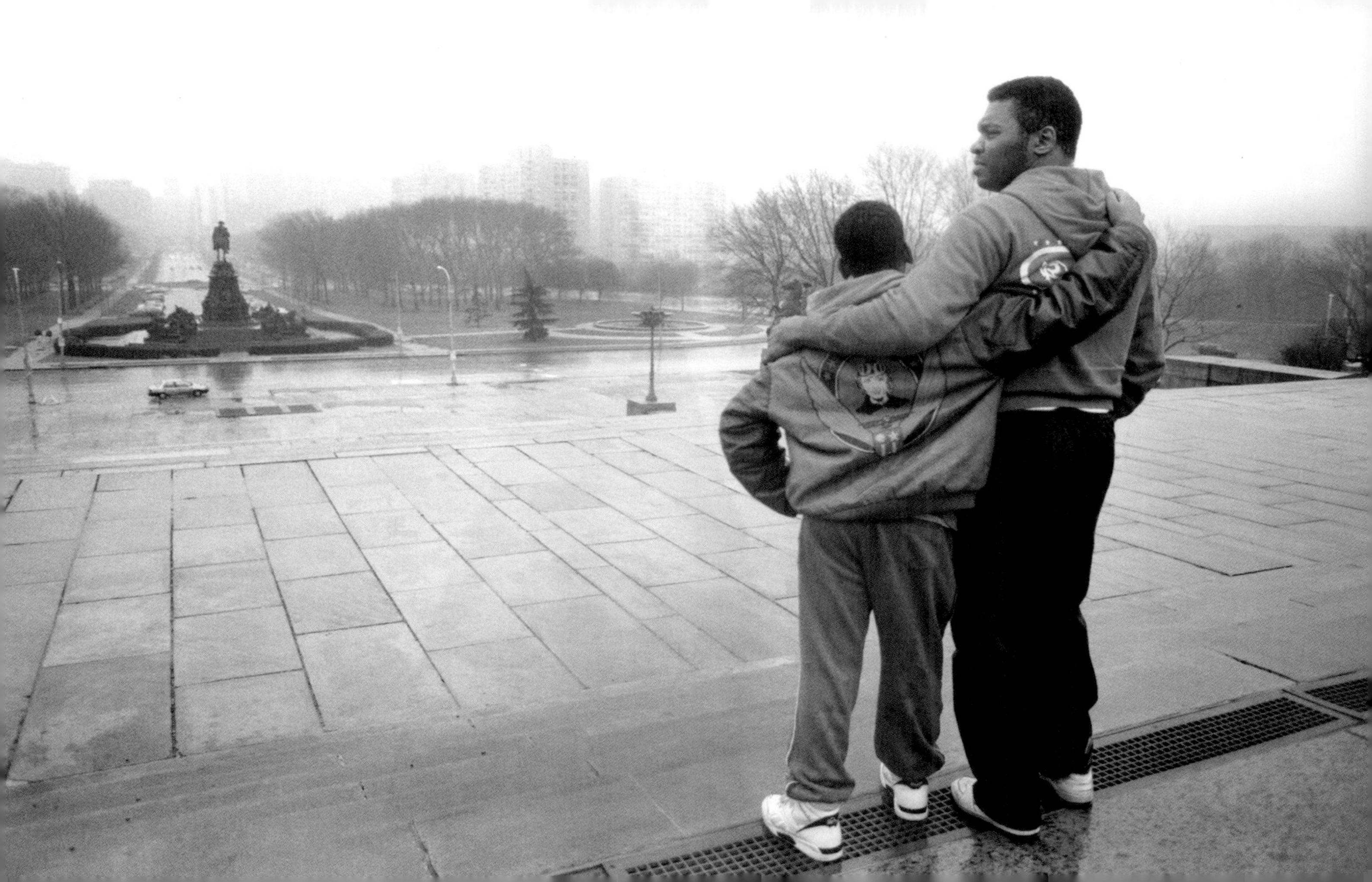

Joe Frazier
Fought Ali three times:
March 8, 1971 at Madison Square Garden, for the Undisputed World Heavyweight Championship; won on points
January 28, 1974 at Madison Square Garden again; lost after twelve rounds
October 1, 1975; Araneta Coliseum, Quezon City, the famous "Thrilla in Manilla"; KO'd in the 14th round.

"The Champ and I had some good times together. I first met him in 1964. He was training for his fight against Doug Jones at the Garden. After training I was asked to go up into the ring and be introduced to the Champ. I was wearing suspenders (braces), he opened my jacket and shouted "Hey, he's wearing a pair of yellow suspenders." I said, "Hey man, that's my style, I like suspenders they keep my pants up."

"When the government had stripped him of his title and I was the Heavyweight Champ, he called me at my gym in Philadelphia. He suggested we stage a fight so we could attract the promoters for a match. I said so long as it was just to stir up the public interest, I would go along with it. He came around to the gym and starts hollerin' and shouting about me being stupid and ugly and we didn't need no white man to allow us to fight. We were both young and crazy then but he said some things that made me mad. Sometimes he would push and push and he would get me steaming and the pot would boil over. I was never really sure if he was joking or if he was for real.

"I once gave him a lift from Philadelphia to New York City so that he could talk to some writer who was doing a story.

He spent the whole journey shouting, 'Smokin Joe you think you can whup me? You think you can whup me, Smokin Joe Frazier? See I wrote a poem, it says *Joe Frazier come out smoking, I'll be poking, pouring water on that smoking.*' He says, 'I might amaze you. I'll retire Smoking Joe Frazier.' All through the whole time from Philadelphia to New York City I had to go through that noise. When we got to New York he starts singing, so I managed to interrupt him and said, 'You stick to fighting and acting—I'll do the singing, and then we will be singing together.'

"He and I had some of the greatest fights of all time. I would say he was the greatest I ever fought. He was the most exciting. I wouldn't say he was the hardest, I think George (Foreman) was the hardest—he had a punch like two mules kicking you. Ali and I was meant for each other, we were two guys brought together by destiny. The good man meant for this to be. I think deep down he is a sincere, true man. He is always trying to help somebody, that's why he has so many people around him.

"I think the people respected me just as much as they did him, but I love him. He was a fine Champion."
Michael Brennan interview, 1980

Frazier, now a successful businessman and entertainer, maintains a string of fighters in his Philadelphia gym.

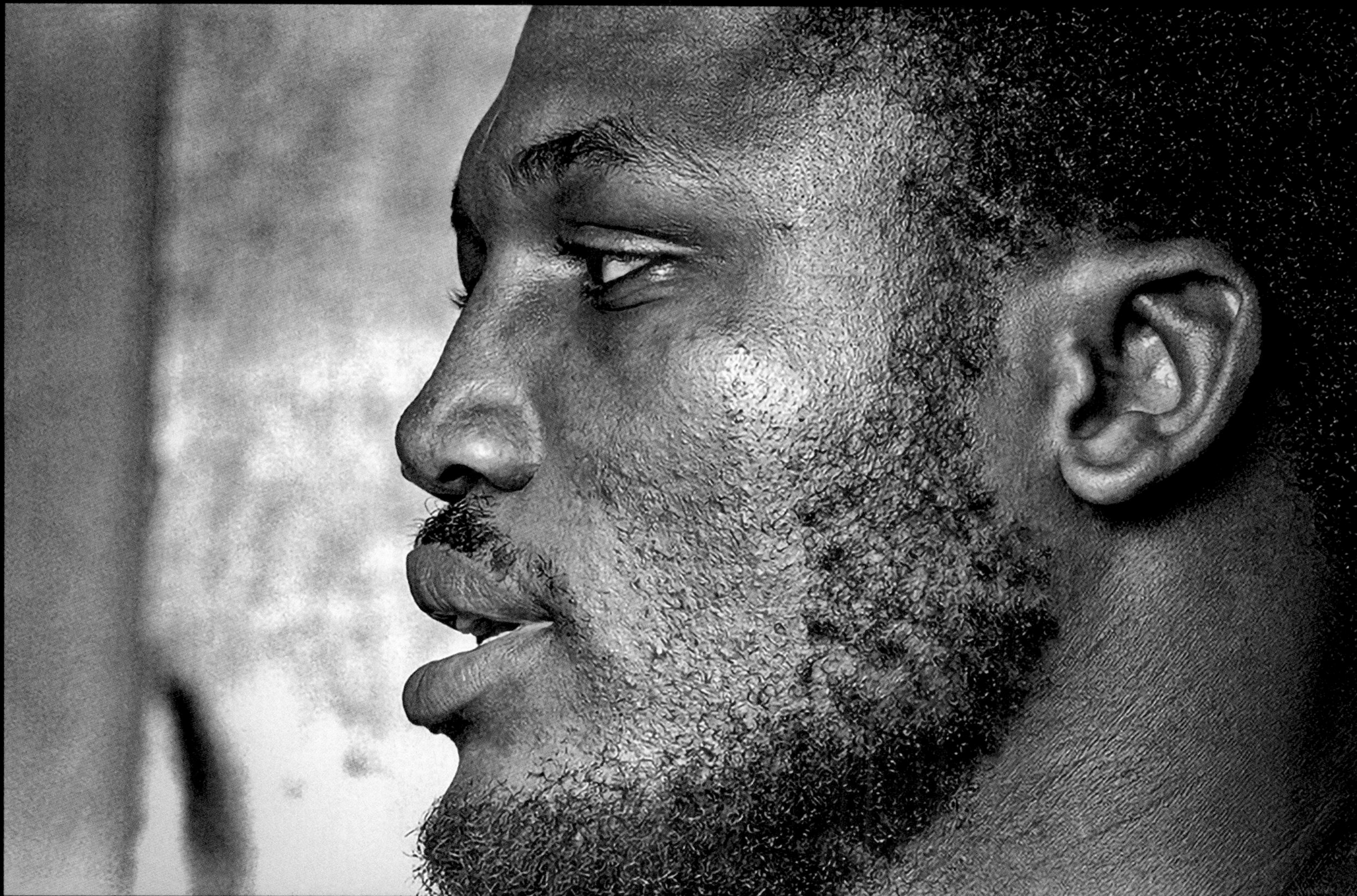

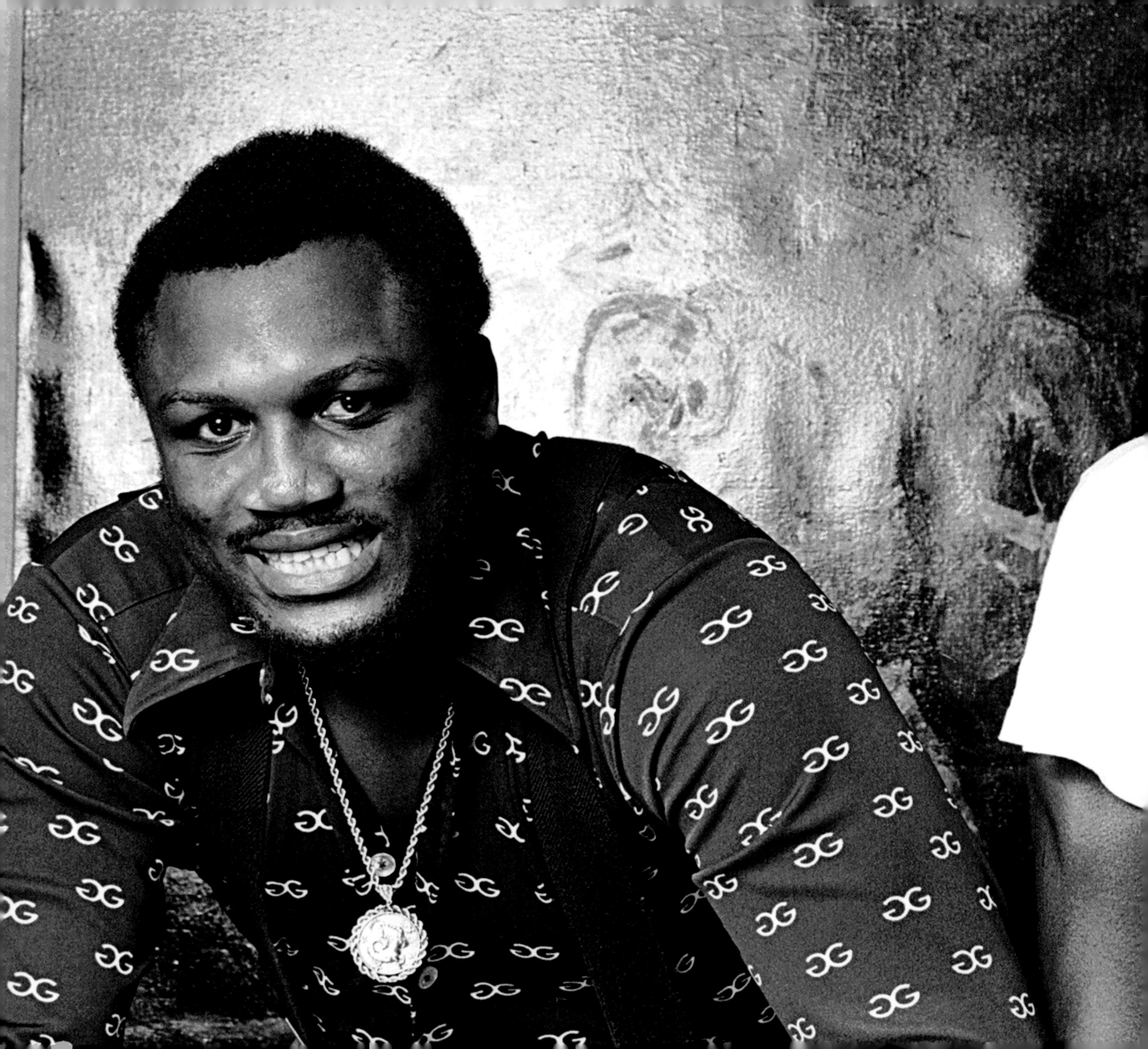

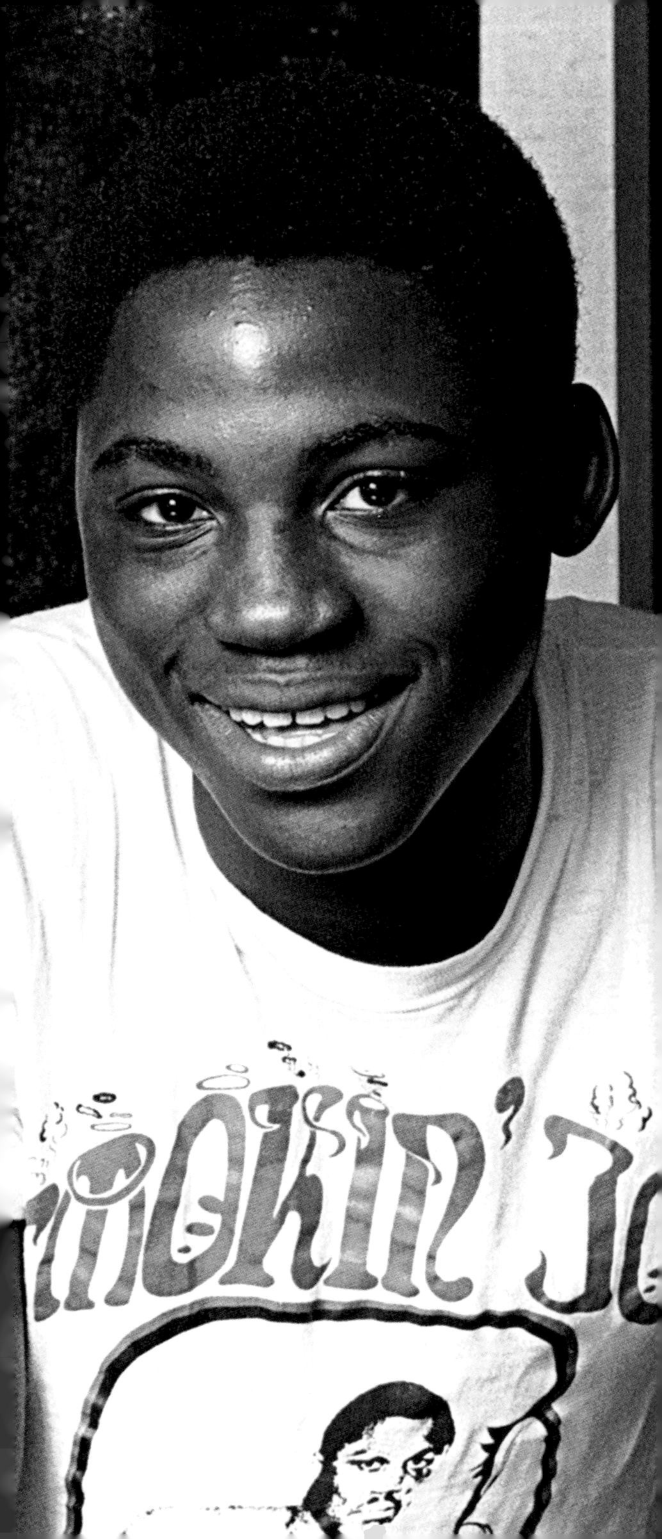

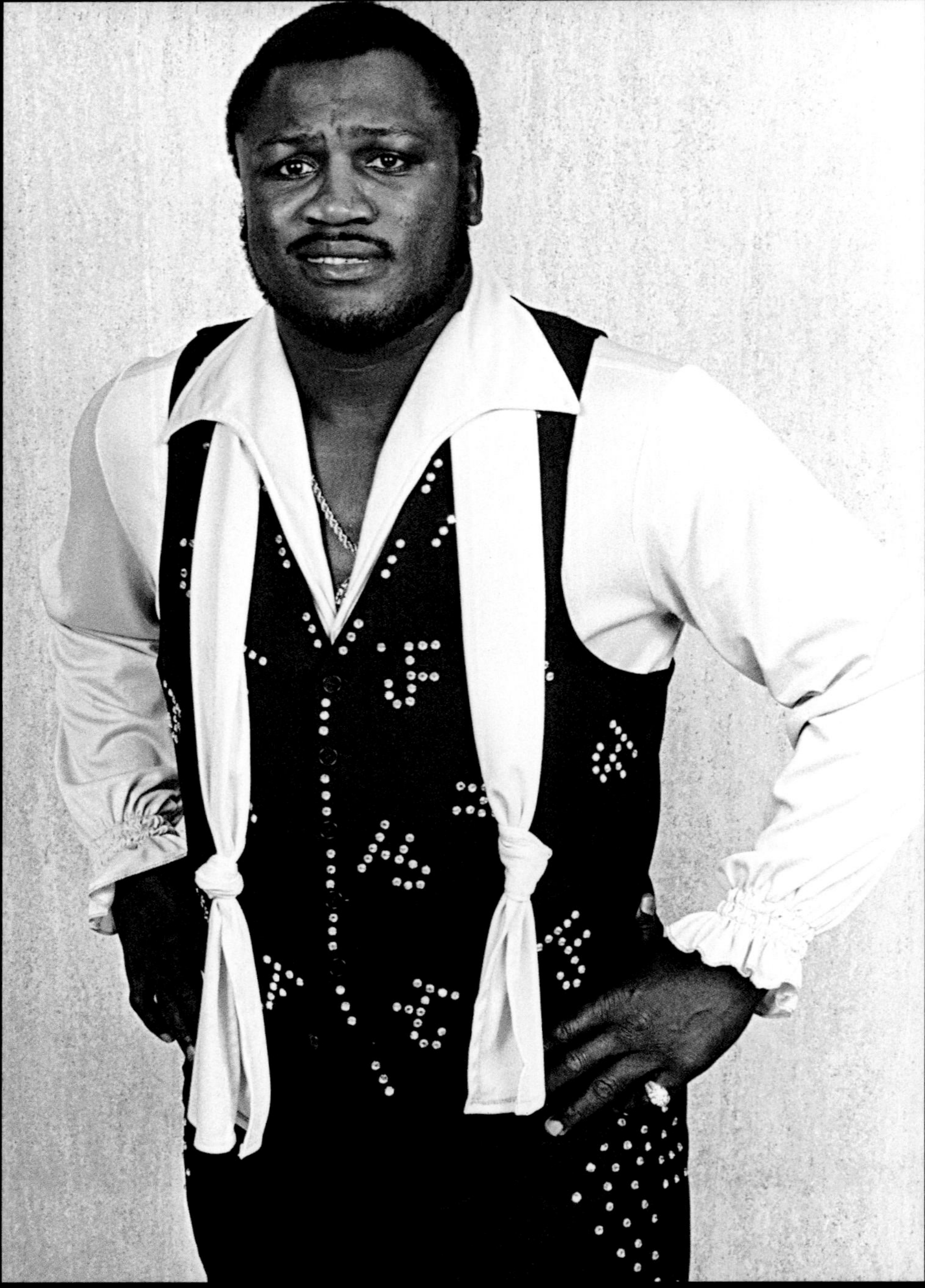

Joe Frazier, backstage at a school in Elmira, NY, June 30, 1979
In retirement, Frazier often went to speak to schools. Here he is seen 'warming-up' before going onstage at a school library in Elmira, NY, with his singing back-up group 'The Knockouts'

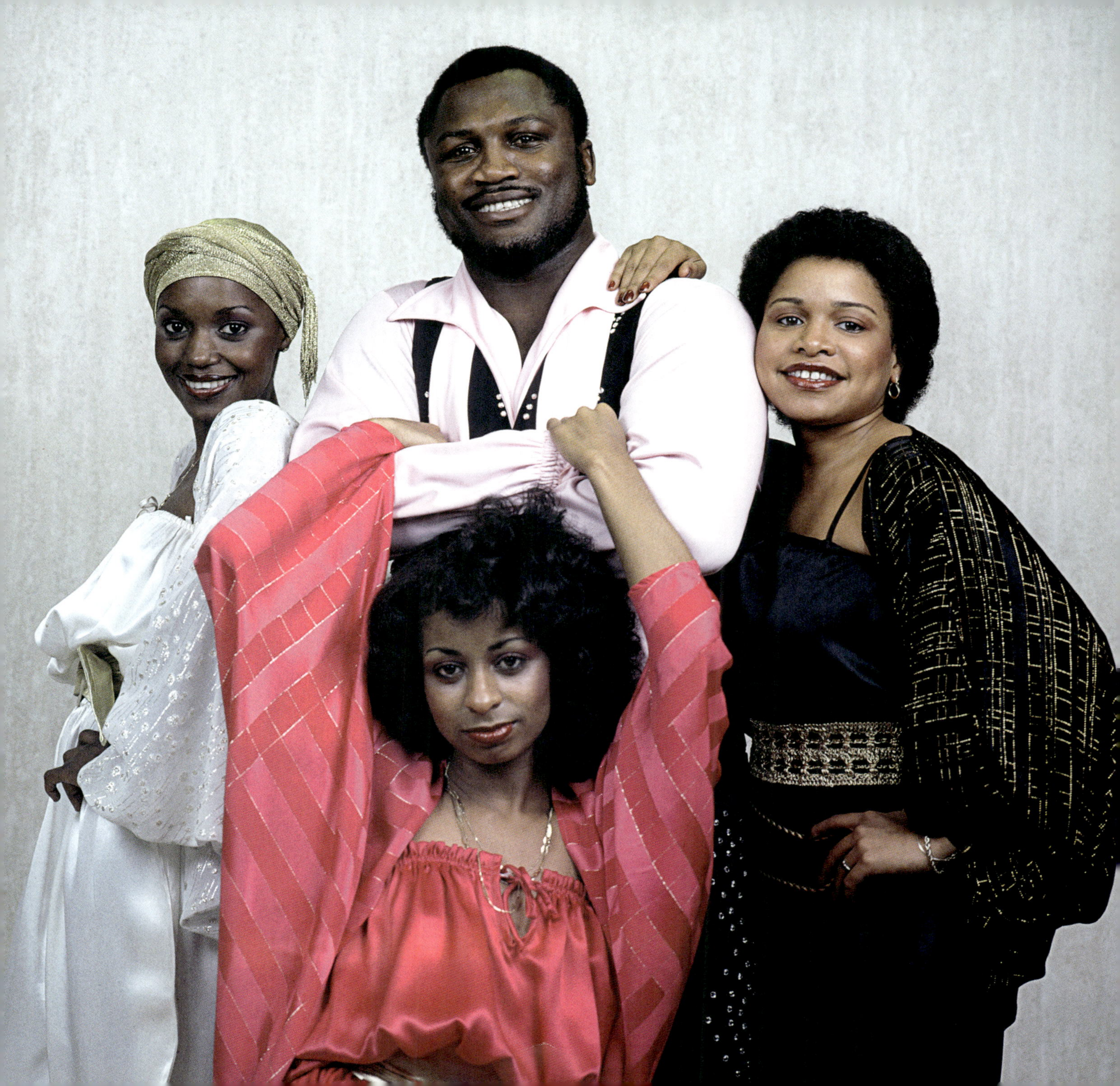

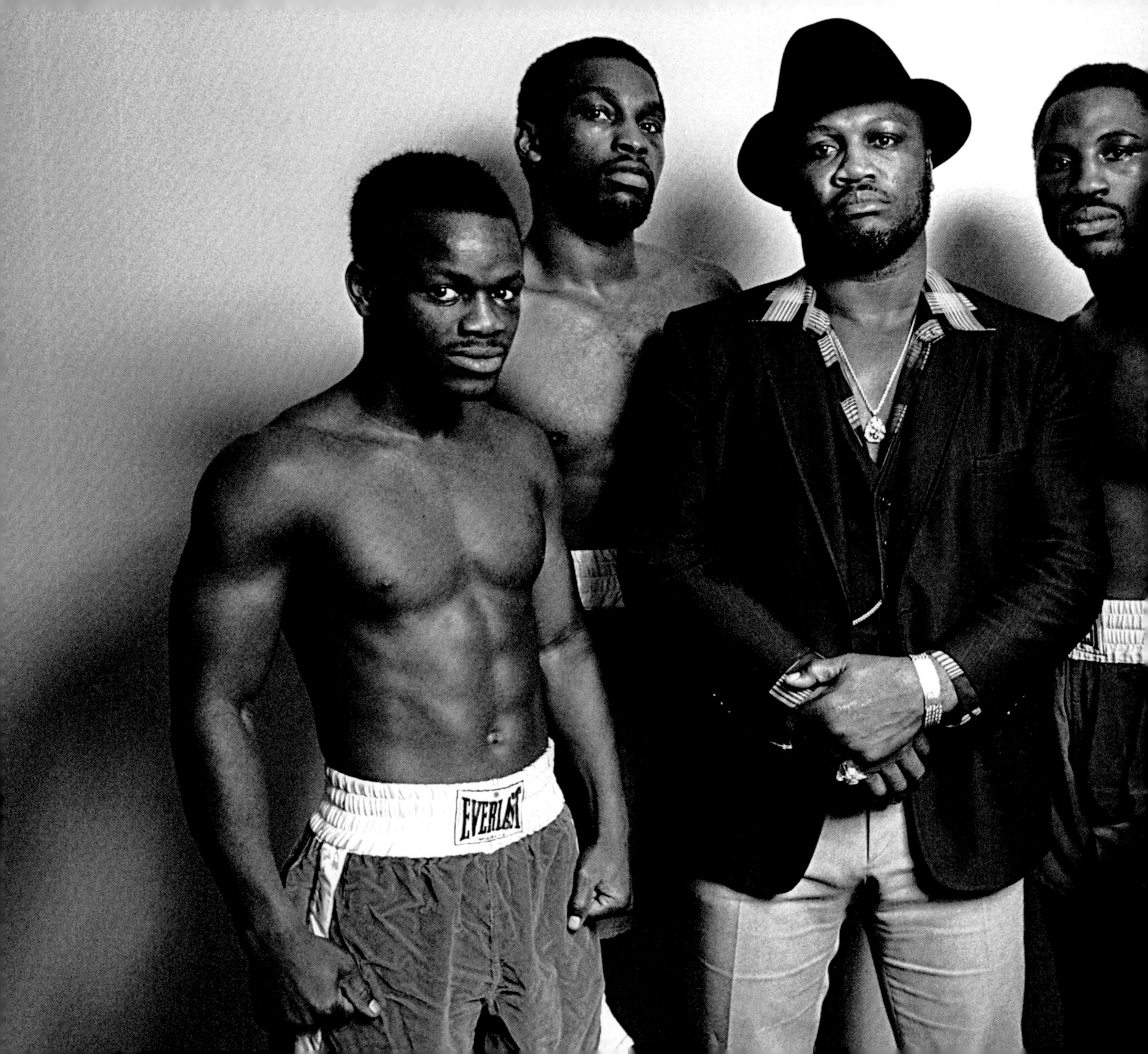
EVERLAST

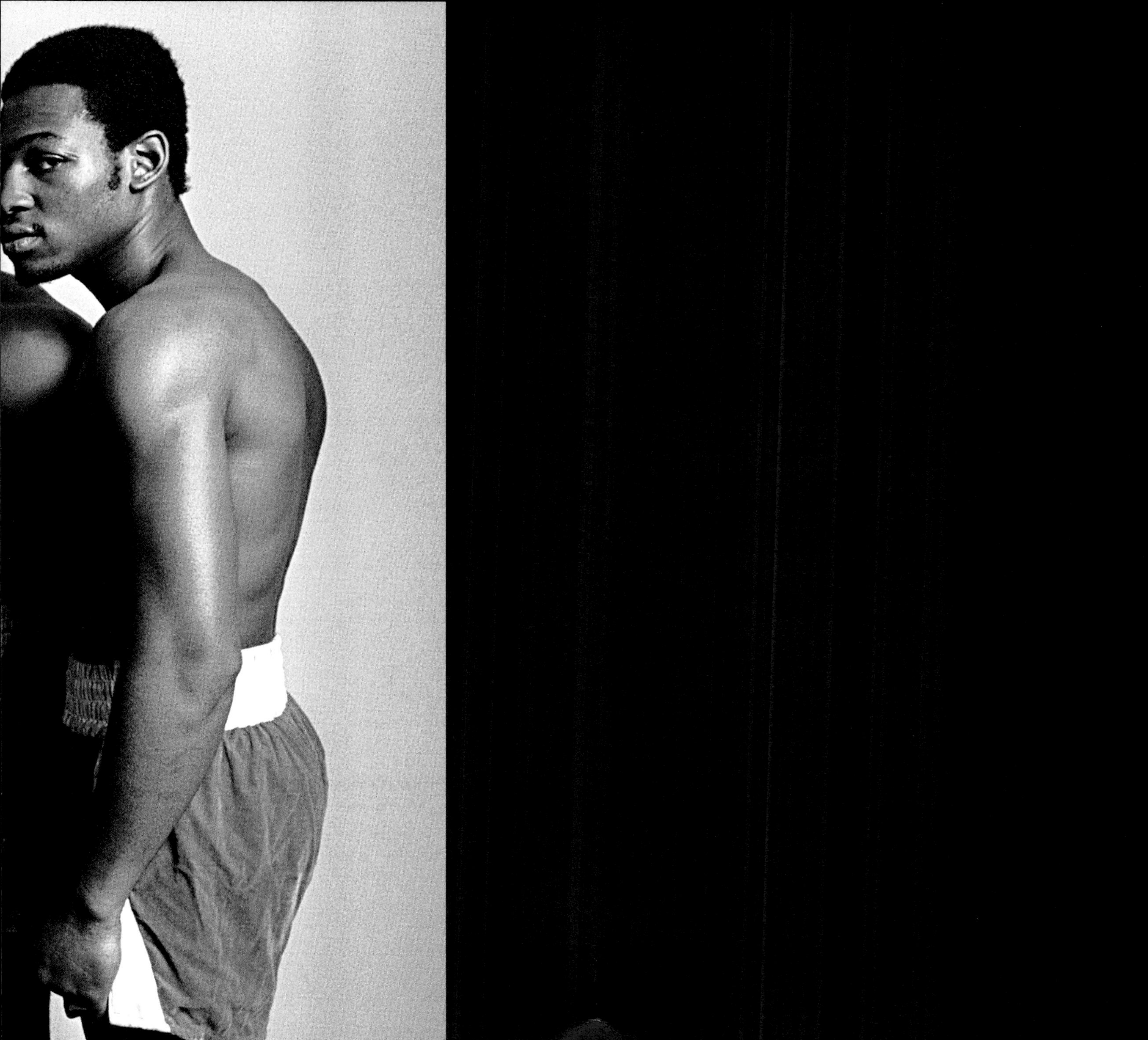

Joe Frazier with his sons and nephews in Philadelphia, 1983

Joe Bugner
Fought Ali twice: first in February 1973, and then two years later in Kuala Lumpur
Lost both times, both times in a UD

In an interview, Bugner claimed he told Elvis Presley to "get stuffed." At a reception prior to his fight with Ali, Bugner told Elvis how much he admired the diamond encrusted robe the singer had bestowed upon Ali and, since he also was a champion, would he consider giving him one. Bugner says that Elvis turned on him and said, "You're no champion"—hence the witty response. Apparently, Bugner was then confronted by Elvis's security, who said, "You don't talk to Elvis that way!" Bugner's reply to the surrounding security detail was less than deferential, suggesting that Mr. Presley was a "dickhead."

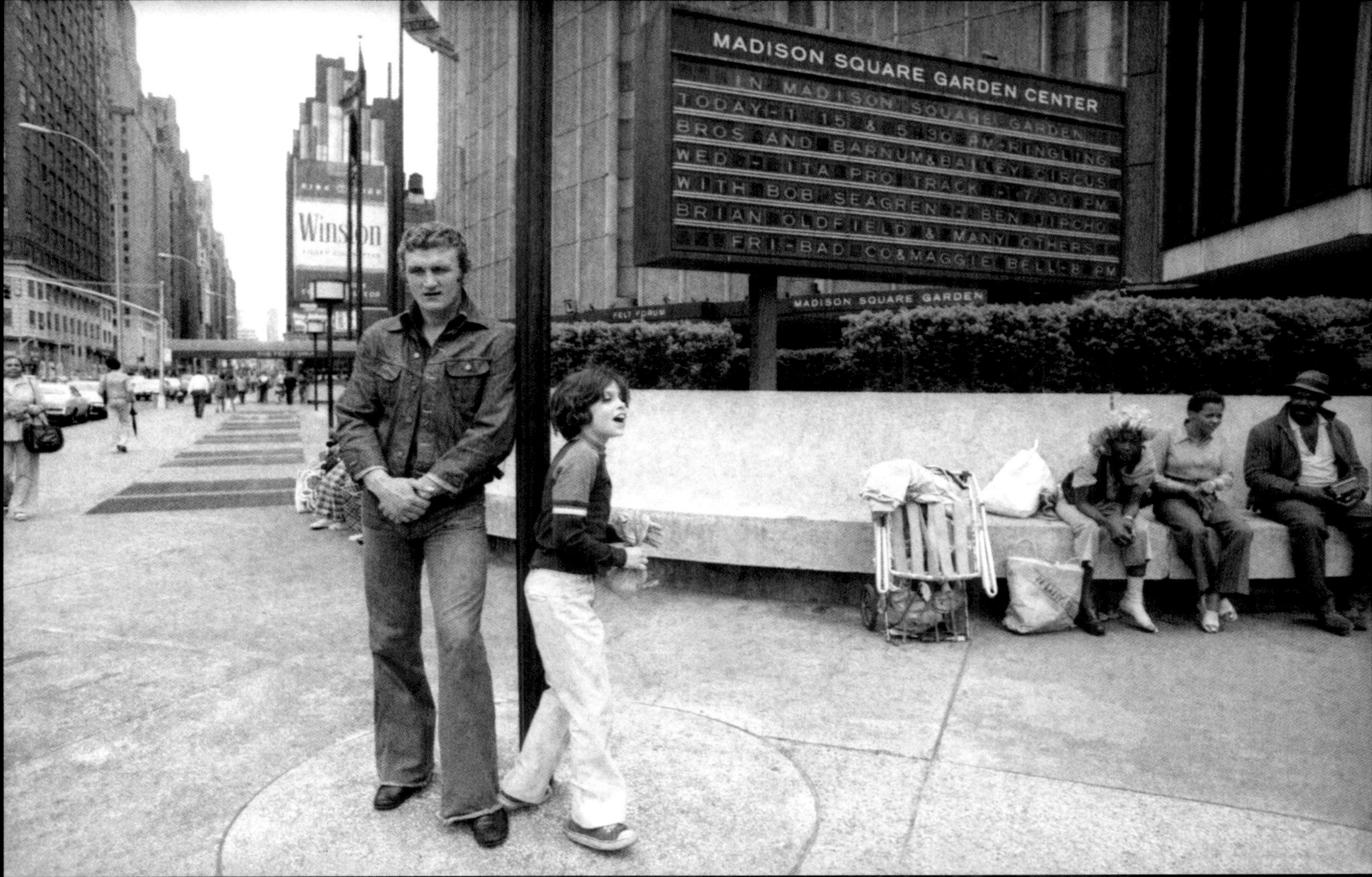
MADISON SQUARE GARDEN CENTER
IN MADISON SQUARE GARDEN
TODAY-1 15 & 5 30 PM-RINGLING
BROS AND BARNUM&BAILEY CIRCUS
WED - ITA PRO TRACK - 7 30 PM
WITH BOB SEAGREN - BEN JIPCHO
BRIAN OLDFIELD & MANY OTHERS
FRI-BAD CO&MAGGIE BELL-8 PM
MADISON SQUARE GARDEN
FELT FORUM
Winston

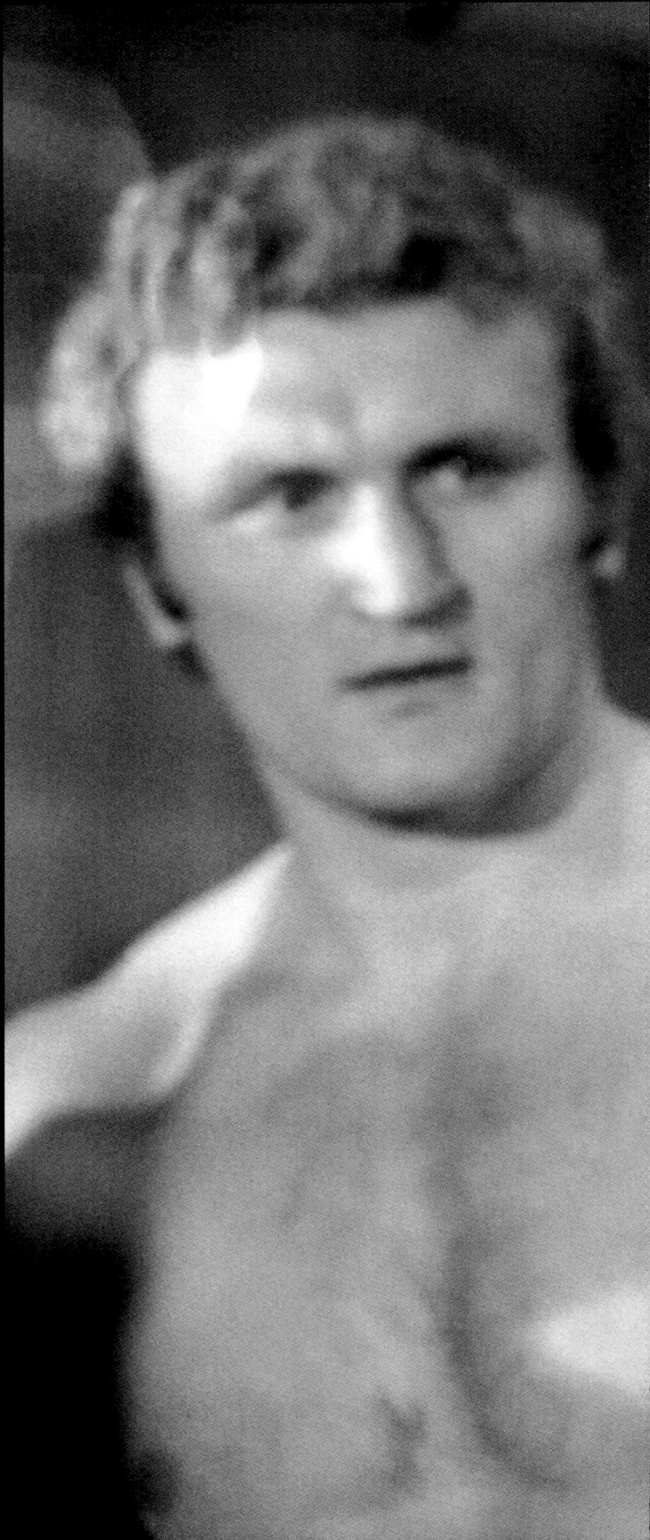

Joe Bugner and Muhammad Ali at Madison Square Garden, June 30, 1975

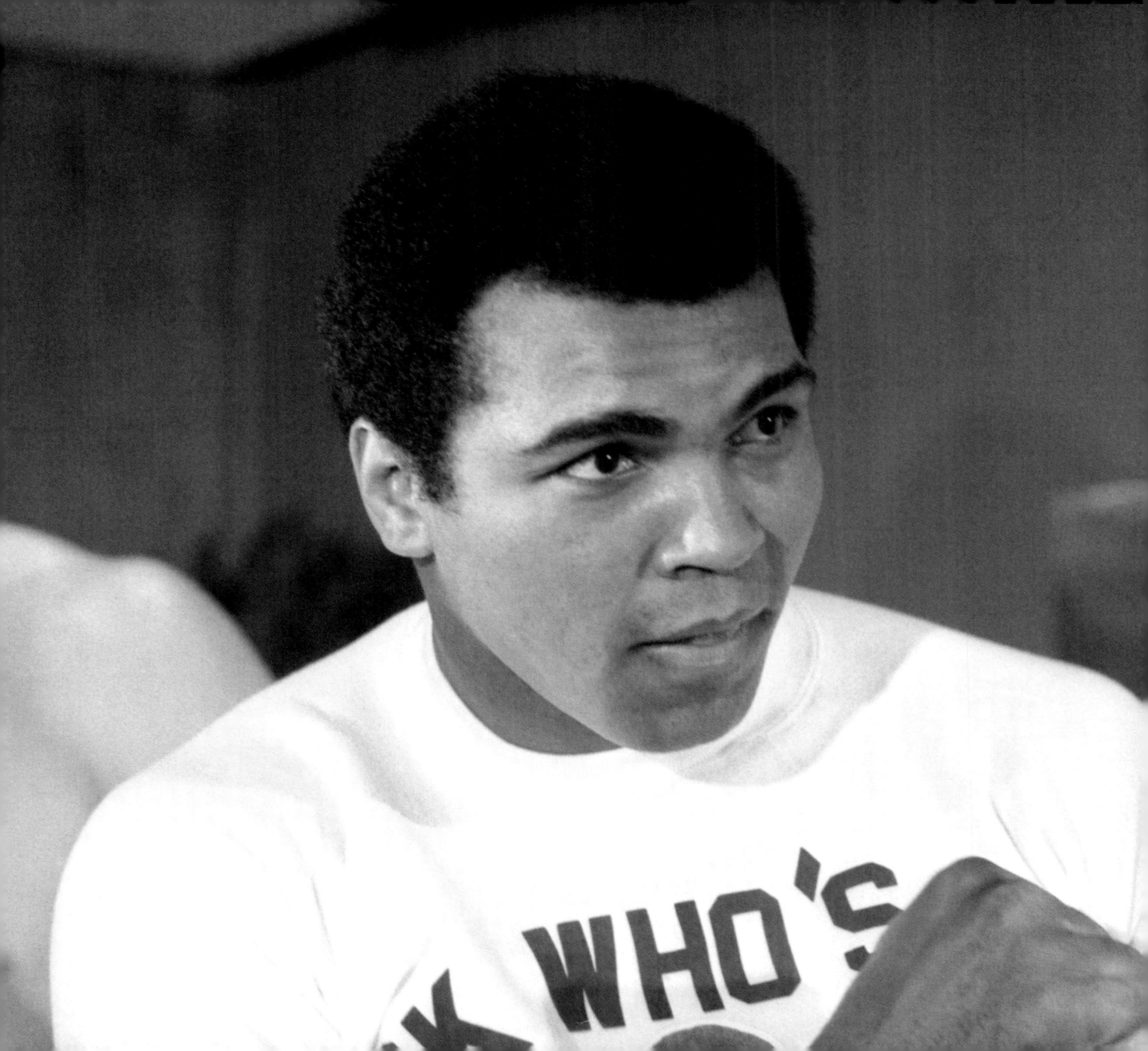
WHO'S

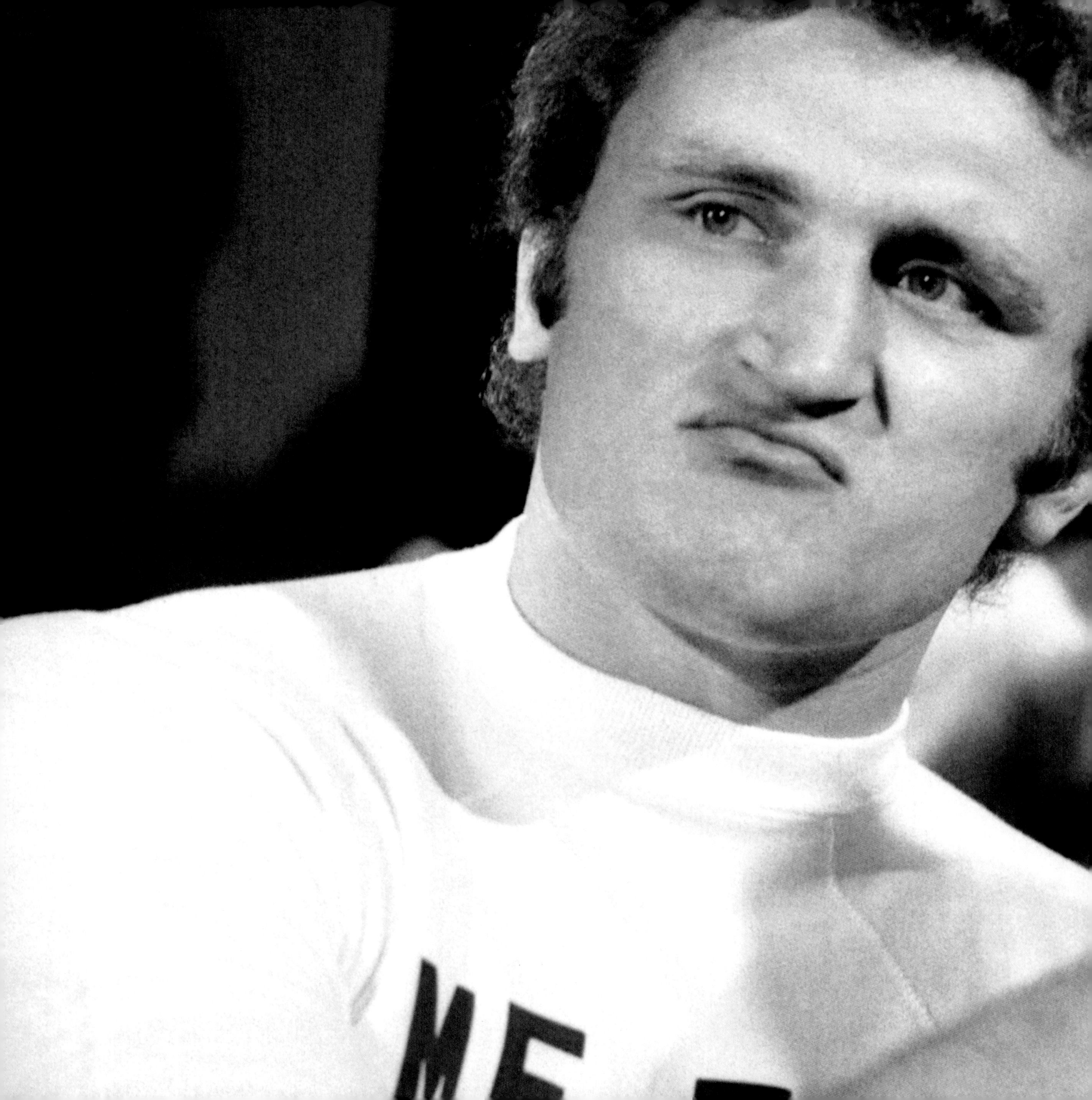

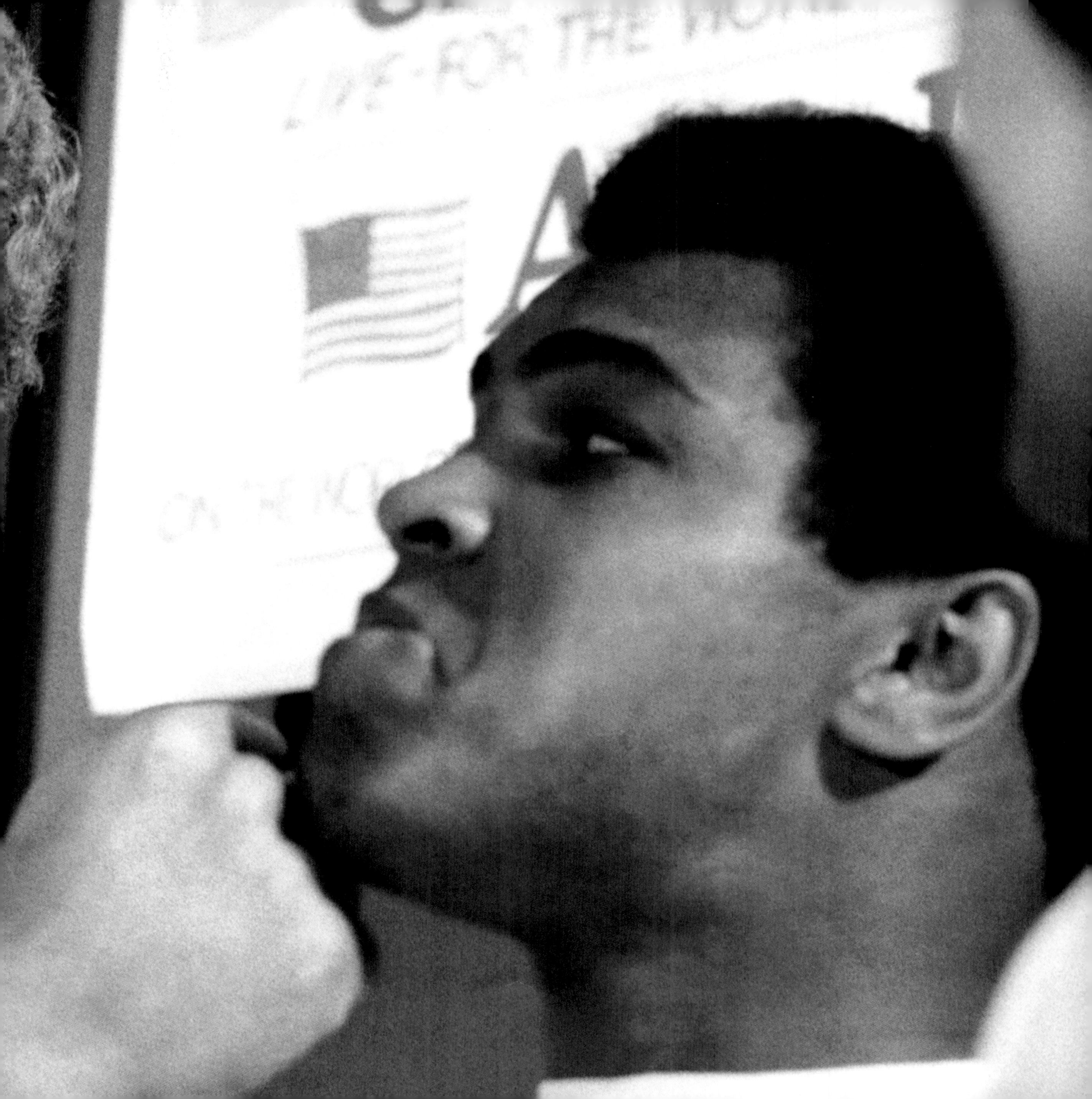
FOR THE

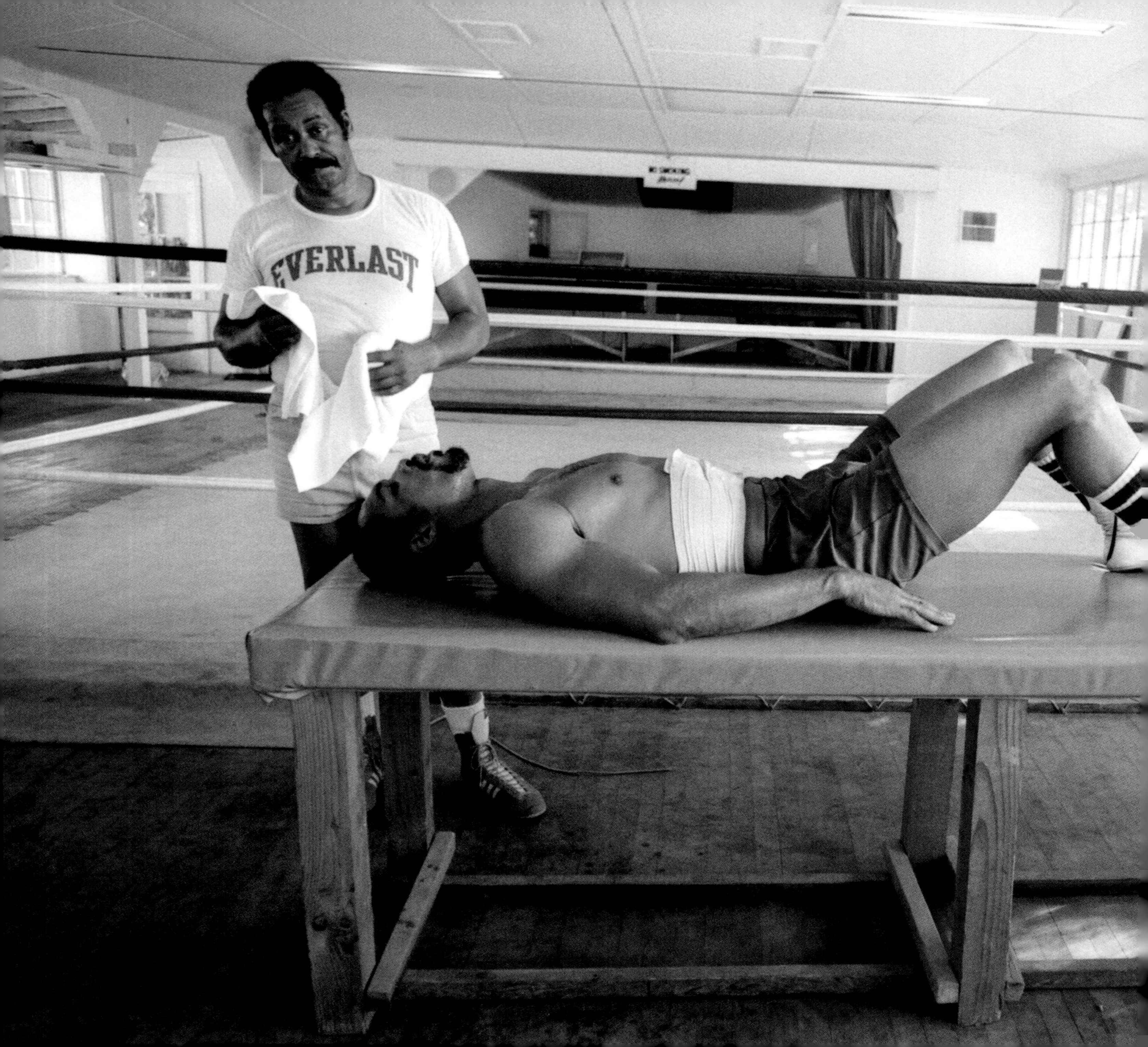
EVERLAST

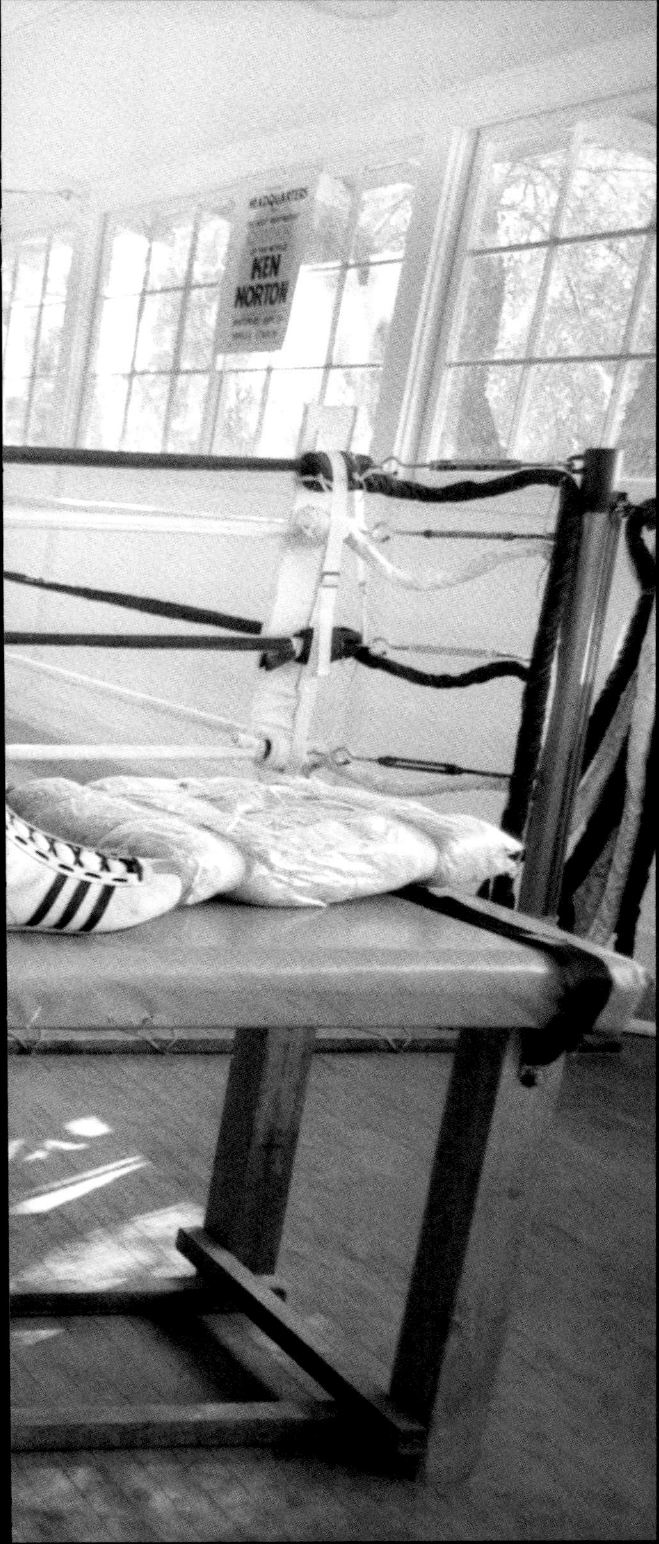

Ken Norton
Fought Ali three times:
San Diego, 1973; won and broke Ali's jaw
LA, 1973; lost
New York's Yankee Stadium, 1976; lost by a controversial decision from the judges at ringside

Ken Norton training at the Massacre Canyon Inn near Los Angeles, August 8, 1976

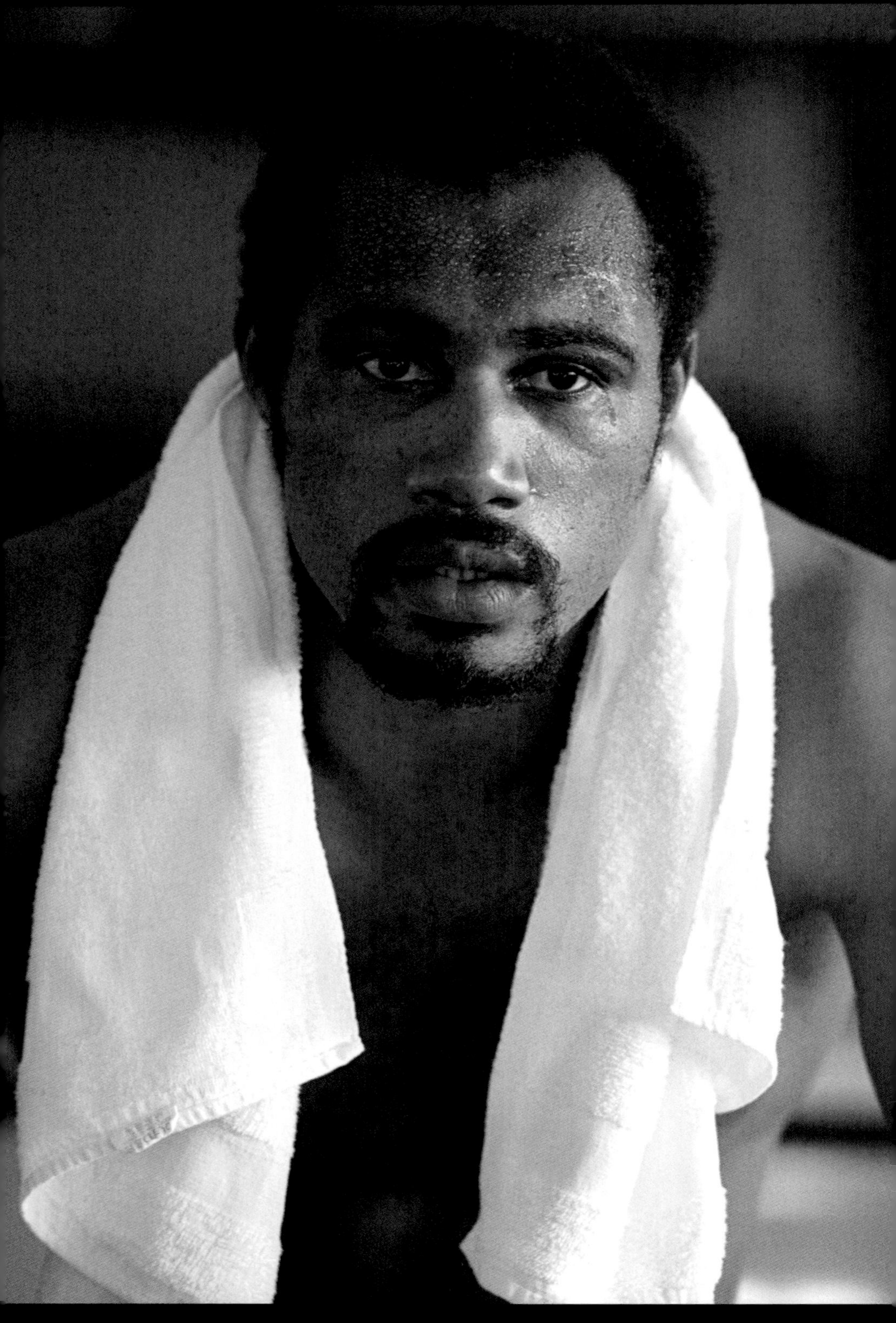

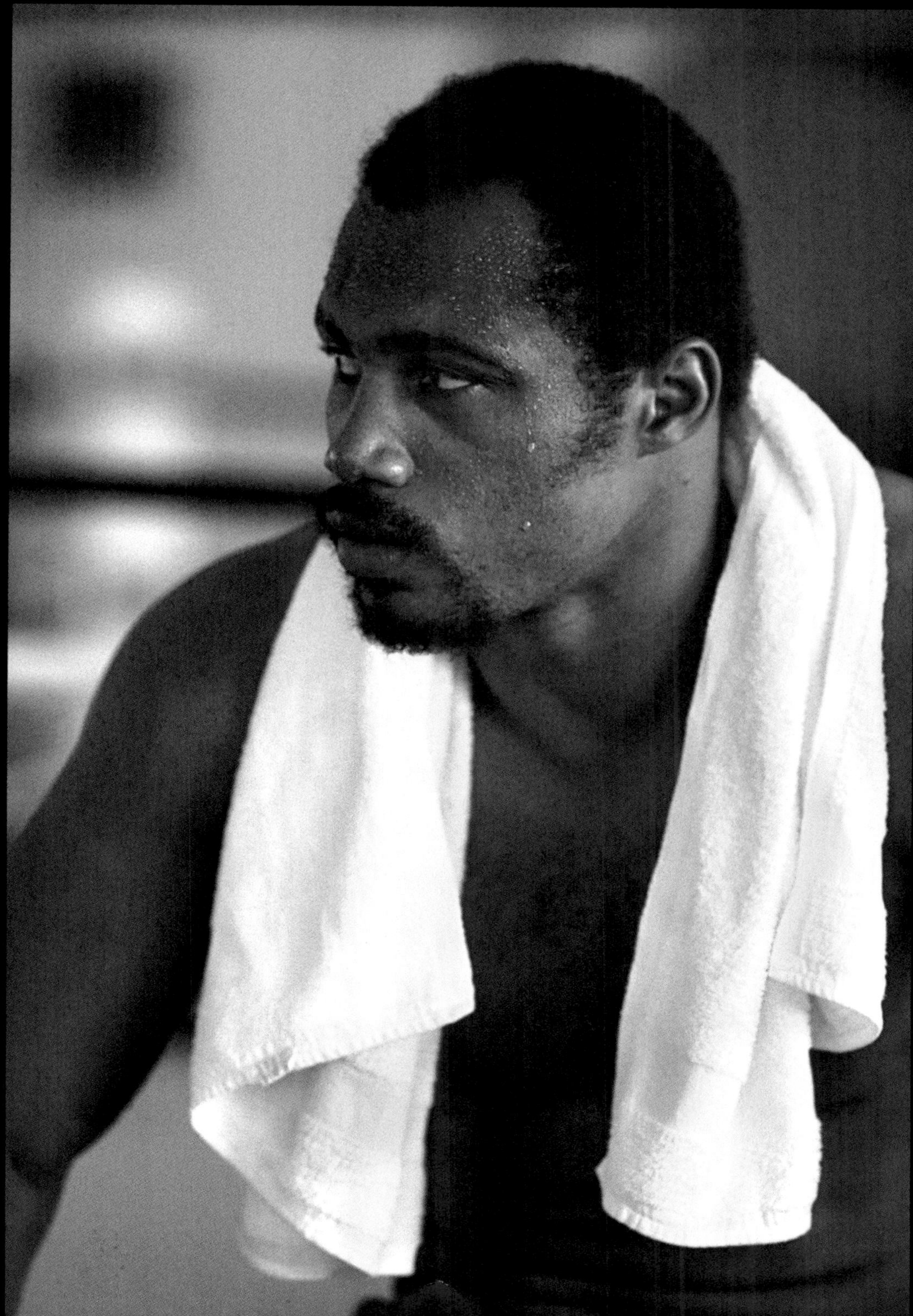

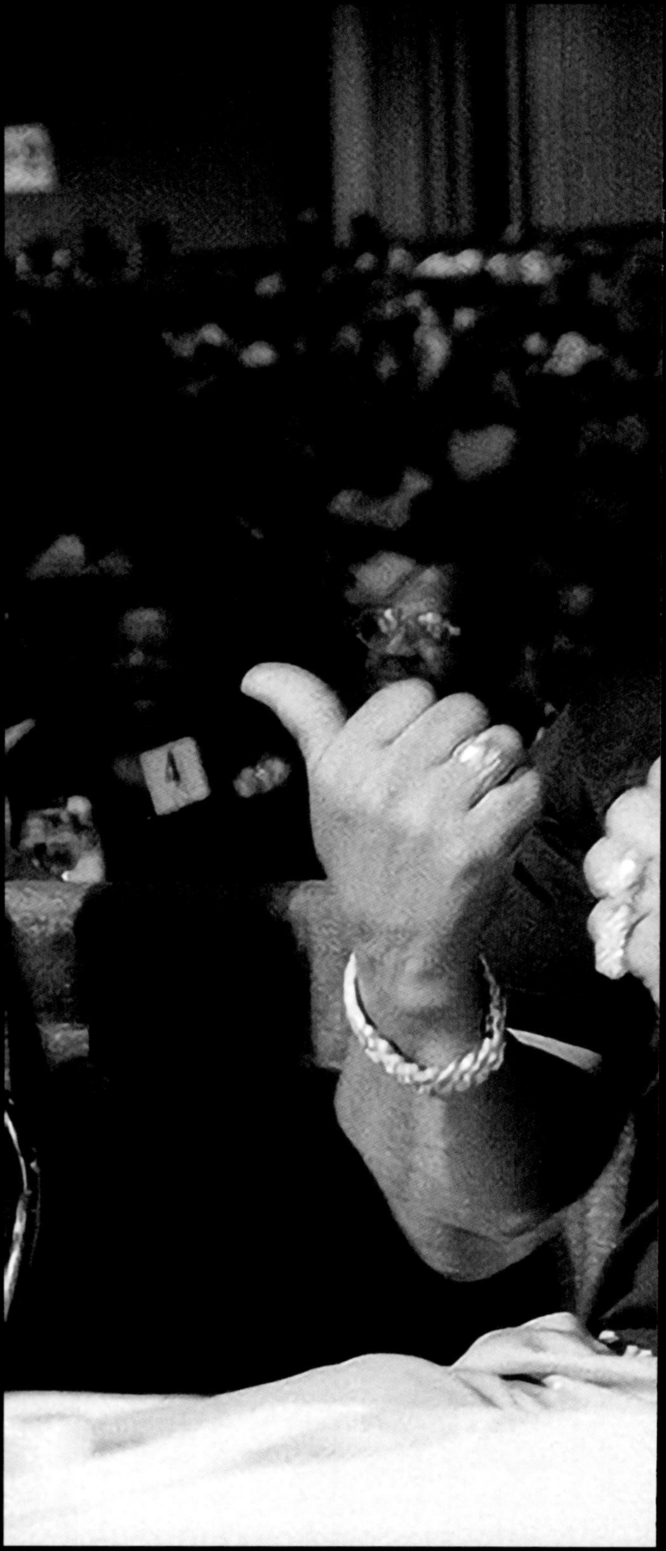

At this meeting in Louisville, Norton jokes that he and Ali should settle things outside, September 20, 1997

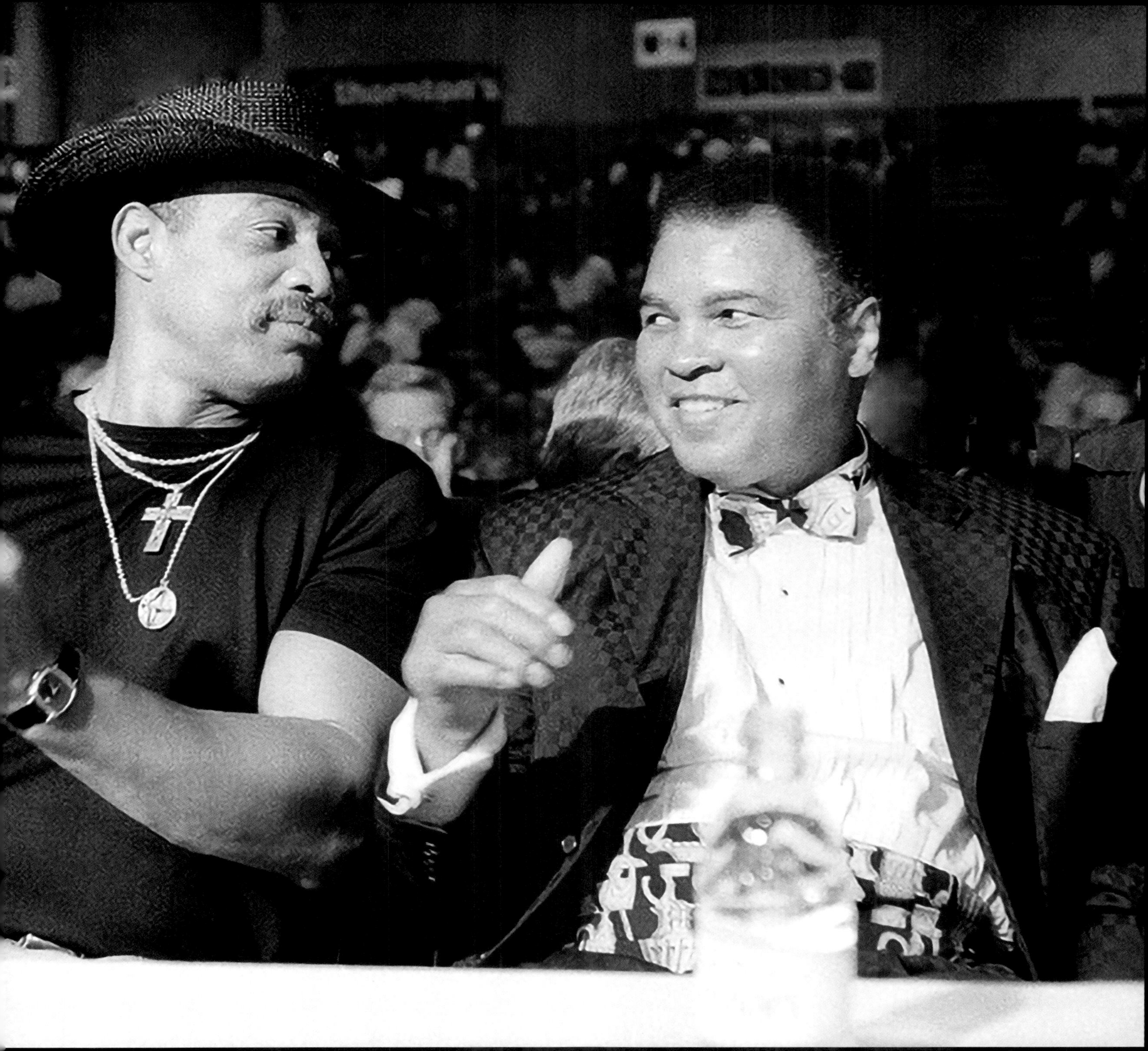

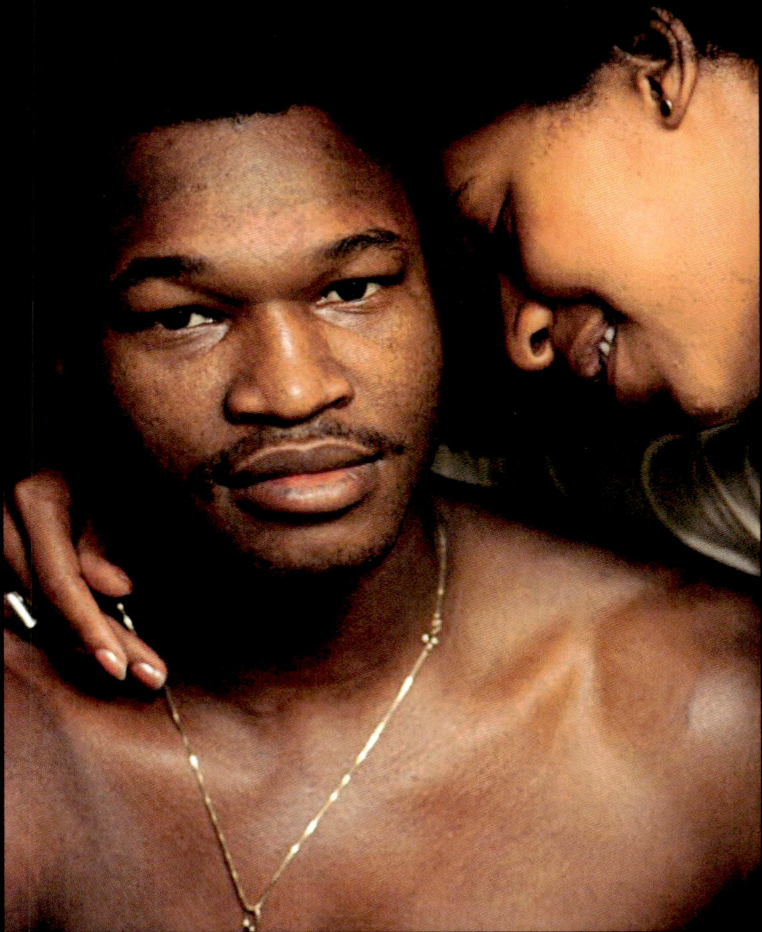

Larry Holmes
Fought Ali on October 2, 1980
Won by a TKO; Angelo Dundee stopped the fight after the 10th

Holmes, once a sparring partner of Ali, later admitted that he took no pleasure in beating his former employer.

Above: *Holmes with his soon-to-be wife, Diane*
Opposite: *A few days after his bruising battle with Ken Norton to win the WBC's Heavyweight title, Larry Holmes tenderly feeds his baby daughter Kandi. Easton, Pennsylvania, June 12, 1978*

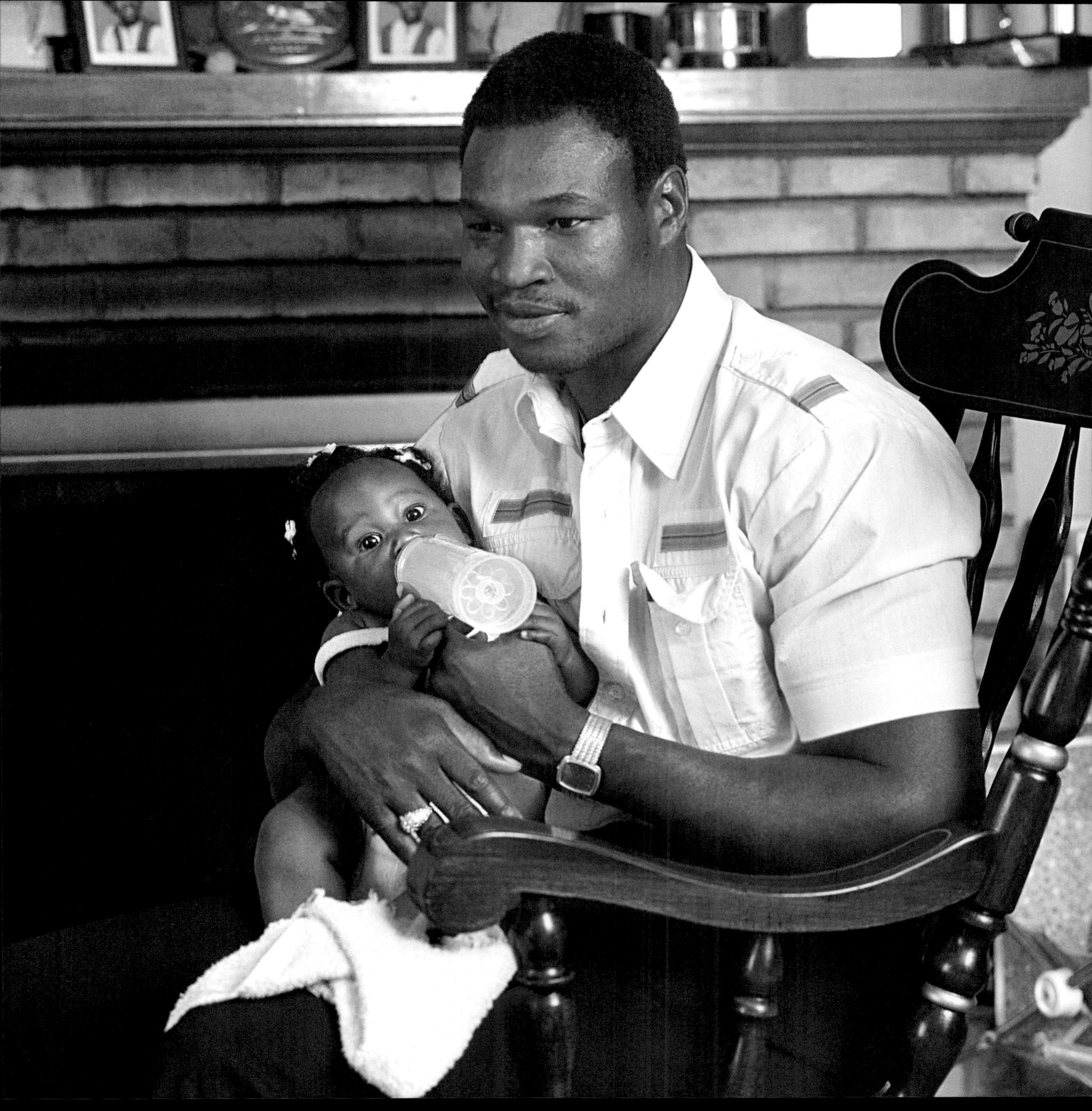

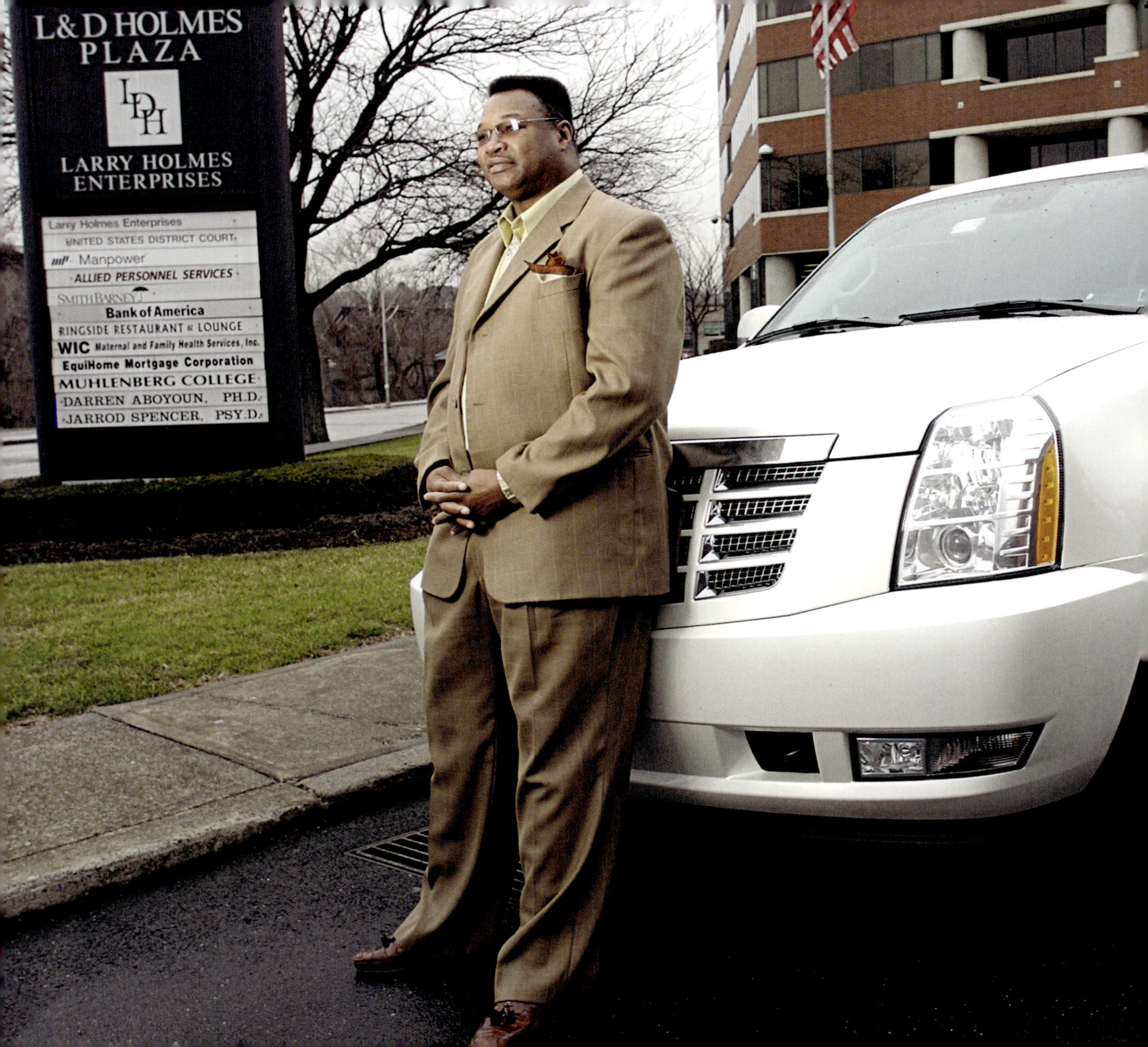
L&D HOLMES
PLAZA
LDH
LARRY HOLMES
ENTERPRISES
Larry Holmes Enterprises
UNITED STATES DISTRICT COURT
Manpower
ALLIED PERSONNEL SERVICES
SMITH BARNEY
Bank of America
RINGSIDE RESTAURANT & LOUNGE
WIC Maternal and Family Health Services, Inc.
EquiHome Mortgage Corporation
MUHLENBERG COLLEGE
DARREN ABOYOUN, PH.D.
JARROD SPENCER, PSY.D.

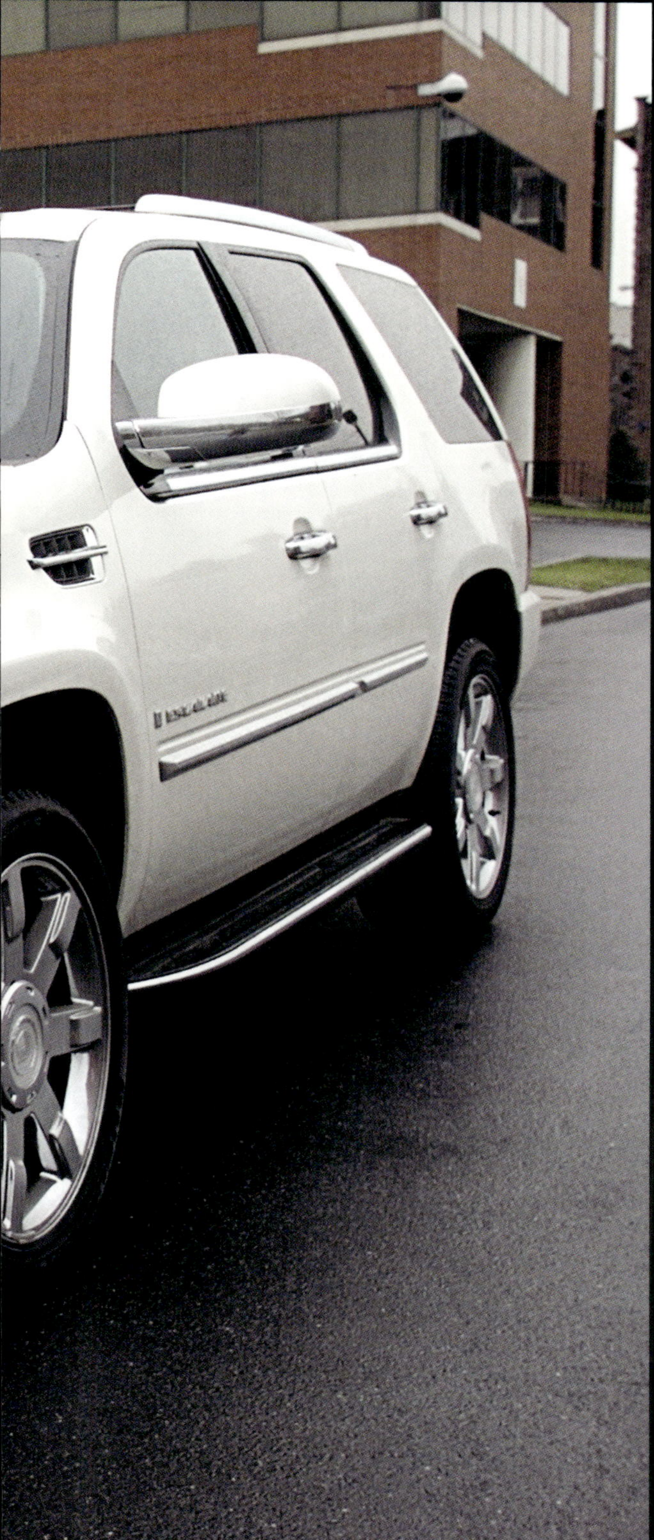

Larry Holmes outside his business complex in his hometown of Easton, Pa., 2006. After retiring from boxing, Holmes invested his earnings into several successful businesses, including a training facility, restaurants and this business complex

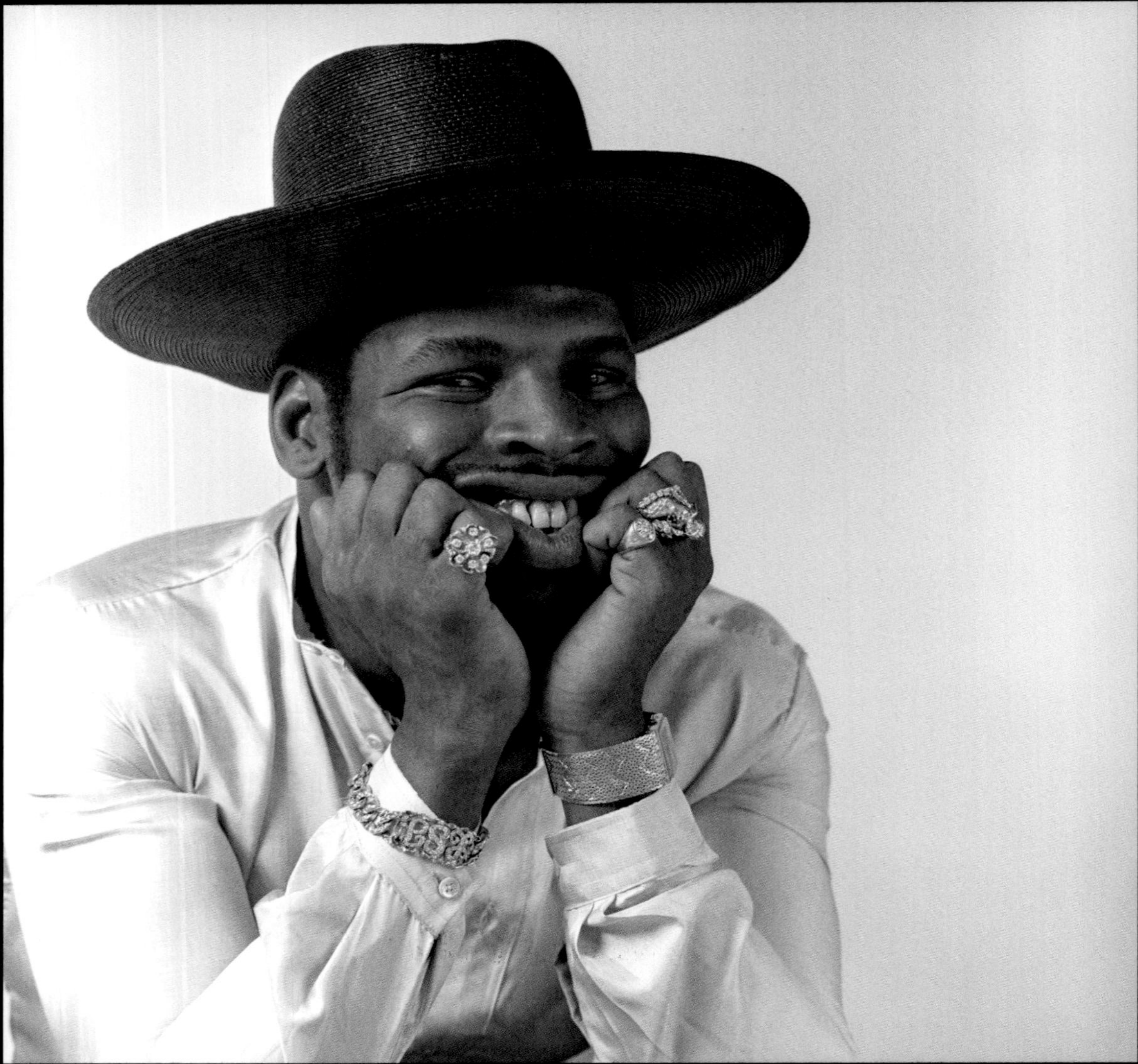

Leon Spinks
Fought Ali twice, both times in 1978
Took the World Championship title from Ali in February in a 15-round split decision; lost in a UD in September

"I congratulated Ali! He is still my idol."
Leon Spinks, two weeks after the fight

Hilton Head Island, South Carolina on June 18, 1978, in-between the Ali fights

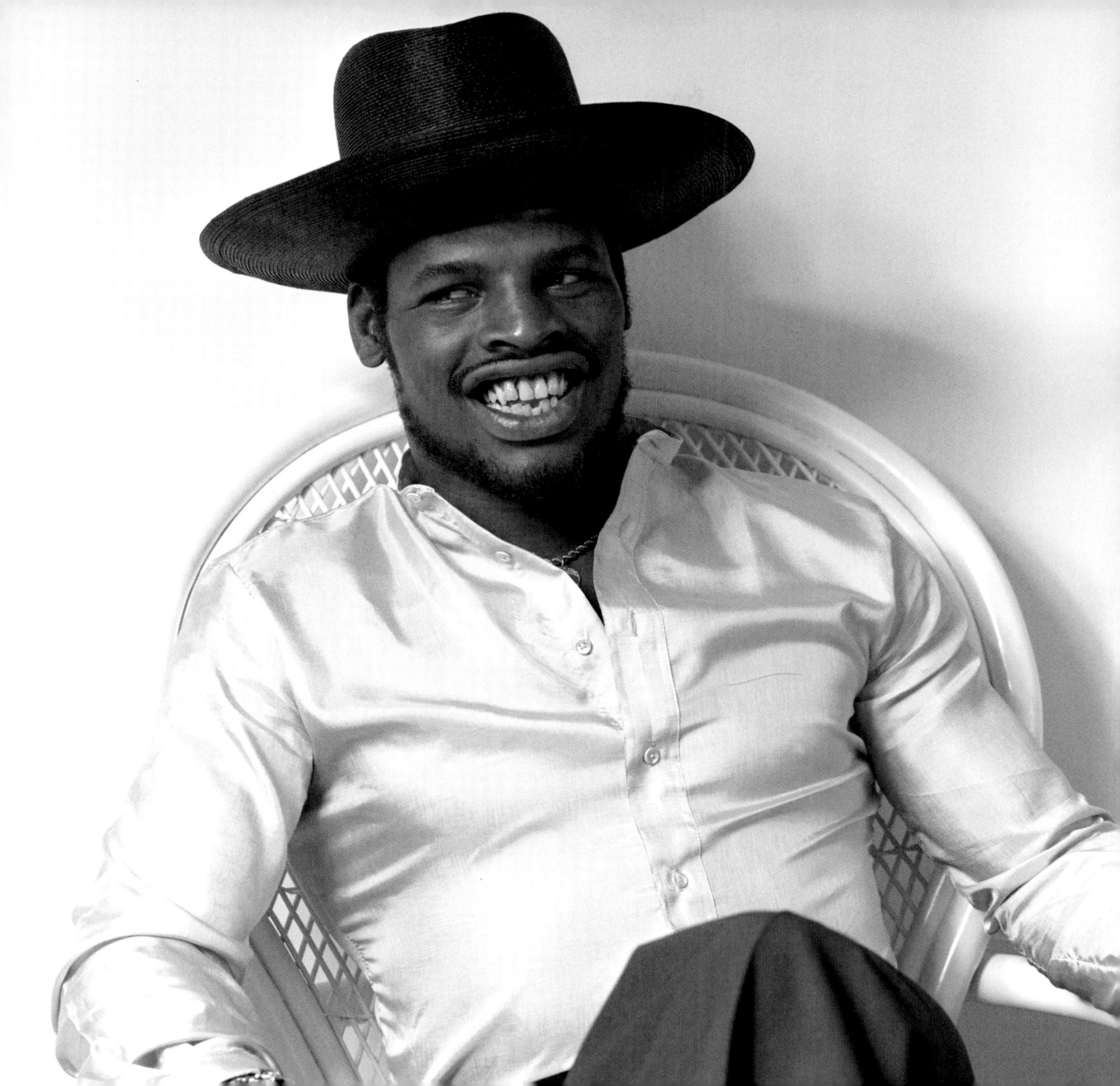

Leon Spinks, after falling on tough times, outside McDonald's in Columbus, Nebraska, where he was working in 2006
McDonald's wouldn't allow me to take photos of Spinks working

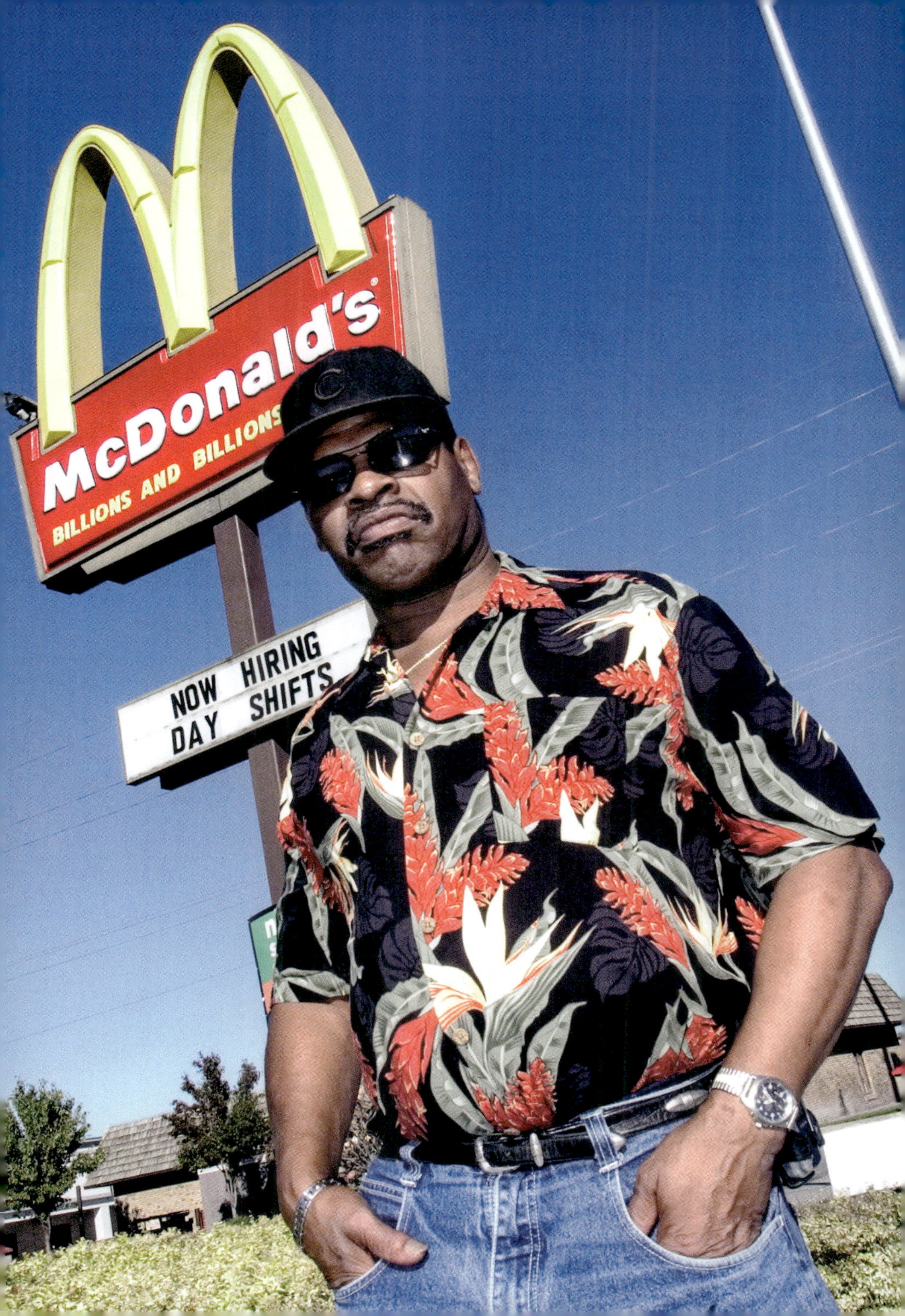
McDonald's
BILLIONS AND BILLIONS
NOW HIRING
DAY SHIFTS

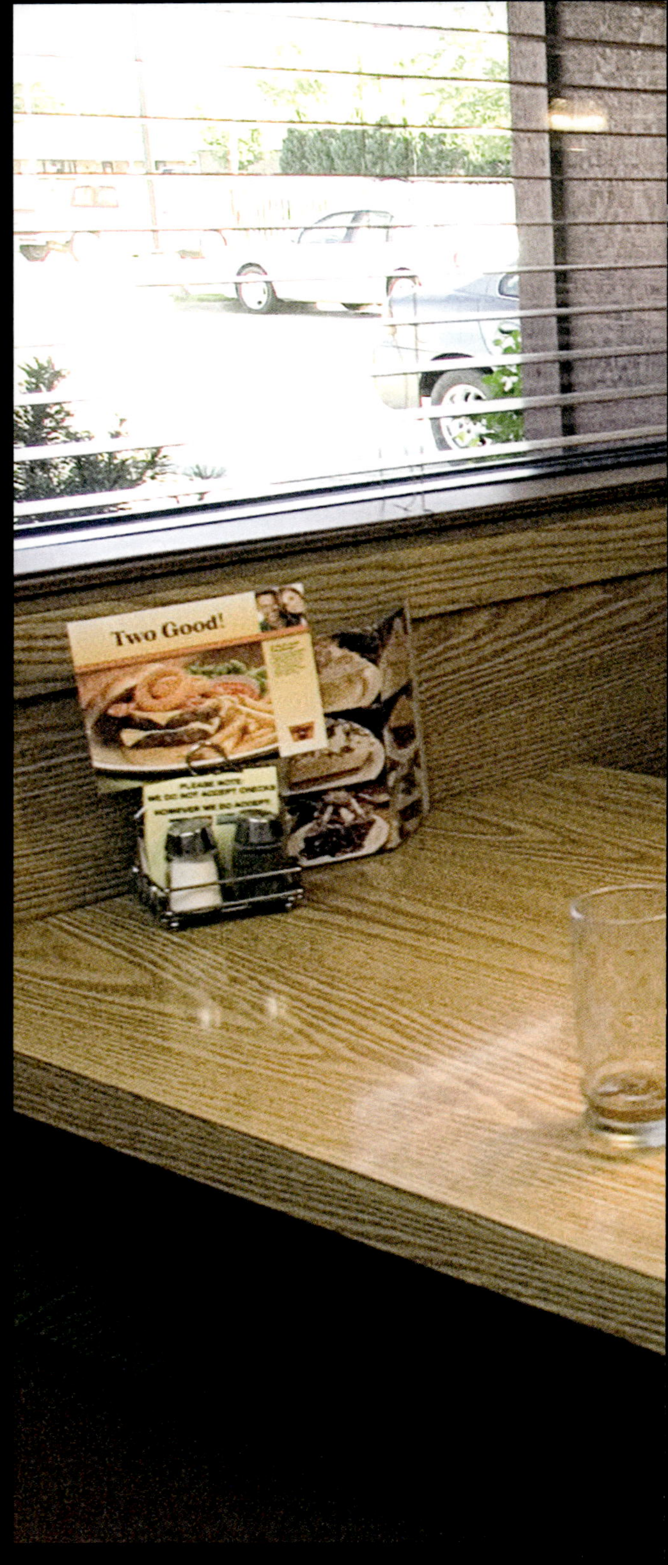

Columbus, Nebraska, September 26, 2006

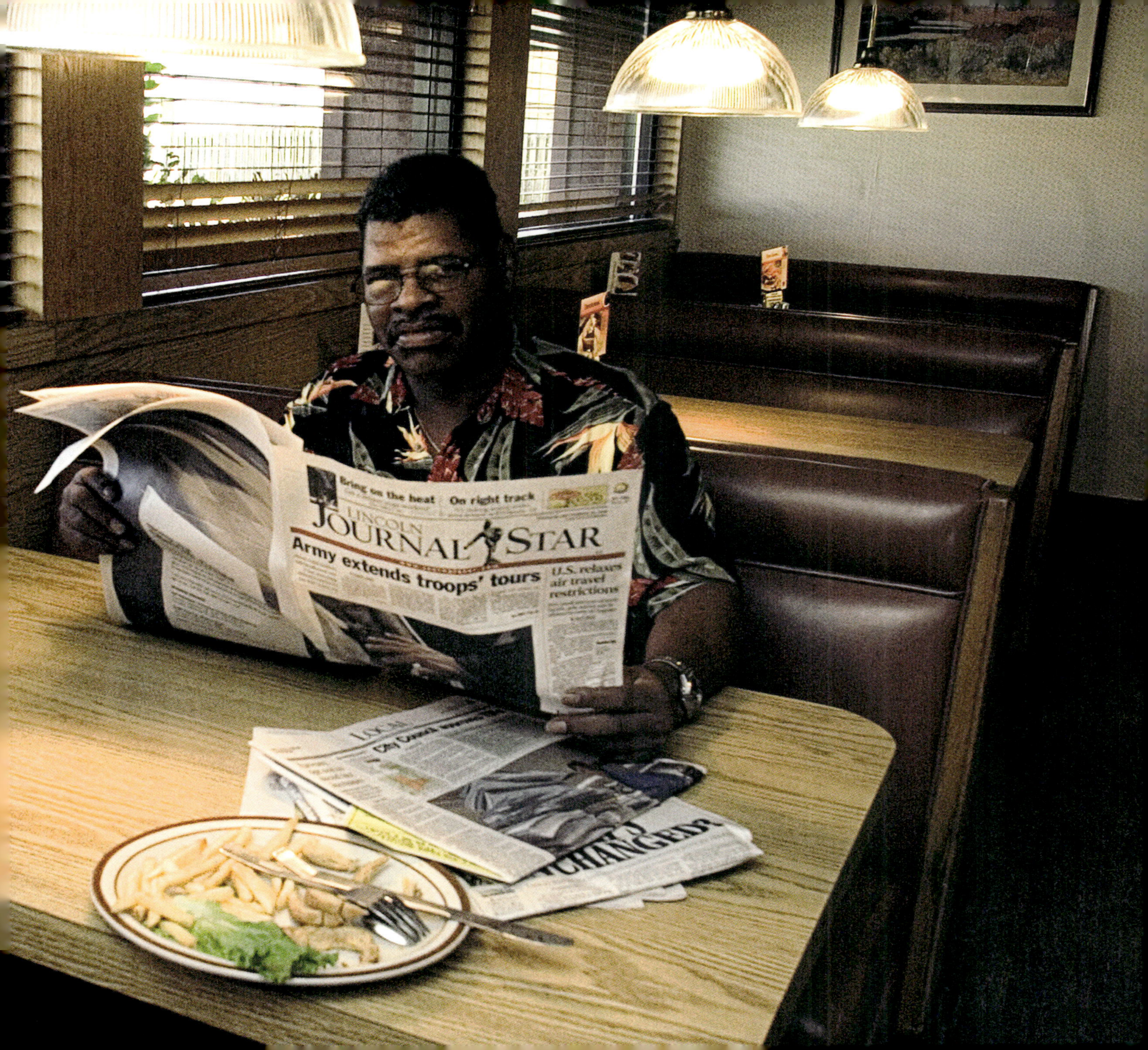
Bring on the heat
On right track
LINCOLN
JOURNAL STAR
Army extends troops' tours
U.S. relaxes air travel restrictions
LOCAL

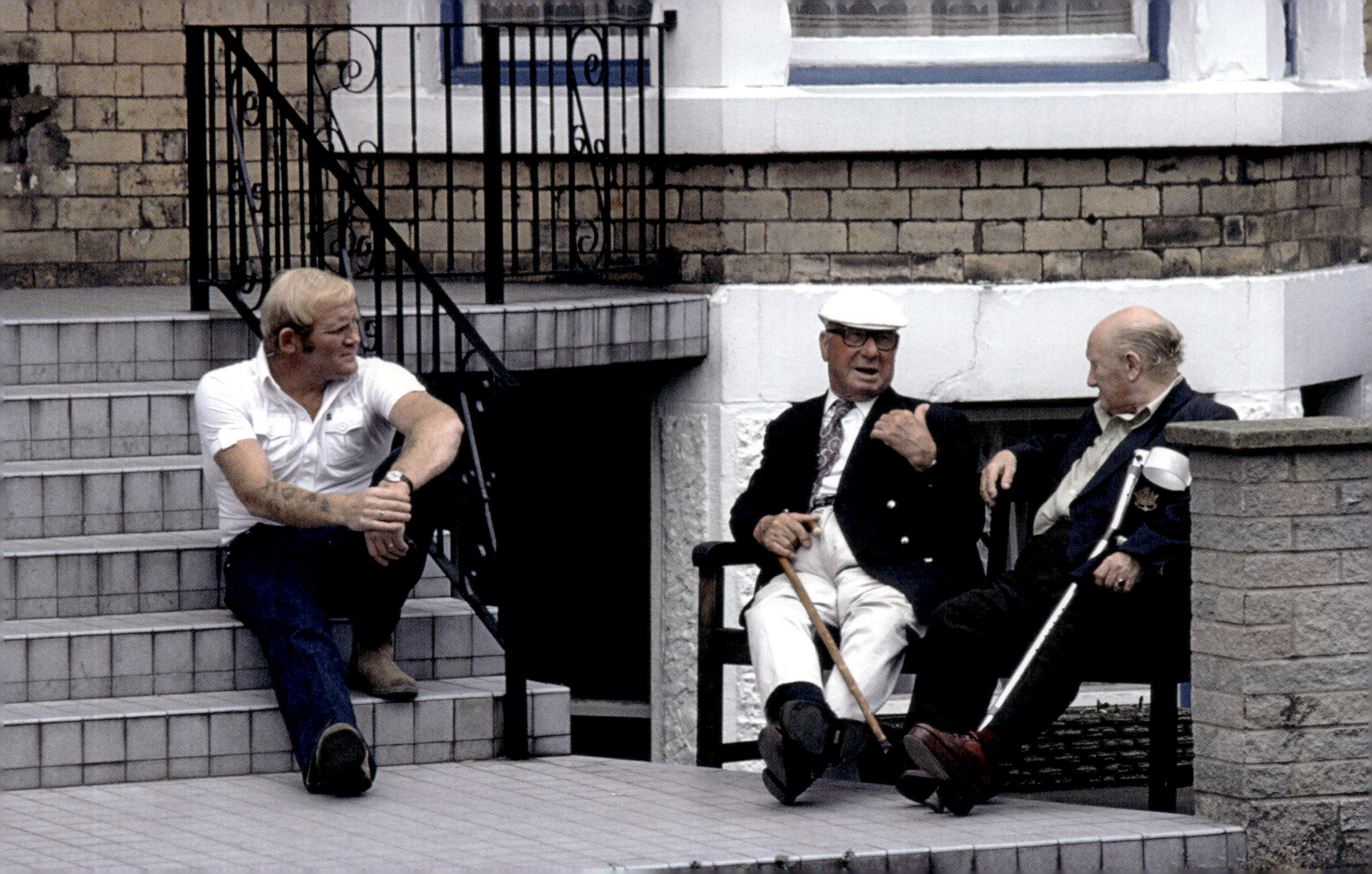

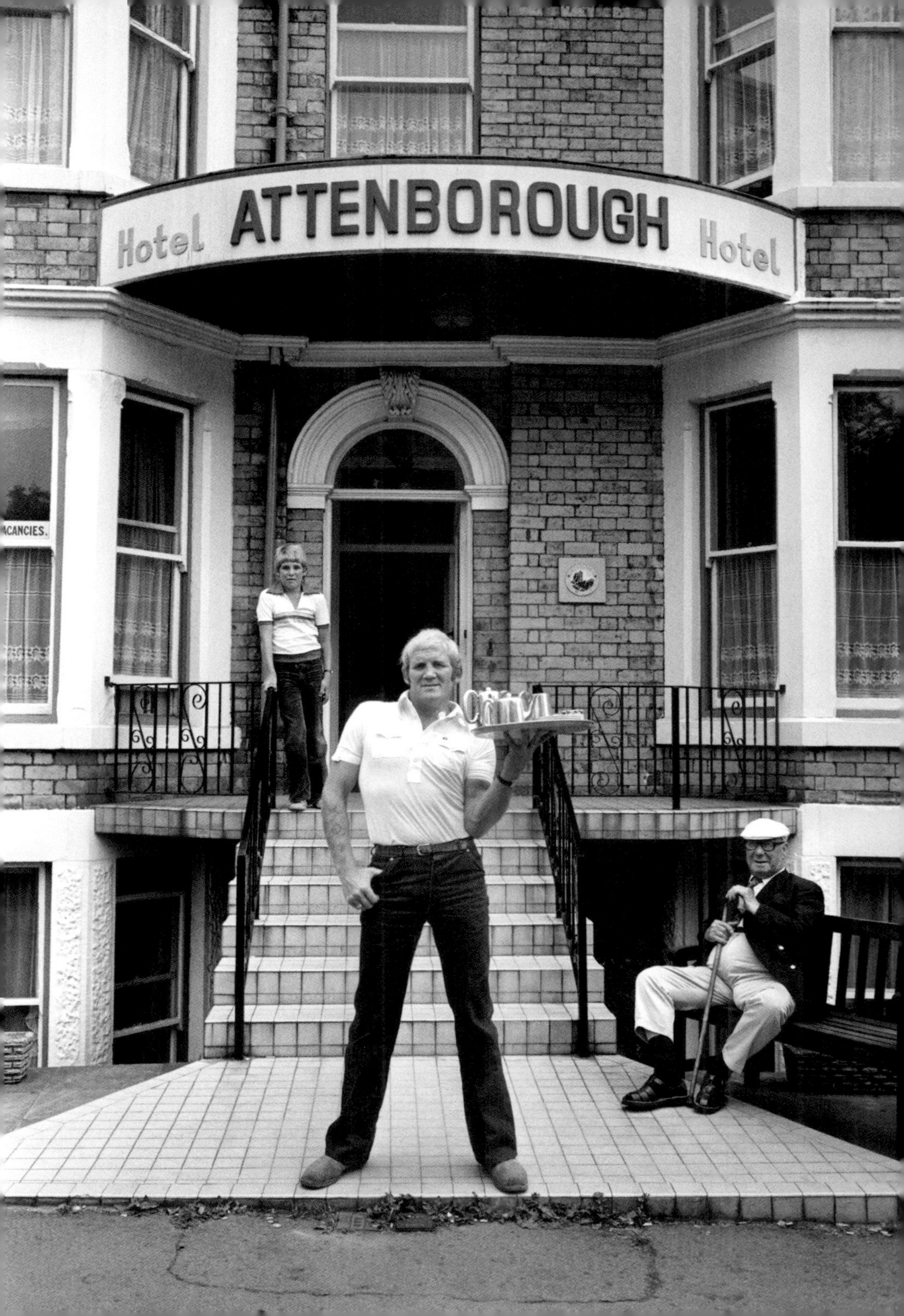
Hotel ATTENBOROUGH Hotel
ACANCIES.

Willi Besmanoff
Fought Cassius Clay in 1961
Lost by TKO in the 7th round

As the son of a Jewish-American father in Nazi Germany, Willi Besmanoff was declared an "enemy of the State" and sent to Buchenwald concentration camp at the age of just 11; his Protestant-German mother managed to secure his release by changing his official religion. After the War, Munich-born Willi Besmanoff became a pro-boxer in Germany before moving to Milwaukee, Wisconsin. After retiring from professional boxing, he started a chain of bakeries and worked with young kids from the Atlanta area.

Willi Besmanoff at the Fulton County Youth Center, Atlanta, Georgia, February 5, 1979

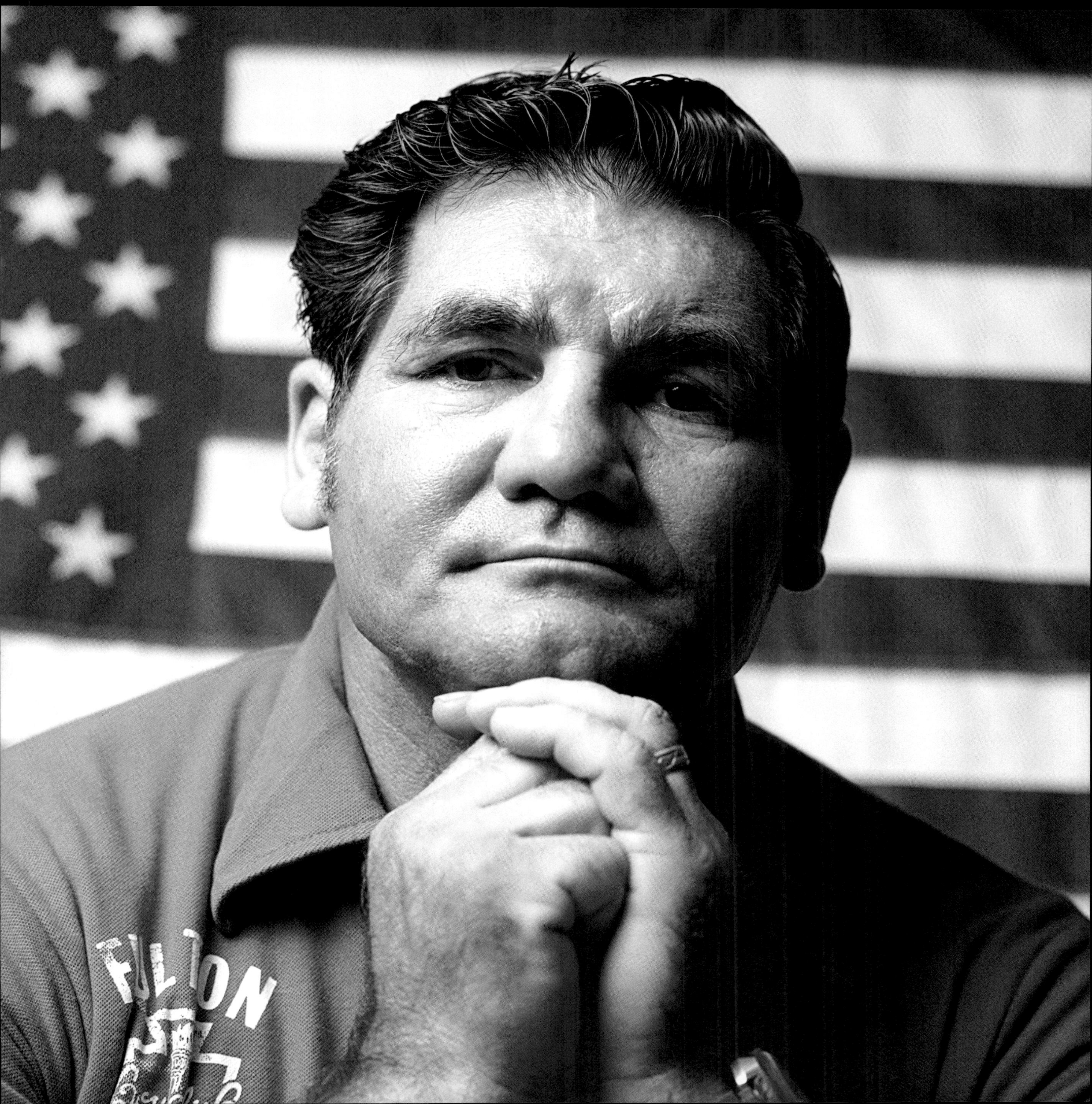

Floyd Patterson
Fought Ali twice: in 1965 and 1972

Lost both times; Patterson retired after his last fight with Ali

Ali was uncharacteristically cruel and cynical toward his opponent. Patterson said later:

"I always called him Cassius Clay. It was nothing personal, but he called all of us names: Liston was the 'Ugly Bear', Joe Frazier was the 'Gorilla' and I was the 'Rabbit'. So, I called him 'Clay'. An order of Sisters of the Poor, who I supported, threw a dinner to raise money. He came 'cos I was involved. He's not in good shape but he turned up. Anyway, I had to speak, and I wanted to show him respect. I broke the habit. For the very first time I called him Muhammad Ali."

Floyd Patterson talking with Patrick Collins from the *Mail on Sunday*. September 26, 1995

"Some of the kids that come here to learn to fight want to be Ali. It don't bother me, I teach all how to fight."

Floyd Patterson in Poughkeepsie, New York, September, 1995

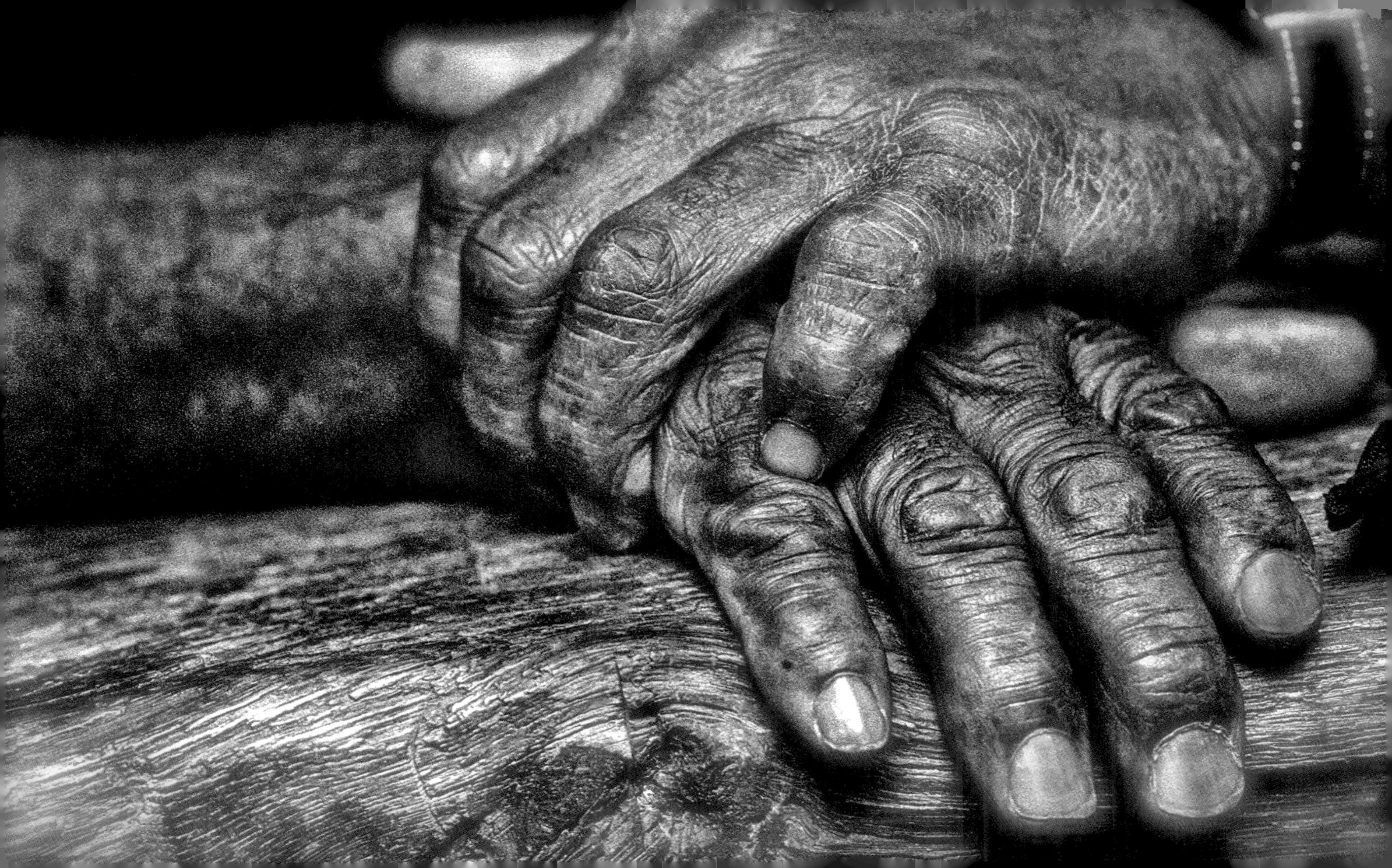

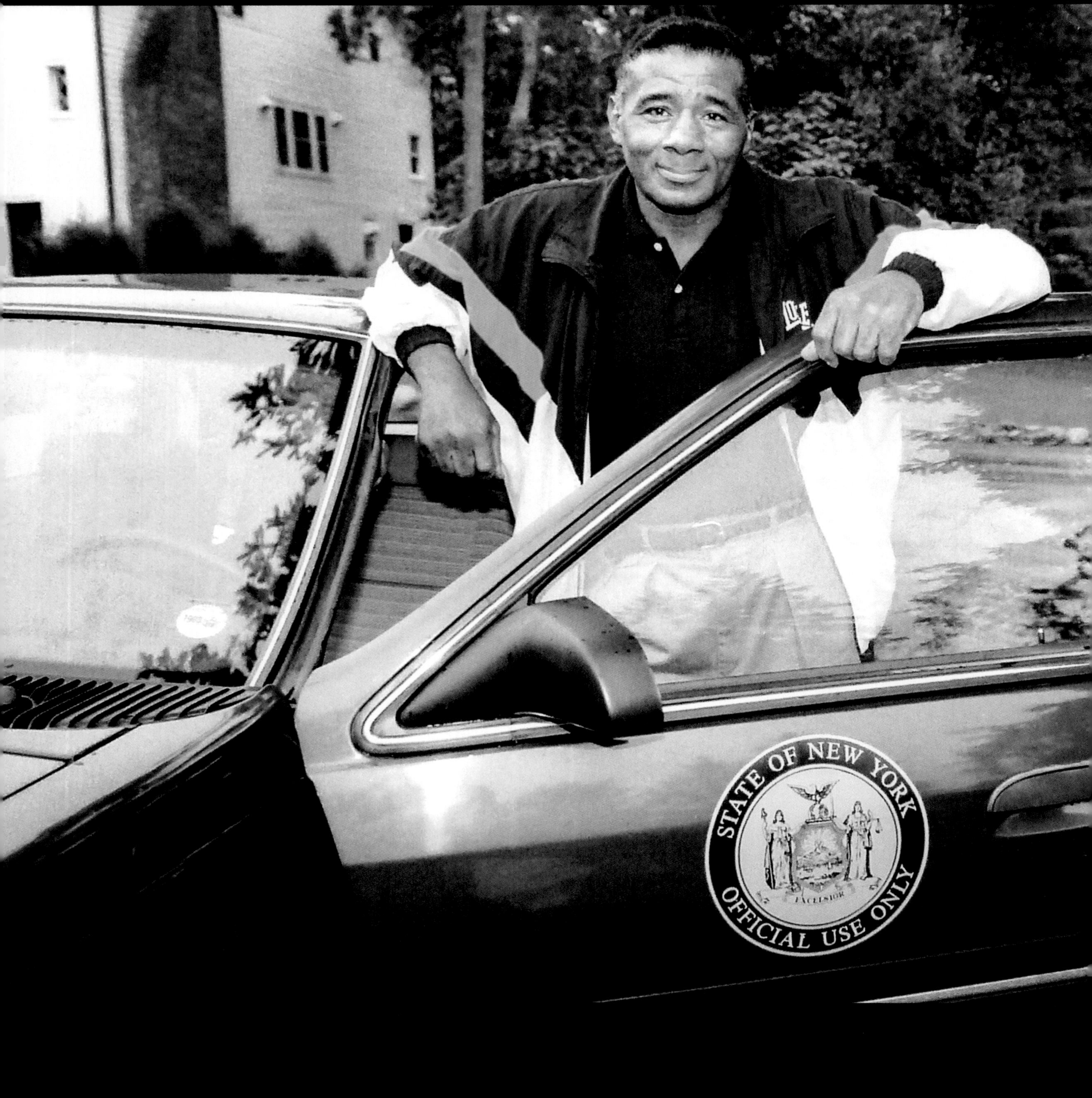
STATE OF NEW YORK
EXCELSIOR
OFFICIAL USE ONLY

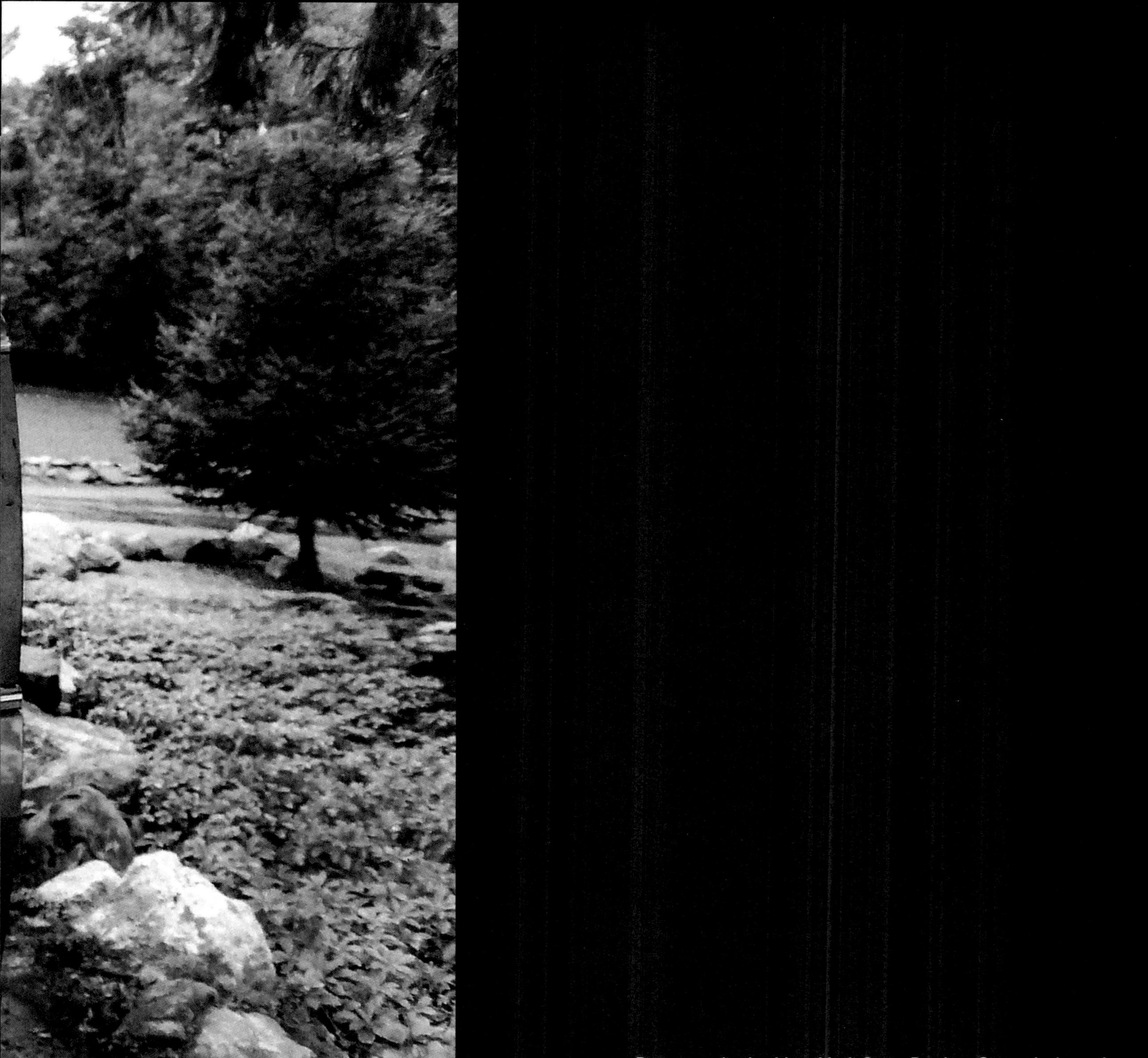

Patterson in the New York State Boxing Commissioner's car

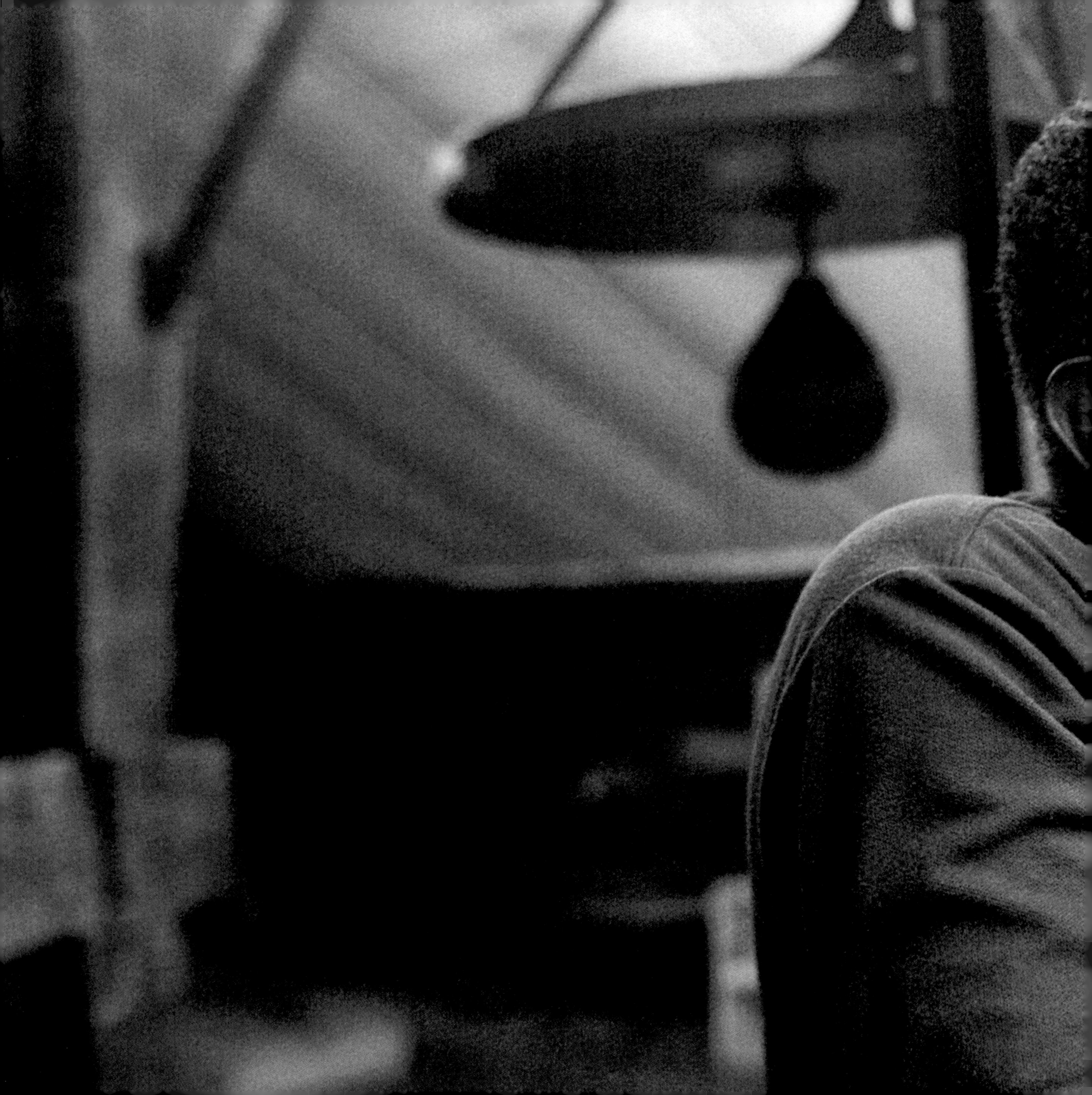

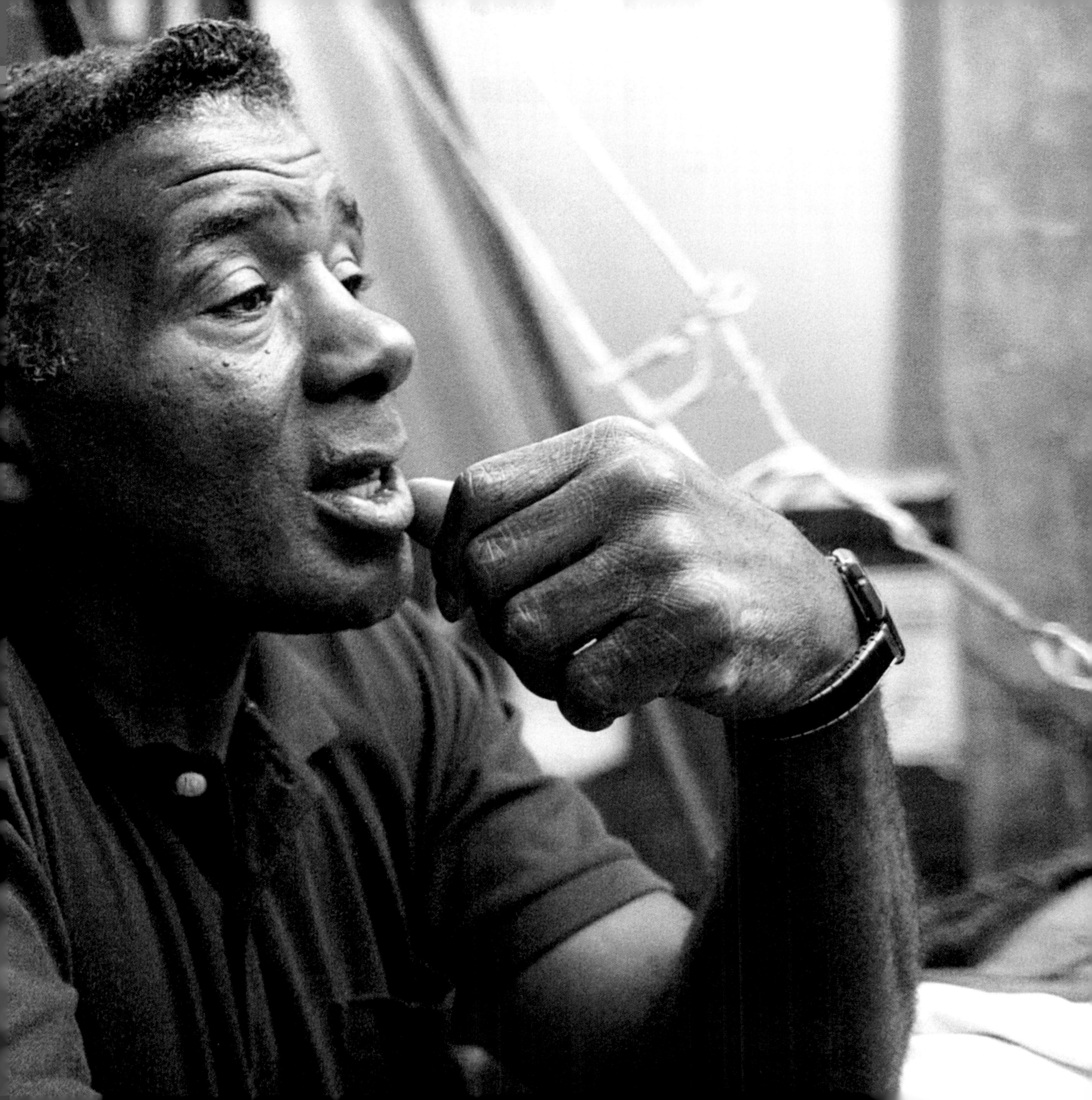

Tunney Hunsaker
Fought Cassius Clay on October 29, 1960 in Louisville, Kentucky
Lost in a 6-round fight

Ali's first professional opponent, Tunney Hunsaker went on to become the police chief of Fayetteville, West Virginia. This interview was conducted in 1978. He died of Alzheimer disease in 2005 at the age of 75.

"I was a policeman at that time. Even then I said given the right chances, Clay could be world champion. He was a nice young man. In no way brash. The day of the fight I ran into him in a downtown department store and he started to clown around with a basketball and a baseball bat, but nothing outrageous. He didn't do that "I'm the greatest" routine until he became more well known.

"The syndicate from Louisville had just given him a brand-new pink Cadillac and he was feeling great. He had just won the gold medal at the Olympics and he was something of a celebrity in Louisville. We drew better than 6,000 people that night.

"When Ali retires, boxing will die. He *is* the greatest. Joe Louis was a good man, a fine champion, but Ali is a showman like there never was and never will be again. I was pulling for him when he fought Spinks the second time. A man like Spinks never had any business being champion.

"But when Clay made his stand on Vietnam, I didn't go for that. He should have served his country.

"He wasn't the toughest fight I ever had, but he was certainly the best fighter I ever fought. He could hit you from any position and you just couldn't knock him off balance. I never saw him again after the fight. I would like to have, because I kept in the game by training some kids.

"It's quiet around here which suits me fine. I've had enough noise for one lifetime."

Police chief, Fayetteville, W. Virginia, October 26, 1978

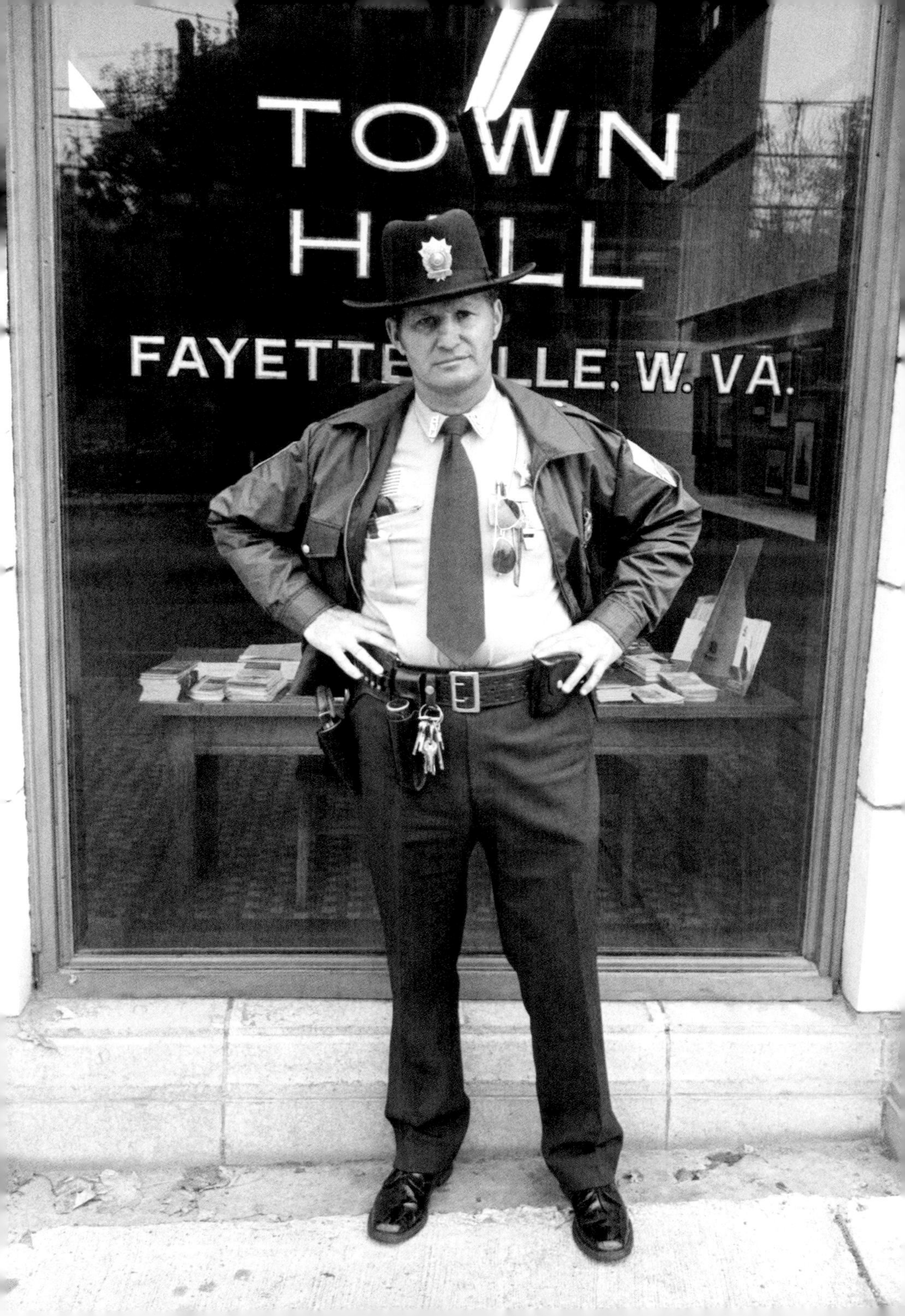
TOWN
HALL
FAYETTEVILLE, W. VA.

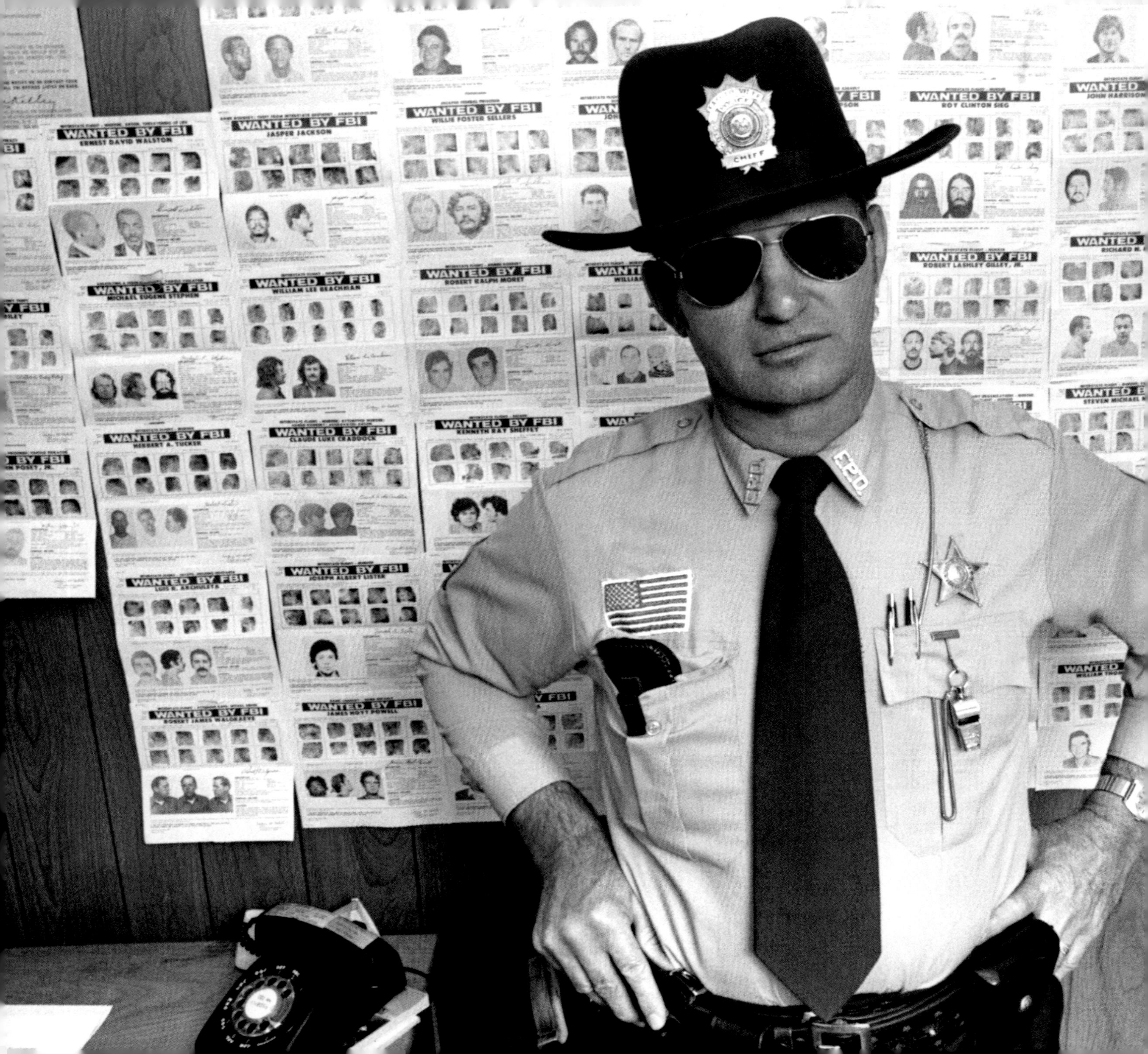
WANTED BY FBI
ERNEST DAVID WALSTON
WANTED BY FBI
JASPER JACKSON
WANTED BY FBI
WILLIE FOSTER SELLERS
WANTED BY FBI
ROY CLINTON SIEG
WANTED BY FBI
JOHN HARRISON
WANTED BY FBI
ROBERT RALPH MOREY
WANTED BY FBI
ROBERT LASHLEY GILLEY, JR.
WANTED BY FBI
HERBERT A. TUCKER
WANTED BY FBI
CLAUDE LUKE CRADDOCK
WANTED BY FBI
KENNETH RAY SHEFFEY
WANTED BY FBI
JOSEPH ALBERT LISTER
WANTED BY FBI
JAMES HOYT POWELL
CHIEF

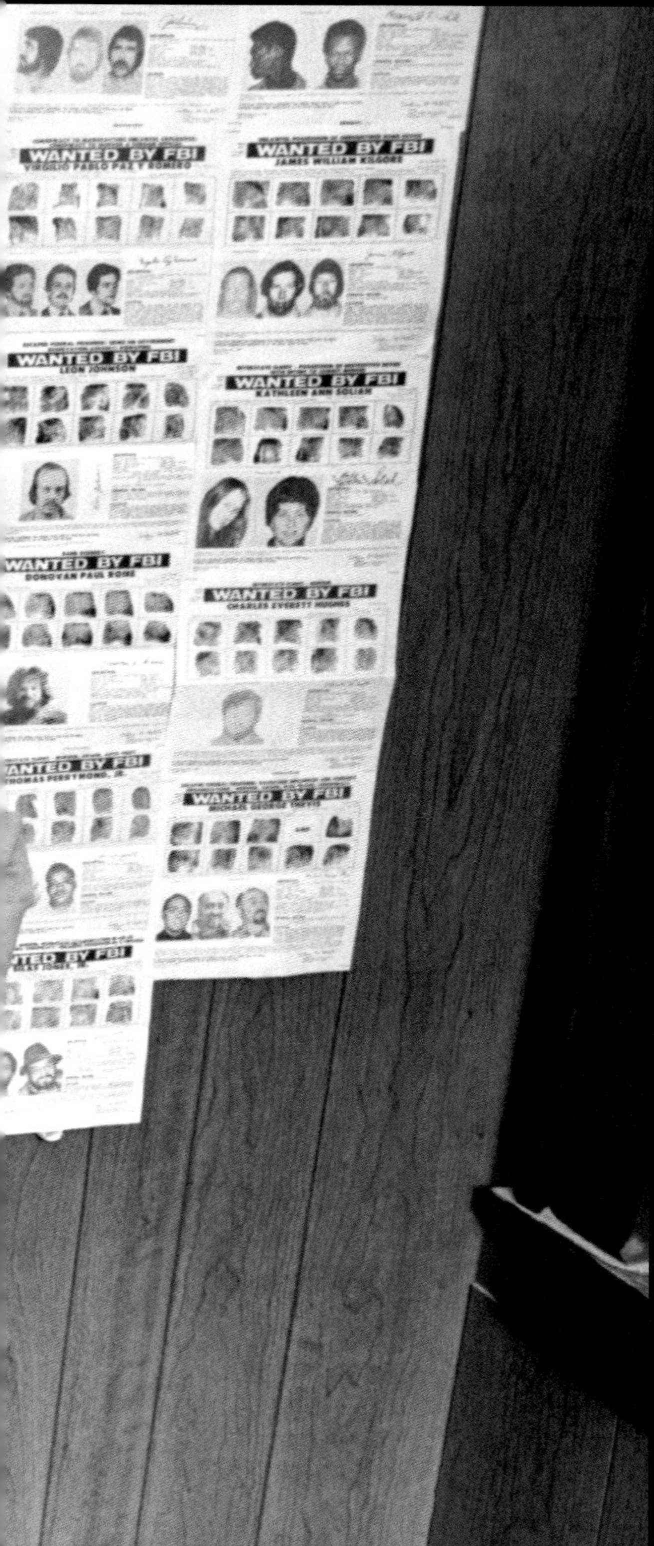
WANTED BY FBI
WANTED BY FBI
JAMES WILLIAM KILGORE
WANTED BY FBI
LEON JOHNSON
WANTED BY FBI
KATHLEEN ANN SOLIAH
WANTED BY FBI
WANTED BY FBI
CHARLES EVERETT HUGHES
WANTED BY FBI
WANTED BY FBI
WANTED BY FBI

Herb Siler
Fought Cassius Clay on December 27, 1960
Lost in a TKO in 4 rounds

"I think I was paid $800 for fighting Clay. They offered me that because they were trying to bring him along – and they knew I was a spoiler. Clay didn't get as much but he had people paying him outside the ring.

"I couldn't find any sparring partners, so I had to work out with my manager, who was only a little guy. I think the people who had money invested in Clay were afraid I would do something drastic and hurt him. It was stopped in the fourth on a TKO because I had a heavy cut in the mouth. He never hurt me, but I wasn't in top shape.

"I was an alcoholic. Even when I was fighting, I was drinking. When I was drunk, I would want to fight anybody; I guess it was my way of getting rid of my tensions and anxieties.

"I was never really into boxing. I had a family to support, so I couldn't travel. I had fought in Texas, Peru and Italy, but I couldn't keep doing it. I never made much money out of fighting. I think my biggest purse was about $2,000.

"The worst thing I ever did through drink is what I served seven years for. I had been drinking and my girlfriend was drunk, too. We got into a fight and she came at me with a butcher knife. I was carrying a gun, so I shot her. She died later in a hospital.

"I'm a reformed alcoholic and have found God. I counselled for AA while I was in prison. If I hadn't had a drink, I wouldn't have been in that joint."

In Miami serving time at a Dade County, Fla., correctional facility, June 28, 1979

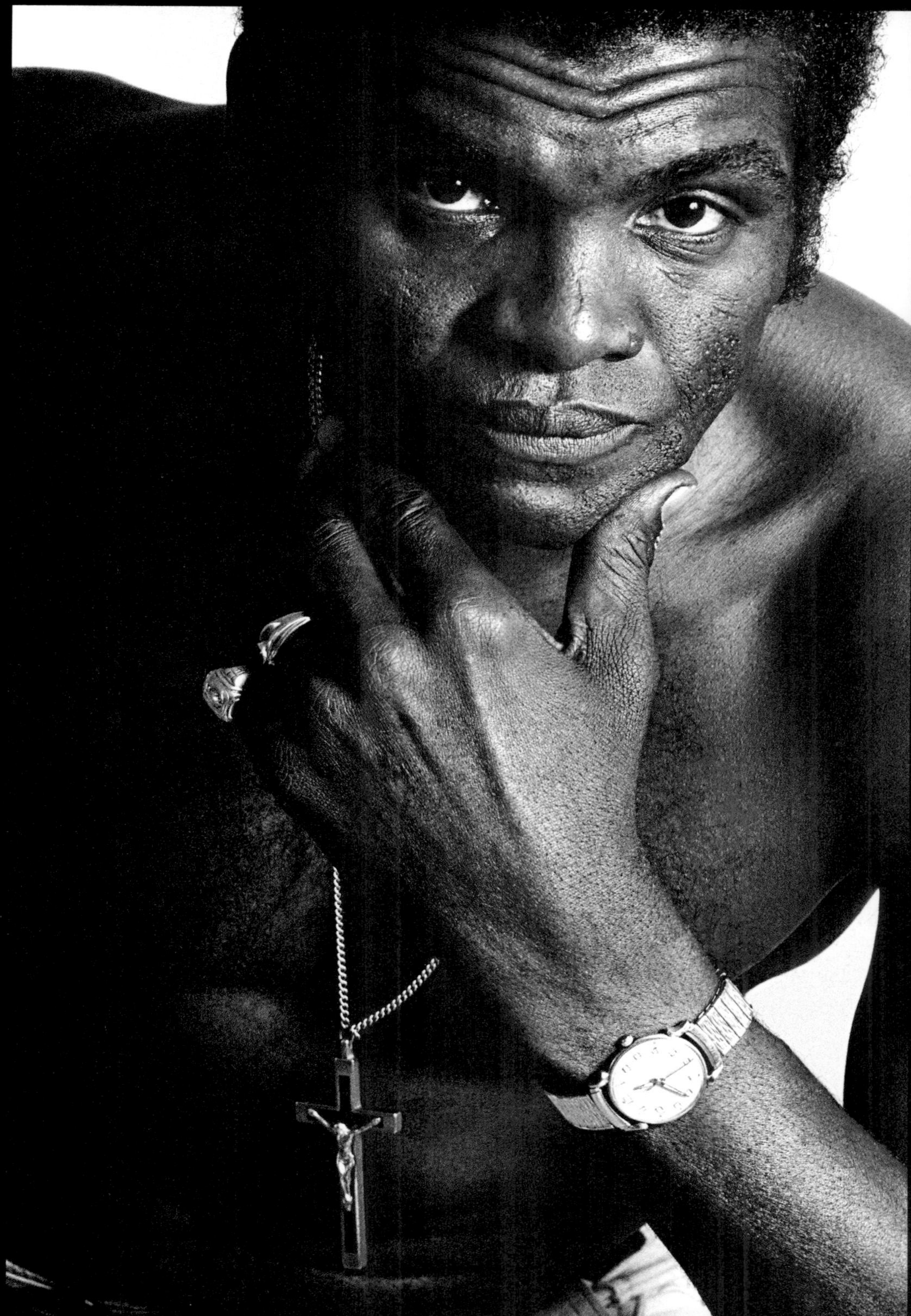

Tony Esperti
Fought Cassius Clay in a 10-round match on January 17, 1961
Lost in a TKO

"I just came out of jail for unlawful entry and fought Ali when I was 28 years old. I used to like going to the gym on Fifth Street in Miami. I was working out one day when Chris Dundee asked me if I wanted to fight some kid called Cassius Clay. I was broke, so I said yeah, O.K.

"I wasn't in any shape, though. I knew he could box, but I didn't know how much heart he had. At the time I fought him I didn't think he had much heart. Now I think he's all right. I think he's a nice guy, and we became friends.

"That happened when we were both in the Dade County jail, when he was getting harassed and they put him inside for five days on account of a traffic violation.

"He was helping in the kitchen while he was inside. I had been inside for two years. When he saw me, he said, 'Hey, that's my man, Tony. How long you been in here?'

"I could probably beat nine out of 10 of the heavyweights around right now, and I'd like to take a shot at one.

"I've been in jail for 13 years now and would like to ask Ali for some help. The trouble is, I can't get to him."

At the Hendry Correctional Institution, Immokalee, Florida, February 7, 1979. Although sentenced to life, Esperti spent time out in the wild landscape of the prison grounds where he shadowboxed while being watched by his only fan, an old feral black & white cat

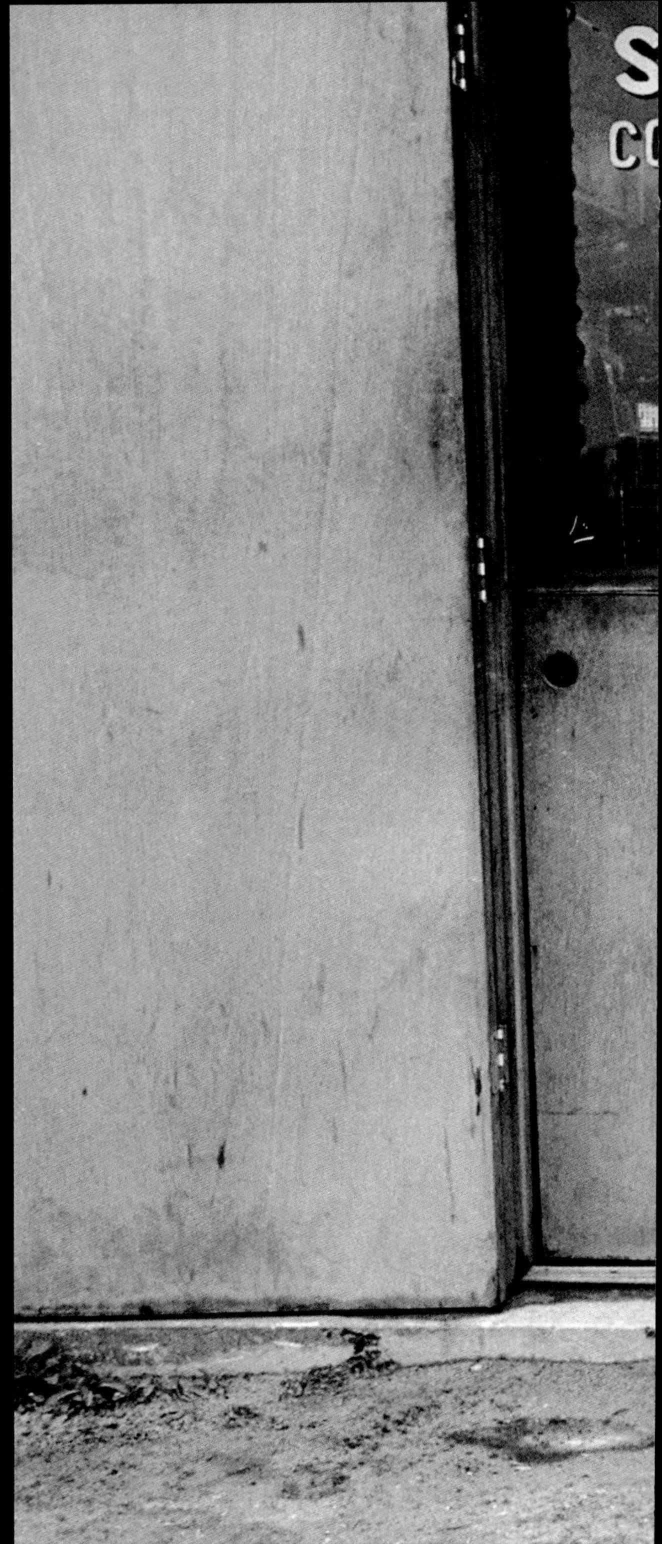

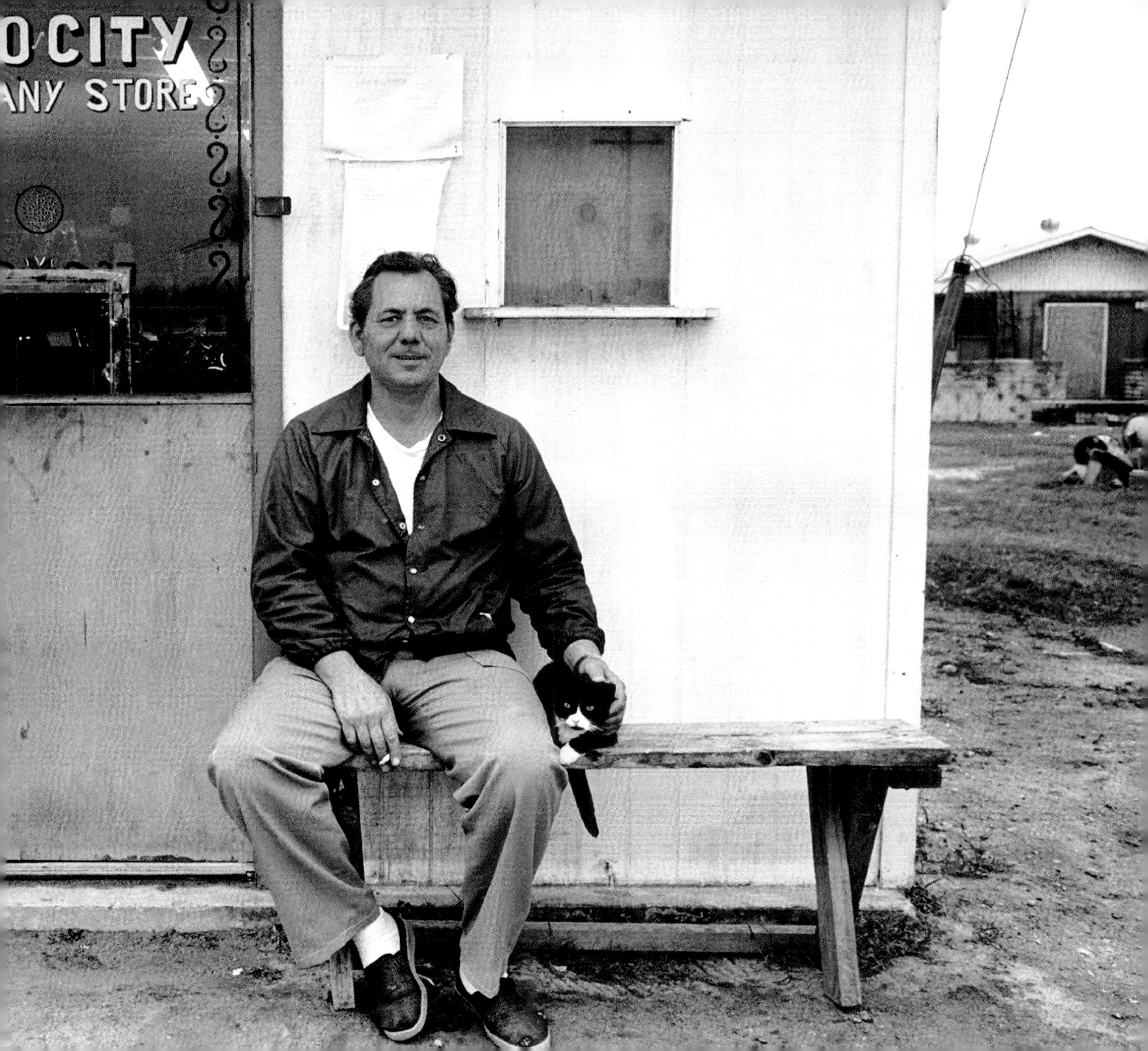
O CITY
ANY STORE

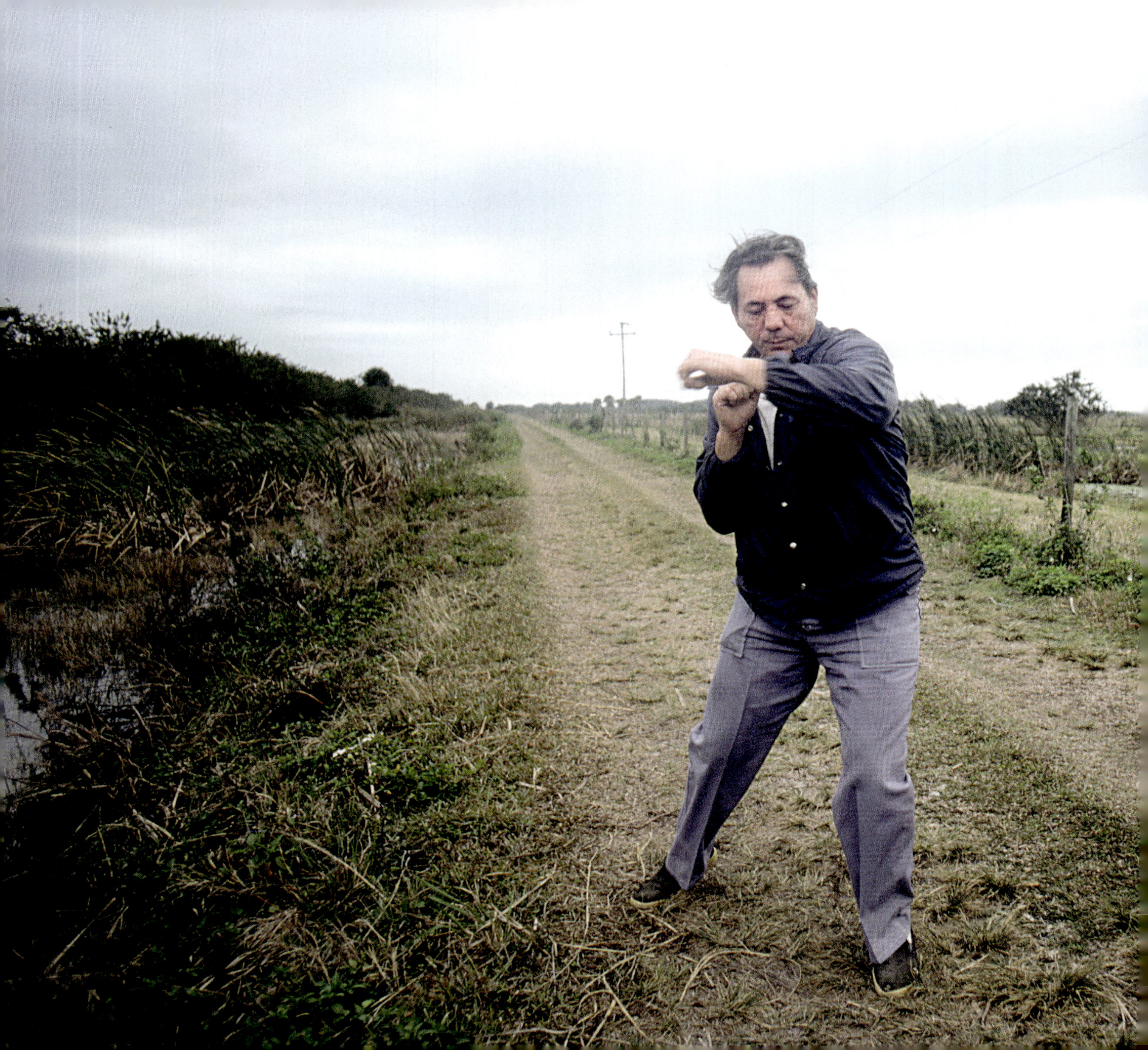

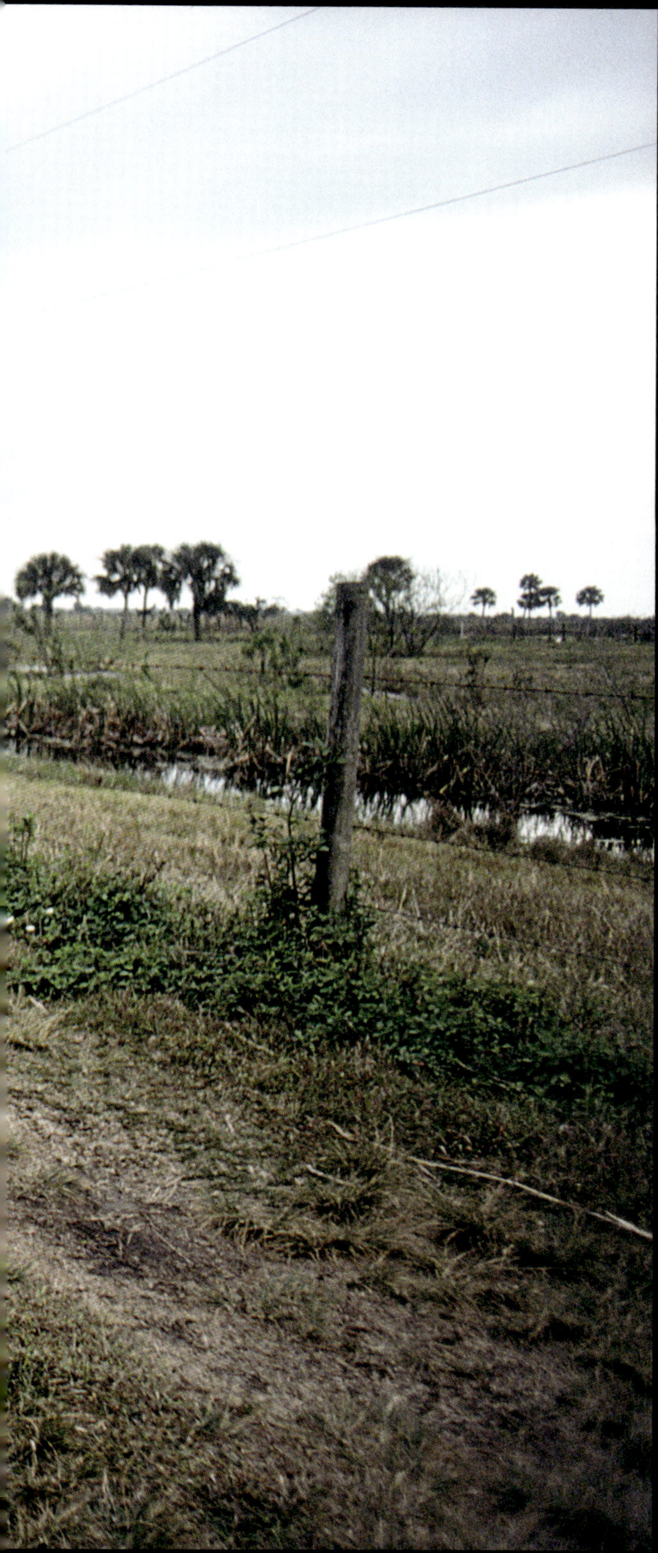

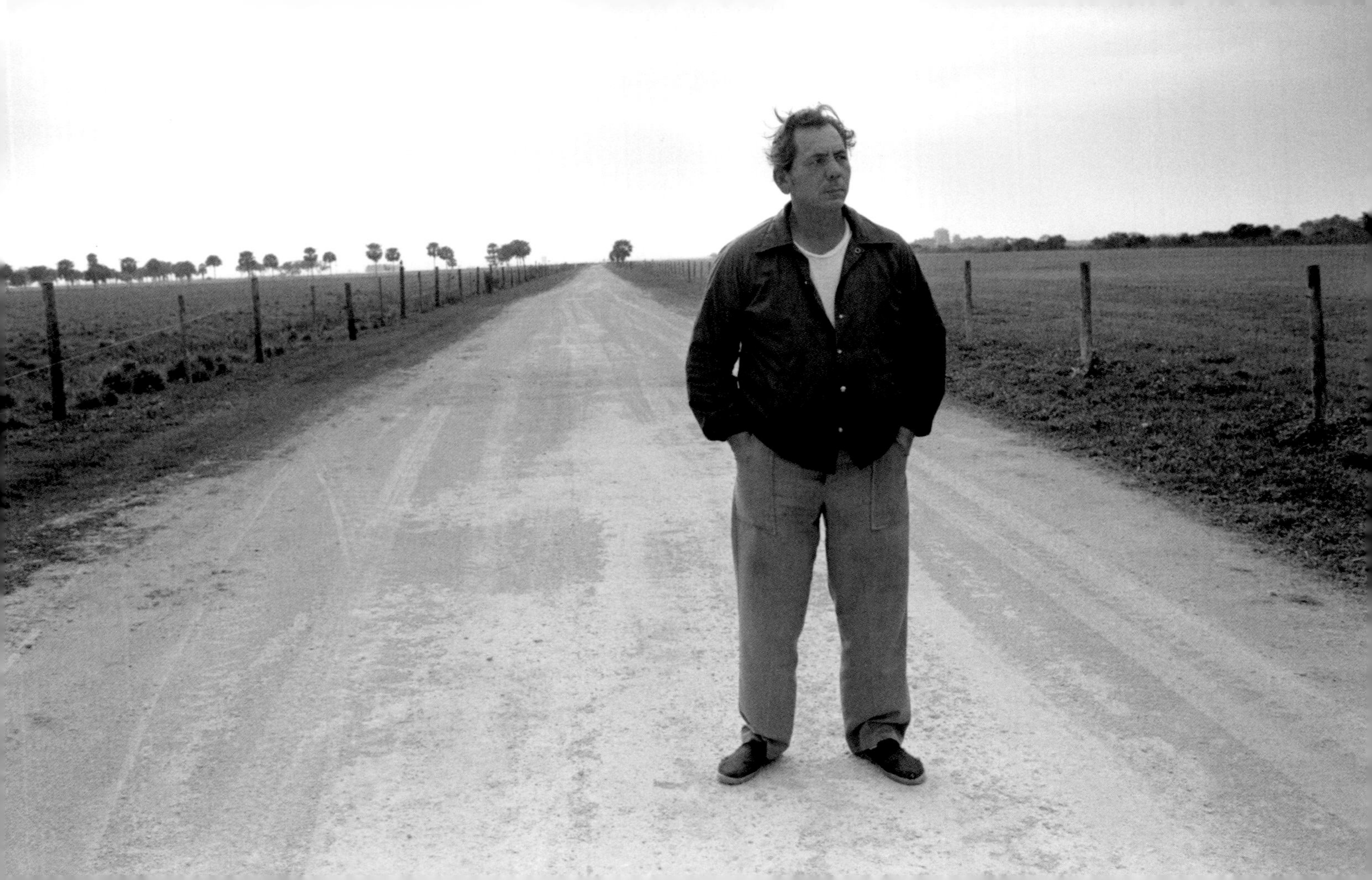

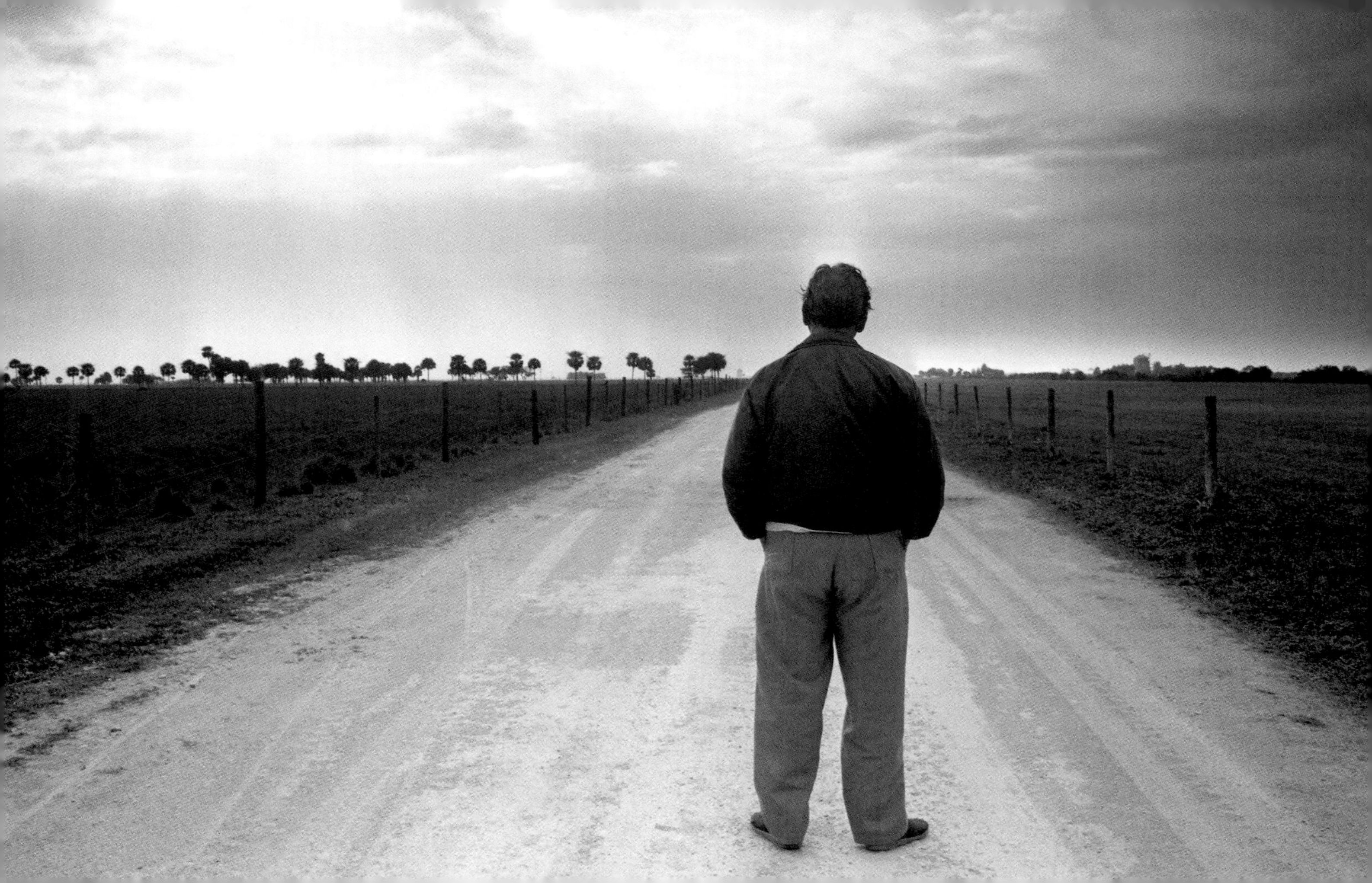

Donnie Fleeman

Fought Cassius Clay on February 21, 1961
RTD in the 6th round because of a rib injury

This was the first time Clay went over six rounds and the first time Fleeman had ever been knocked out. Fleeman retired after this fight.

"I had fought Pete Rademacher a few weeks before in Washington, and he had cracked my ribs and damaged my spleen. Clay was going to be one of my last fights anyway. I shouldn't have fought him, in fact, because the doctor said I shouldn't have been fighting anybody.

"I had 47 pro fights but I never really took fighting seriously. There was no money to be made. For Clay I got a guarantee of $3,000. I don't know what he got. It wasn't very much.

"I remember he was very fast and that he hit me with a right hand where it hurt me most. It seemed that he was well coached and knew just where I was having trouble. He moved real good and if he could have punched harder, he would have been a great fighter.

"Ali's business is fighting, and that's all he lives for. He's made boxing a big sport and he's the one who's put money into the sport. There was no money in it until he came along. Look at Joe Louis. He didn't make as much in his whole career as what Ali makes for just one public appearance.

"I'd have to say that even in politics he proved himself. He fought them all and they tried to throw him out of fighting. On Vietnam he had a point and he stood up for it. Maybe at that time I didn't think he was right, but times change, and he turned out to be right. He was a brave man."

Folklore has it that Fleeman's first opponent was a stubborn mule causing trouble at a local farm. Donnie KO'd him (the mule) in the first round.

Maintenance engineer, Dallas, June 10, 1980

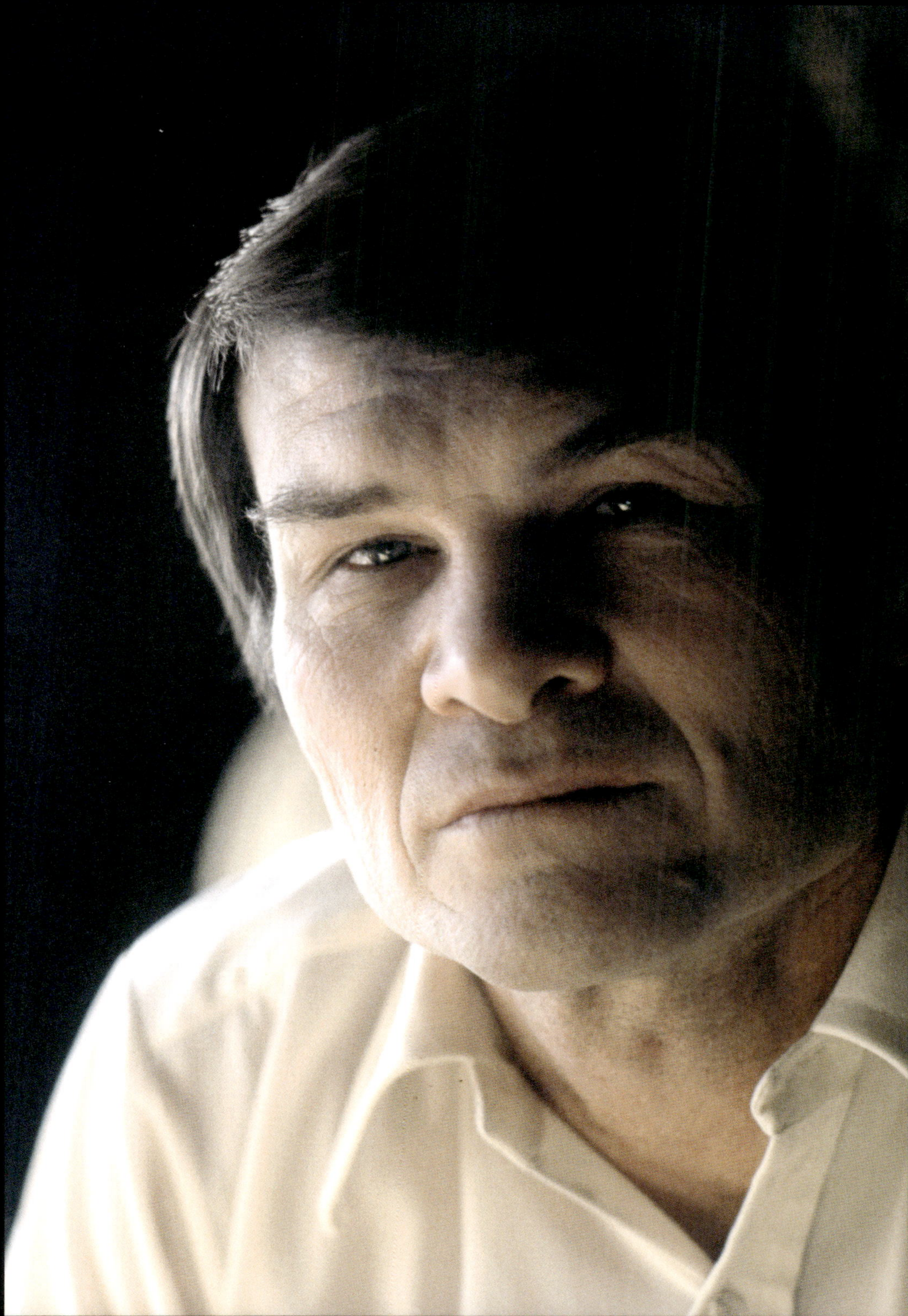

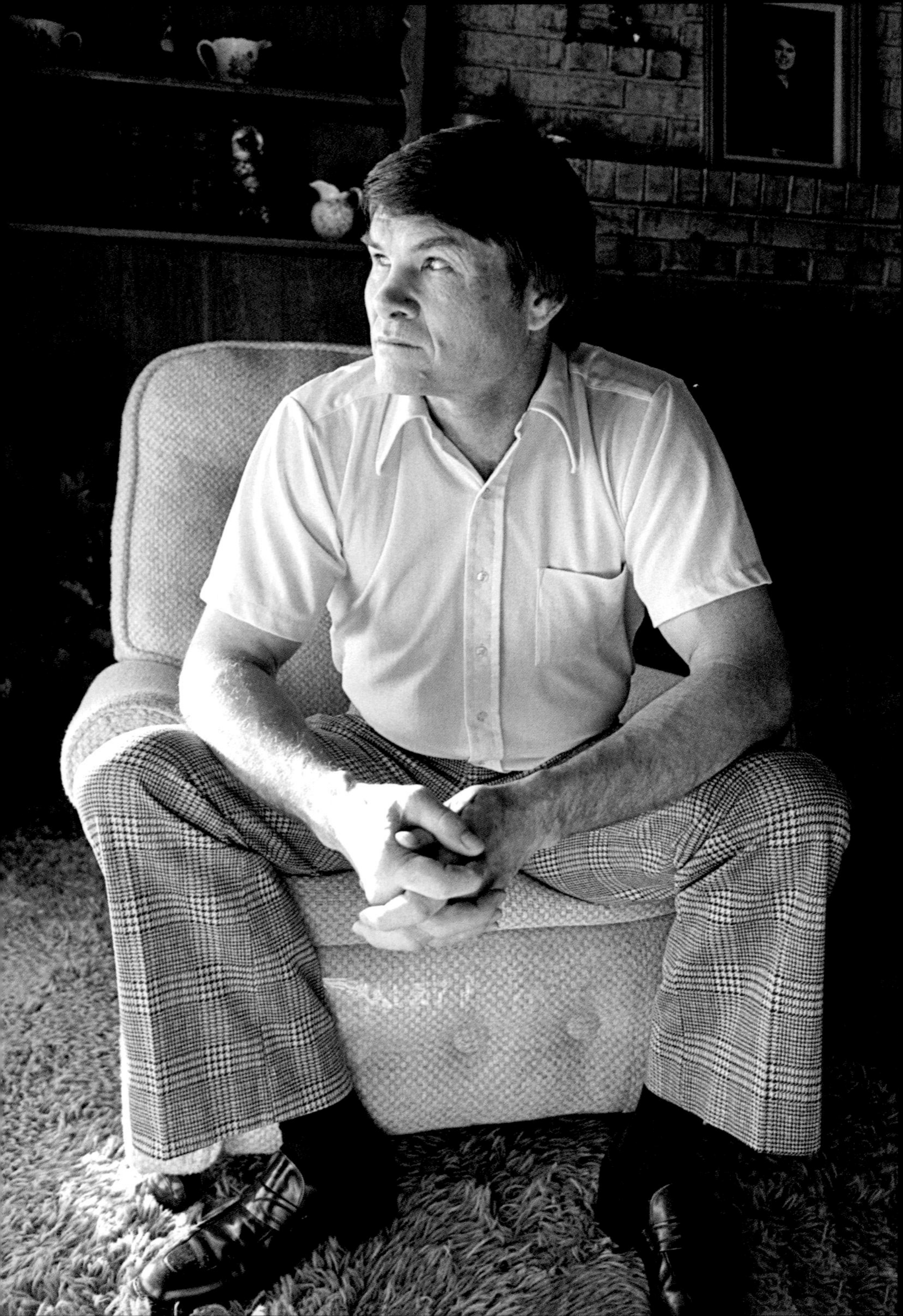

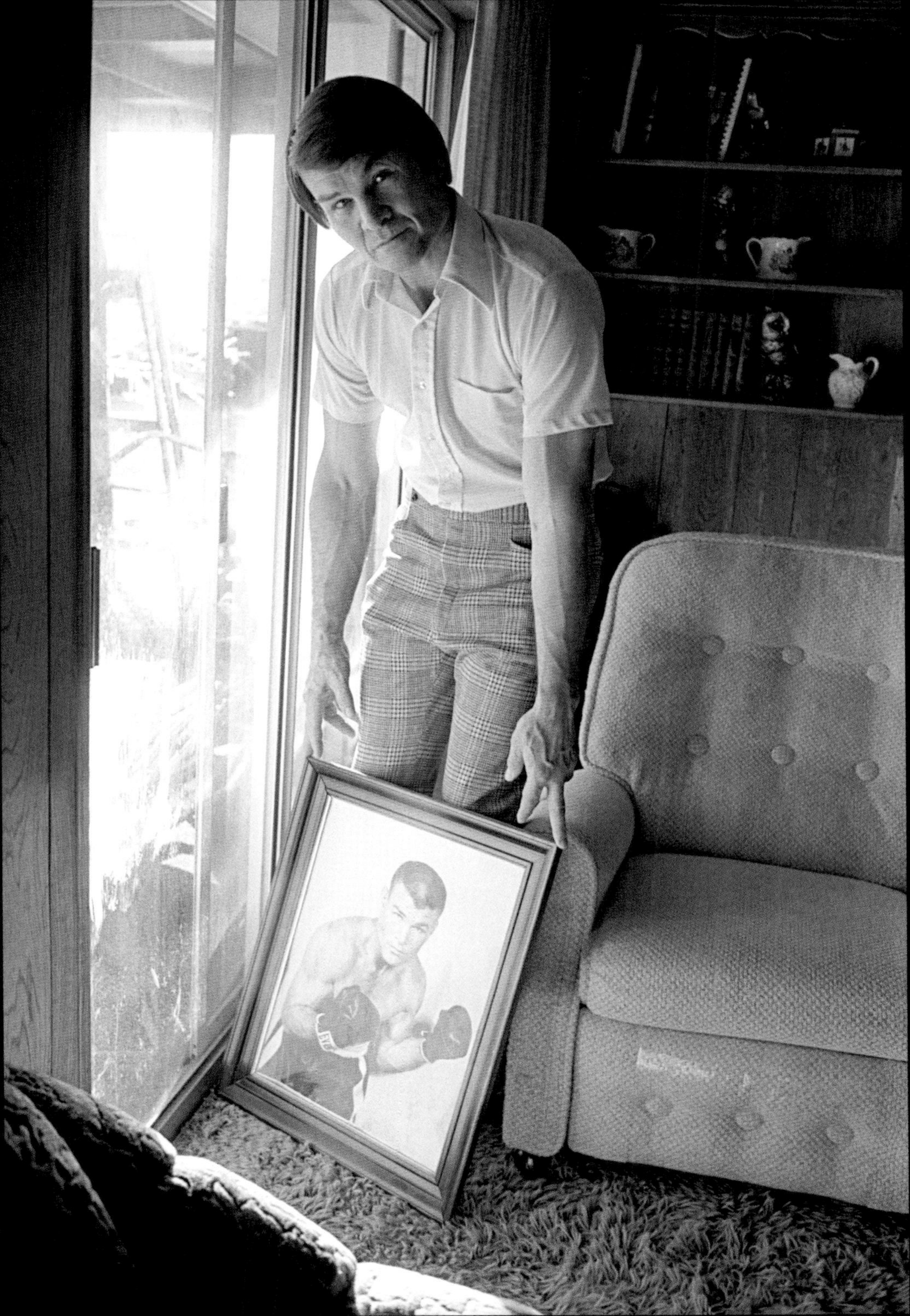

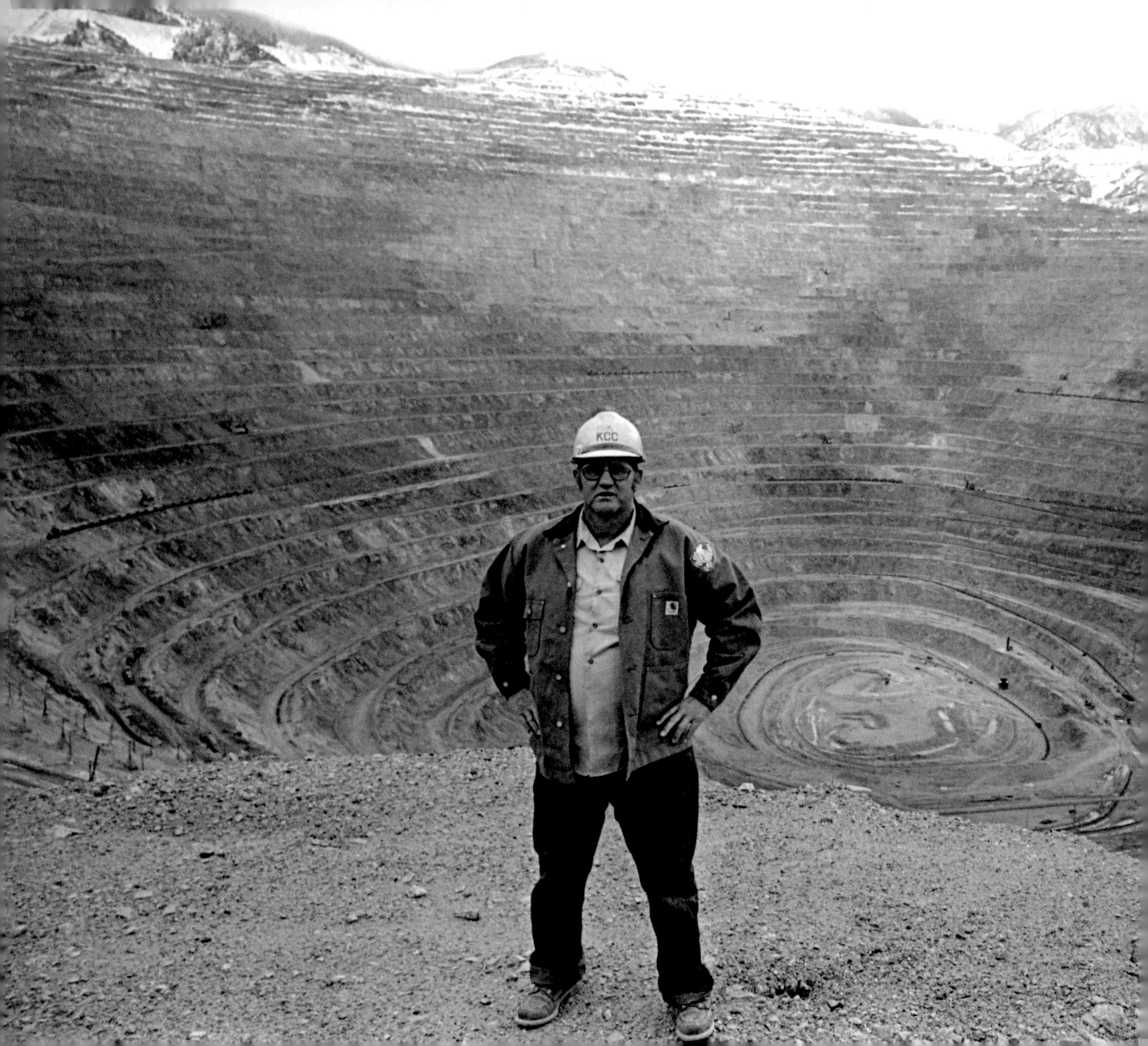
KCC

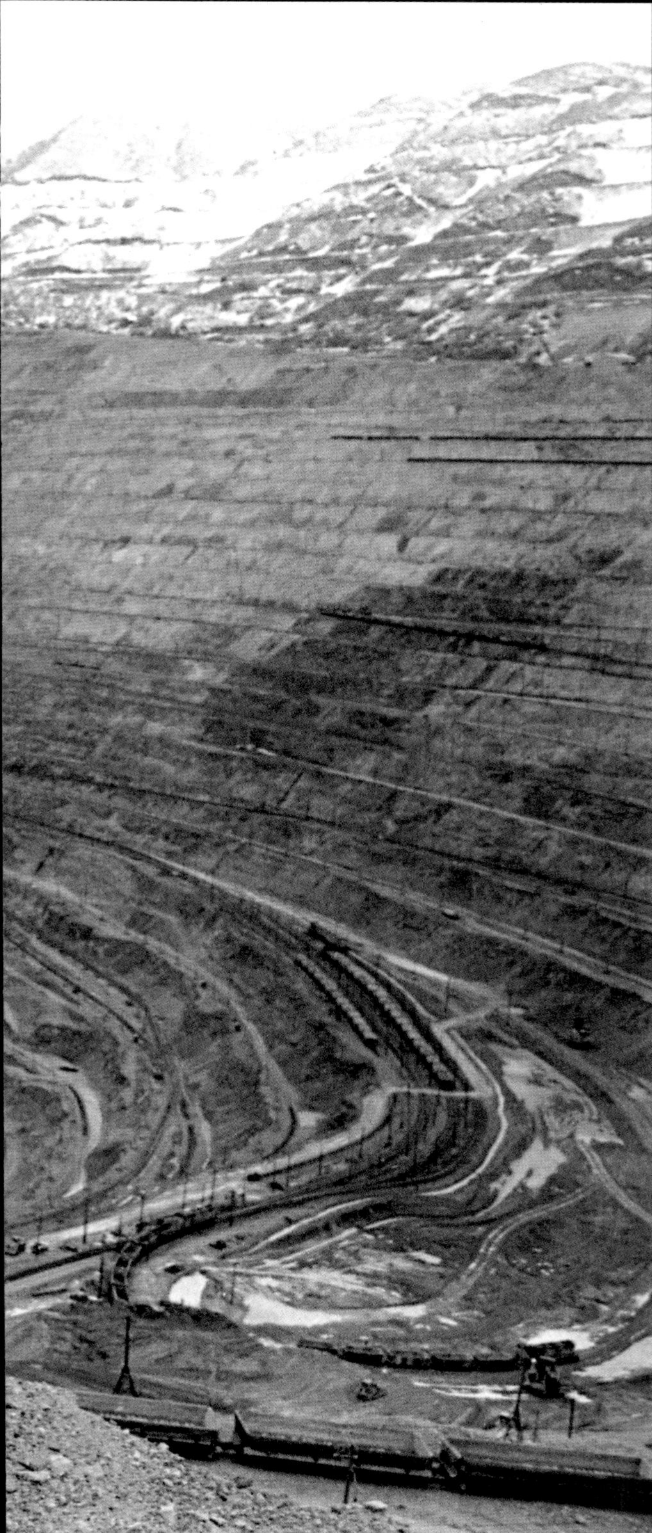

LaMar Clark
Clark fought Cassius Clay on April 19, 1961
Lost with a KO in the 2nd round and retired from boxing soon after

"I first met him at the weigh-in. He was as cocky as he is now. He gives the people a good show. He made up a poem about me and called me the 'Utah farmer.' Afterward he drove out to see me and said, 'LaMar, what I said wasn't to put you down or insult you, it was to create interest.'

"I had ideas about being the champion, if I had fought as a light-heavy-weight I think I would have been. But I was doing so much fooling around at that time … I wish I had married earlier. The first fight I ever had I was scared to death, but once I put my shoes on, everything was all right. My measurements were about the same as Rocky Marciano's. I had 51 pro fights, 45 KO's, two decisions and three losses, all by knockouts.

"Ali said before that fight that he was going to retire me and, in fact, it was my last fight. It only went two rounds. He caught me with a left and a right and broke my nose. There were tears in my eyes. When he came out to see me after the fight, he apologized for hurting me.

"I think he would make a good ambassador somewhere—he really has the gift of the gab that you need."

Mine gang boss, Salt Lake City, Utah, May 16, 1980
Special clearance was needed for me to be escorted down into the huge crater where they were mining. I was introduced to Mr. Clark, who was overseeing repairs with a crew of workmen in a blinding blizzard

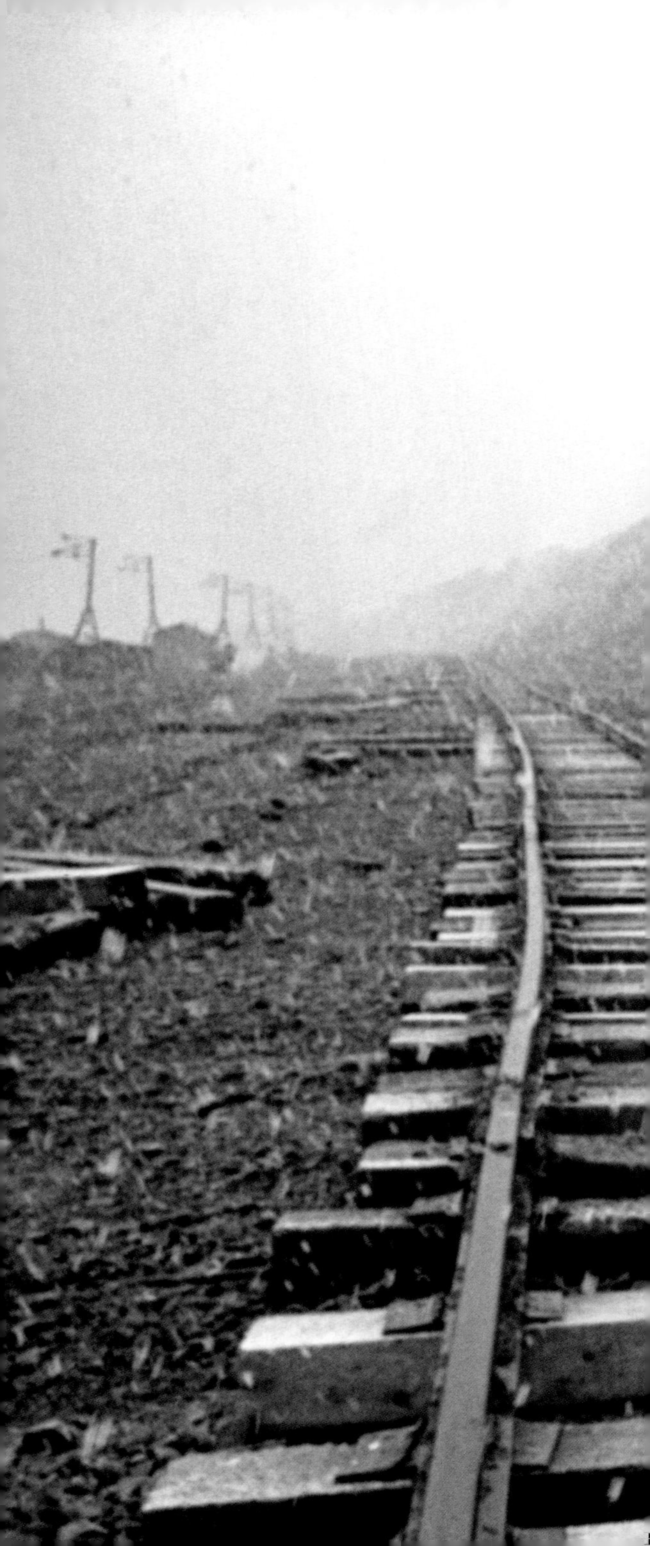

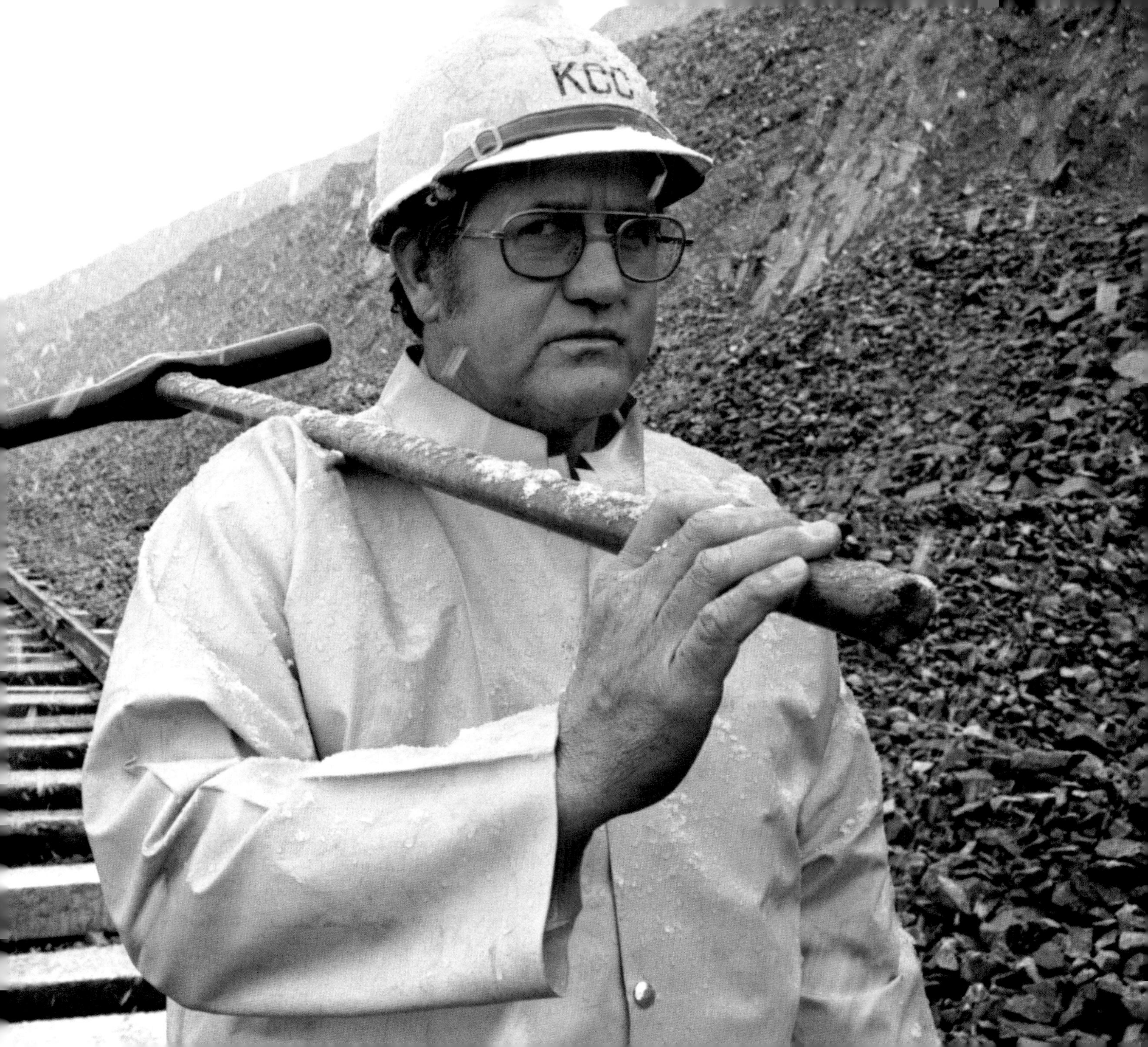
KCC

192 **Duke Sabedong**
Fought Cassius Clay in Las Vegas on June 26, 1961
Lost in a UD

"I never really knew Ali that well. The longest time we ever spent in each other's company was that 45 minutes in the ring. He kept saying, 'The big guy from Hawaii will go in four.' I was 6'7'' and when he saw me, he looked over at Angelo Dundee as if to say, 'What the hell do I do with this guy?' I was so much taller than him.

"I had trouble hitting him; he was very fast. I threw a couple of low punches just to let him know I was there. The first time I hit him low, his eyes went as big as saucers. I was going to bite his ear. You know when you are in the clinches you get the guy's ear between your teeth and give it a little tug, that usually would bring water to their eyes. Deep down, though, I never really had it to motivate myself to go into the ring and beat someone to a pulp. But I would walk 10 miles to get into a barroom brawl; I used to love it. I'm quite happy now. I'm not bitter about anything. I have a good wife, a good job, I'm in good health, I have a good life.

"I don't think Ali was the greatest I fought. Howard King, he was the best."

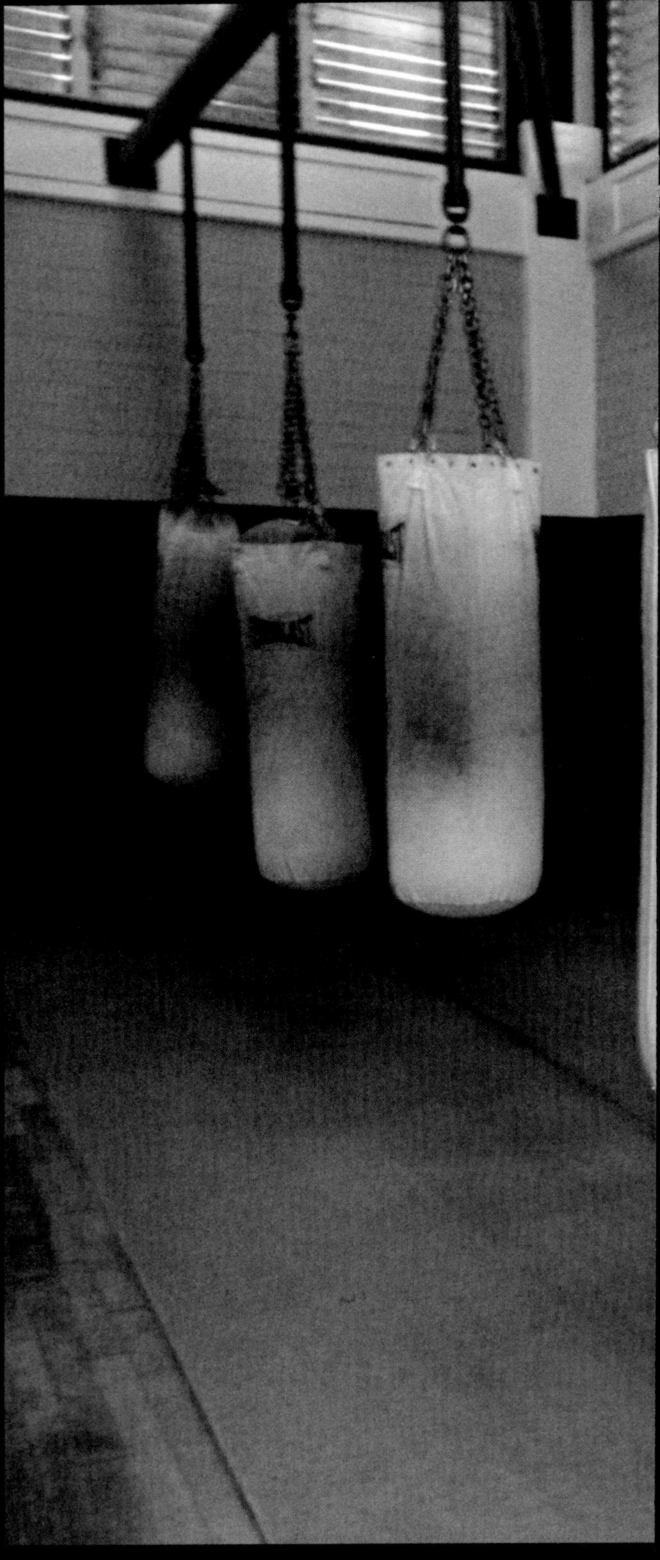

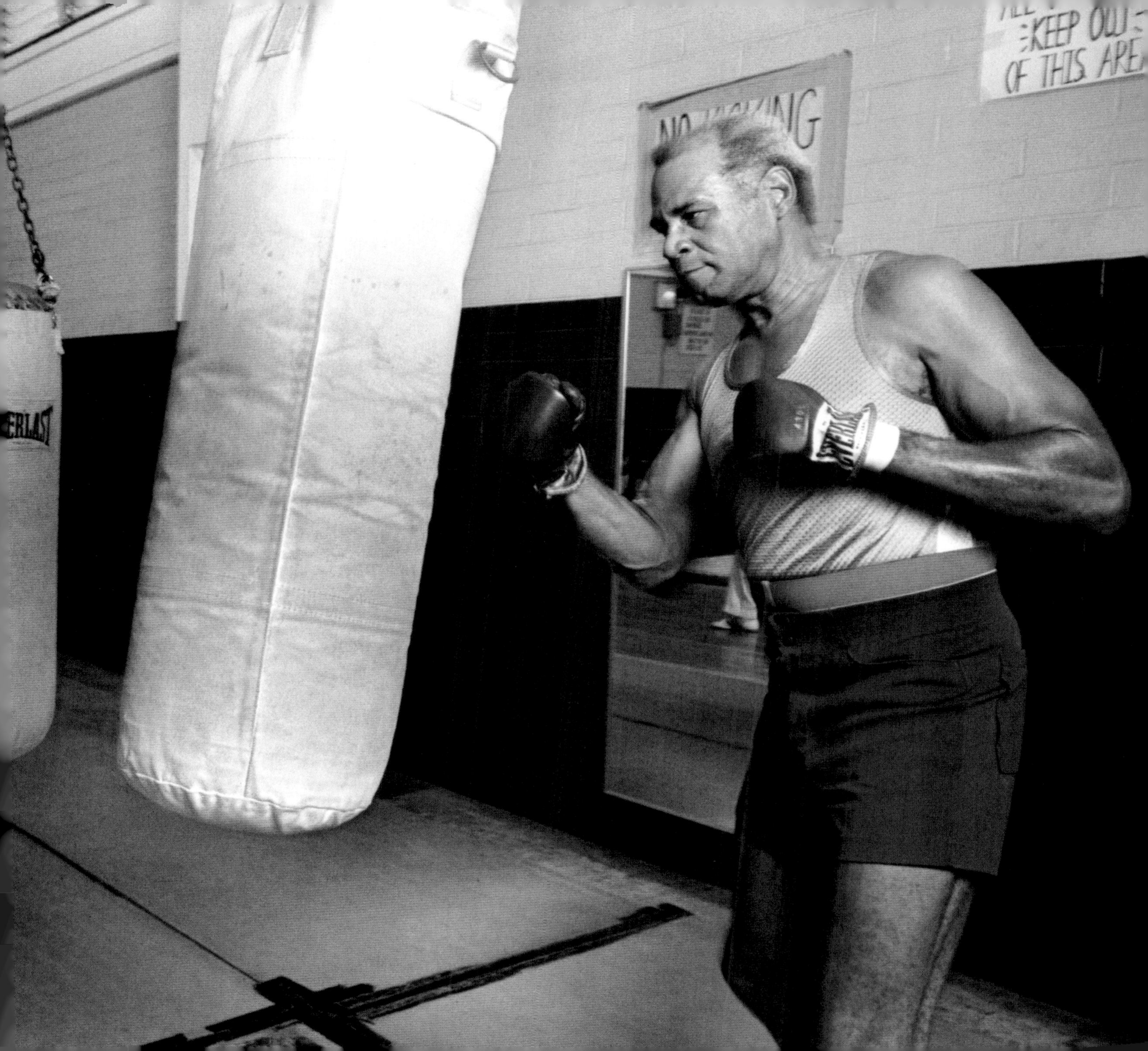
KEEP OU
OF THIS ARE

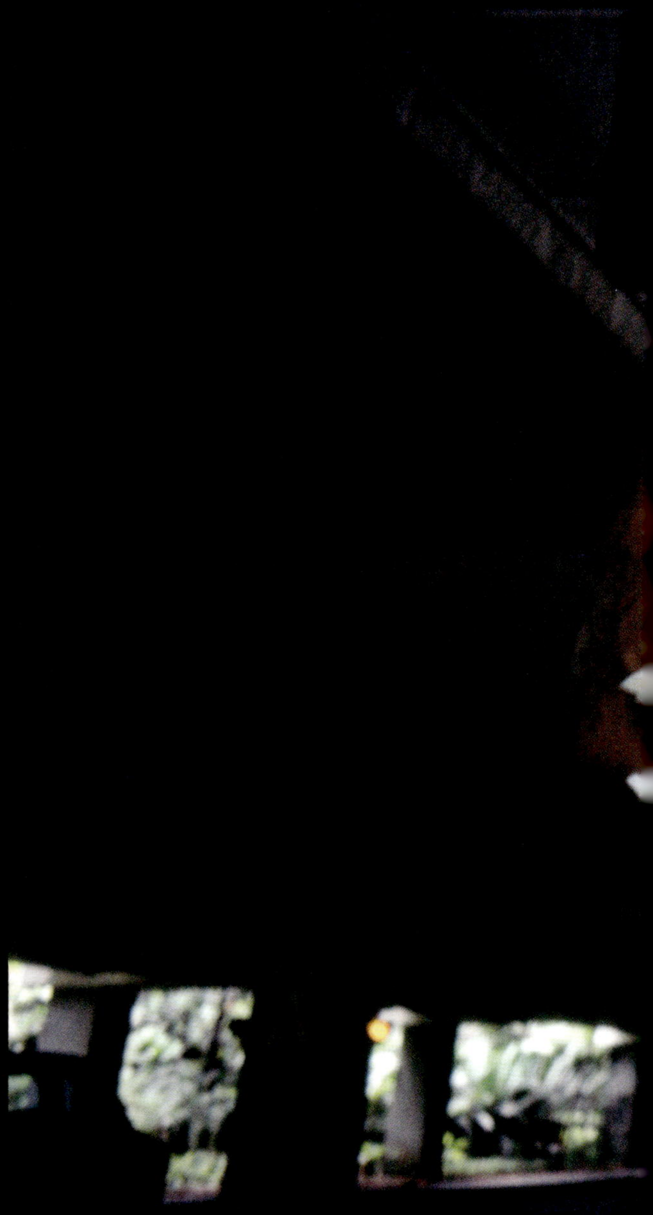

When I disembarked at the airport in Honolulu a very tall man was handing out leis to arriving tourists (I declined). After an hour on the phone at my hotel trying to locate Mr. Sabedong he turned up at the hotel still carrying the leis—the same gentleman who had greeted my arriving aircraft!

The ex-fighter chuckled when he reflected on how Ali had flown in from Chicago in the morning, given some interviews, made a couple of TV appearances, had his picture taken and returned to Chicago later that afternoon. Ali confessed to Sabedong, "I ain't too good at being on vacation in paradise. I'm better off hangin' with some brothers on a street corner in Chicago!"

Travel coordinator, Honolulu, Hawaii, June 7, 1980

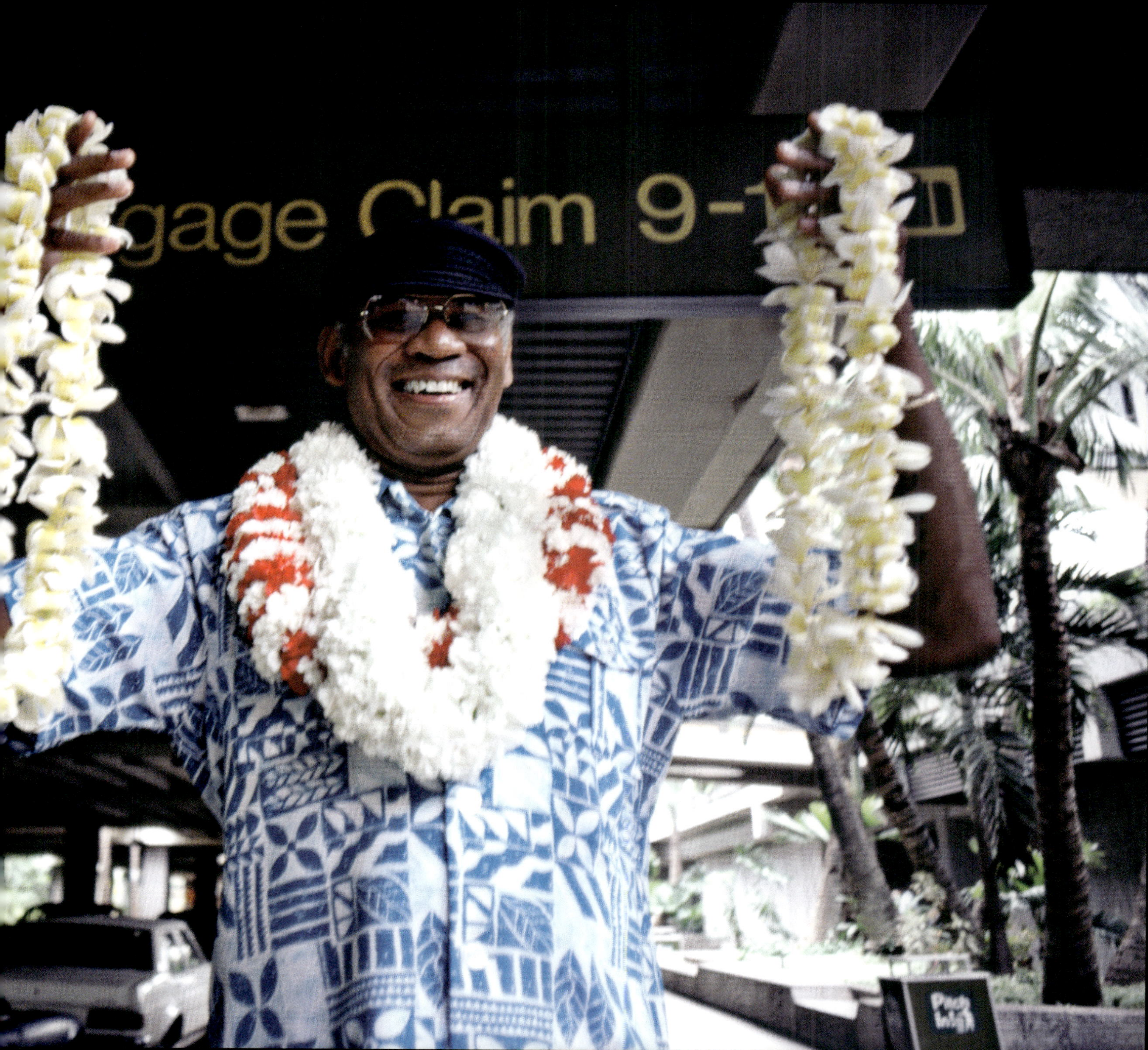
gage Claim 9-1

Alex Miteff
Fought Cassius Clay on October 7, 1961, in Louisville, Kentucky
Lost in a TKO in the 6th round

"He was a young kind who didn't have much to say. It was after he fought me that he started his predictions. I think back now and say to myself I have known two very great men. The first was the ex-President of my country, Argentina, Juan Peron, and the other is Muhammad Ali. He was no puncher, he didn't punch hard at all. But he had me on the canvas in the sixth round. The referee stopped the fight.

"I hated boxing. The managers and promoters treat you like a piece of meat. At home, in my country, there was just the manager and he was the trainer also. Here everybody is trying to get a slice of you. I thought that boxing was a good way of making some quick money. I didn't enjoy being punched on the head and risking permanent damage.

"Ali and I became friends after we fought. He and I were in a movie together. It was called *Requiem for a Heavyweight,* with Anthony Quinn. I was the double for Quinn and Ali was the guy who knocks him out. He was like a little kid, always asking for autographs. He even asked one of the stars, I think it was either Jackie Gleason or Mickey Rooney, to sign a $100 bill for him.

"Ali was right in making his stand against the war."

I found Alex Miteff hustling as a Limousine service owner outside Radio City Music Hall on Sixth Avenue in Manhattan, NYC, June 5, 1979

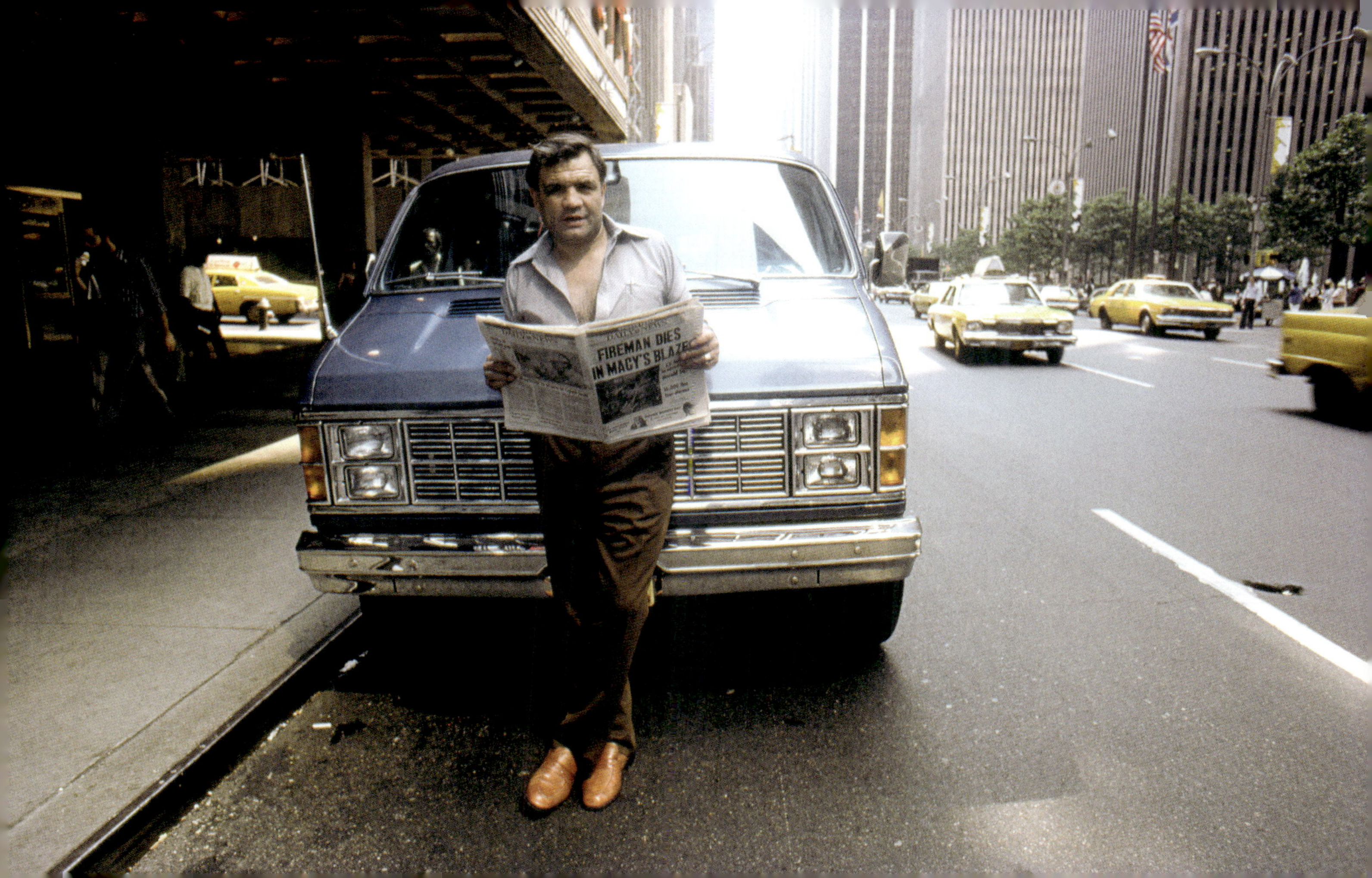
FIREMAN DIES
IN MACY'S BLAZ

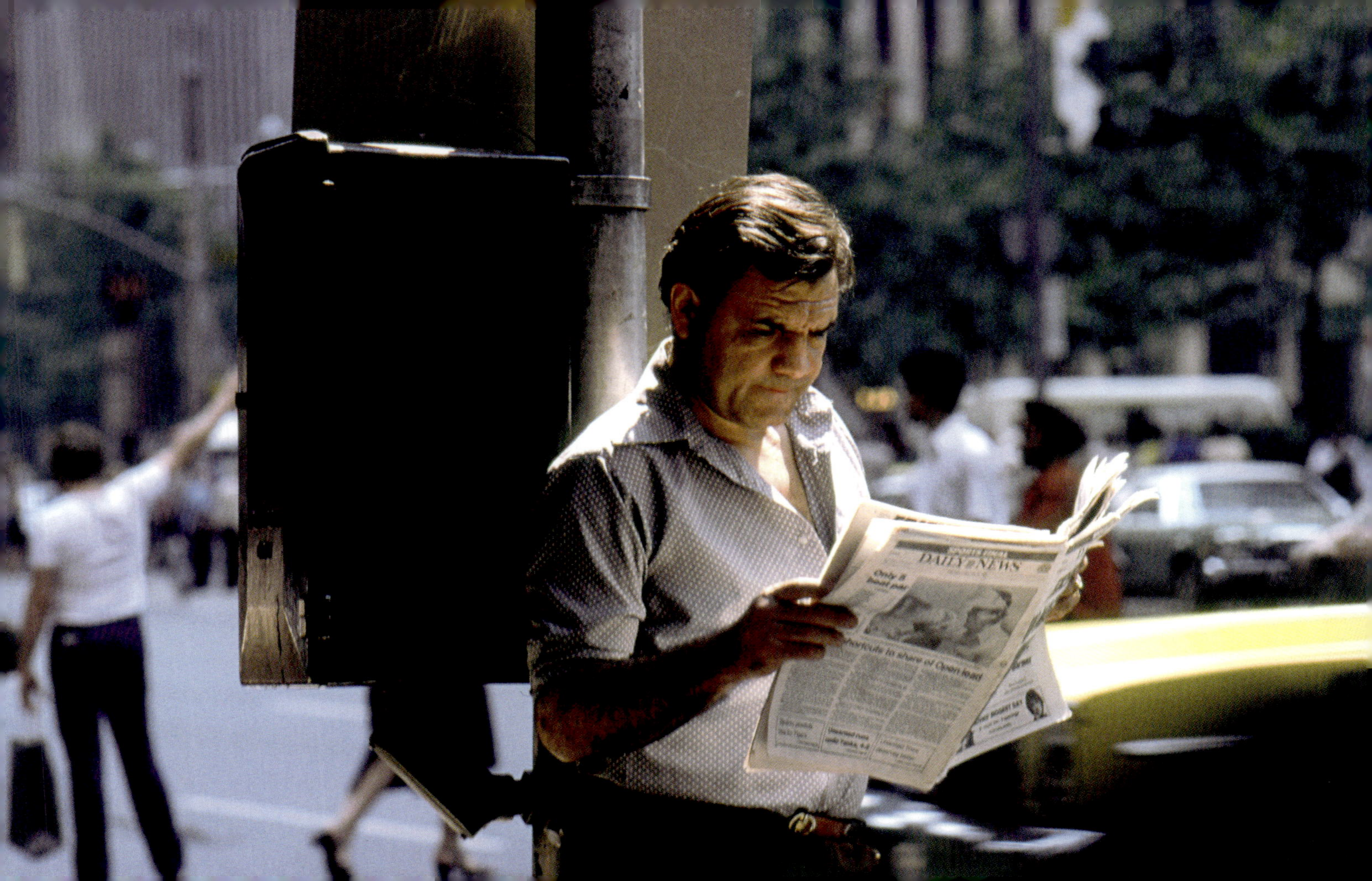
DAILY NEWS

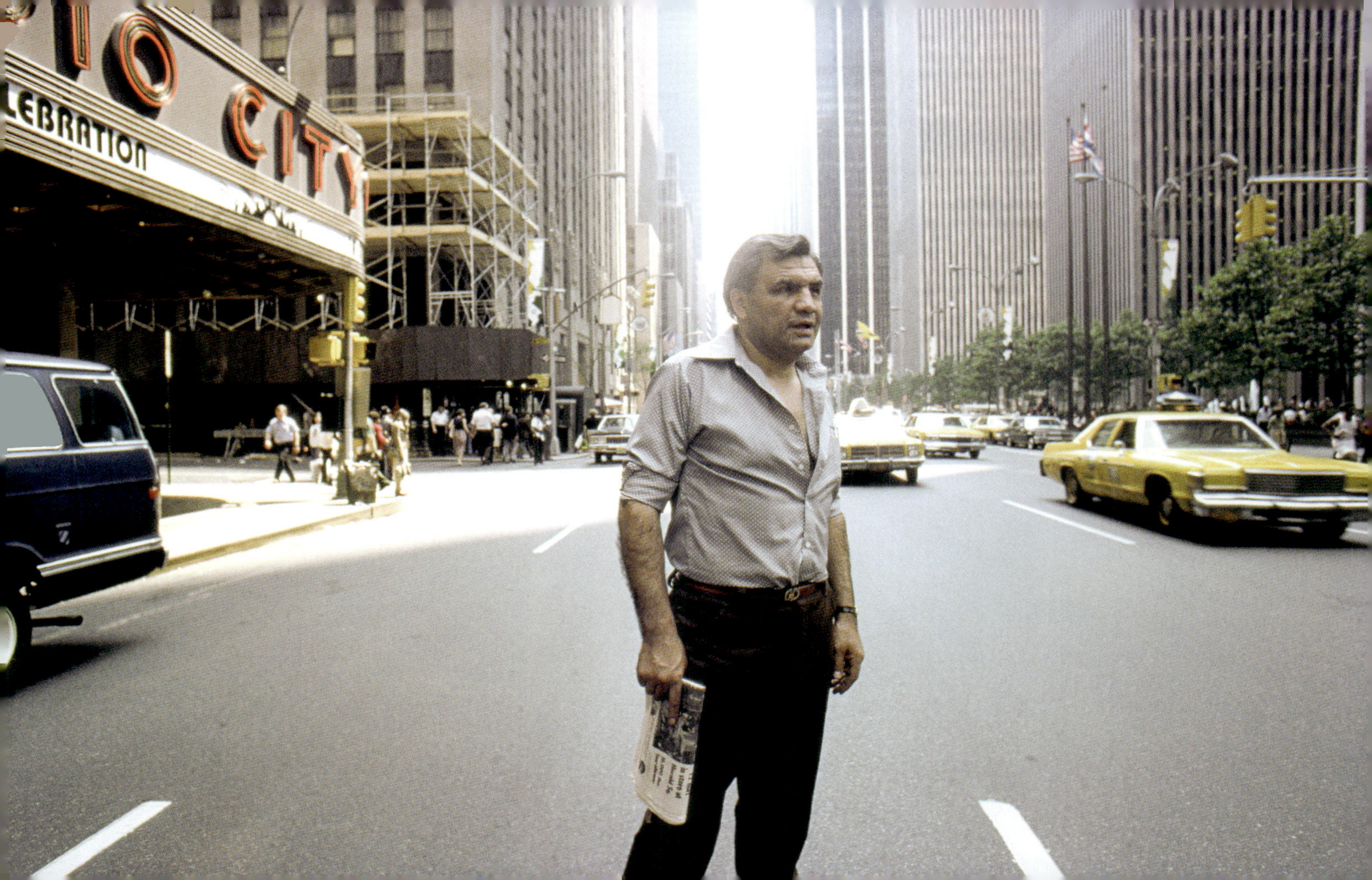
IO CITY
LEBRATION

Charlie Powell
Fought Cassius Clay at the Civic Arena in Pittsburgh on January 24, 1963
KO'd in the 3rd round

Prior to becoming a boxer, Powell played for the San Francisco 49ers for five seasons. At aged 19, he was the youngest player in NFL history.

Charlie Powell, September 1977

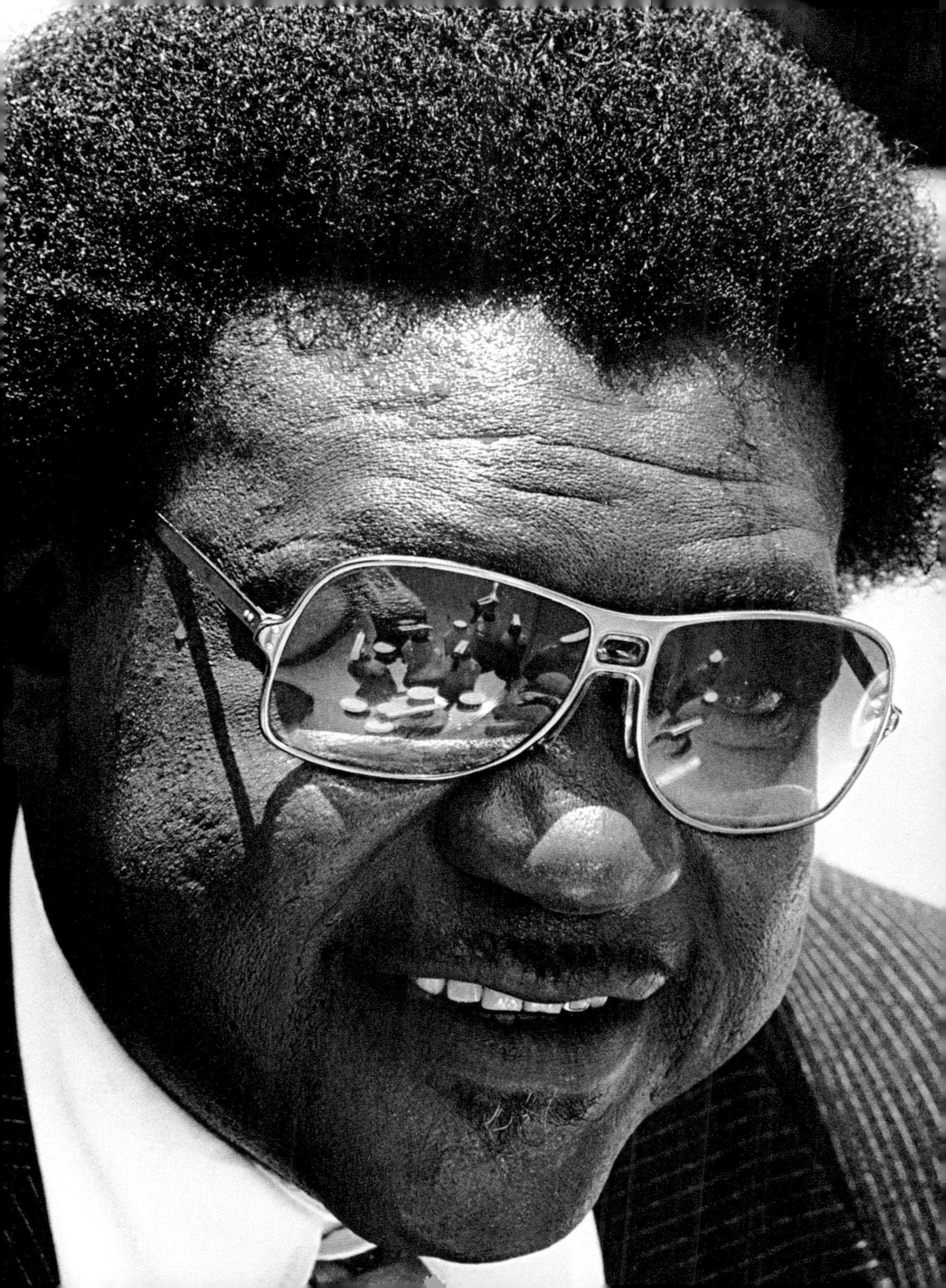

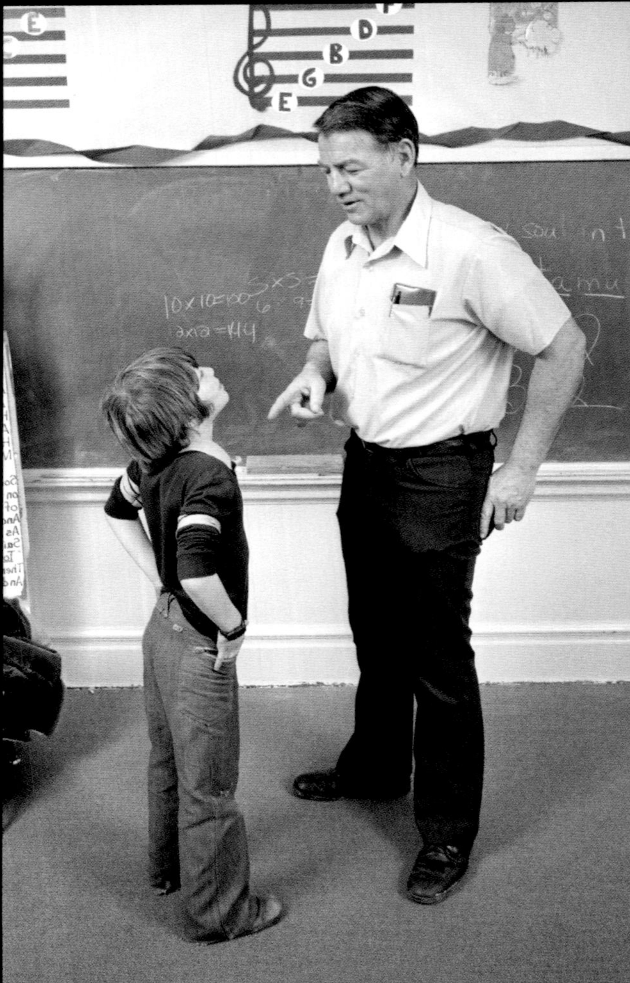

George Logan
Fought Cassius Clay on April 23, 1962 in Los Angeles, Ca.
Lost in a TKO in the 4th round

“I gave up fighting because I was turned off by the whole cotton-picking thing. Many times, some drunk would call me up in the middle of the night and say, ‘Hey, Logan, come on down here. I’ll whip your butt off.’

“If Ali had gone to fight for his country, there would be no question, no doubt, that he was the greatest.

“Sometimes a kid will ask me what I did before this job. I tell them I boxed against Muhammad Ali.”

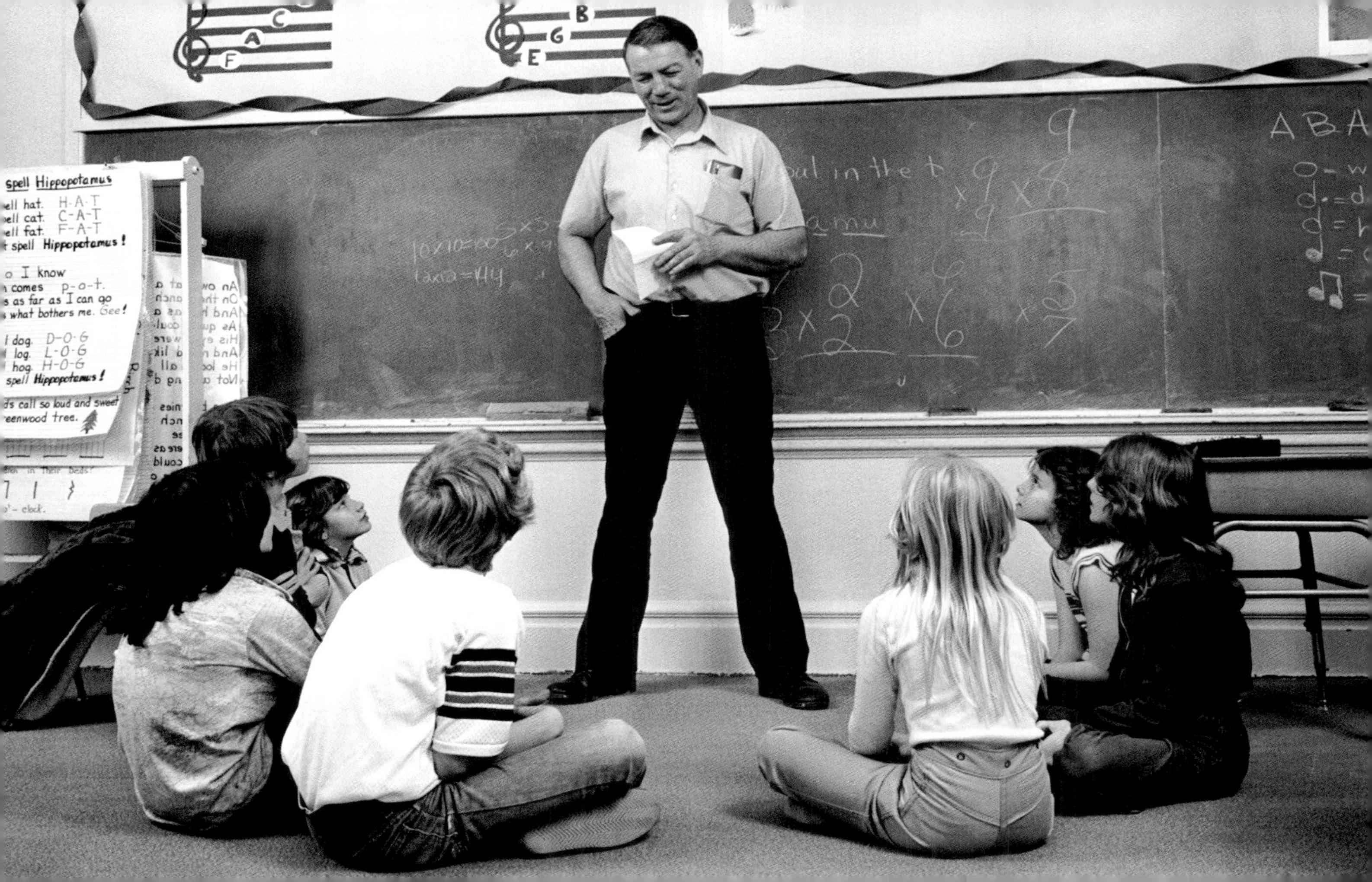
spell Hippopotamus
H-A-T
C-A-T
F-A-T
spell Hippopotamus!
I know
comes p-o-t.
as far as I can go
what bothers me. Gee!
dog. D-O-G
log. L-O-G
hog. H-O-G
spell Hippopotamus!
call so loud and sweet
10x10=100
ABA

Henry Cooper
Fought Ali twice:
Non-title fight (when he was still called Cassius Clay), 1963 at Wembley Stadium; lost in a TKO
1966 at Arsenal Football Stadium, Highbury, London; lost in a TKO

"In the first of our two fights, I hit Clay with a genuine left hook with all my power behind it. He fell on the ropes and slid gently to the canvas. There was a count of five, and the bell went.

"There was panic in his corner. Suddenly they found Clay had a split glove. By the time the referee had been called over and they tried to find a spare pair of gloves, easily half to three-quarters of a minute had gone by. Half a minute to a fit guy is a lifetime.

"They started the fifth round with Clay wearing the split glove. With the second or third punch he caught me in the eye and it started to gush blood. If he had wrapped sandpaper around his gloves, he couldn't have done better with an eye like mine.

"He told me later, 'You're not as dumb as you look. I have never been hit so hard in my life.' Afterwards he always admitted that it was the finest punch that ever hit him.

"Of the great fighters he was definitely one of the top five. Not the greatest, but surely right up there with the Dempseys and Marcianos."

Cooper as a company director, London, November 28, 1978
While posing for pictures, Cooper remarked, "Blimey, you want me to wear that titfer? I'm going to look a right idiot!" 'Titfer' (tit for tat) is cockney rhyming slang for hat!

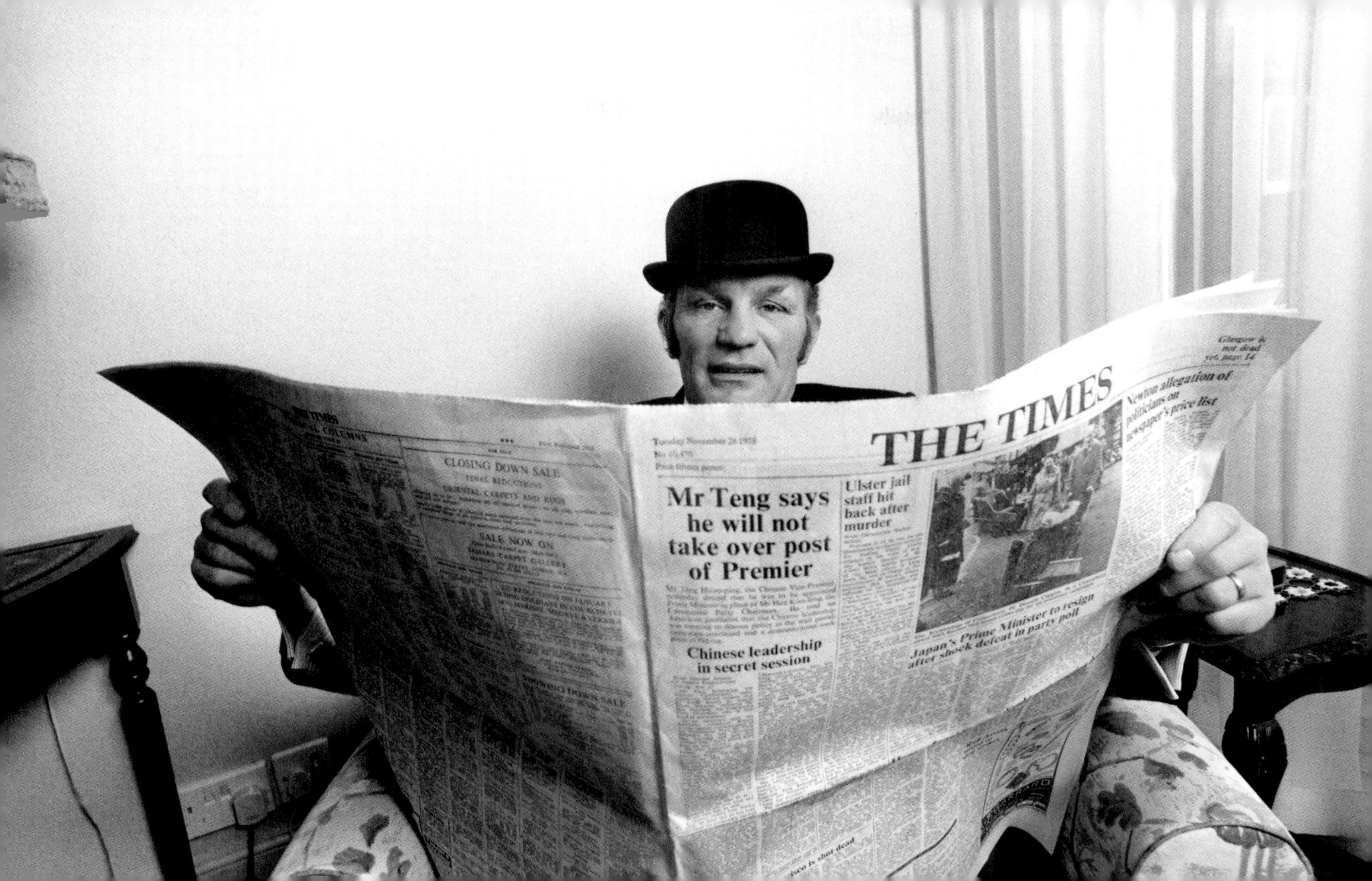

THE TIMES
Mr Teng says he will not take over post of Premier
Chinese leadership in secret session
Ulster jail staff hit back after murder
Japan's Prime Minister to resign after shock defeat in party poll
Newton allegation of politicians on newspaper's price list
Glasgow is not dead yet, page 14
CLOSING DOWN SALE
SALE NOW ON

Buster Mathis
Fought Ali on 17 November 1971 in Houston
Lost over 12 rounds, knocked down four times

"I thought he was a terrific person, the biggest b.s. artist in the whole world. He kept saying, 'I'm gonna do to Buster what the Indians did to Custer.' That was O.K., he was just drumming up publicity and boosting the ticket sales. He kept telling me how he was going to beat me. He kept chastising me, it does play on your mind.

"I fought the hell out of him. He had me down in the 11th and 12th rounds. He hit me with some good shots, but he's not a great puncher; he didn't hurt me. Joe Frazier was the hardest puncher I ever met. Joe could hit you on your big toe and knock you out. After the fight, Ali told me not to quit because I was a good fighter, the fastest he ever fought.

"But now I try to stay away from boxing because it bothers me. I 'almost' went to the Olympics but I was injured… I was 'almost' World Heavyweight Champion… Those things still haunt me. I guess it's all water under the bridge. I have come a long way from where I started from. I was from a poor family. I was marked for prison. I'm pretty proud of myself.

"Ali, he wakes up every morning with his money. Me, at 4am I'm loading trucks just to get by."

Buster Mathis died of a heart attack in 1995.

Truck loader, Grand Rapids, Michigan, July 7, 1979

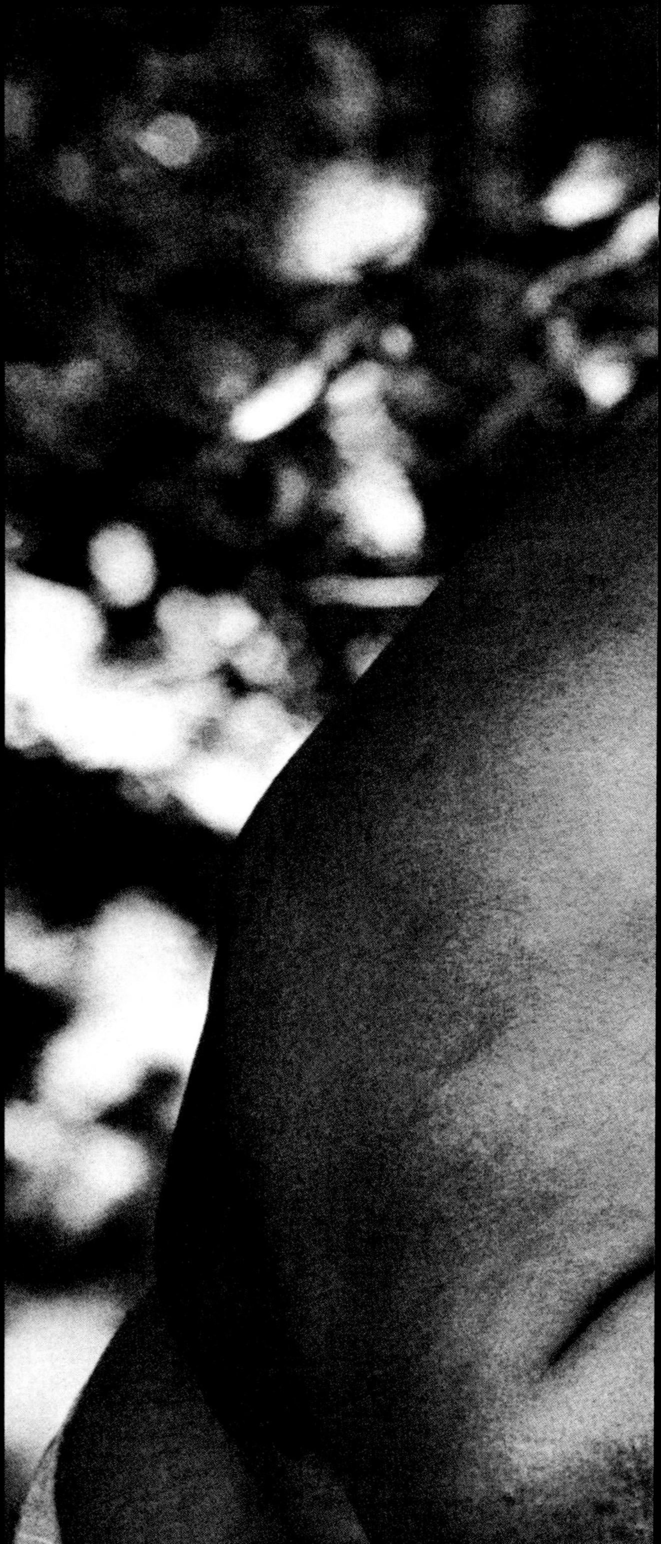

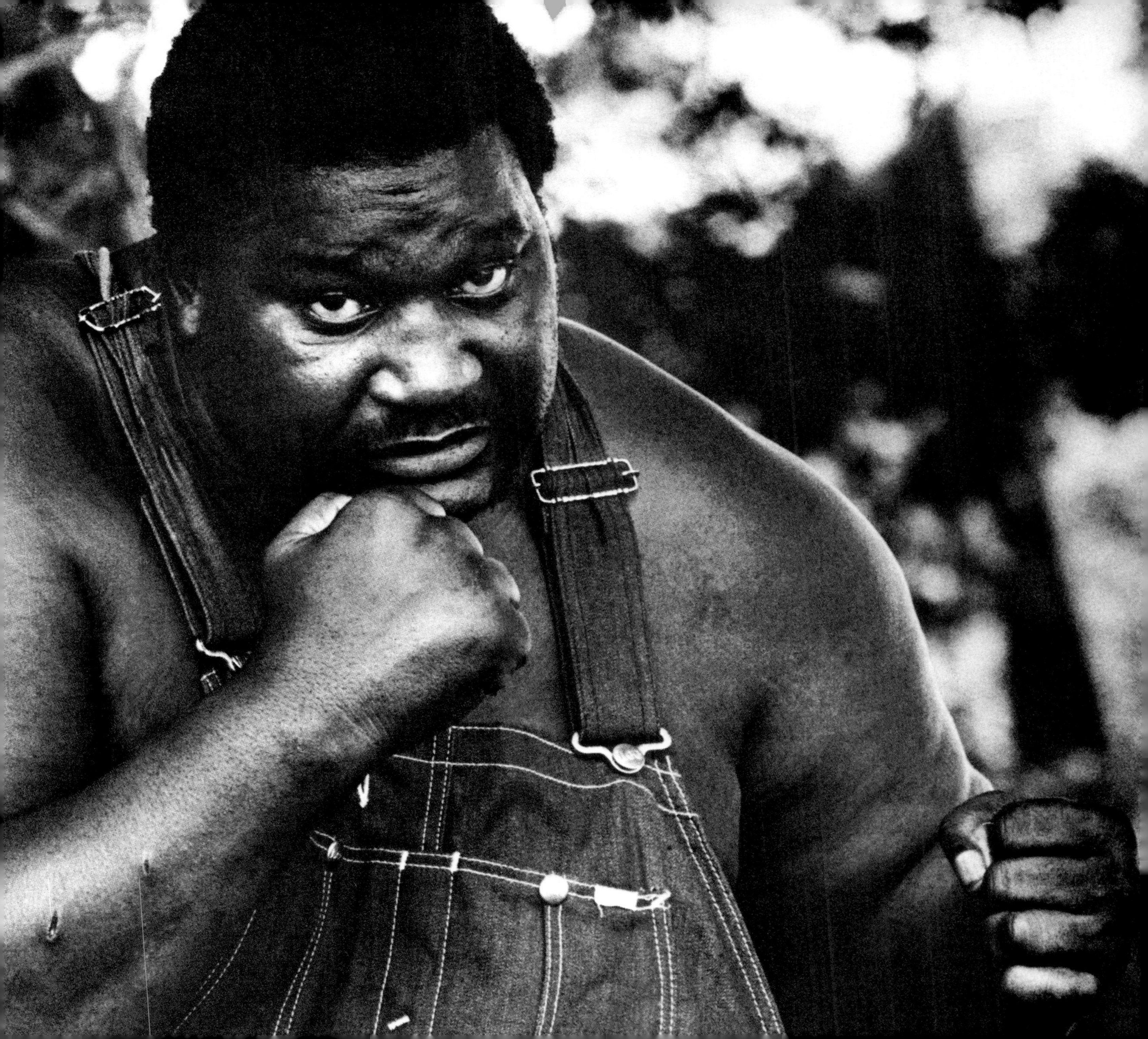

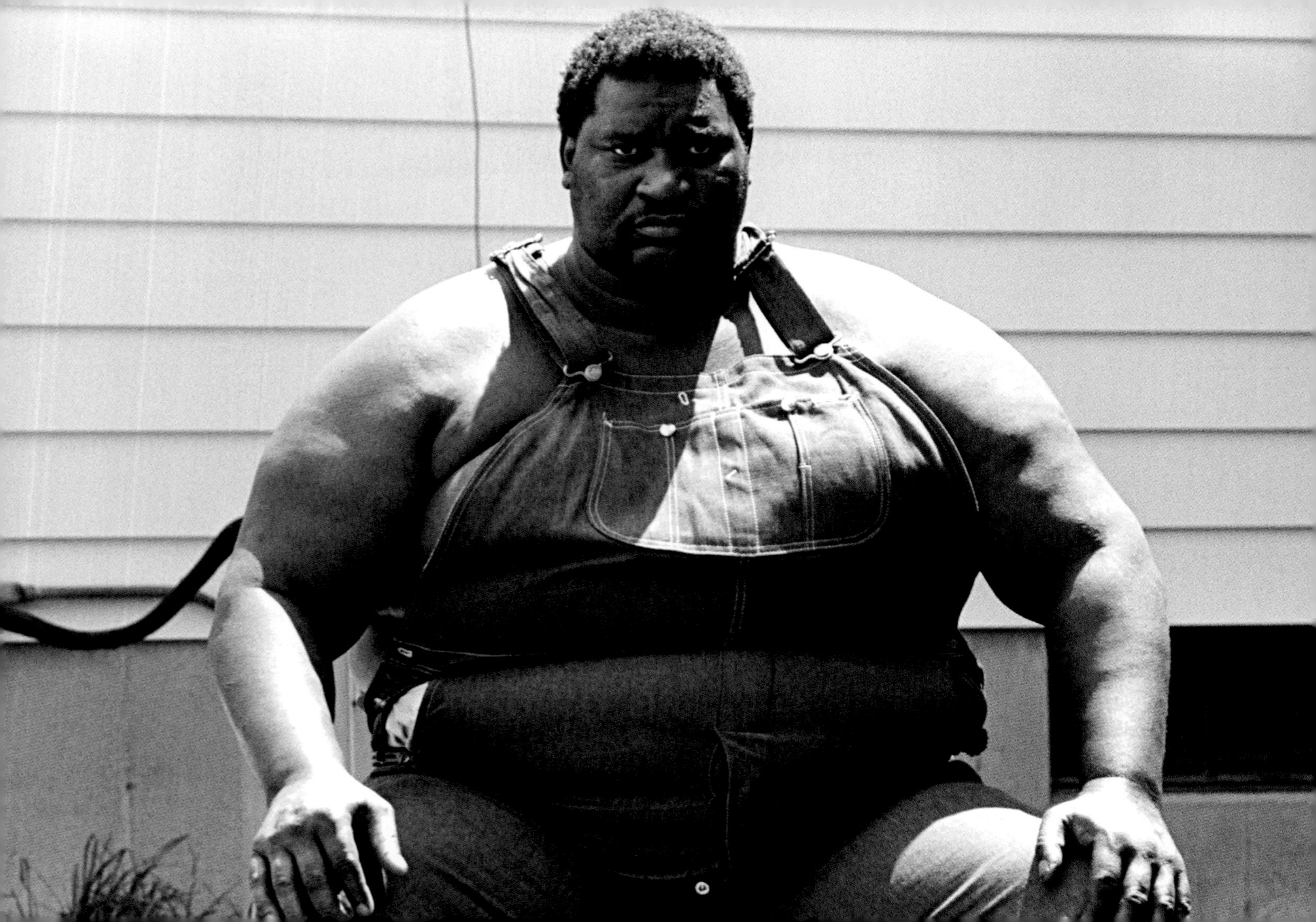

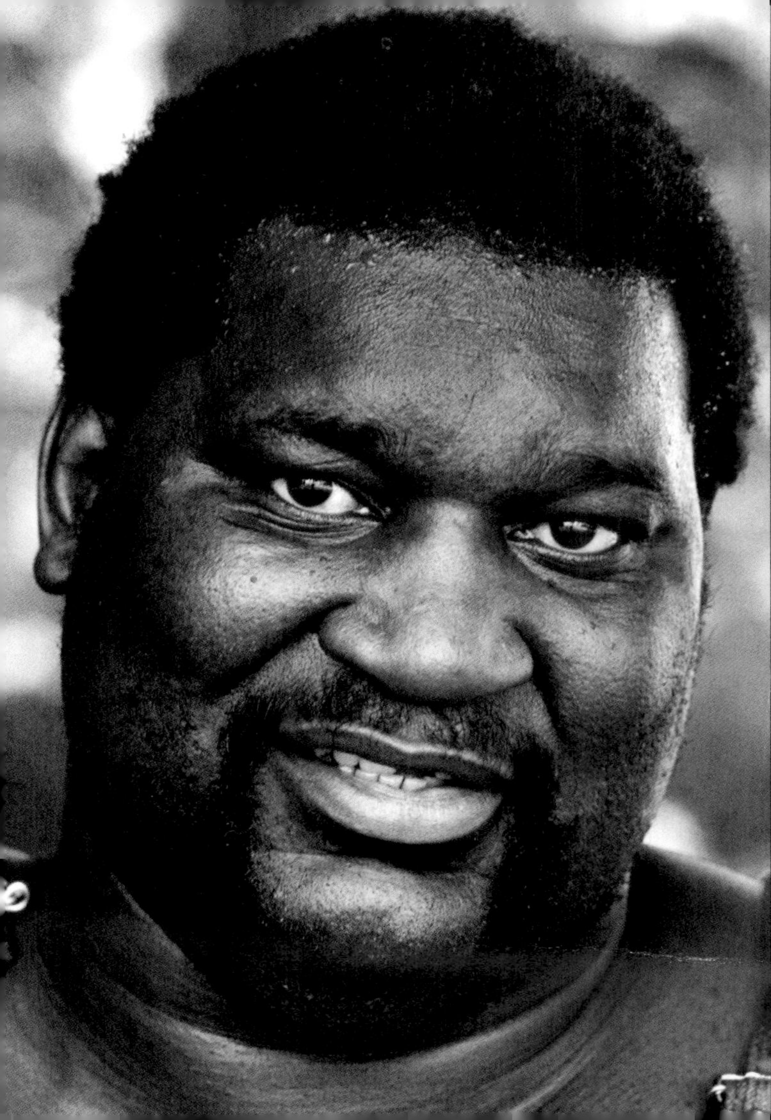
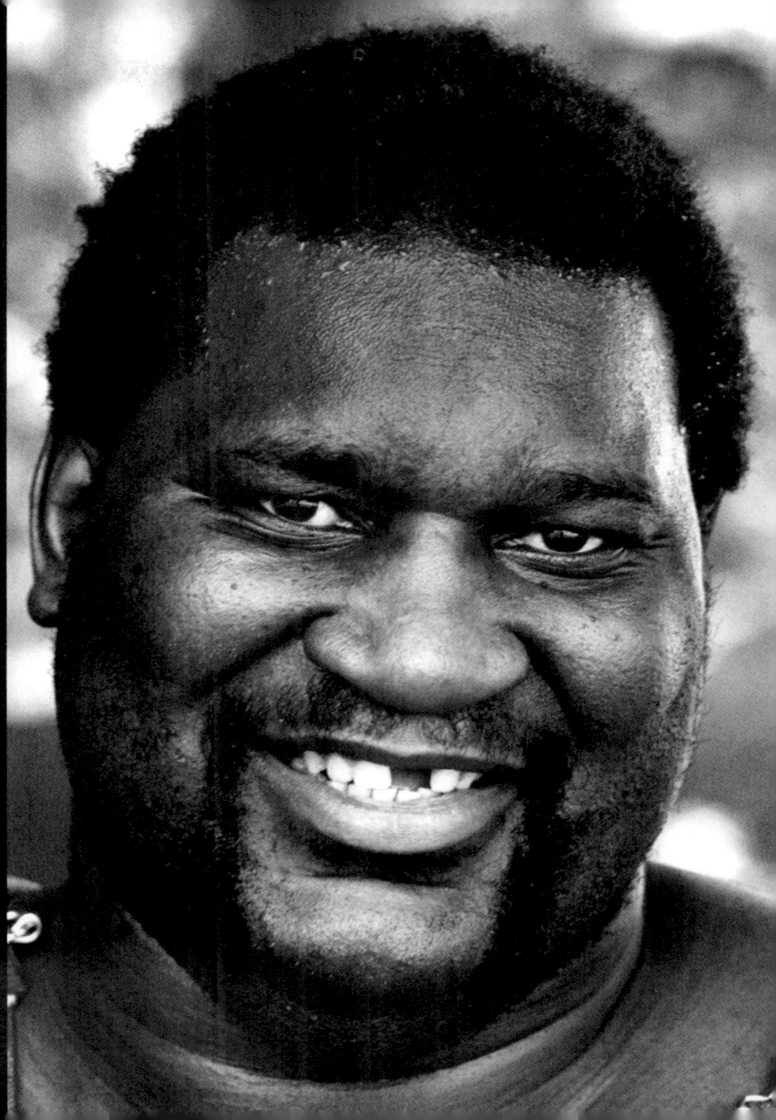

"Sweet Jimmy" Robinson
Fought Cassius Clay on February 7, 1961
Lost by a KO in the first round

"There's only been one sighting since then. In 1979, a photographer shooting pictures for *Sports Illustrated* went to find Ali's earliest opponent. Michael Brennan located Jim Robinson, who people down in Miami called 'Sweet Jimmy.' Most of what's known about his life comes from a brief blurb that ran with the photos. He lived off veteran's benefits. He claimed he was born around 1925. He claimed he was wrongfully convicted of armed robbery. Most days, he just hung out in the seedy Overtown neighborhood, at the pool hall owned by Miami concert promoter Clyde Killens.

"The photos show a haunted man. His jaw juts out, like he's lost teeth. His eyebrows are bushy; once, they probably seemed delicate. A visor throws a shadow across his eyes. A deep scar runs along his left cheekbone. In one, he leans up against the wall of a Winn-Dixie. In another, he walks down railroad tracks, the skyline of Miami rising behind him. He never smiles.

"Brennan shot the photos on a Friday night and Saturday morning. Sweet Jimmy smelled of booze and Camel cigarettes. Brennan remembers the last time he saw him. It was in the morning, on the railroad tracks, and he slipped the old fighter 20 bucks. Sweet Jimmy turned and walked off, negotiating the crossties. He never looked back.

'Tell Clay I ain't doing too good,' he said."

Wright Thompson, *ESPN* magazine

Welfare recipient living in cheap hotels, Overtown, Miami, Florida, November 9, 1979

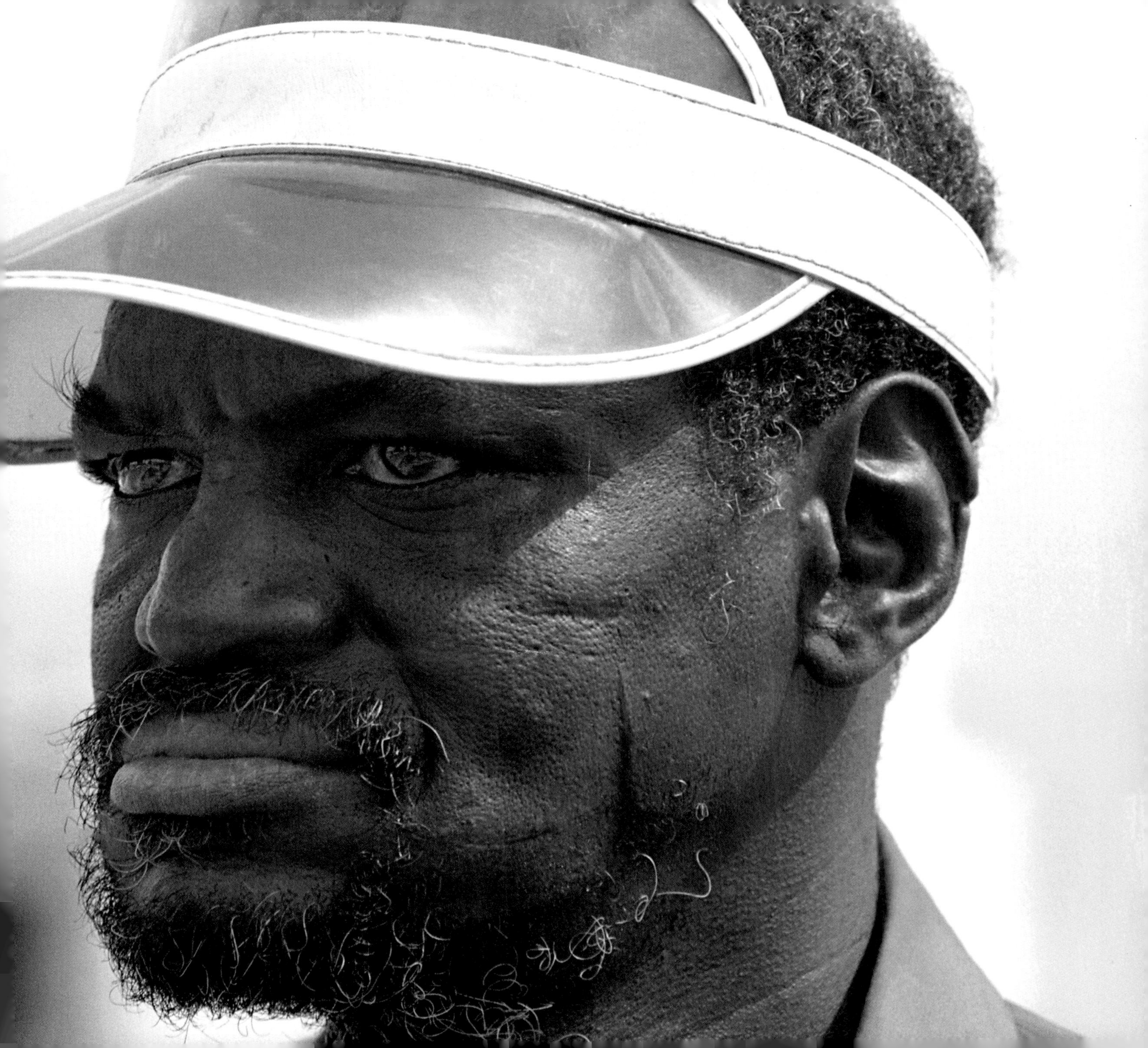

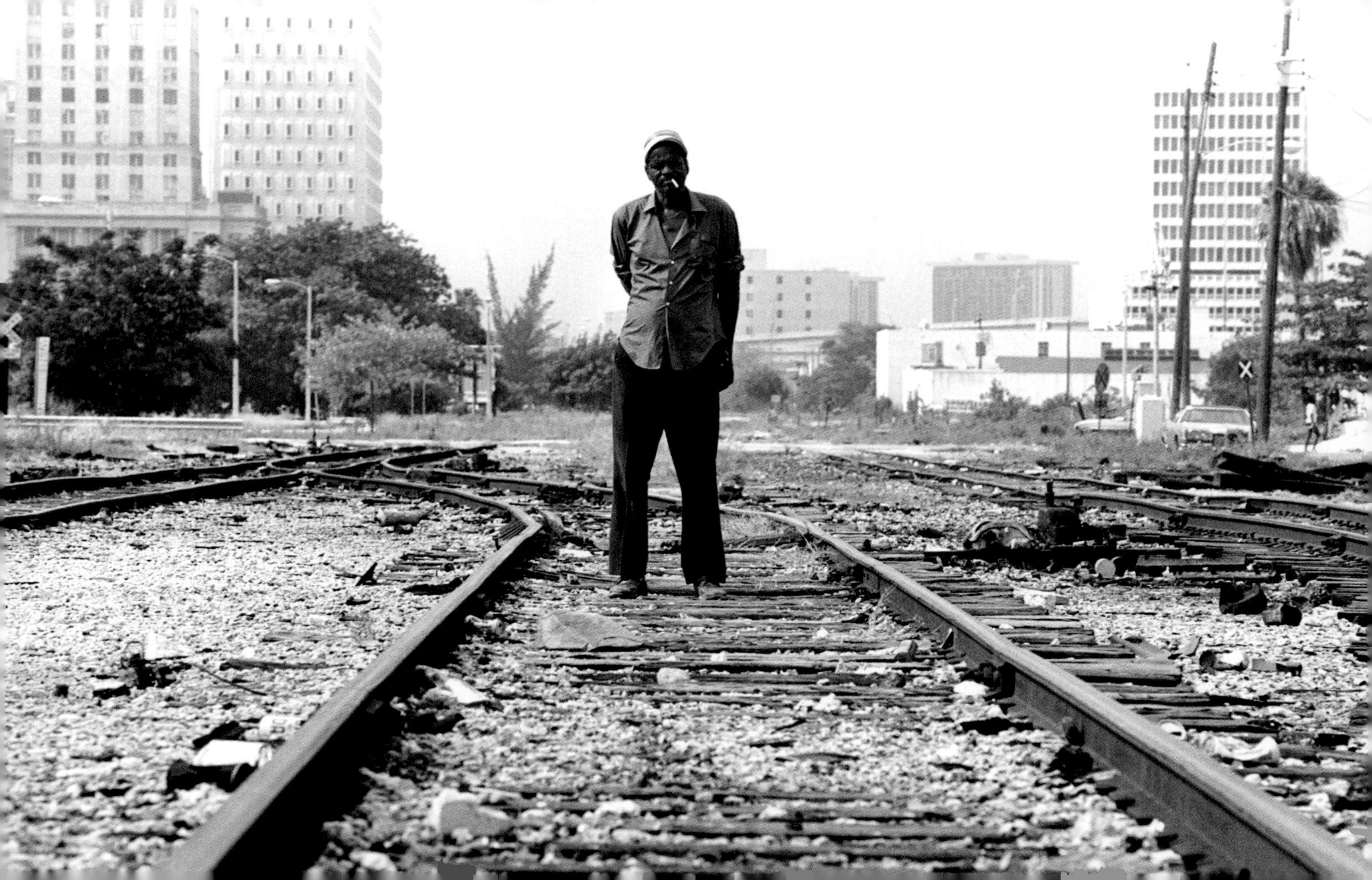

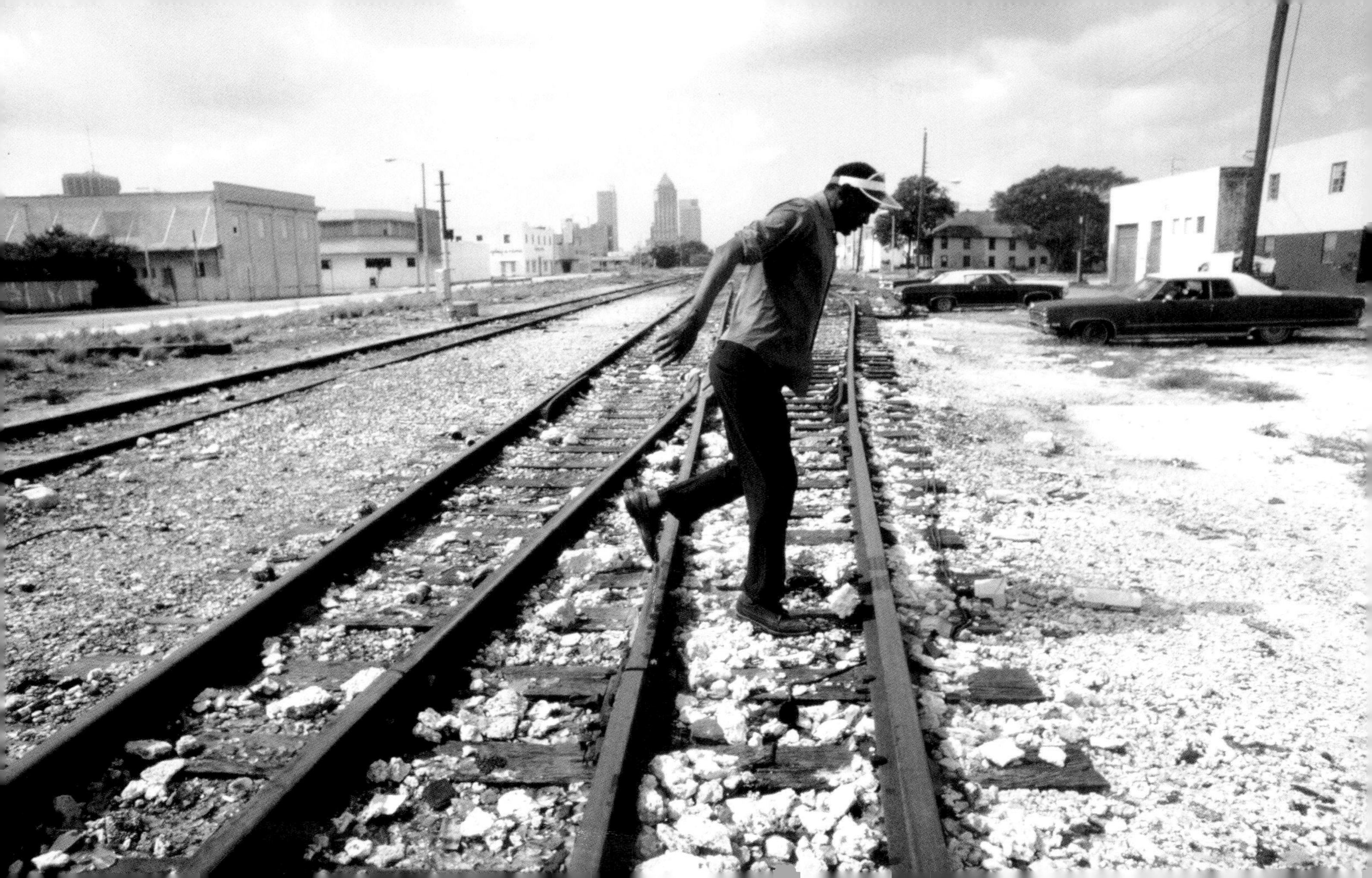

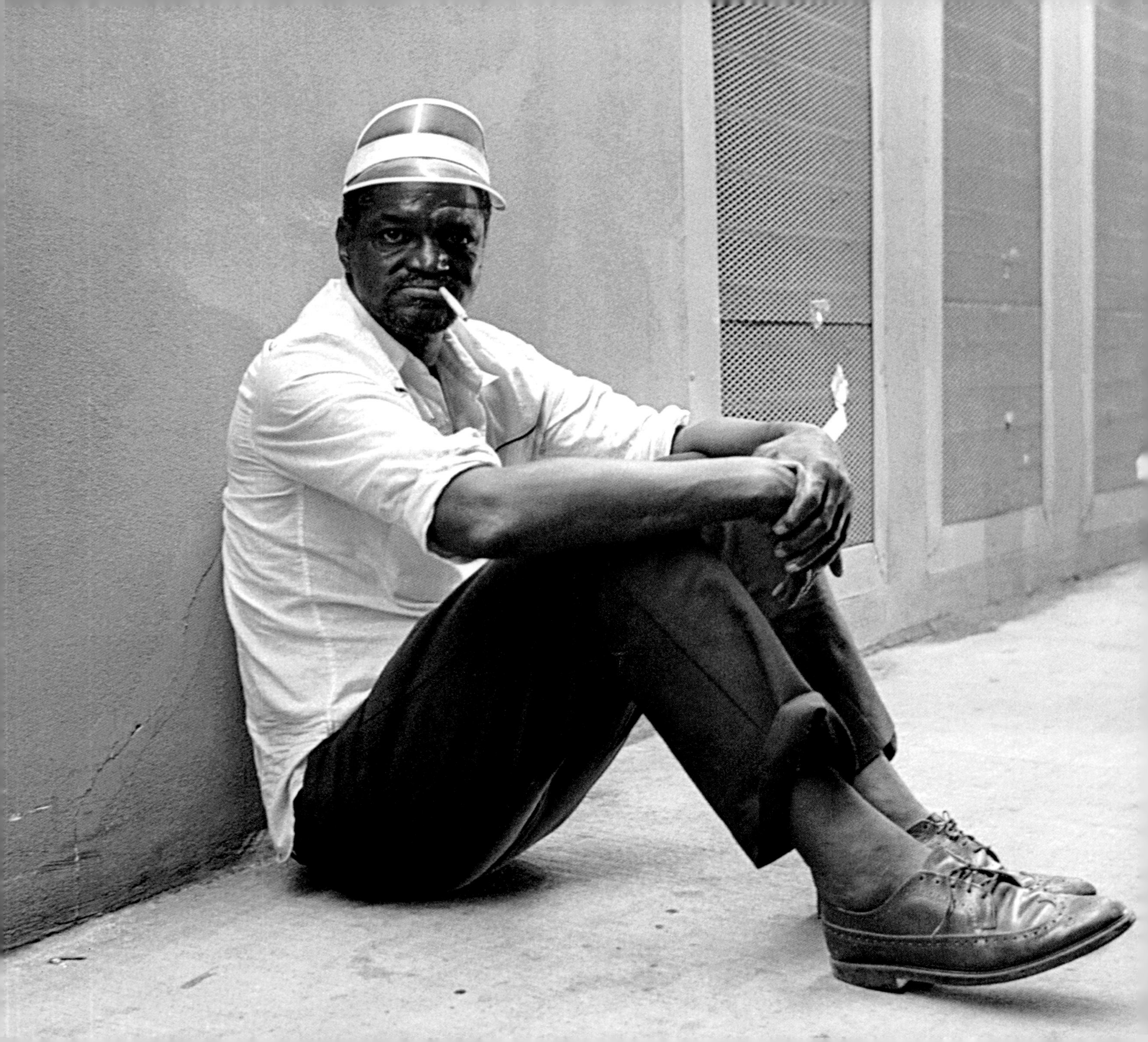

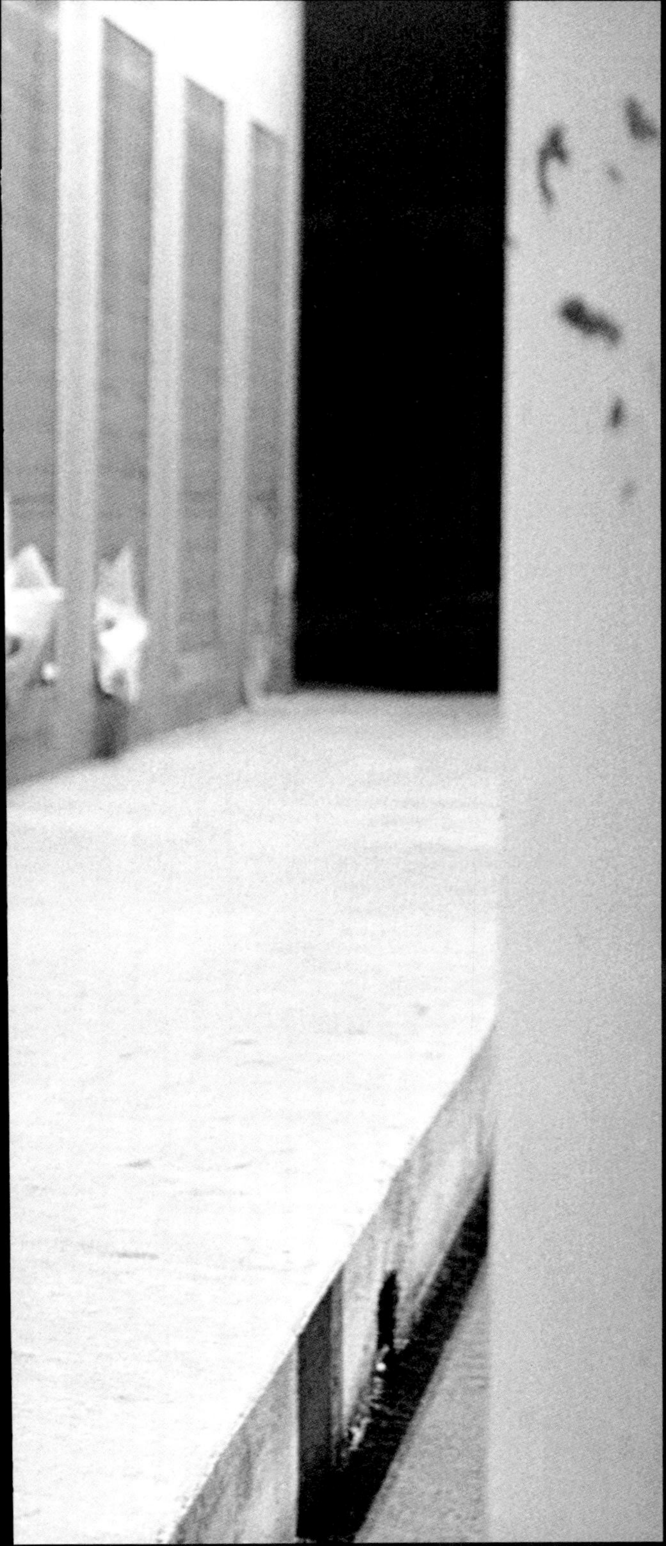

Of all the old opponents, "Sweet Jimmy" was the hardest to track down. Having left messages all around Overtown, Miami, he turned up at my hotel late on a Friday night. He talked of Ali and how they had "hung-out" together.

"I had read about Clay in the papers, but I didn't know much about him. My manager asked me if I wanted to fight him. I said I couldn't because I only weighed 158 pounds. He said, 'We'll work something out.' At the weigh-in, I was standing on the scales when he took my little finger and pressed down until the scale registered 178 pounds.

"In the first round, Clay bloodied my nose but I was a smart fighter; I had been fighting before he was born. But he caught me with a heavy right hand and I went down. I sat on my knees and took a nine count before getting up. The referee looked at my nose and stopped the fight. Clay had fast hands but he never had one great punch. He couldn't have lived with Joe Louis.

"He and I were good friends. I would drive him around in his pink Cadillac. The last time I saw him was in 1967. I went around to a barbershop where he was having his hair cut. I was doing bad at that time, and he said, 'Sit down, I want to talk to you.' Then he pressed $200 in my hand.

"I had a lot of fights after the one with Clay. I would fight three or four times a month in Florida. I retired in 1969. I was 44. After I quit, I was found guilty of armed robbery, a crime I didn't commit. I spend my days down in Clyde Killens's pool hall. I do a little bit of gambling and a little drinkin."

Sonny Liston
Fought Ali twice:
February 25, 1964, title fight, Miami Beach; RTD after 6th round.
25 May 1965, Lewiston, Maine; KO'd in the 1st round
Two of the only four losses in this champion's life. A few days after the first fight Cassius Clay announced his conversion to Islam and changed his name from to Cassius X. The rematch, originally scheduled for 16 November 1964 in Boston, was postponed when Cassius X needed emergency operation for a strangulated hernia. By the time of the second fight, he had changed his name to Muhammad Ali

'When Sonny retired from the ring, he had some dough stashed, but not very much, and he was looking for action. Some very tough citizens were running a loan-shark factory out of East Las Vegas, and since Sonny used to be a head knocker for the unions around St. Louis, they figured he'd make a perfect collector and they hired him. But he wasn't satisfied. He wanted a bigger piece of the action.

'Meanwhile, Sonny was getting drunk around town, making scenes and putting pressure on these guys. So, one night they took him out on a party. After he got stinking drunk, they took him home, jabbed him with an OD and that's the end of Sonny.

"I talked to a guy I knew in the Vegas sheriff's office, and here's what he said: 'He got what was coming to him.' I don't buy that. He had some good qualities, but I think he died the day he was born."

Harold Conrad's memoirs,
Dear Muffo: 35 Years in the Fast Lane. Stein & Day, 1982

Liston was found dead of a heroin overdose in his Las Vegas home on January 5, 1971. He is buried in Paradise Memorial Gardens near McCarran Airport.

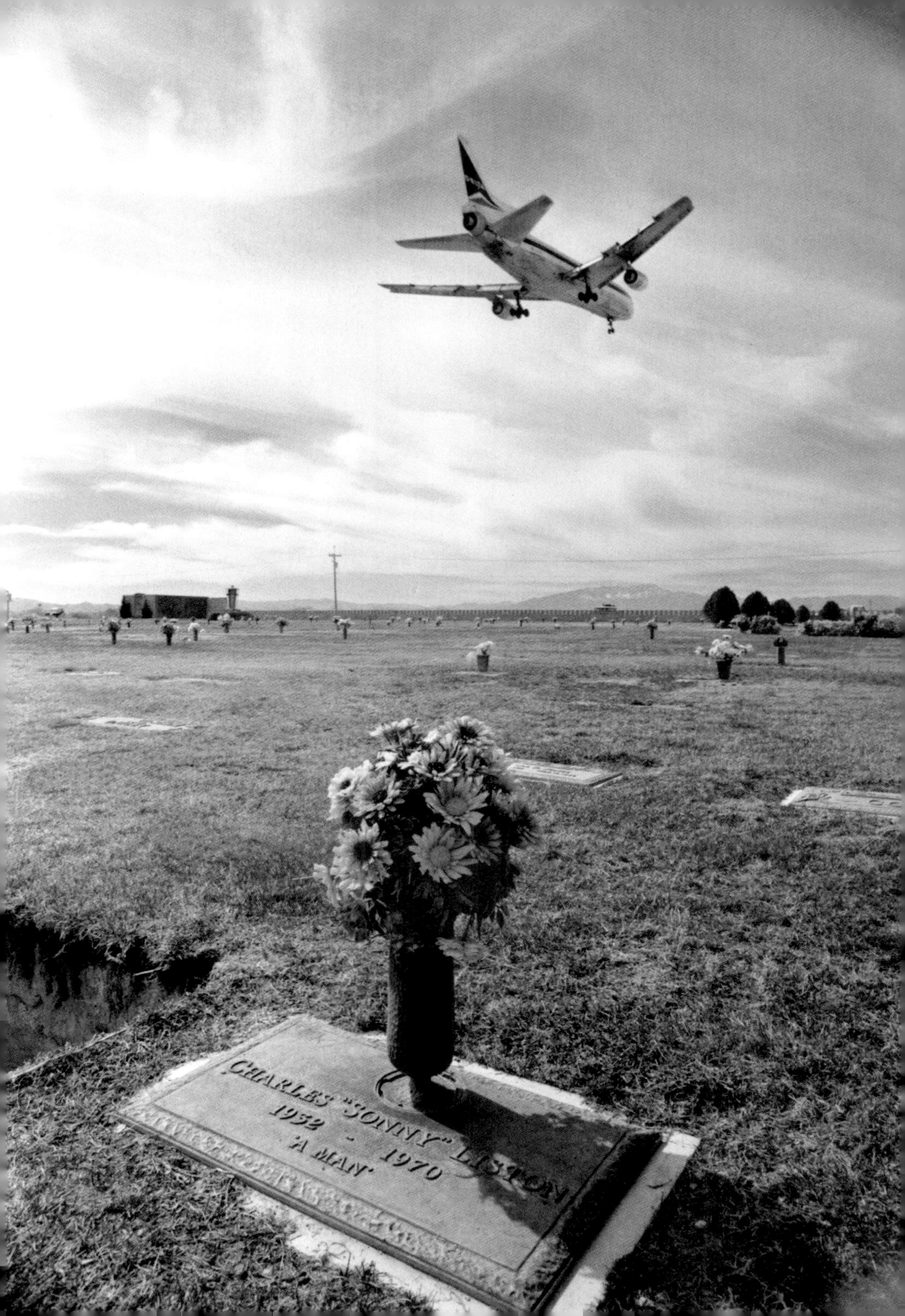
CHARLES "SONNY" LISTON
1932 - 1970
'A MAN'

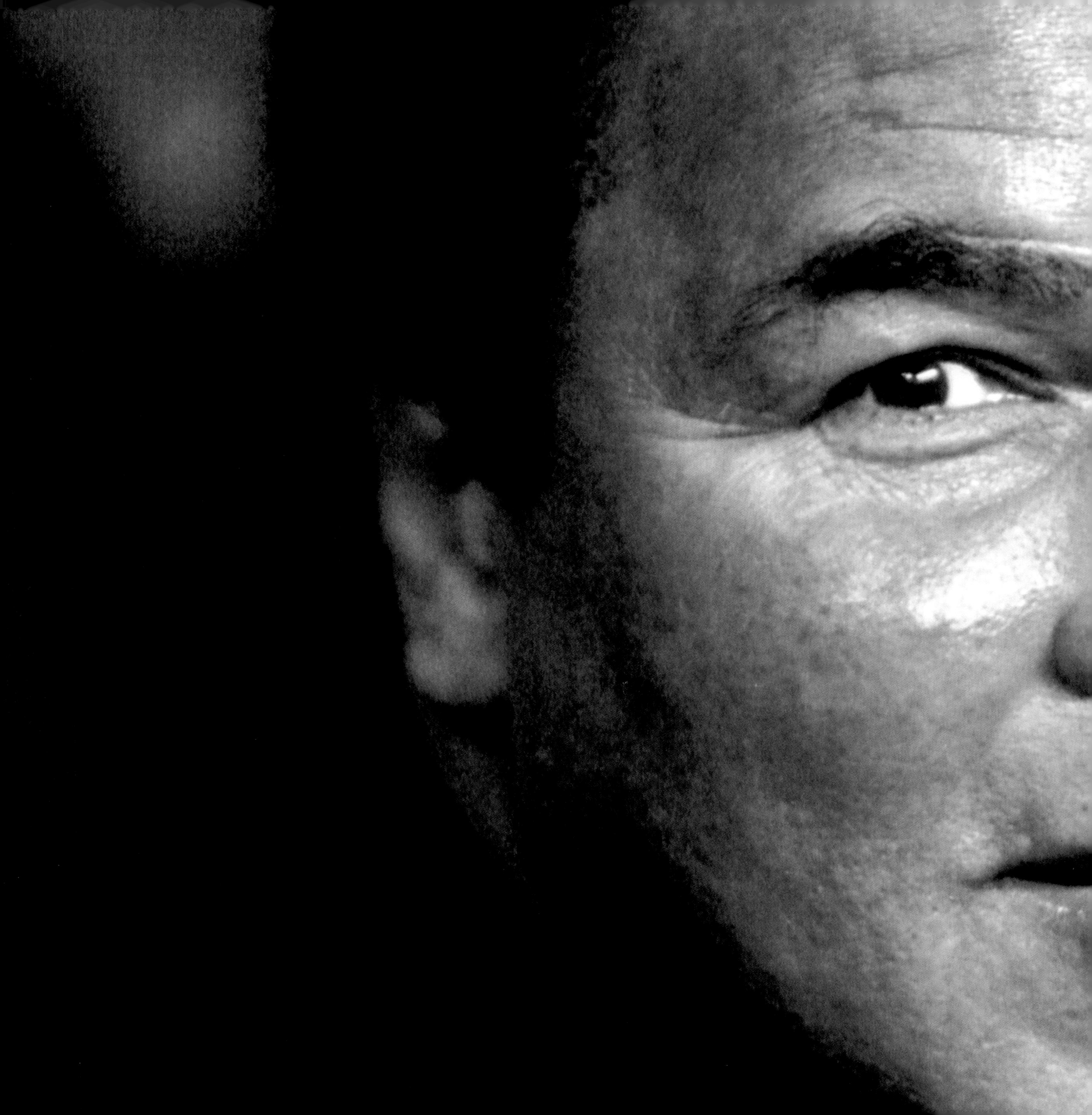

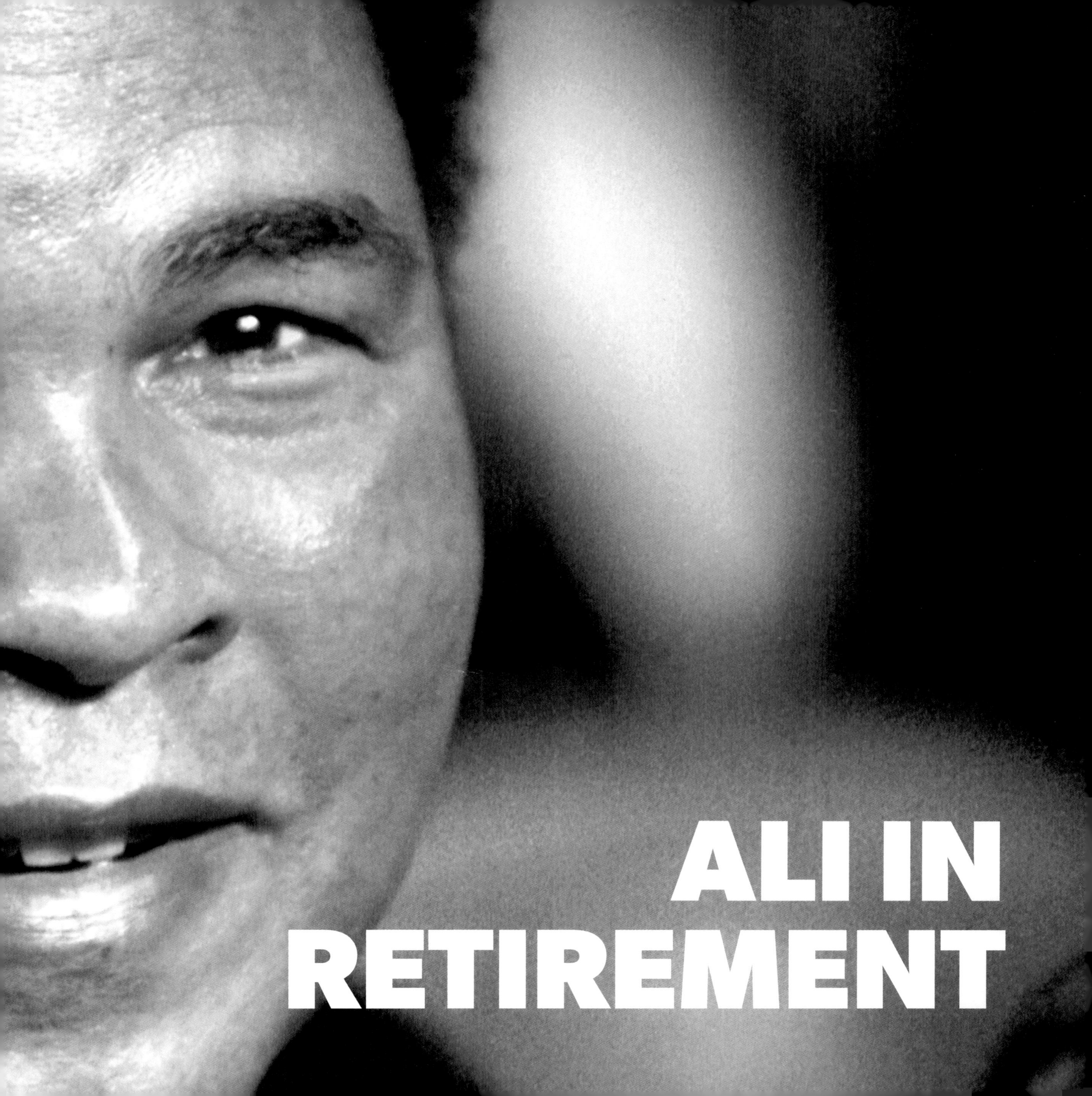

ALI IN RETIREMENT

The Deafening Silence
Muhammad Ali in retirement, Los Angeles
Wednesday February 23, 1983

Number 55 Fremont Place is a gated community off Wilshire Blvd; downtown Los Angeles. An assistant opens the door and attempts to put some ground rules in place. Clearly she hasn't worked for Ali for too long. Ground rules indeed.

'The Greatest' sits alone, although somewhat greater than his fighting weight he still is tall, powerful and a commanding presence. He doesn't formally acknowledge our arrival. However, with his first words, "Limey, you seen this one?" he produces three equal lengths of rope and somehow makes them, with his 'magic powers', appear as one long length.

And so it goes on, trick after magic trick, with a grand finale of Ali levitating from his living room floor. The thunderous applause consists of three observers politely clapping.

The gravelly, slow, almost inaudible voice gives rise to the question of brain damage. He says, "Sure, everybody asks me that but I went to a doctor at UCLA recently who told me I was in fantastic shape. My voice gets tired when I'm bored. I was always so noisy, I was shoutin' and hollerin' all the time, now I just like my peace."

A manservant arrives and offers us coffee. Laughing, Ali says, "He's my man, I stole him from the King of Morocco."

"I'm tired of crowds, everyone around the World has known me. Royalty, politicians, film stars." Ali is on a roll now. Shades of his boisterous past emerge as he continues. "I'm gonna hitch-hike around the World, I can go anywhere and not pay for anything. I'll start in LA and thumb my way to New York. Someone will buy me a ticket to go to England, will go stay with your Mama, Limey!" He laughs as he sees the mock alarm on my face.

Moving over to an antique desk, Ali opens a draw and pulls out a pile of photographs. "Look, there I am with Pele, two of 'The Greatests' together, there's Travolta, there's Sinatra. I still can't go anywhere without being mobbed. I'm going to Pakistan soon and a million people will meet me at the airport. All the reporters keep calling and saying, 'Where's Ali? What's he doin'? Has he any money left? Is he all beat up, all washed up?'"

He takes us upstairs where, in a glass case, is a diamond-studded, full-length robe with 'The Second Coming' written with precious stones on the back. He proudly tells me, "Elvis gave me that before I fought Joe Bugner!"

As the time comes to depart, it's obvious he would rather we stuck around. "Don't go yet, I got Brooke Shields, Diana Ross and Sophia Loren coming by at around two."

However, he asks his secretary Marge to call a taxi to take us to the airport. When the taxi arrives he graciously escorts us and bids farewell.

As the cab draws away, the view from the back seat is of the three-time World Heavyweight Boxing Champion—and one of the most recognizable persons on the face of the earth—shadow boxing.....on an empty street.

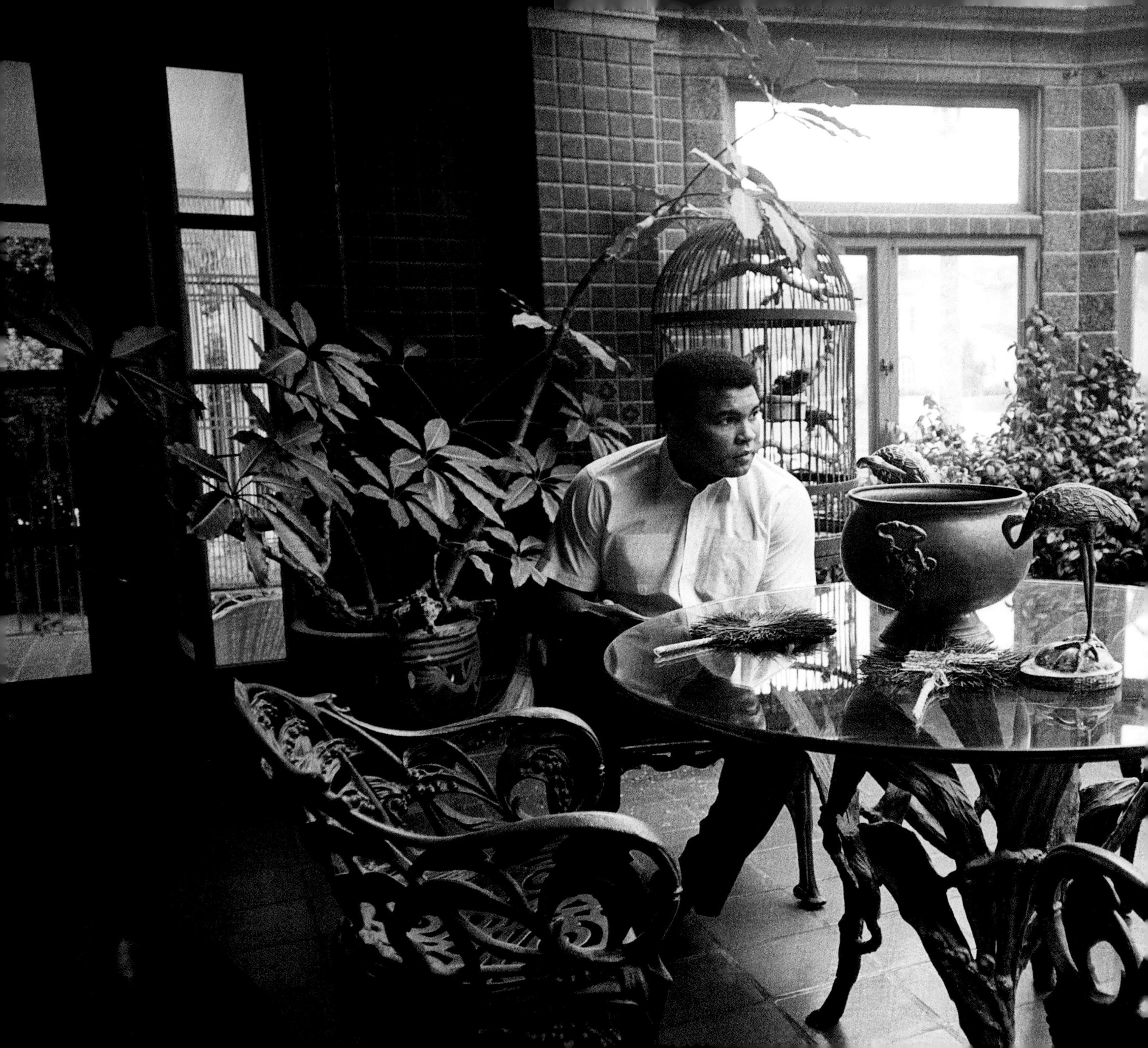

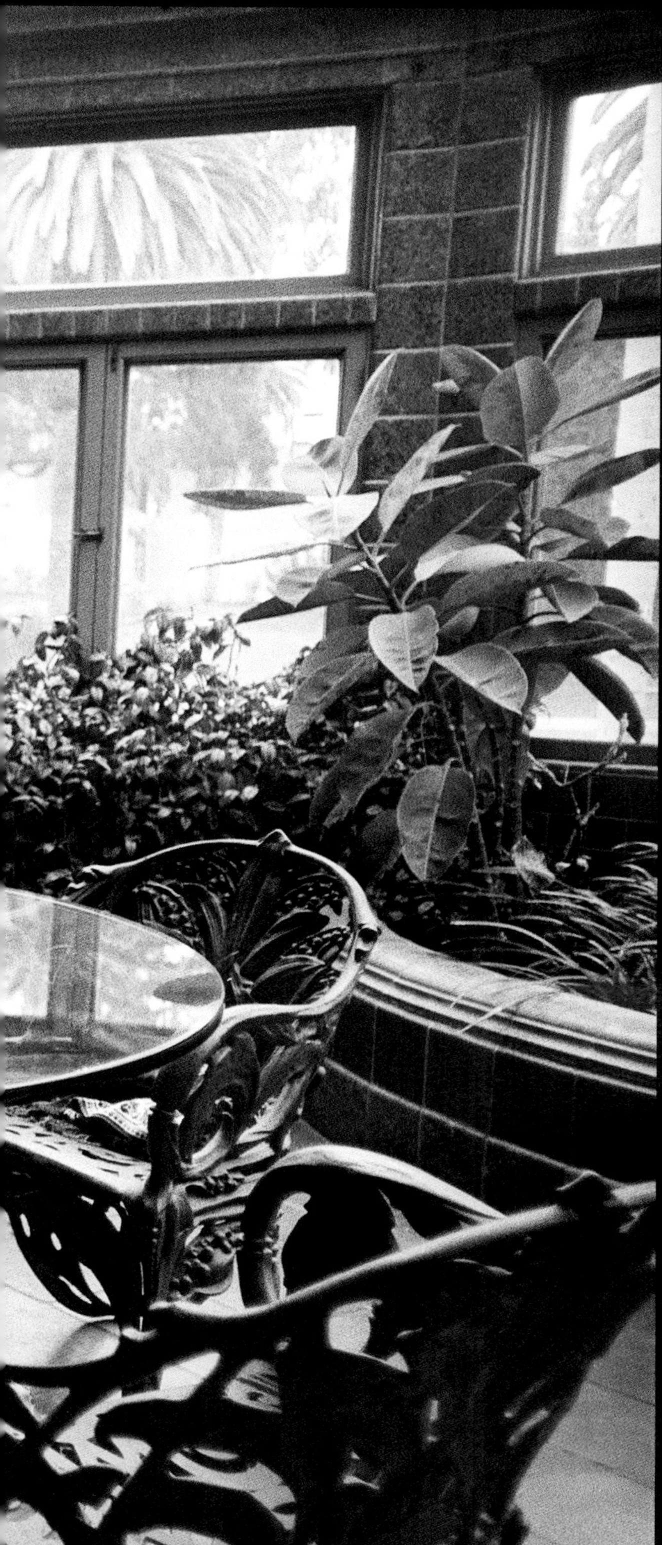

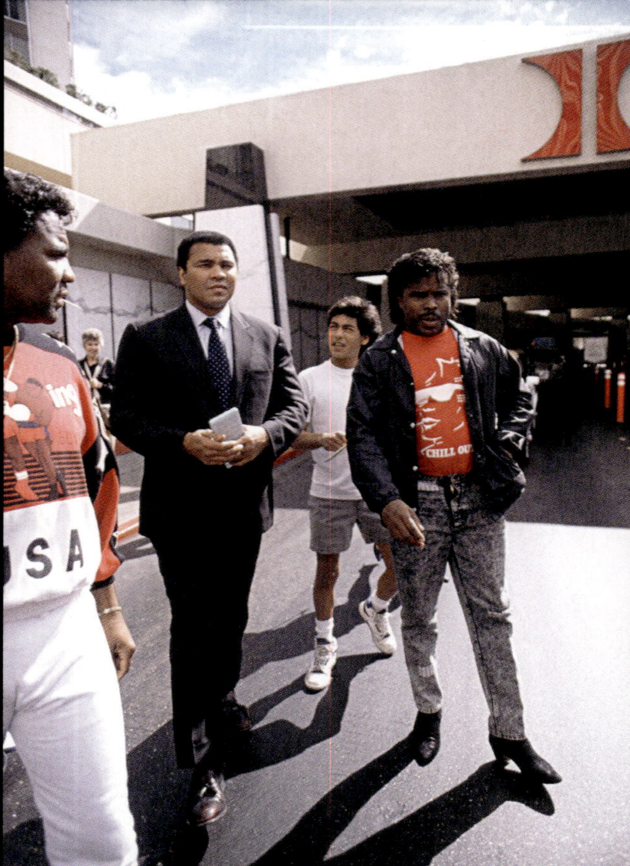

The Mike Tyson v Frank Bruno press conference
Las Vegas Hilton Hotel, Las Vegas, Nevada
Wednesday February 22, 1989

The pre-fight press conference had seen Muhammad Ali dominate for a near thirty-five years. He had made you laugh, made you angry. He had used comedy, civil rights, sleights, innuendo. He had forecasted, bombasted, intimidated, persecuted, seldom praised, made political belief's public and more. Now, here he was, casually walking with another fighter outside the Las Vegas Hilton in the town he helped make more famous with only the casual autograph seeker checking him out. Not being center stage any more didn't disturb him—he felt his job was done.

Muhammad Ali outside the Las Vegas Hilton after the Tyson v Bruno press conference

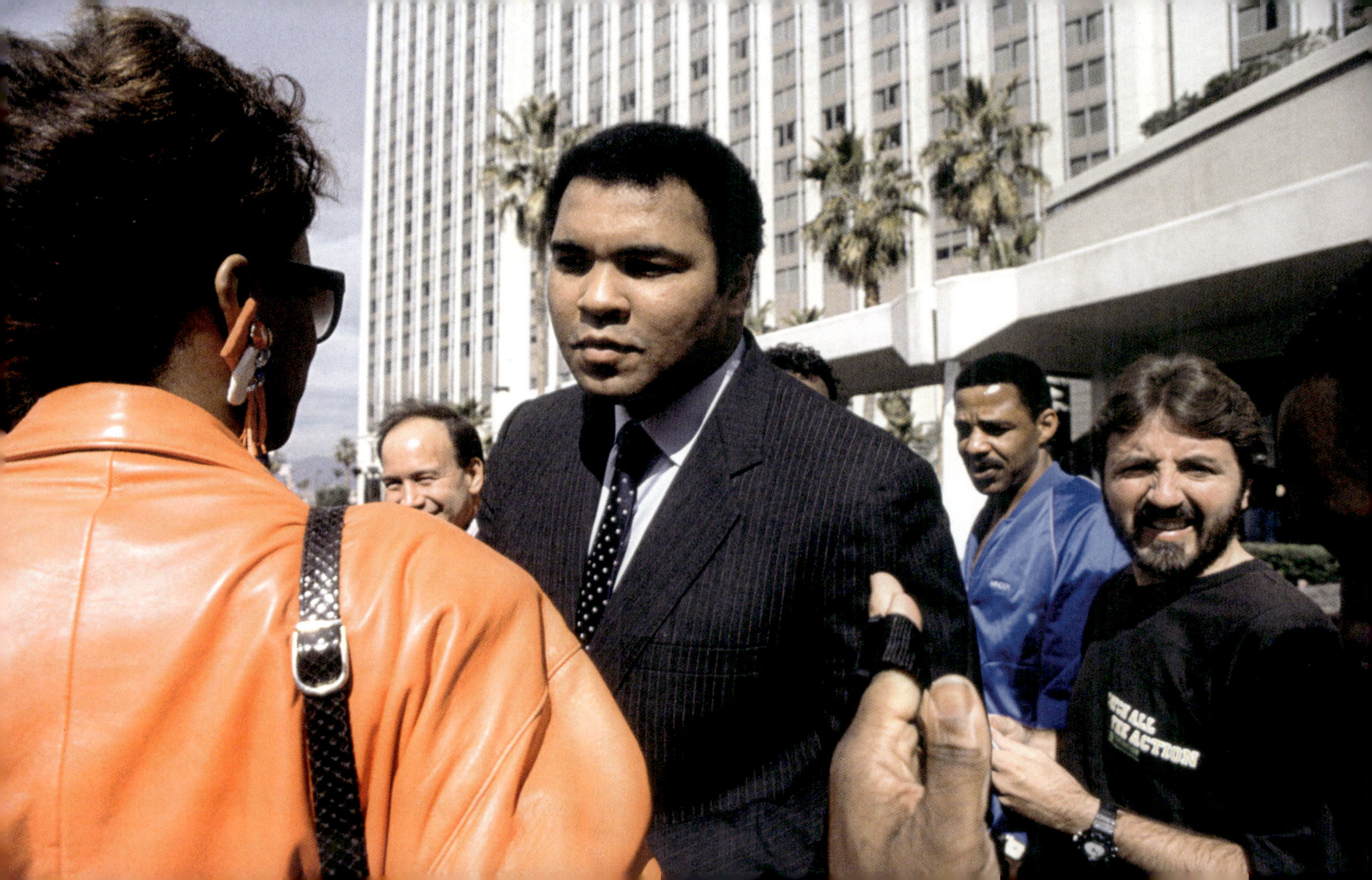

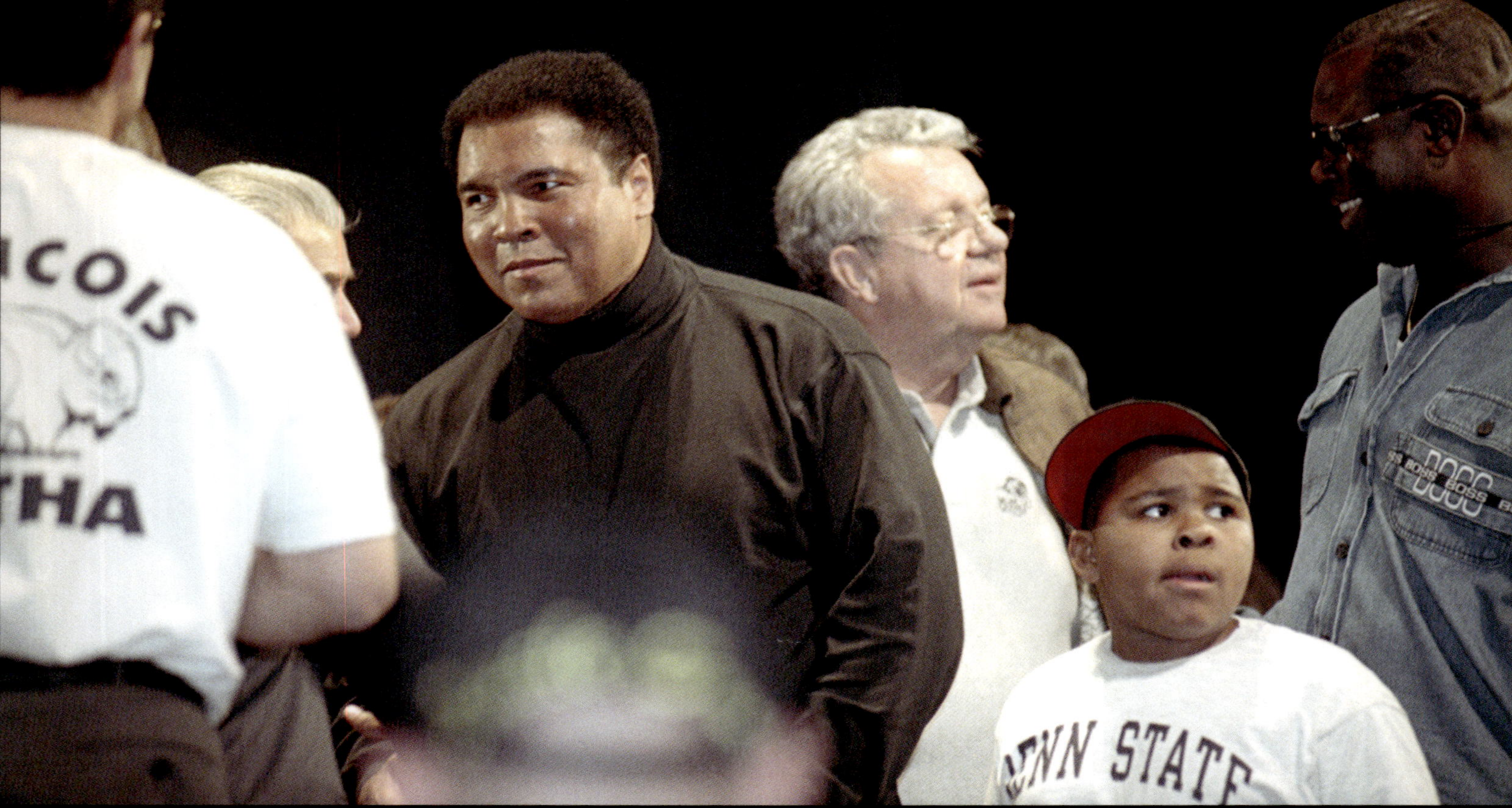

Mike Tyson v Frans Botha
Grand Garden Arena, MGM Grand Hotel, Las Vegas, Nevada
January 1999

Center stage once again. Ali arrives to tumultuous applause. A grand entrance for the man who made these things happen!

Muhammad Ali along with his adopted son Asaad and long-time friend Gene Kilroy and at the Tyson v Botha pre-fight press conference. Thursday January 14, 1999

Muhammad Ali and daughter Laila attend the Tyson v Botha fight. Saturday January 16, 1999

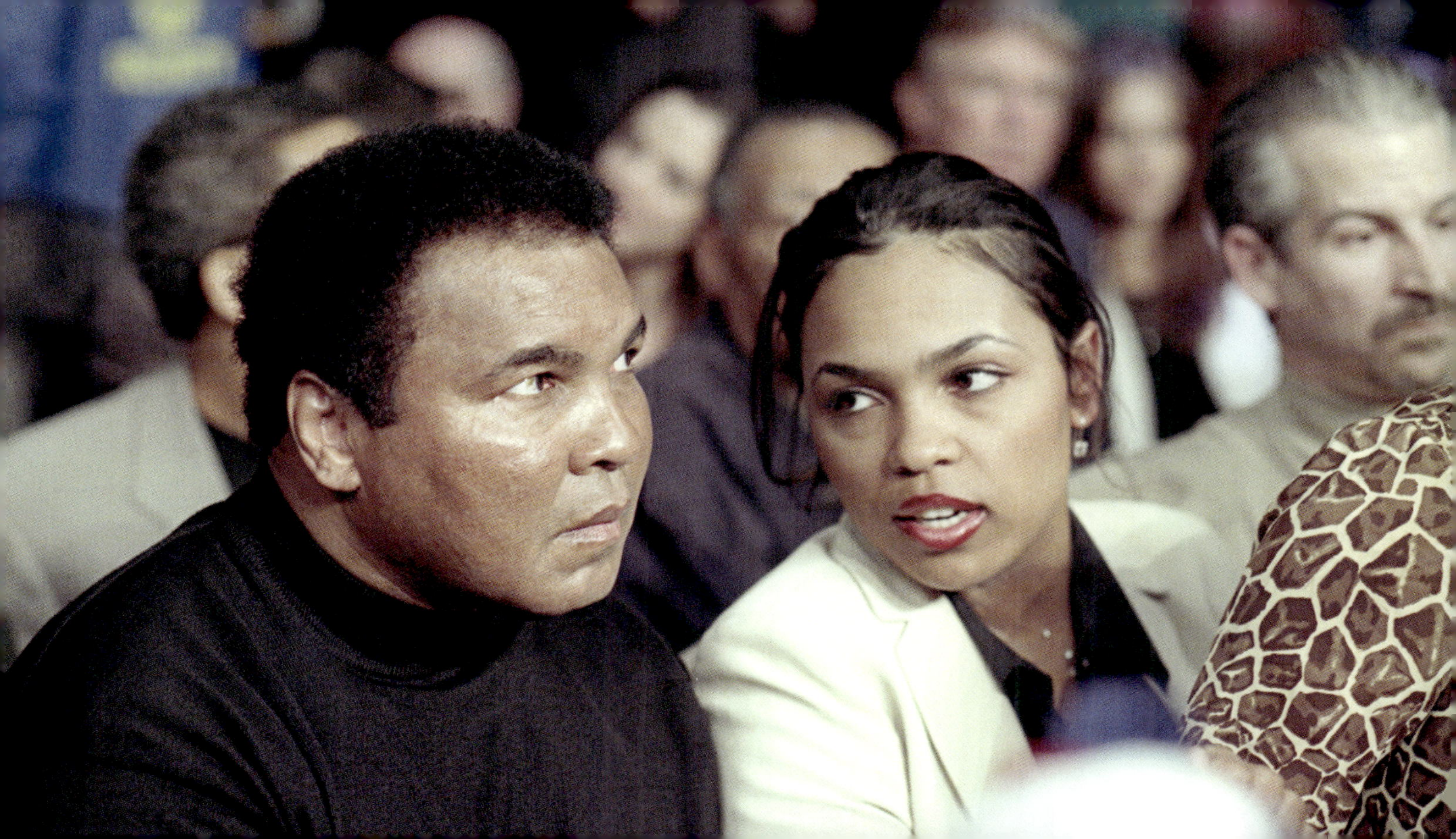

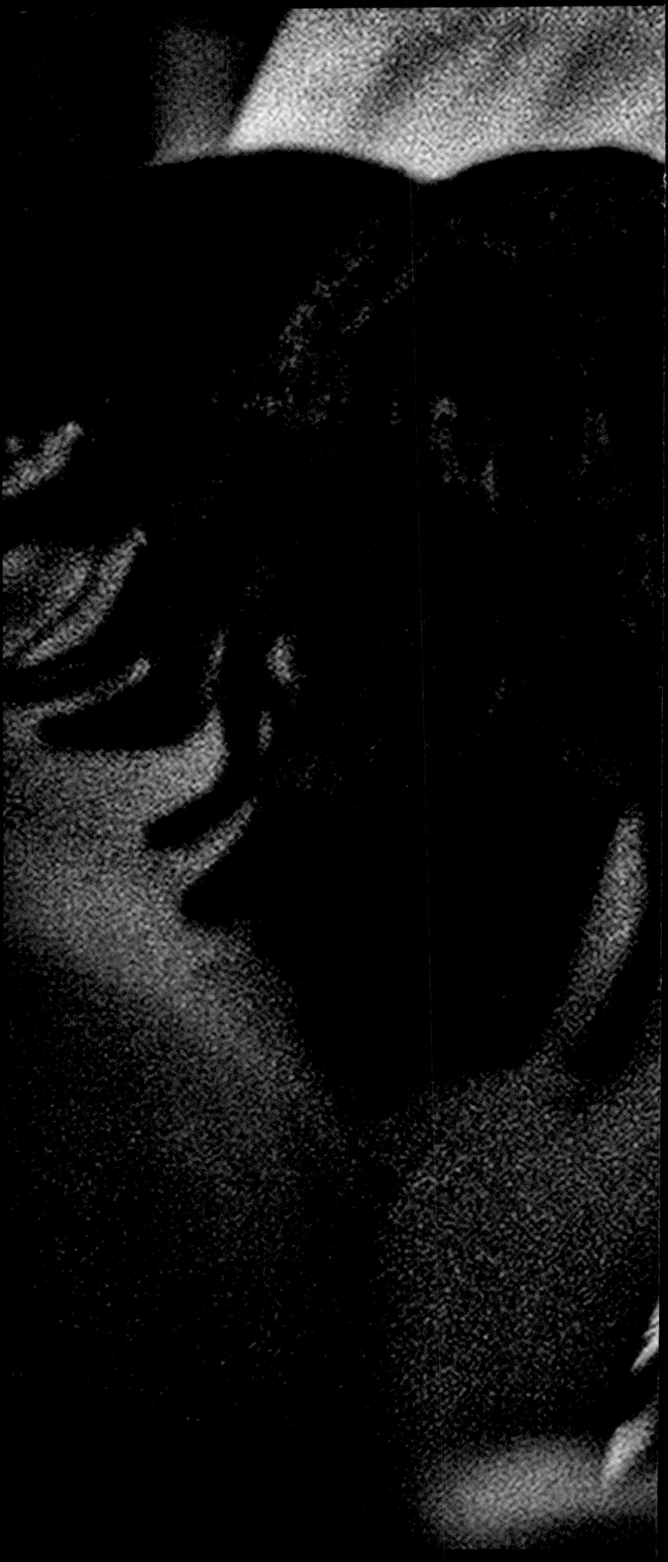

Ali enjoys some popcorn at the Mike Tyson v Andrew Golota fight at The Palace, Auburn Hills, Michigan, October 20, 2000

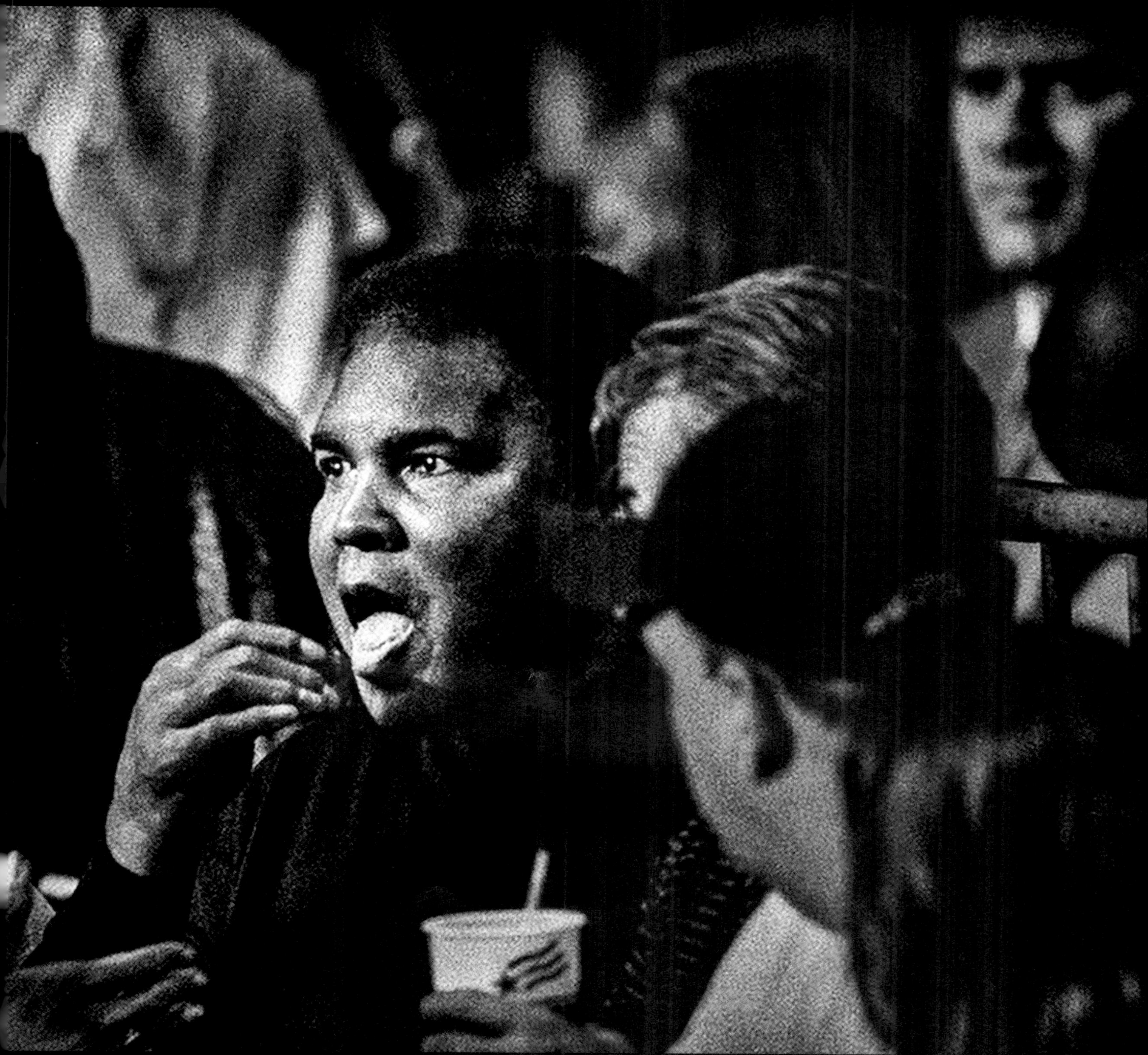

New York City
February 1997

Muhammad Ali was in Manhattan to meet with his agent Barry Frank at the New York headquarters of the mighty IMG global talent management agency. Along with sports journalist Ian Wooldridge, we were to meet with Ali at the Upper East Side offices. With his wife Lonnie by his side, it was clear that Ali was weary but he answered as best he could to Ian's questions. However, the interview was terminated by Lonnie when Ali fell asleep mid-sentence.

It was around 4pm on a weekday when I found myself with Ali on East 76th Street. It was around the time when drivers would change shift, so taxis were scarce. After an uncomfortable twenty minutes of trying to hail a cab to take Ali and Lonnie back to their hotel, a taxi with its "off-duty" sign lit was stopped by one of the IMG men standing in the middle of the road. The driver remonstrated noisily with the IMG guy, who shoved a number of large denomination dollar bills through the driver's window and told him to turn round and see who his passenger was; Ali had already niftily jumped in the back with Lonnie by this point. The driver looked over his shoulder through the partition and almost started crying when he recognised Ali. "You should have said it was The Greatest!" he wailed. He happily wound his window up and sped off with his famous passenger. He didn't try to hand back the cash though!

New York City
2000

It was just a small gesture, just a slight smile but, nevertheless, a recognition.

Muhammad Ali walked unaided into the ballroom of The United Nations Plaza Hotel on Manhattan's East 45th Street, New York City to be guest of honor to some World charity event. As he walked past me, he fleetingly turned and clicked his fingers above my left ear and walked on, a sure sign he remembered "The Limey."

Wherever Ali went, crowds and the press followed and this event was no exception. Across the road from the UN building, the event was packed with diplomats, politicians and UN personnel, all of whom were trying for a glimpse or perhaps an audience with the great man. Although slowed by his biggest defeat—the vile onslaught of Parkinson's disease—Ali still knew how to work the room.

I took it as a huge compliment that Muhammad Ali had remembered me; Ali, the three-time world heavyweight boxing champion, humanitarian and, as *TIME* magazine had once proclaimed, "The most instantly recognised human being in the World." I felt the need to scratch my left ear in gratitude.

Muhammad Ali passed away on June 3, 2016.

"I can feel the texture of all that sweat and hard work. I can feel my life."

Ali reminisces with Michael Brennan after seeing Brennan's photography

December 2, 1981, Nassau, Bahamas

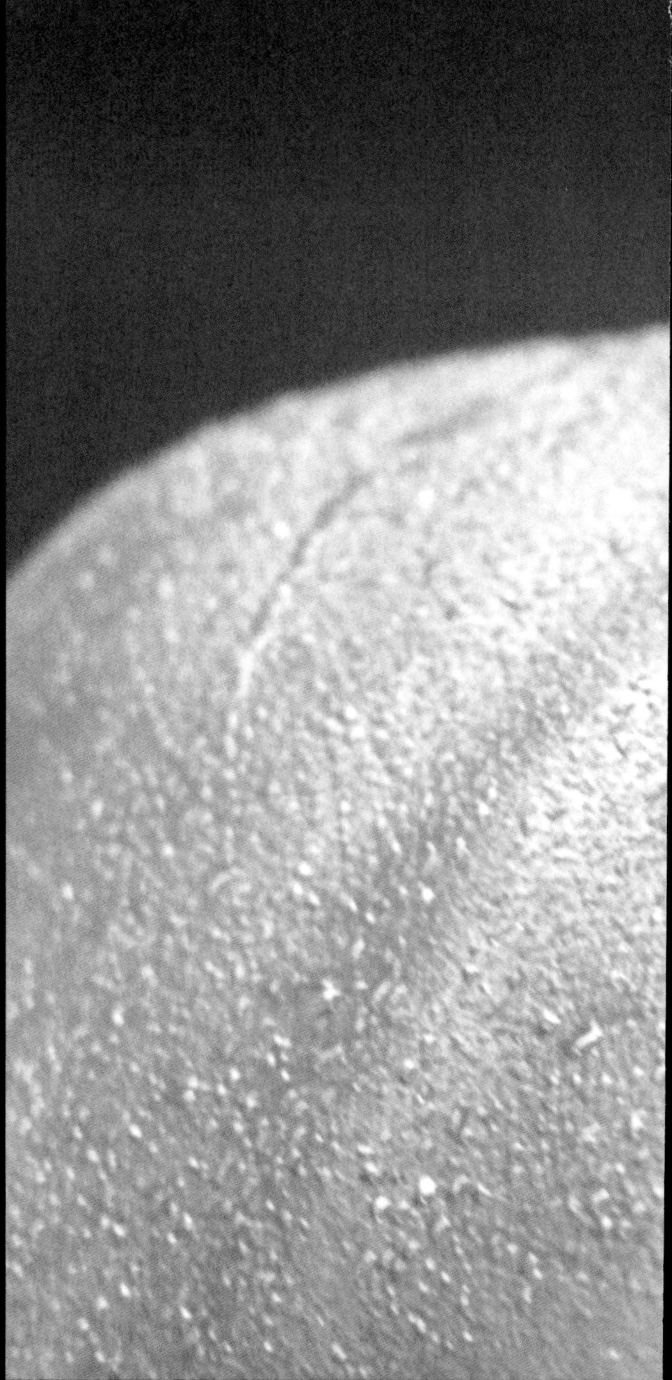

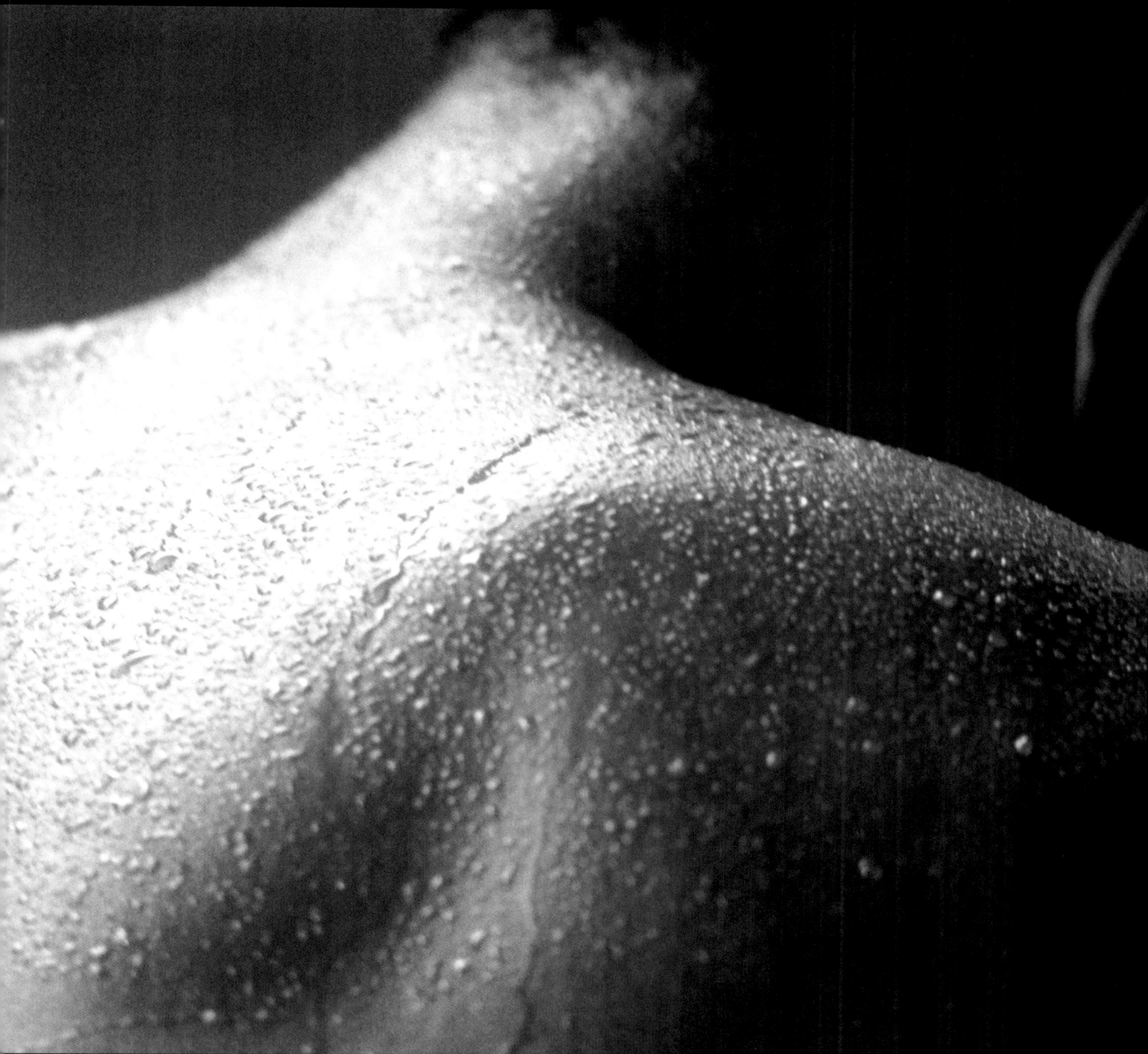

About Michael Brennan.

I sauntered into the Holiday Inn at Tampa Bay and, as instructed, I headed straight to the bar. The tallest among the patrons turned to me and said, "If you are Mick, what are you having?" There he was with his mates, in full majesty! The great 1966 captain of England's World Cup-winning football team, Bobby Moore... asking me what I would like to drink!
Well, what a way to earn a living this is. It doesn't get any better than this.
I replied with appropriate humility, "I'll have a Heineken thanks, Bob."

Photographer Michael Brennan was born in England, on August 13, 1943 in Sheffield, Yorkshire. His father Thomas was an Irish immigrant who went to Britain looking for work as a farm laborer and who then served in the British Army during the war. His mother Dorothy, a native of Hertfordshire, was a housewife who stayed home raising Michael and his two siblings, while their father worked as a cab driver in post-war London.

At age 15, Michael landed his first job, working as a messenger for the national Sunday newspaper: *The People*.

Sometime in 1959, Croydon, UK.

My mother was having her hair "done" at Allders Department Store, at the Ladies Salon. Hairdressers, haircutter, barbers... call them what you will... male or female, they are professionally inquisitive of their clients, it's part of the job.

"My boy wants to work in the 'papers'," my mother said. "Well that's amazing," says the hairdresser. "My husband George is a photographer with The People and he was saying, just last night they were looking for a new copy boy."

A little later saw myself wearing short trousers and being escorted by my mother to the editor's secretary Kate Wadleigh on a Saturday morning to interview for the position of copy boy.

Actually, I was quite good at it. Whatever "it" was.

Brennan remembers it as a great job since many of his friends worked digging roads. *The People* was a newspaper known at the time for its massive circulation and for publishing sensational stories exposing vice bosses and London Mafia kingpins. One of Brennan's duties was to offer assistance to some of the paper's celebrity "buy-ups." One charge he remembers was the legendary Irish playwright Brendan Behan, who did most of his writing in The Enterprise, a Covent Garden pub. Keeping an eye on Behan was an unforgettable experience.

Covent Garden had the distinction of the pubs being open at times when other pubs were closed to allow the porters and workers at the market to enjoy a drink at all hours. Brendan figured that out very early during his short tenure at *The People*. His pub of choice was The Enterprise on Long Acre.

One Friday morning as the editor was chomping about Behan's very late column, I was dispatched to The Enterprise to ask Mr. Behan would he care to return to the office since Mr. Campbell was a bit fed-up.
"I'm not leaving here until you, you wee fucker, has a drink with me!" "Thank you, Mr. Behan, could I have a light ale?"
Three light ale's later, Mr. Behan escorted me back to the office where ....I fell asleep. I really do believe that Brendan Behan was the first to render me paralytic drunk.

Brennan learned what he calls the "then well respected trade of newspaper photography" after taking a job with South London's *Croydon Times*. One of Brennan's neighbors growing up had been George Phillips, a photographer who influenced Michael and who gave him tips on photography. Although Brennan owned a Yashica-Mat, a compact crank advance camera, most of the work he did for the *Croydon Times* involved taking group shots with an extremely heavy glass plate camera. "Fifty years later, I can say without equivocation that I gained nothing except a stiff neck from using those contraptions."

Learning the ropes as a photographer, there were some memorable mishaps. "My first week," recalls Brennan, "I had to do a group shot of a Catholic diocese." While trying to get all his subjects into the frame, Brennan told the head priest "Get a little closer to your wife." Brennan's career took off in the early '60s when he worked in Manchester, which he remembers as being the "Las Vegas of Britain." On January 4, 1967 he took a series of terrifying photographs of the Englishman Donald Campbell crashing and dying while attempting the world water speed record on Lake Coniston.

A frigid January morning in Cumberland, 1967. Campbell had sat atop and around his jet-propelled vehicle for weeks without moving any distance. The hint of a lack of funds ran around the Bluebird camp with the chance of a quick two hundred quid from the Daily Sketch *newspaper that might finance a quick dangerous record water attempt. The Wednesday morning of the 4th saw the likes of myself and every major daily newspaper camped out along the shores of Coniston. My representation for the newly minted* Sun *was a bit hampered by the fact that I didn't have a long enough lens. Some one hour before Campbell's attempt at the World Record, a deal was struck between myself and the much experienced* Daily Mail *photographer Peter Howard. It was agreed I could borrow the* Daily Mail's *spare 400mm Novoflex and if I "got lucky" then my images would be distributed among all the competing newspapers. A small promontory off the lake and facing the town of Coniston found us waiting for the much anticipated event. I clung tightly to the* Mail's *400mm Novoflex attached to a hand driven Pentax 35mm body (physically moving the wind-on lever to the next exposure on the film).*

Campbell came down the lake from right to left. While impressive, it clearly hadn't broken any records. Anyone present would testify (and I think some did) that a huge 'wash' was apparent from the boat's initial run. Apparently, a million demons, not the least of which was the fact that he was running out of money, must have compelled Campbell to immediately turn the boat around and throttle the vehicle to full power in the opposite direction. The fact that the wash was still bouncing around the lake must have completely skipped his plans.

Hearing the whine of the jet engine as the vehicle came toward me was a help to know on what track and where to focus. Seeing the boat coming closer I kept the focus on one near spot (I would guess somewhere around four hundred yards away). As Campbell hit my point of focus Bluebird *lurched upward, the way a jet would at take-off. I clicked one frame and instinctively panned right and clicked again. The third frame was of the aftermath of the crash. Actually, I don't remember any loud explosions. In fact, after the vehicle hit the lake the only sound was the "popping" of small plastic bags coming to the surface. They had been installed within the boat to protect the wiring.*

After half an hour or so fellow photographers gathered and tried to assess who had what. I didn't know of my outcome so therefore I set off back to Manchester. I stopped at a public phone box on the way and phoned The Sun's *northern office to speak to picture editor Ron Graham. Before I could tell my story, Ron passed on the sobering news that the Editor Arthur Brown had told him, "should Brennan not have the pictures of Campbell dying in* Bluebird *then let him know to not bother returning to the office...he's fired."*

In the darkroom, Pete Redfern warmed up the D76 developer and put the two rolls in the tank. He emerged with the sequence of Donald's Campbell's death.

I went to Manchester with my exclusive pics of Donald Campbell dying in Bluebird *while attempting the World's Water Speed record in January 1967.*

Brennan's photos, which appeared in *Life* magazine, won him the prestigious British News Picture of the Year award.

After returning to London in 1969 Brennan worked for Rupert Murdoch's *Sun* newspaper. In his first year with the *Sun* he was awarded British photography's highest accolade Photographer of the Year, which was presented to him by Princess Anne. With celebrity culture "not yet on the horizon" Brennan's pictures from that era covered serious topics, including the emerging troubles in Northern Ireland, The Indo-Pakistani War and other international skirmishes.

After the *Daily Mail* assigned him to New York in 1973, Brennan began a more than 30-year stint in New York, also shooting photos for *Sports Illustrated*. When Brennan spent time in Pennsylvania covering Muhammad Ali's training sessions, the champ took a liking to Brennan, giving him unprecedented access. "His generosity knew no boundaries," says Brennan. "His humor, friendship and goodwill are legendary." His iconic portrait of Muhammad Ali entitled "1977" found a permanent home at the National Portrait Gallery, Smithsonian Institute in 2011 and was included in a group exhibition there later that year.

In addition to his iconic portraits of Muhammad Ali, Brennan has photographed some of the best-known personalities of our time, including HM Queen Elizabeth II, Nelson Mandela, Princess Diana, Pelé, George Best, Led Zeppelin, Mick Jagger, John Lennon and literary figures, including Norman Mailer and P.G. Wodehouse.

Now retired in Costa Rica, Michael Brennan says self-deprecatingly that he was "reasonably good at what he did." Looking back, he sees the '60s and '70s as a "fun period" before paparazzi took over photojournalism. For Brennan, photography wasn't just about who was being photographed; it was about the atmosphere. His great photo of Muhammad Ali is about much more than the man, it was also about the sweat covering his face and the far seeing look in his eyes.

Although Brennan says that he regrets that "great photojournalism has been violated by the celebrity culture that is now lumped in with the same," he notes with optimism that "There were, and still are, great artists who carry on the tradition of wonderful photography." Without a doubt, Michael Brennan is one of those greats himself.

© Michael Brennan
pp6-7 text © Simon Van Booy
pp12-13 text © Jimmy Breslin
World copyright reserved

ISBN: 978 1 78884 018 7

The right of Michael Brennan to be identified as author of this work has been asserted by him in accordance with the Copyright, Designs and Patents Act 1988

All rights reserved. No part of this publication may be reproduced, stored in a retrieval system, or transmitted in any form or by any means electronic, mechanical, photocopying, recording or otherwise, without the prior permission of the publisher

British Library Cataloguing-in-Publication Data
A catalogue record for this book is available from the British Library

Dates and places as noted in the book are all to the best of Michael Brennan's recollections, date books, clippings and notes. Fight dates and information are sourced from www.BoxRec.com. Any errors are wholly unintentional.

FSC www.fsc.org MIX Paper from responsible sources FSC® C110418

Printed in Slovenia
for ACC Art Books Ltd., Woodbridge, Suffolk, England

www.accartbooks.com

ACC ART BOOKS

ICONICIMAGES
FINEART ARCHIVES PUBLISHING CREATIVE

THEY MUST FALL

Muhammad Ali and the Men He Fought

CEO, Iconic Images
Robin Morgan

Editor
Carrie Kania

Production
Adam Powell

www.iconicimages.net

Publisher, ACC Art Books
James Smith

Editor
Susannah Hecht

Design
Craig Holden

Production
Stephen Mackinlay

www.accartbooks.com

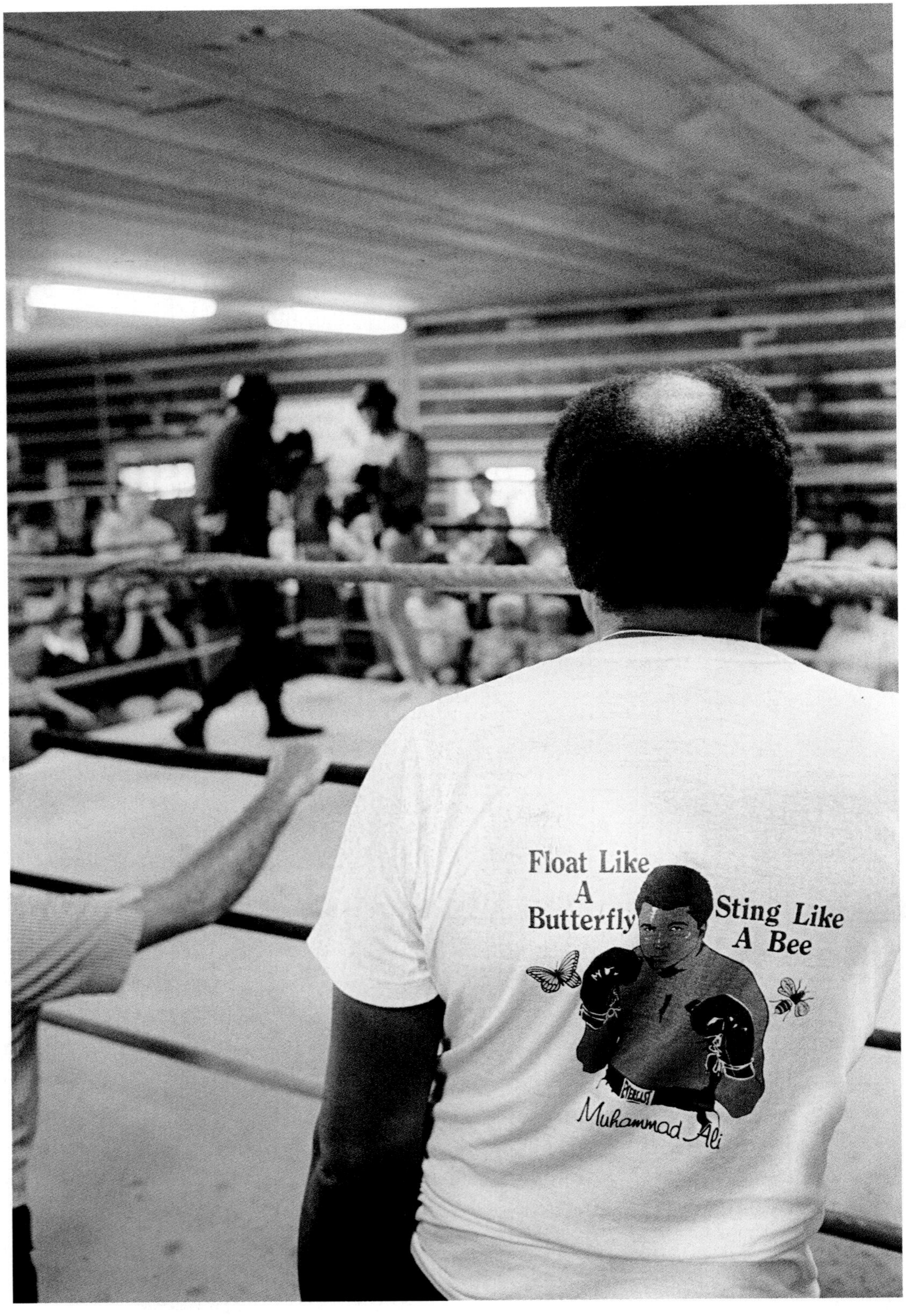
Float Like
A
Butterfly
Sting Like
A Bee
Muhammad Ali